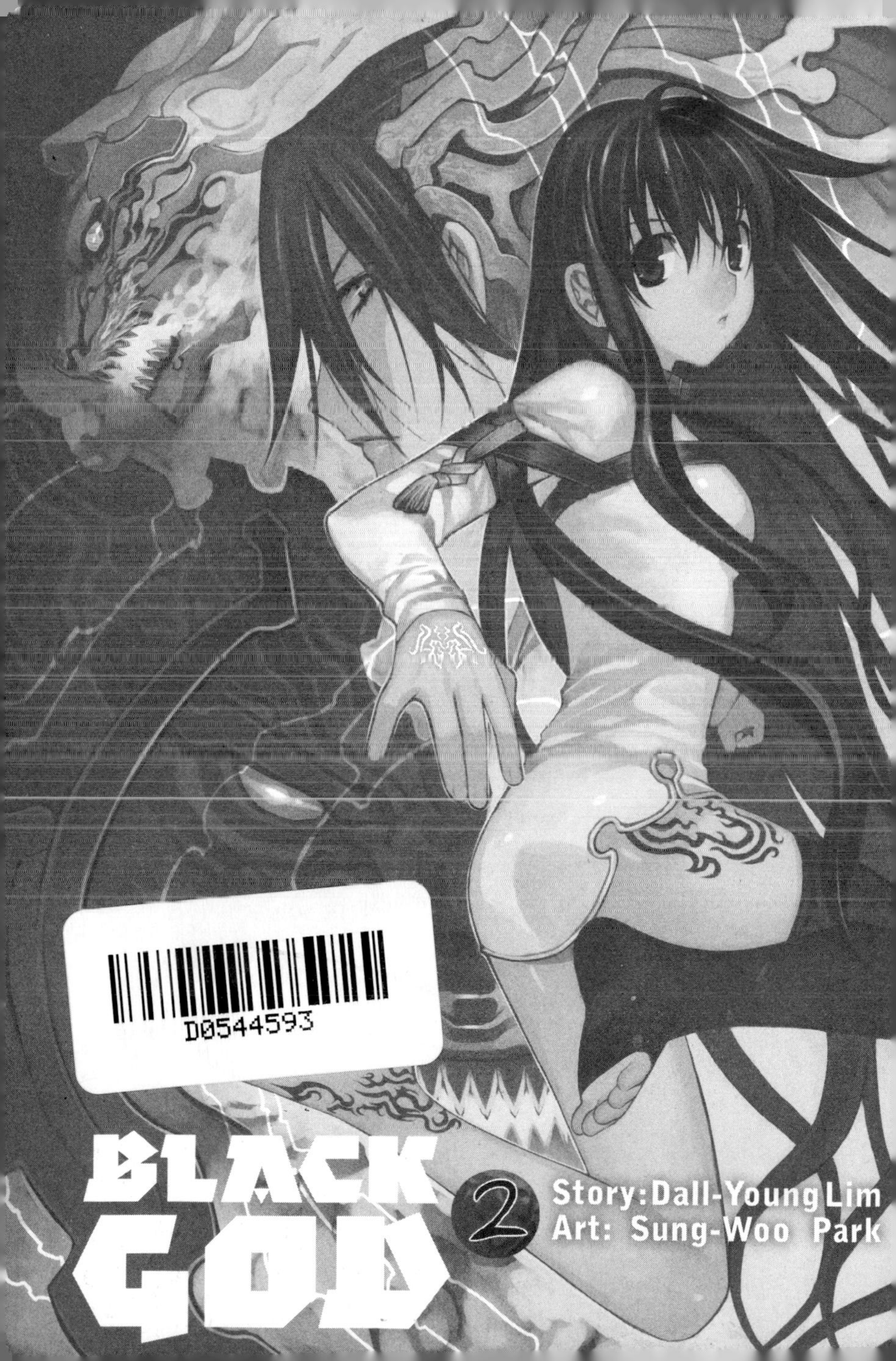
BLACK GOD
2
Story: Dall-Young Lim
Art: Sung-Woo Park

CONTENTS

FATE. 6   CONTACT · EXPERIMENT   3

FATE. 7   CROSS · CHANCE   27

FATE. 8   IMPATIENCE · INSPIRATION   53

FATE. 9   CLASH · CANCEL   85

FATE. 10   TRANSCENDENCE · SHARING   117

FATE. 11   EXECUTION · bURdEN   145

FATE. 12   REST · TRAINING   177

FATE. 13   SORROW · WITNESS   199

EVEN IF THERE ARE WORDS HERE YOU DON'T UNDERSTAND, PLEASE DON'T WORRY AND READ ON! (HA!)

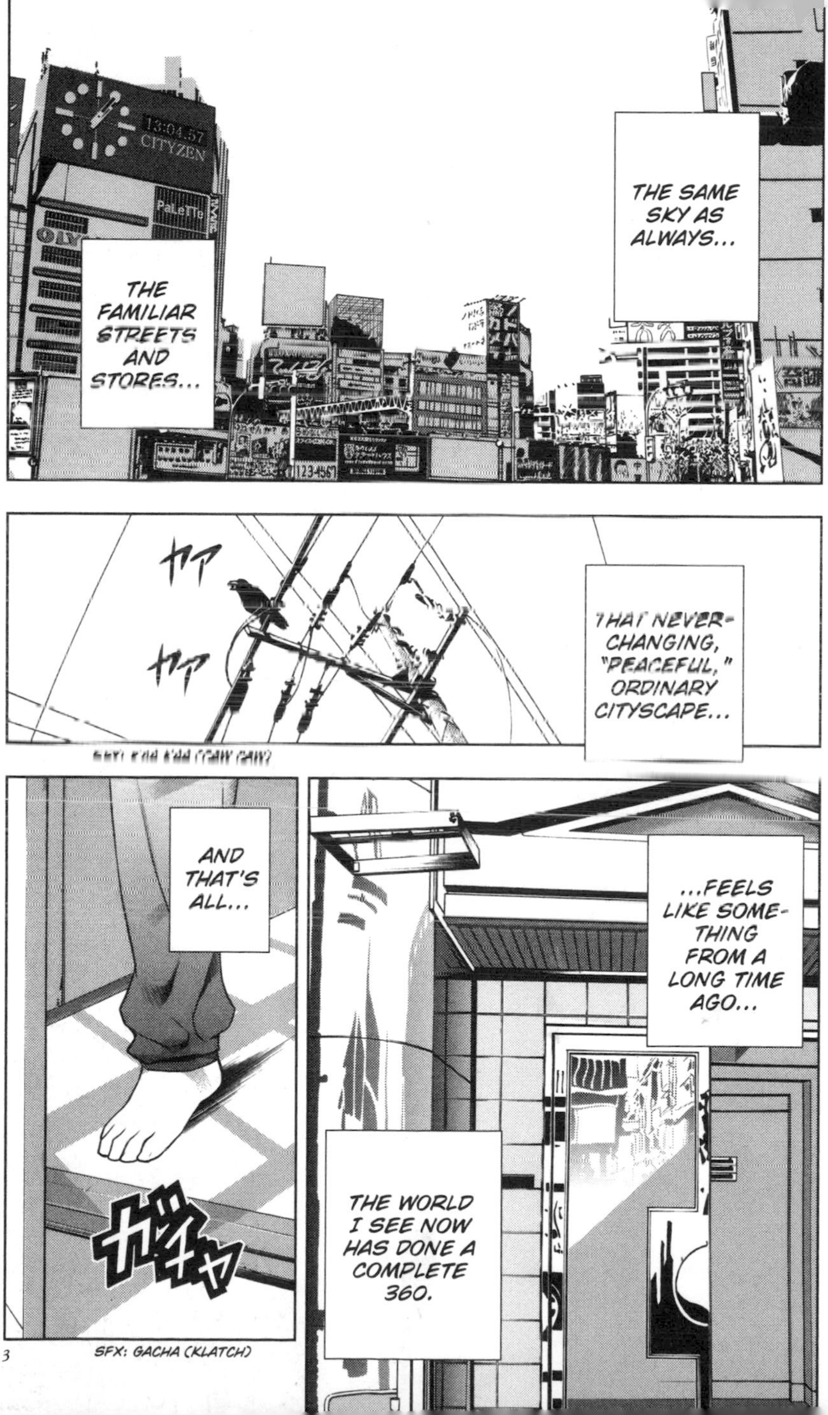
THE SAME SKY AS ALWAYS...
THE FAMILIAR STREETS AND STORES...
13:04.57
CITYZEN
PaLeTTe
THAT NEVER-CHANGING, "PEACEFUL," ORDINARY CITYSCAPE...
...FEELS LIKE SOMETHING FROM A LONG TIME AGO...
THE WORLD I SEE NOW HAS DONE A COMPLETE 360.
AND THAT'S ALL...
ガチャ
SFX: GACHA (KLATCH)

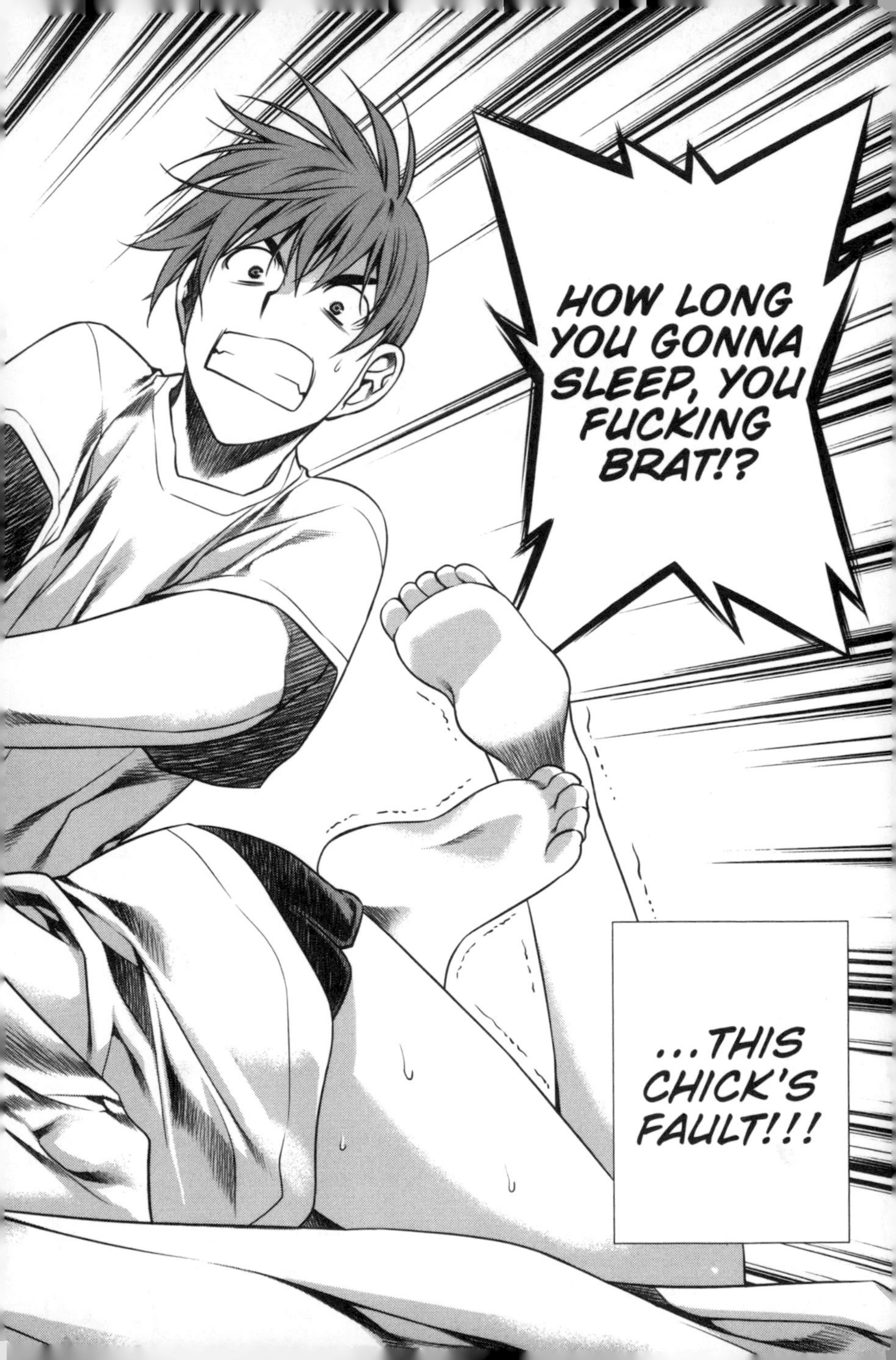
HOW LONG YOU GONNA SLEEP, YOU FUCKING BRAT!?
...THIS CHICK'S FAULT!!!

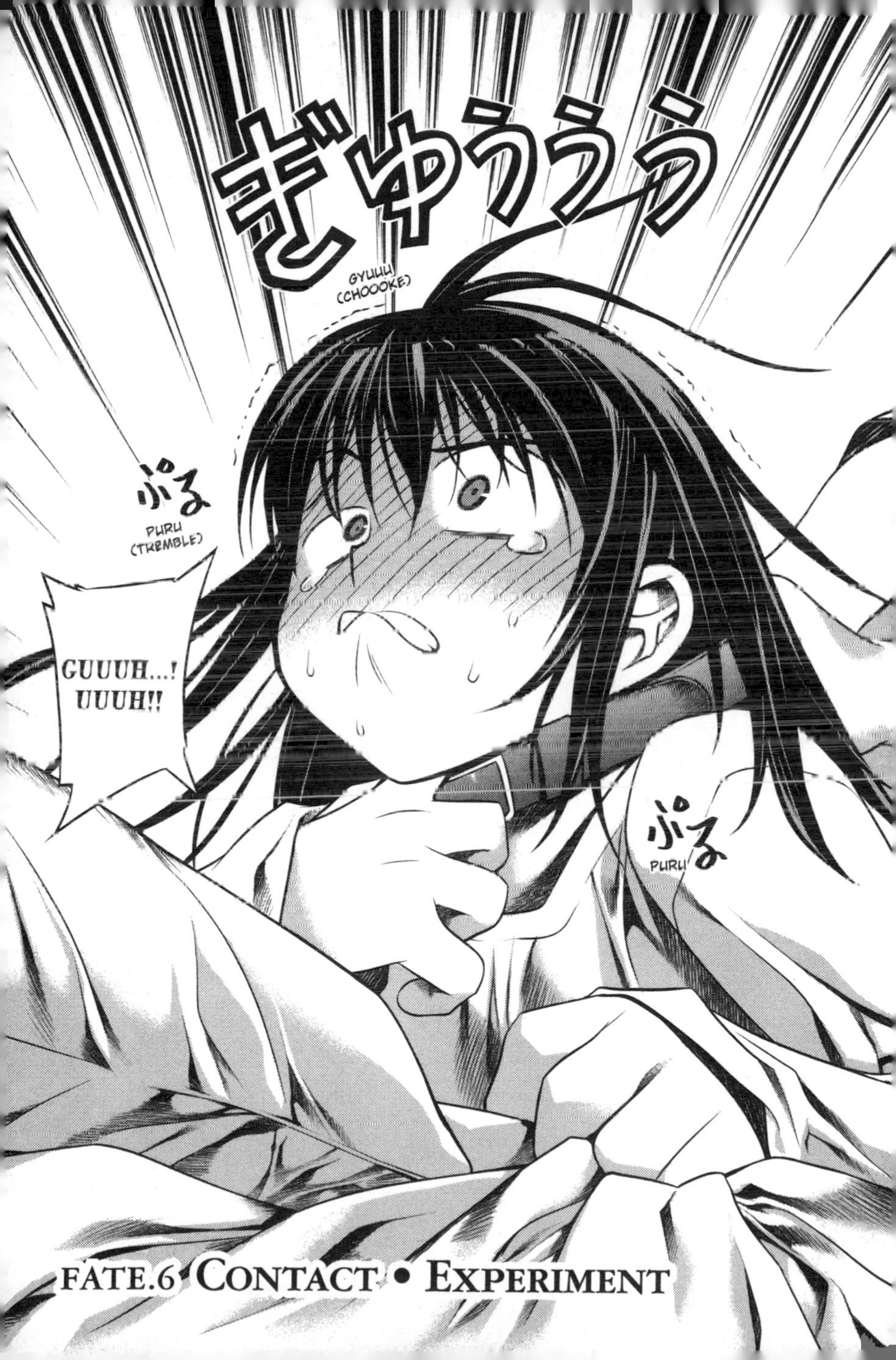
ぎゅううう
GYUUU (CHOOOKE)
ぷる
PURU (TREMBLE)
GUUUH...! UUUH!!
ぷる
PURU

FATE.6 CONTACT • EXPERIMENT

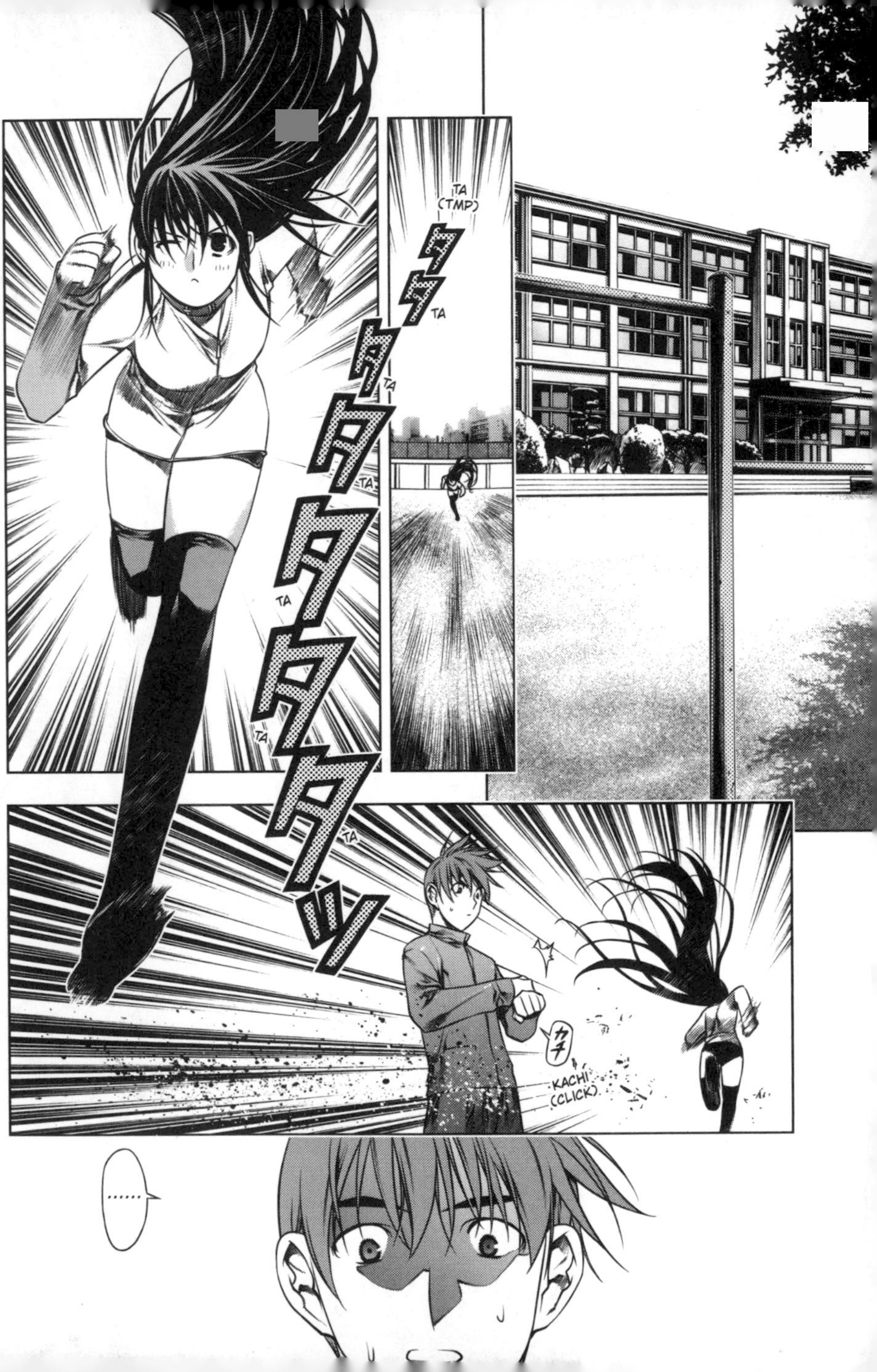
TA (TMP)
TA
TA
TA
TA
TA
TA
カチ
KACHI (CLICK)
......

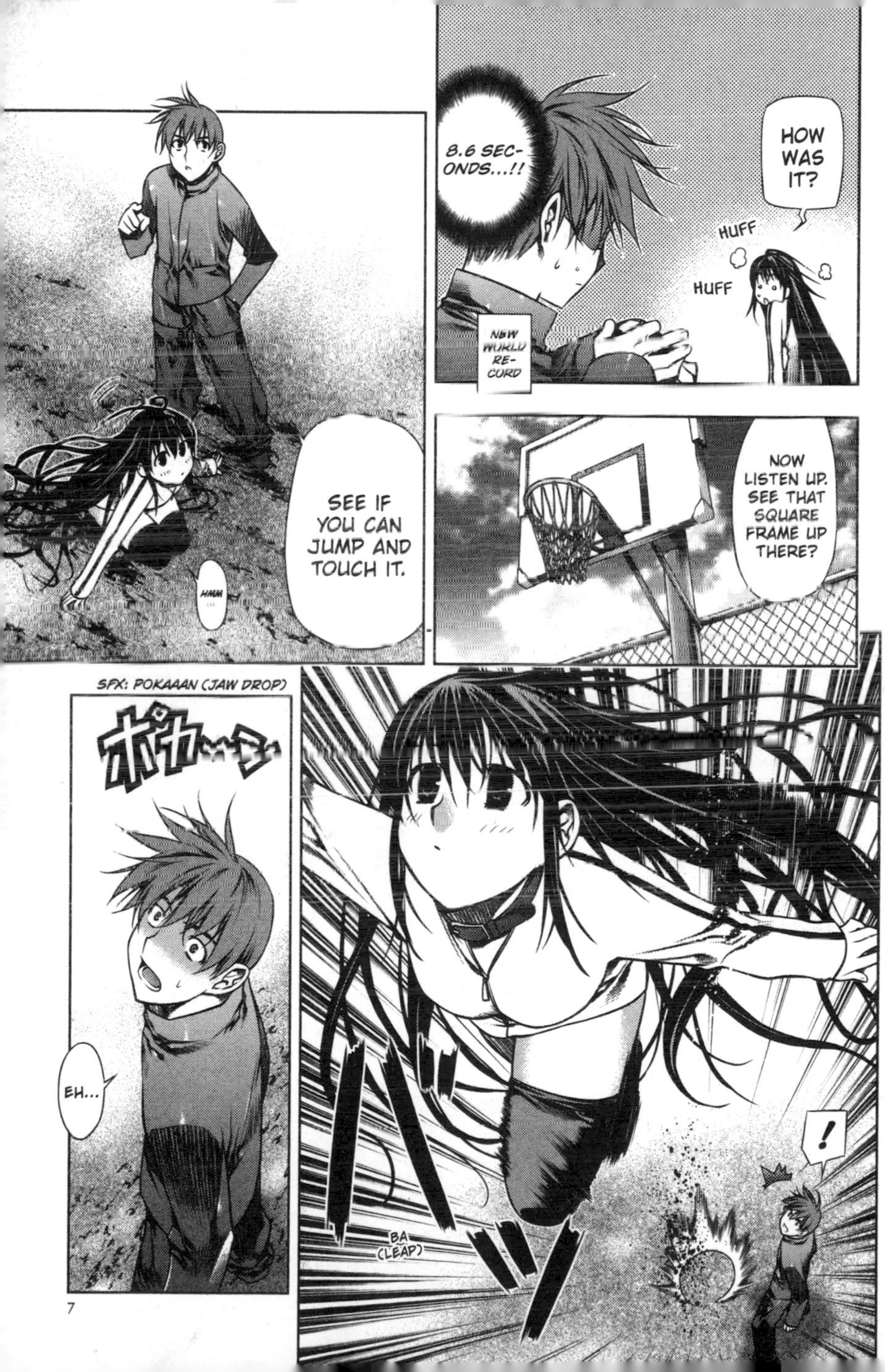
HOW WAS IT?
HUFF
HUFF
8.6 SECONDS...!!
NEW WORLD RECORD
NOW LISTEN UP. SEE THAT SQUARE FRAME UP THERE?
SEE IF YOU CAN JUMP AND TOUCH IT.
HMM ...
!
BA (LEAP)
SFX: POKAAAN (JAW DROP)
ポカ～ン
EH...

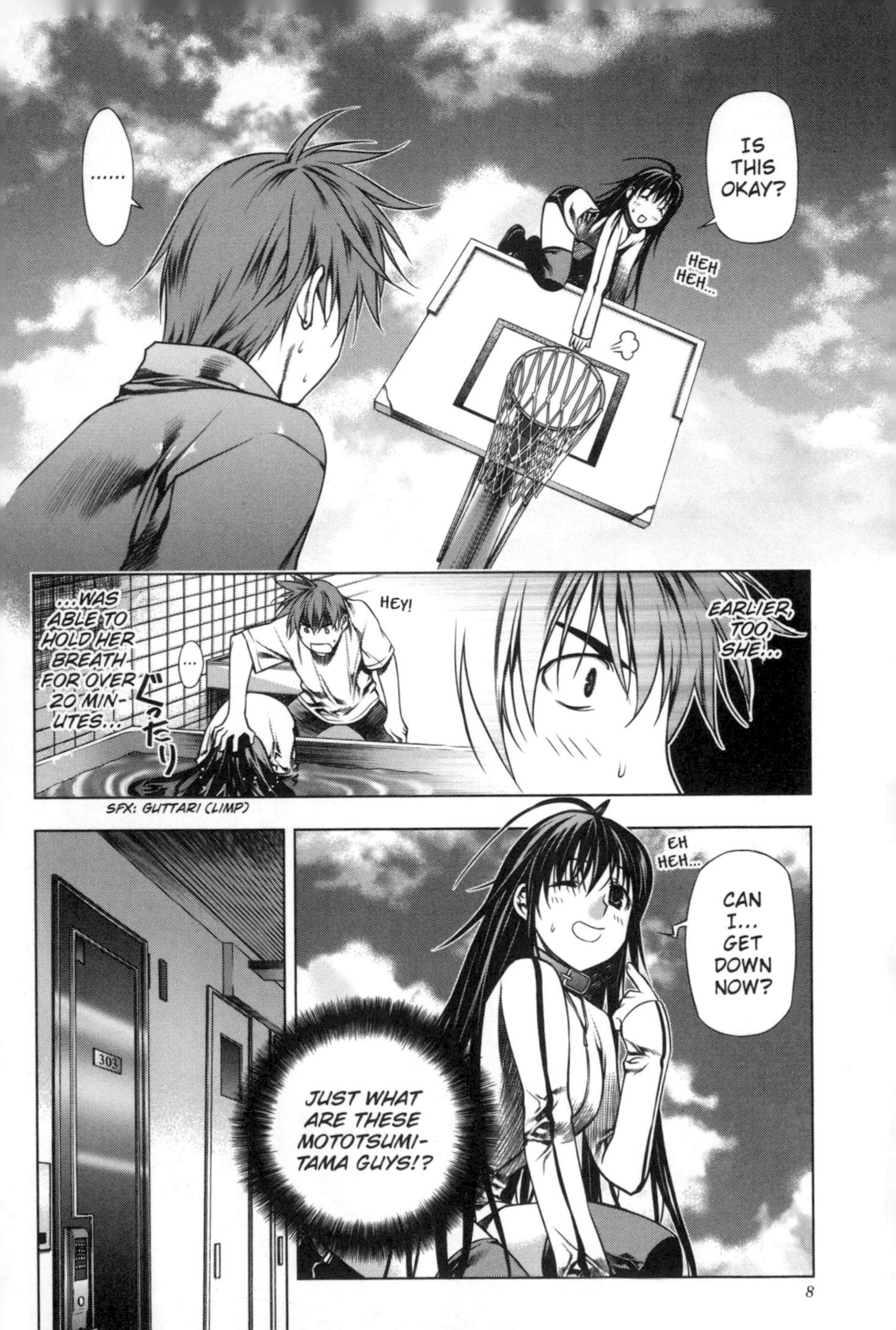

IS THIS OKAY?
HEH HEH...
......
EARLIER, TOO, SHE...
...WAS ABLE TO HOLD HER BREATH FOR OVER 20 MIN-UTES...
HEY!
...
ぐったり
SFX: GUTTARI (LIMP)
EH HEH...
CAN I... GET DOWN NOW?
JUST WHAT ARE THESE MOTOTSUMI-TAMA GUYS!?
303

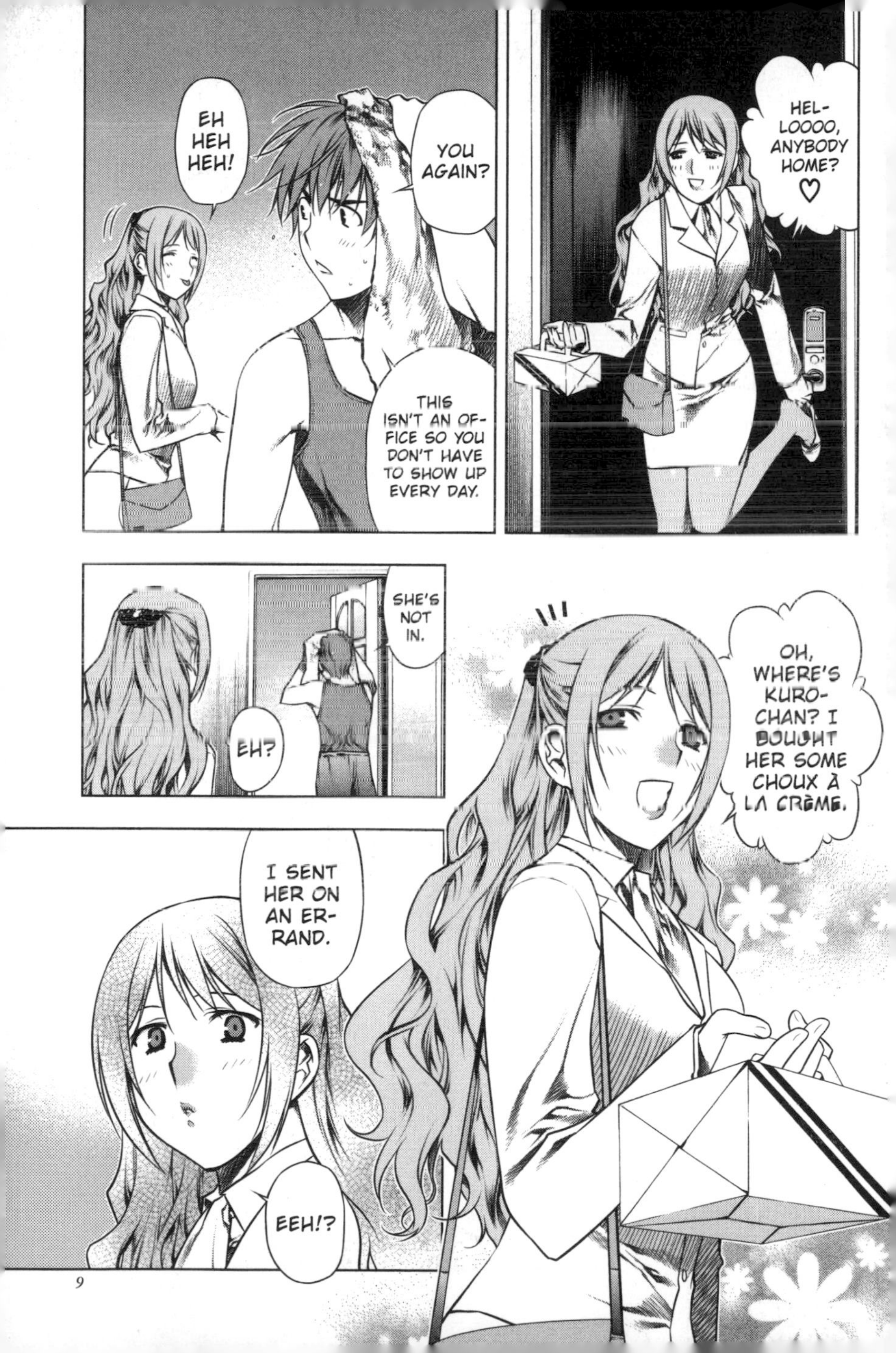
HEL-LOOOO, ANYBODY HOME? ♡
YOU AGAIN?
EH HEH HEH!
THIS ISN'T AN OF-FICE SO YOU DON'T HAVE TO SHOW UP EVERY DAY.
OH, WHERE'S KURO-CHAN? I BOUGHT HER SOME CHOUX À LA CRÈME.
SHE'S NOT IN.
EH?
I SENT HER ON AN ER-RAND.
EEH!?

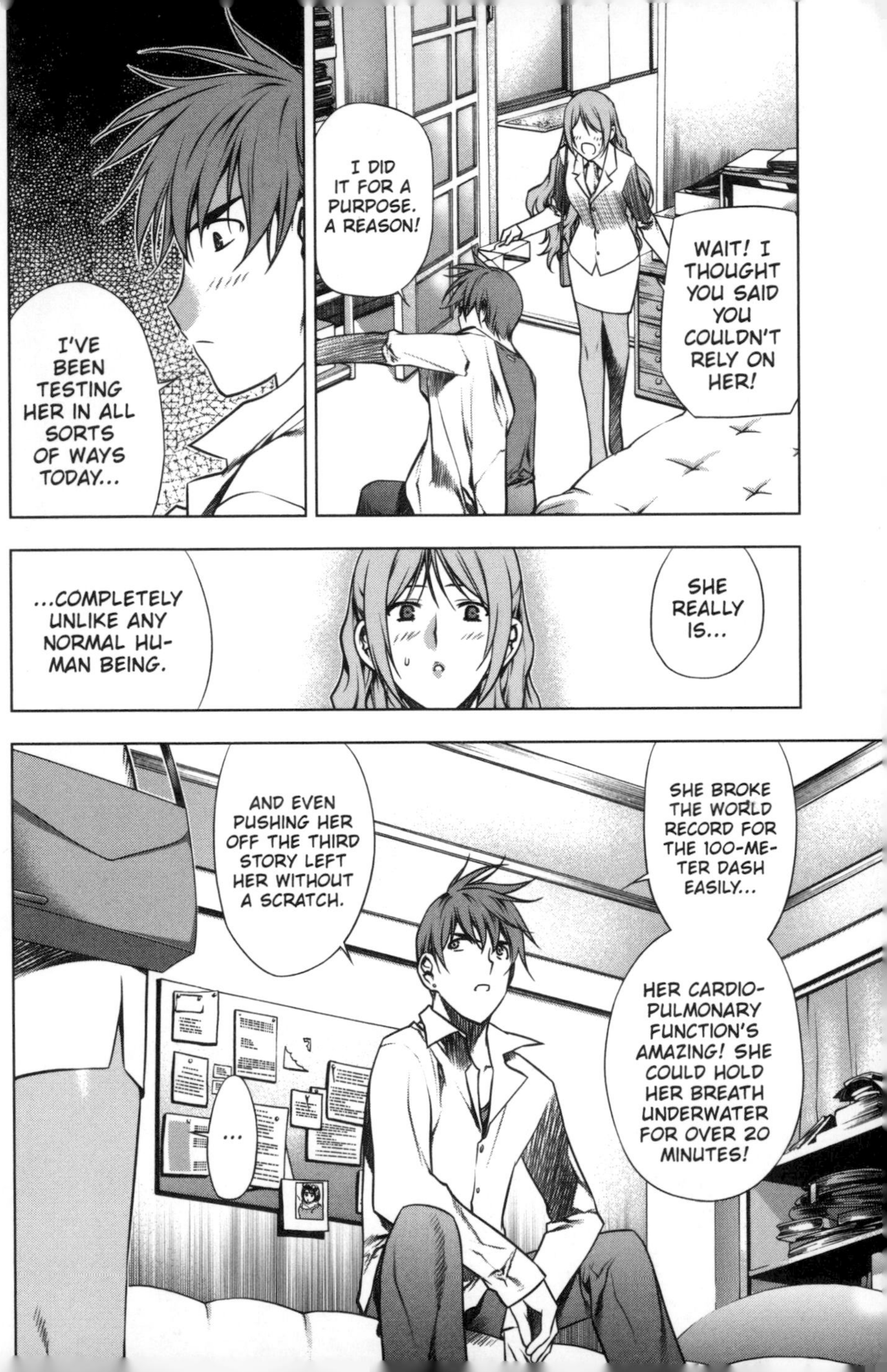
WAIT! I THOUGHT YOU SAID YOU COULDN'T RELY ON HER!
I DID IT FOR A PURPOSE. A REASON!
I'VE BEEN TESTING HER IN ALL SORTS OF WAYS TODAY...
SHE REALLY IS...
...COMPLETELY UNLIKE ANY NORMAL HU-MAN BEING.
SHE BROKE THE WORLD RECORD FOR THE 100-ME-TER DASH EASILY...
HER CARDIO-PULMONARY FUNCTION'S AMAZING! SHE COULD HOLD HER BREATH UNDERWATER FOR OVER 20 MINUTES!
AND EVEN PUSHING HER OFF THE THIRD STORY LEFT HER WITHOUT A SCRATCH.
...

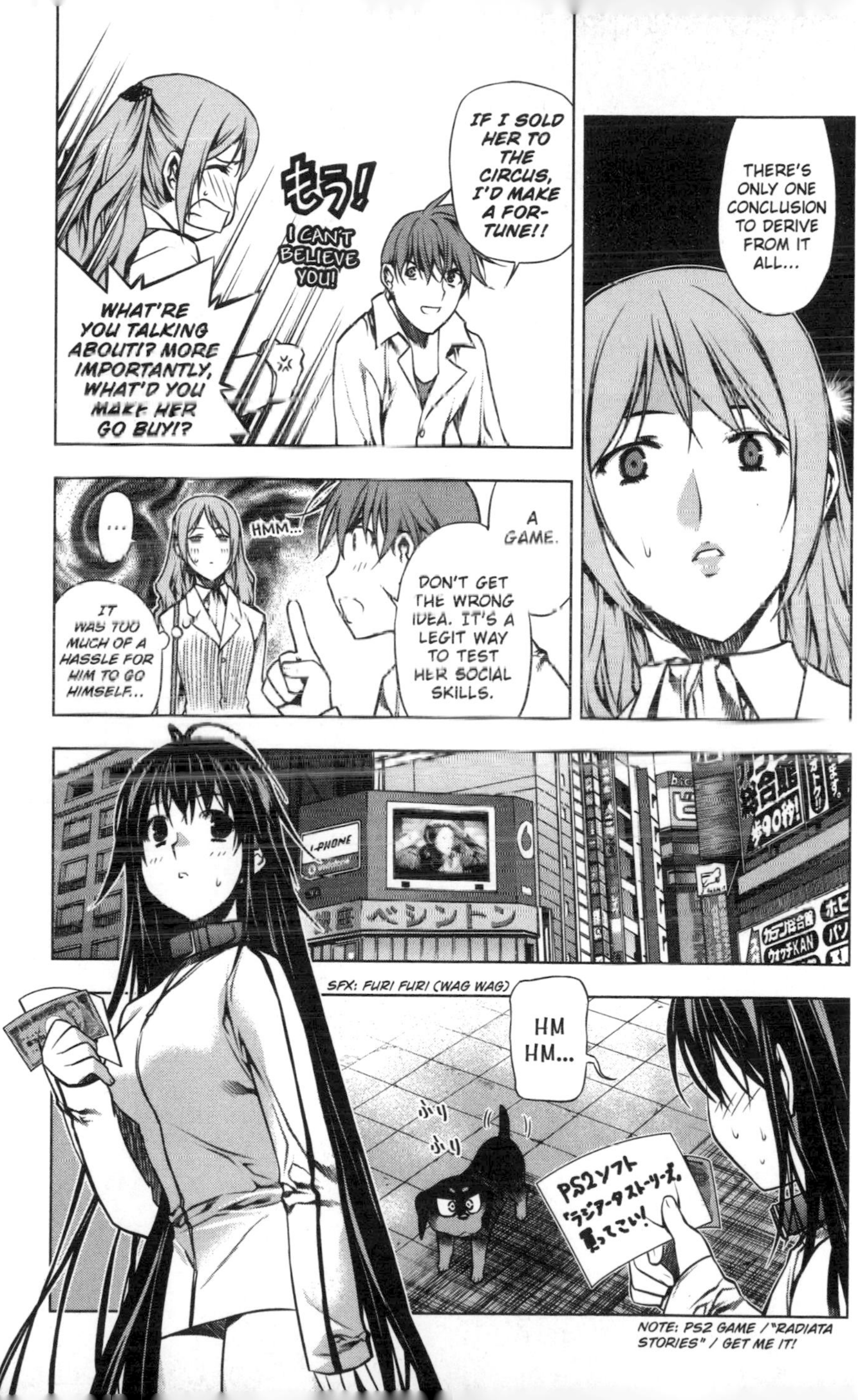

THERE'S ONLY ONE CONCLUSION TO DERIVE FROM IT ALL...
IF I SOLD HER TO THE CIRCUS, I'D MAKE A FOR-TUNE!!
もう!
I CAN'T BELIEVE YOU!
WHAT'RE YOU TALKING ABOUT!? MORE IMPORTANTLY, WHAT'D YOU MAKE HER GO BUY!?
A GAME.
DON'T GET THE WRONG IDEA. IT'S A LEGIT WAY TO TEST HER SOCIAL SKILLS.
HMM...
...
IT WAS TOO MUCH OF A HASSLE FOR HIM TO GO HIMSELF...
I-PHONE
ベシントン
SFX: FURI FURI (WAG WAG)
HM HM...
ふり
ふり
PS2ソフト
「ラジアータストーリーズ」
買ってこい!
NOTE: PS2 GAME / "RADIATA STORIES" / GET ME IT!

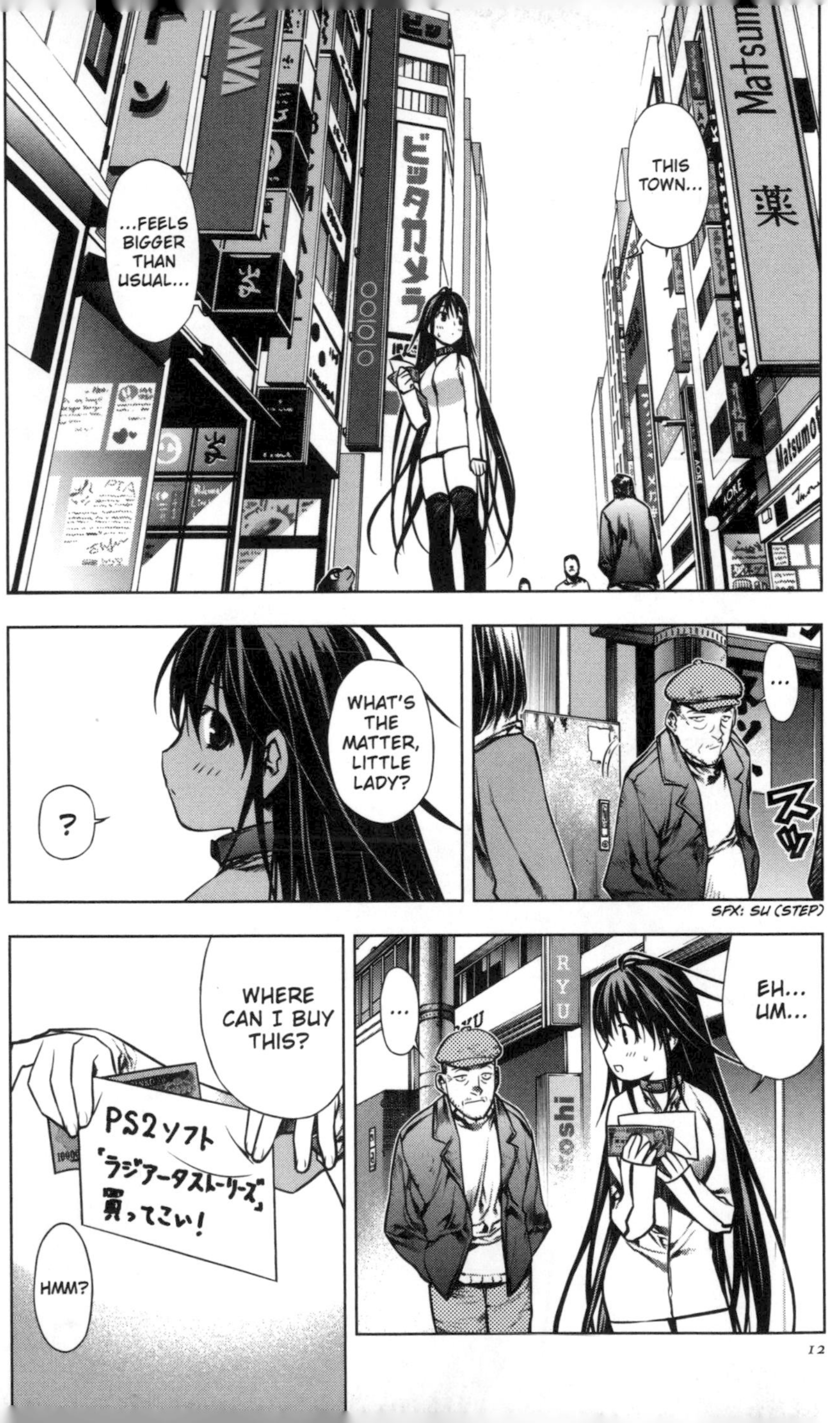
THIS TOWN...
...FEELS BIGGER THAN USUAL...
...
スッ
SFX: SU (STEP)
WHAT'S THE MATTER, LITTLE LADY?
?
EH... UM...
...
WHERE CAN I BUY THIS?
PS2ソフト「ラジアータストーリーズ」買ってこい！
HMM?

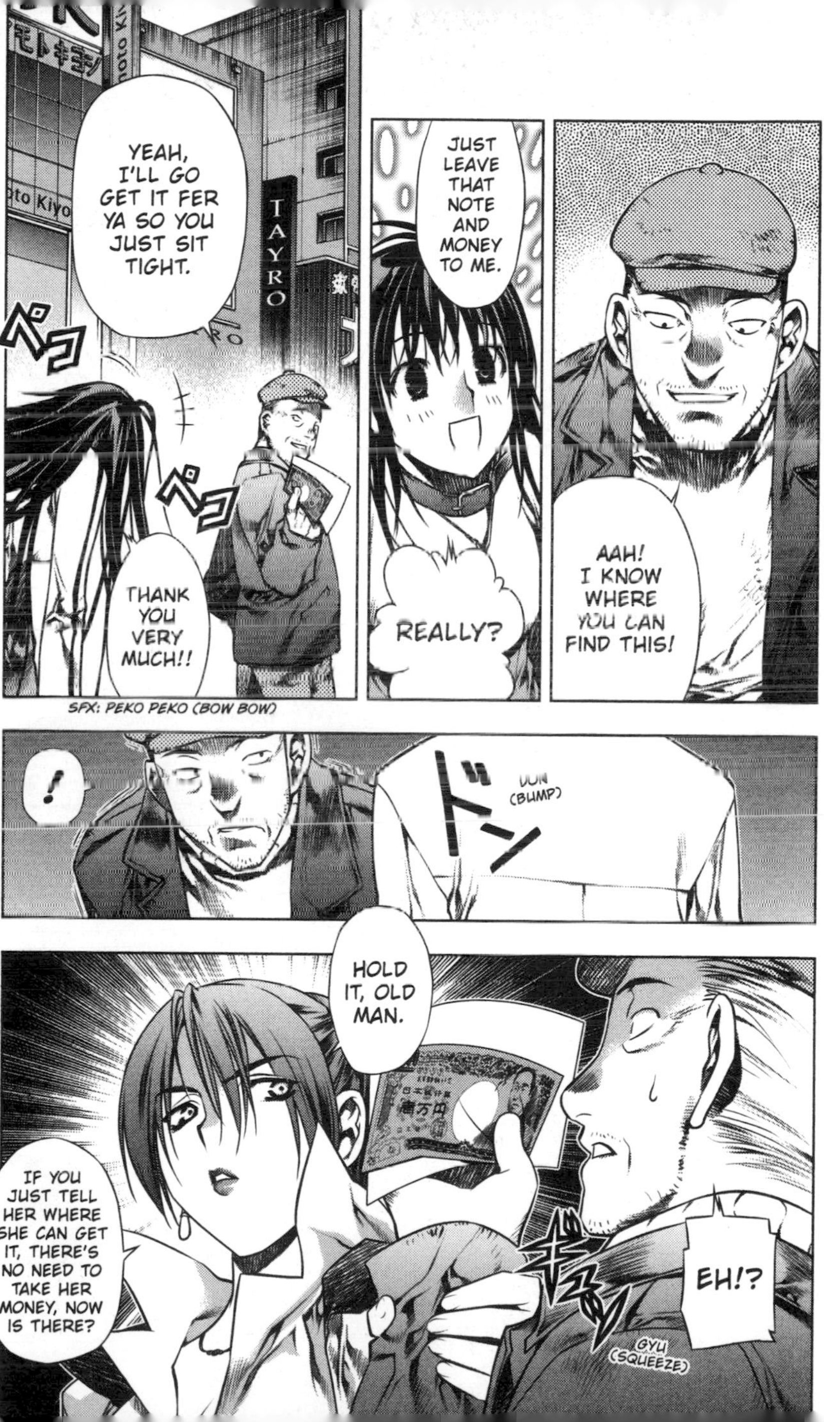
AAH! I KNOW WHERE YOU CAN FIND THIS!
JUST LEAVE THAT NOTE AND MONEY TO ME.
REALLY?
TAYRO
YEAH, I'LL GO GET IT FER YA SO YOU JUST SIT TIGHT.
ペコ
ペコ
THANK YOU VERY MUCH!!
SFX: PEKO PEKO (BOW BOW)
ドン
(BUMP)
!
HOLD IT, OLD MAN.
EH!?
GYU (SQUEEZE)
IF YOU JUST TELL HER WHERE SHE CAN GET IT, THERE'S NO NEED TO TAKE HER MONEY, NOW IS THERE?

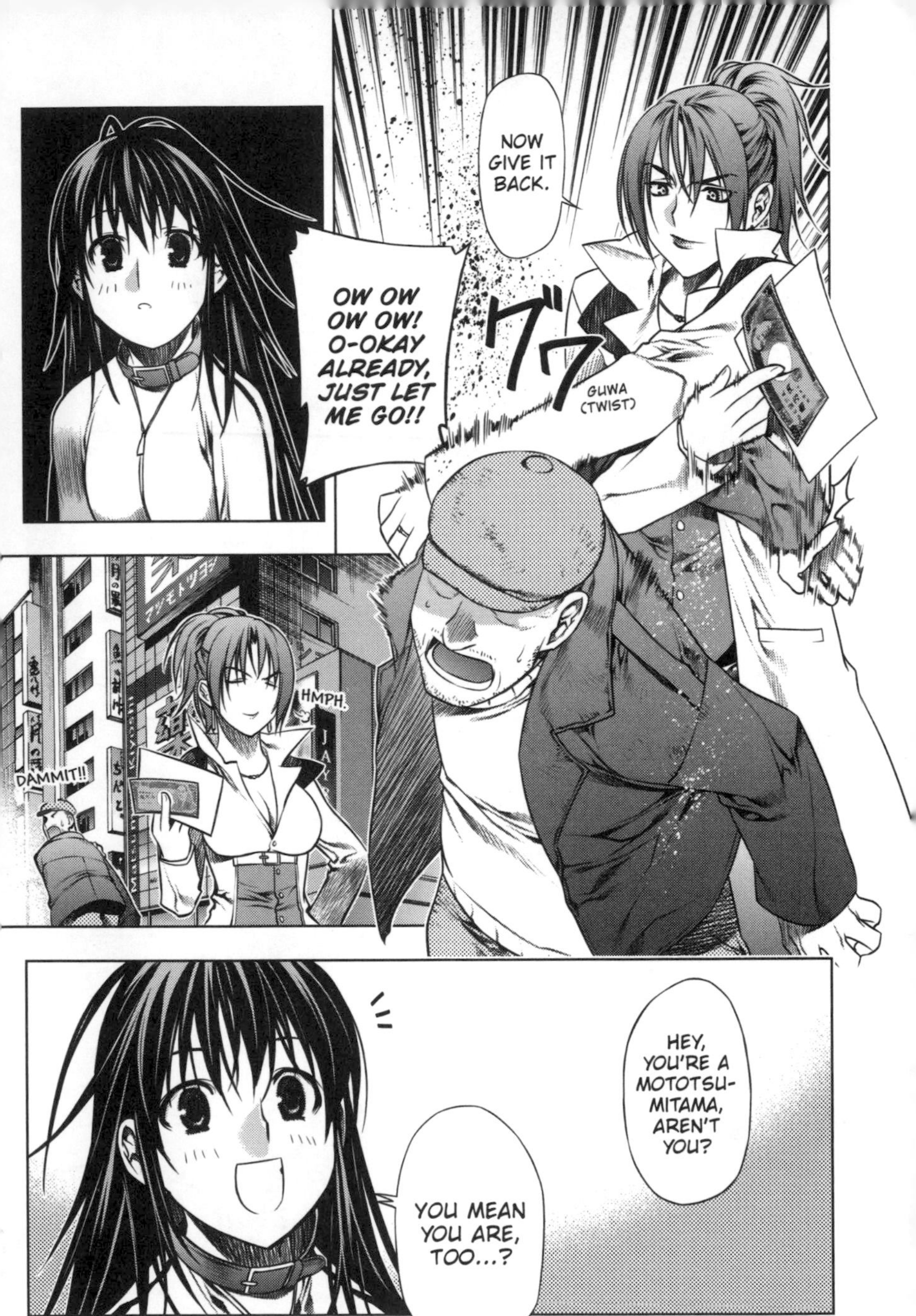
NOW GIVE IT BACK.
OW OW OW OW! O-OKAY ALREADY, JUST LET ME GO!!
グワ
GUWA (TWIST)
HMPH.
DAMMIT!!
HEY, YOU'RE A MOTOTSU-MITAMA, AREN'T YOU?
YOU MEAN YOU ARE, TOO...?

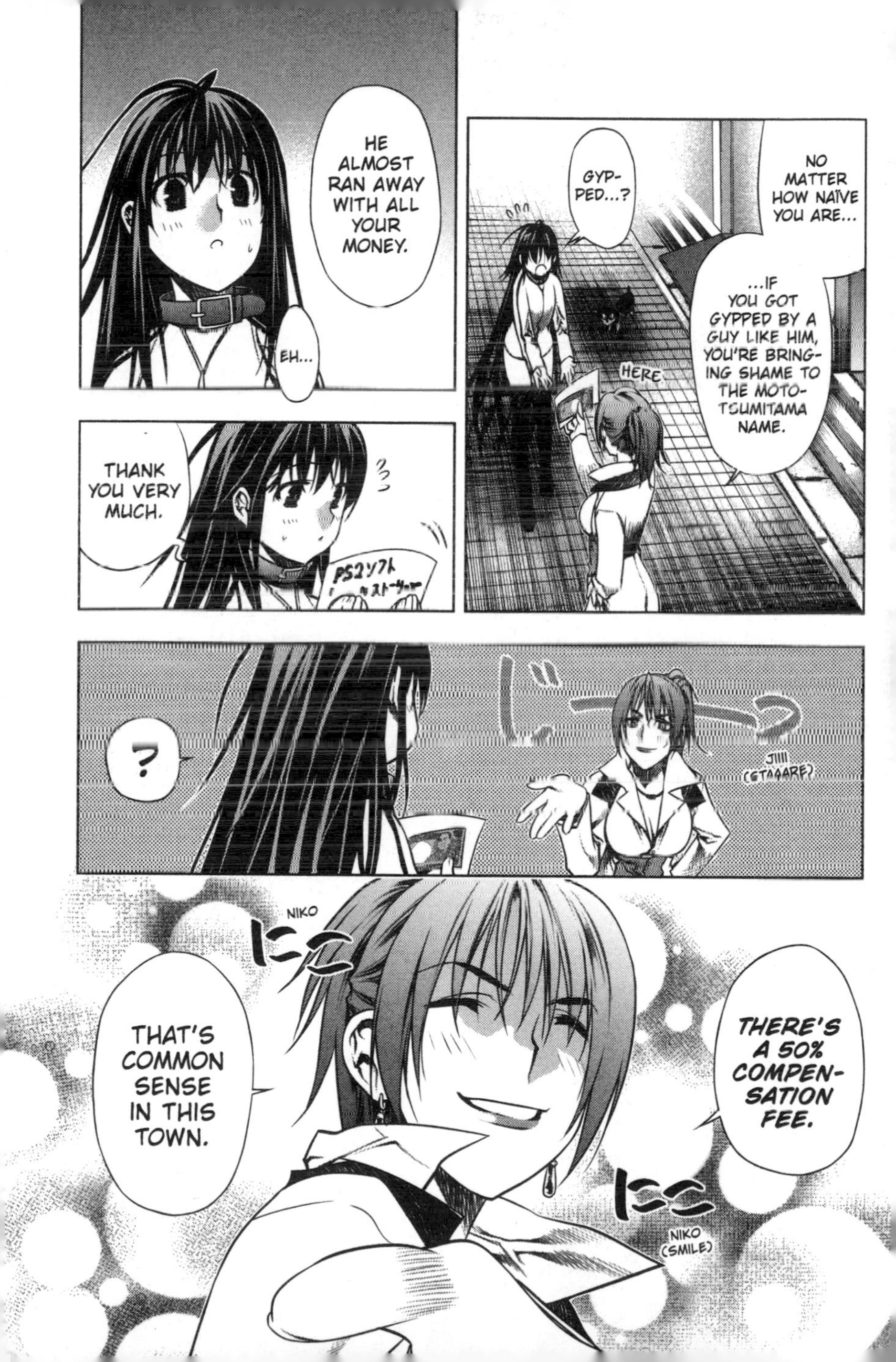
NO MATTER HOW NAÏVE YOU ARE...
GYP-PED...?
...IF YOU GOT GYPPED BY A GUY LIKE HIM, YOU'RE BRING-ING SHAME TO THE MOTO-TSUMITAMA NAME.
HERE.
HE ALMOST RAN AWAY WITH ALL YOUR MONEY.
EH...
THANK YOU VERY MUCH.
PS2ソフト
じーっ
JIIII (STAAARE)
?
THERE'S A 50% COMPEN-SATION FEE.
にこ
NIKO (SMILE)
にこ
NIKO
THAT'S COMMON SENSE IN THIS TOWN.

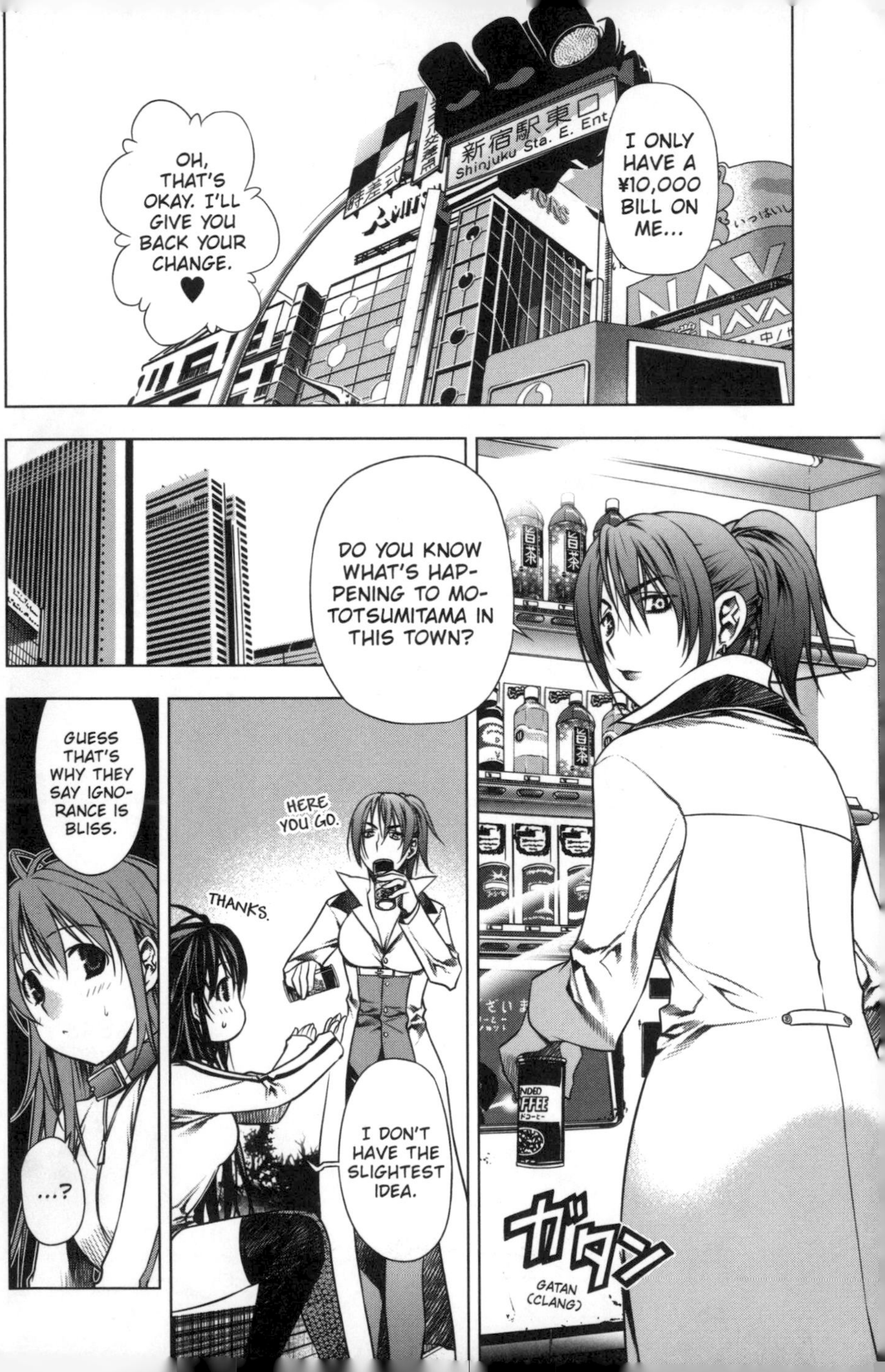
新宿駅東口
Shinjuku Sta. E. Ent.
I ONLY HAVE A ¥10,000 BILL ON ME...
OH, THAT'S OKAY. I'LL GIVE YOU BACK YOUR CHANGE. ♥
DO YOU KNOW WHAT'S HAP-PENING TO MO-TOTSUMITAMA IN THIS TOWN?
GATAN (CLANG)
HERE YOU GO.
THANKS.
I DON'T HAVE THE SLIGHTEST IDEA.
GUESS THAT'S WHY THEY SAY IGNO-RANCE IS BLISS.
...?

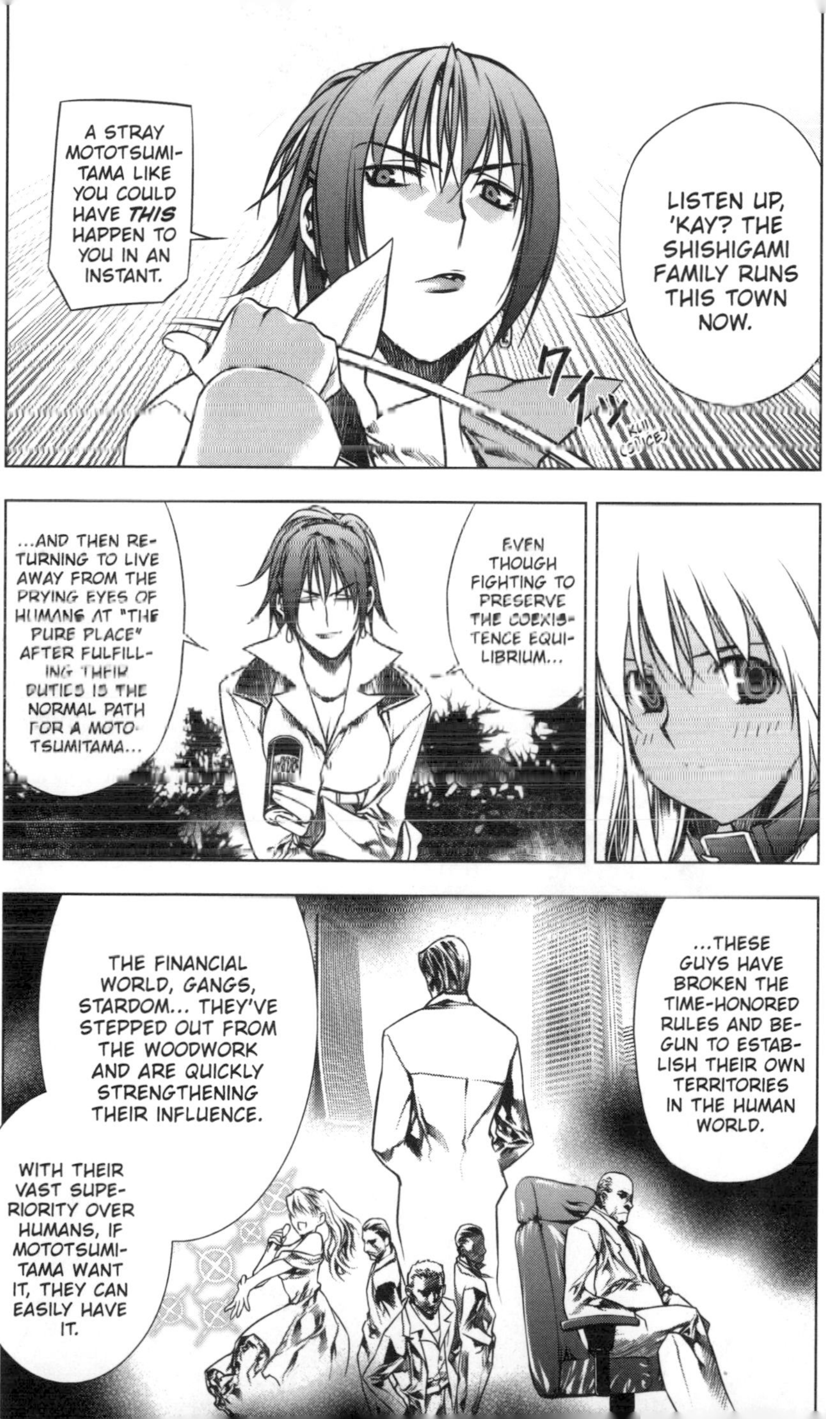
LISTEN UP, 'KAY? THE SHISHIGAMI FAMILY RUNS THIS TOWN NOW.
クイッ
KUII (SLICES)
A STRAY MOTOTSUMI-TAMA LIKE YOU COULD HAVE *THIS* HAPPEN TO YOU IN AN INSTANT.
EVEN THOUGH FIGHTING TO PRESERVE THE COEXISTENCE EQUILIBRIUM...
...AND THEN RETURNING TO LIVE AWAY FROM THE PRYING EYES OF HUMANS AT "THE PURE PLACE" AFTER FULFILLING THEIR DUTIES IS THE NORMAL PATH FOR A MOTOTSUMITAMA...
...THESE GUYS HAVE BROKEN THE TIME-HONORED RULES AND BEGUN TO ESTABLISH THEIR OWN TERRITORIES IN THE HUMAN WORLD.
THE FINANCIAL WORLD, GANGS, STARDOM... THEY'VE STEPPED OUT FROM THE WOODWORK AND ARE QUICKLY STRENGTHENING THEIR INFLUENCE.
WITH THEIR VAST SUPERIORITY OVER HUMANS, IF MOTOTSUMITAMA WANT IT, THEY CAN EASILY HAVE IT.

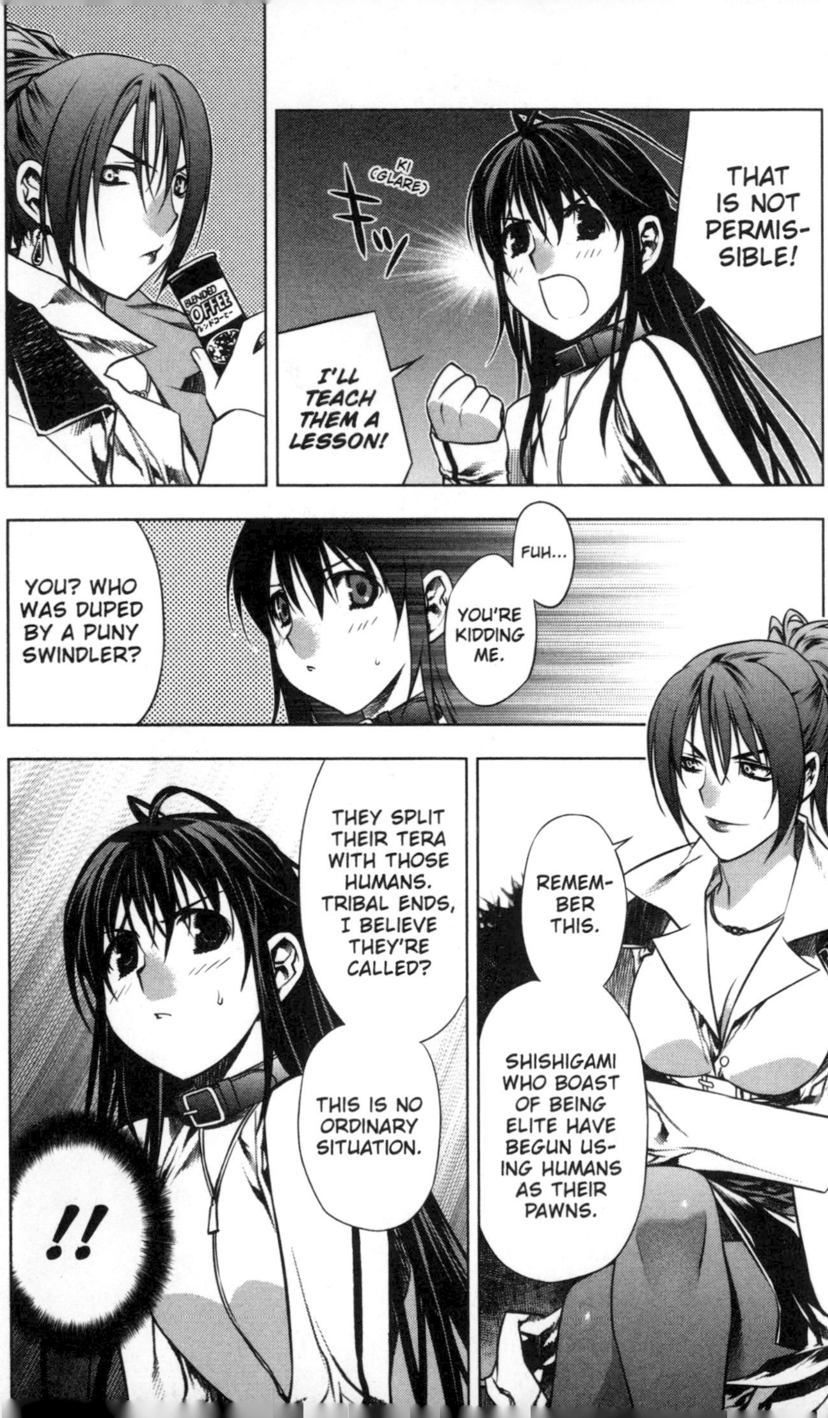
THAT IS NOT PERMIS-SIBLE!
KI (GLARE)
I'LL TEACH THEM A LESSON!
BLENDED
OFFEE
FUH...
YOU'RE KIDDING ME.
YOU? WHO WAS DUPED BY A PUNY SWINDLER?
REMEM-BER THIS.
SHISHIGAMI WHO BOAST OF BEING ELITE HAVE BEGUN US-ING HUMANS AS THEIR PAWNS.
THEY SPLIT THEIR TERA WITH THOSE HUMANS. TRIBAL ENDS, I BELIEVE THEY'RE CALLED?
THIS IS NO ORDINARY SITUATION.
!!

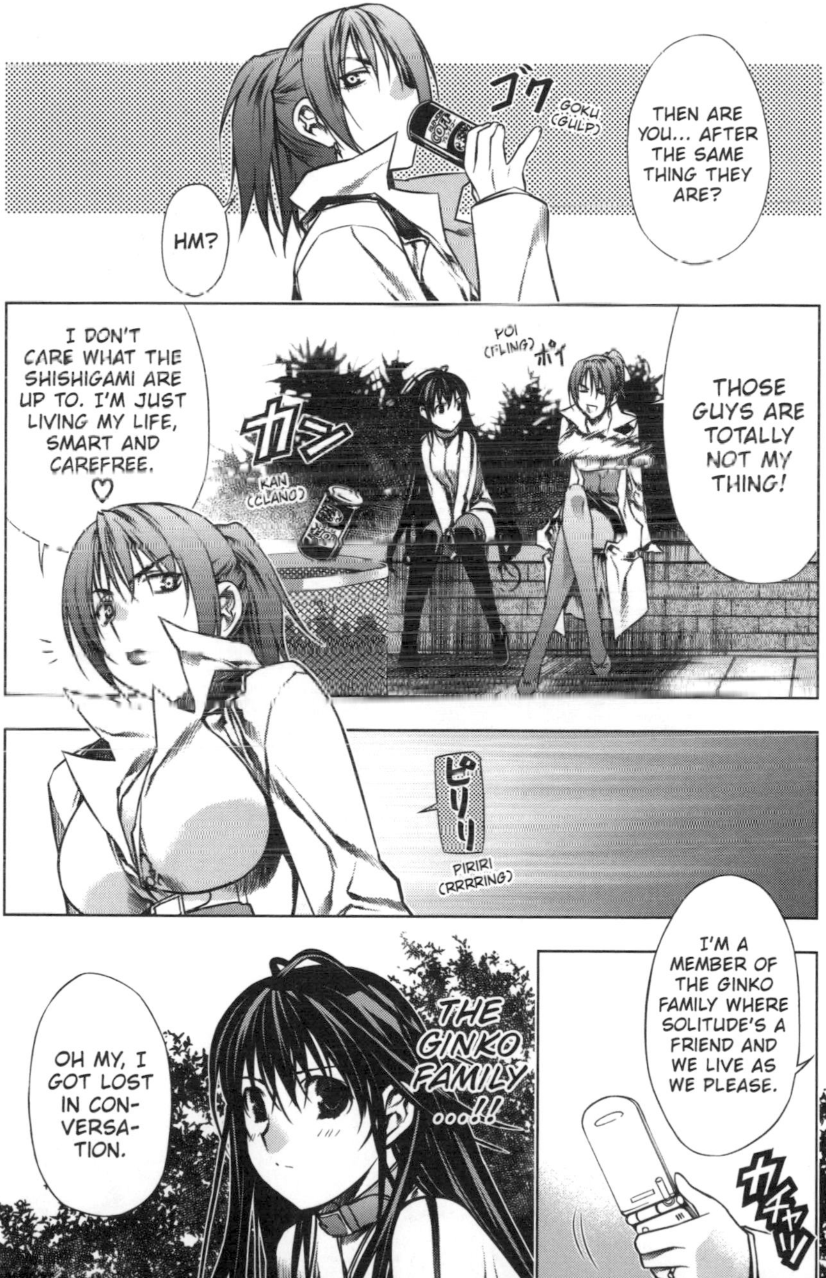
THEN ARE YOU... AFTER THE SAME THING THEY ARE?
ゴク GOKU (GULP)
HM?
THOSE GUYS ARE TOTALLY NOT MY THING!
ポイ POI (FLING)
カン KAN (CLANG)
I DON'T CARE WHAT THE SHISHIGAMI ARE UP TO. I'M JUST LIVING MY LIFE, SMART AND CAREFREE. ♡
ピリリ PIRIRI (RRRRING)
I'M A MEMBER OF THE GINKO FAMILY WHERE SOLITUDE'S A FRIEND AND WE LIVE AS WE PLEASE.
THE GINKO FAMILY.....!!
OH MY, I GOT LOST IN CON-VERSA-TION.
SFX: KACHA (K-CLICK)

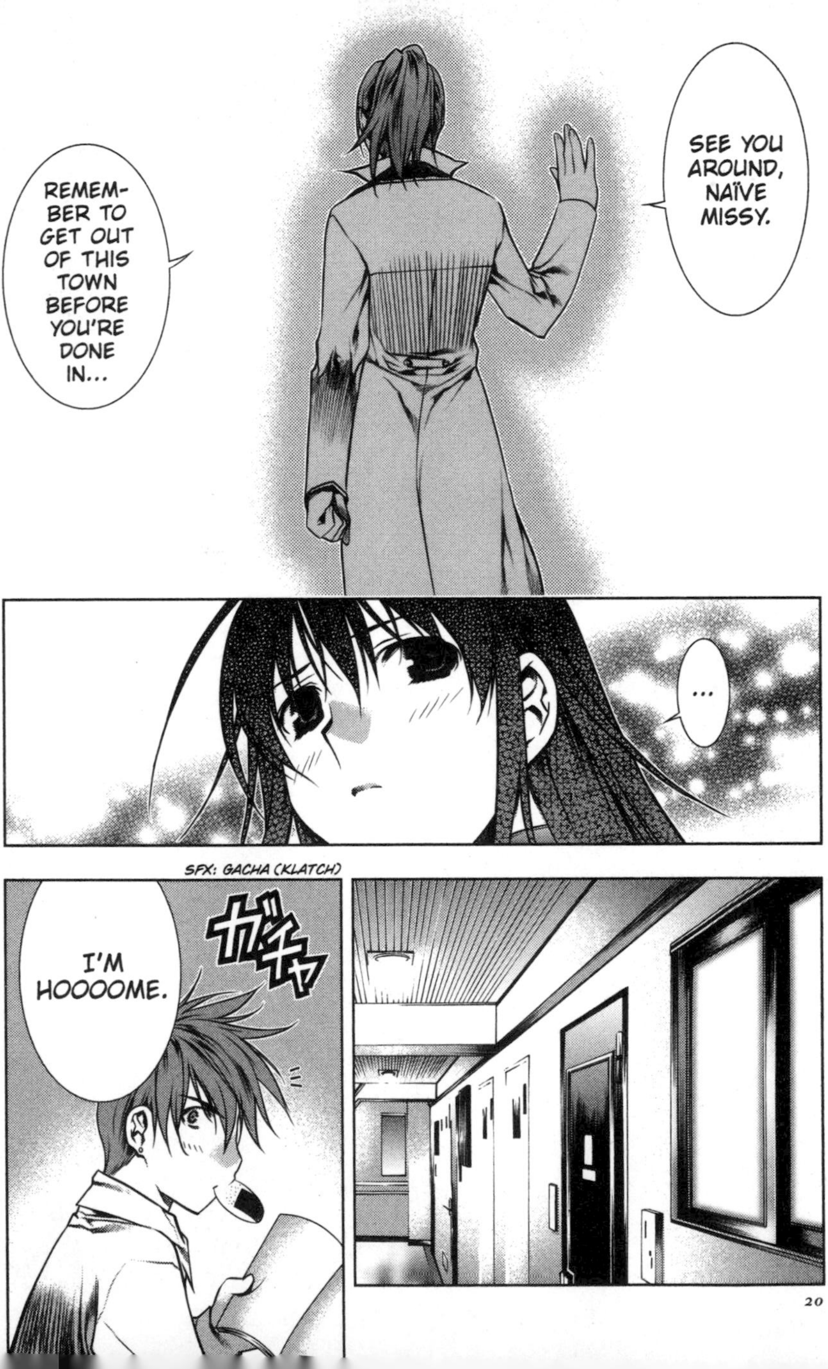
SEE YOU AROUND, NAÏVE MISSY.
REMEM-BER TO GET OUT OF THIS TOWN BEFORE YOU'RE DONE IN...
...
SFX: GACHA (KLATCH)
ガチャ
I'M HOOOOME.

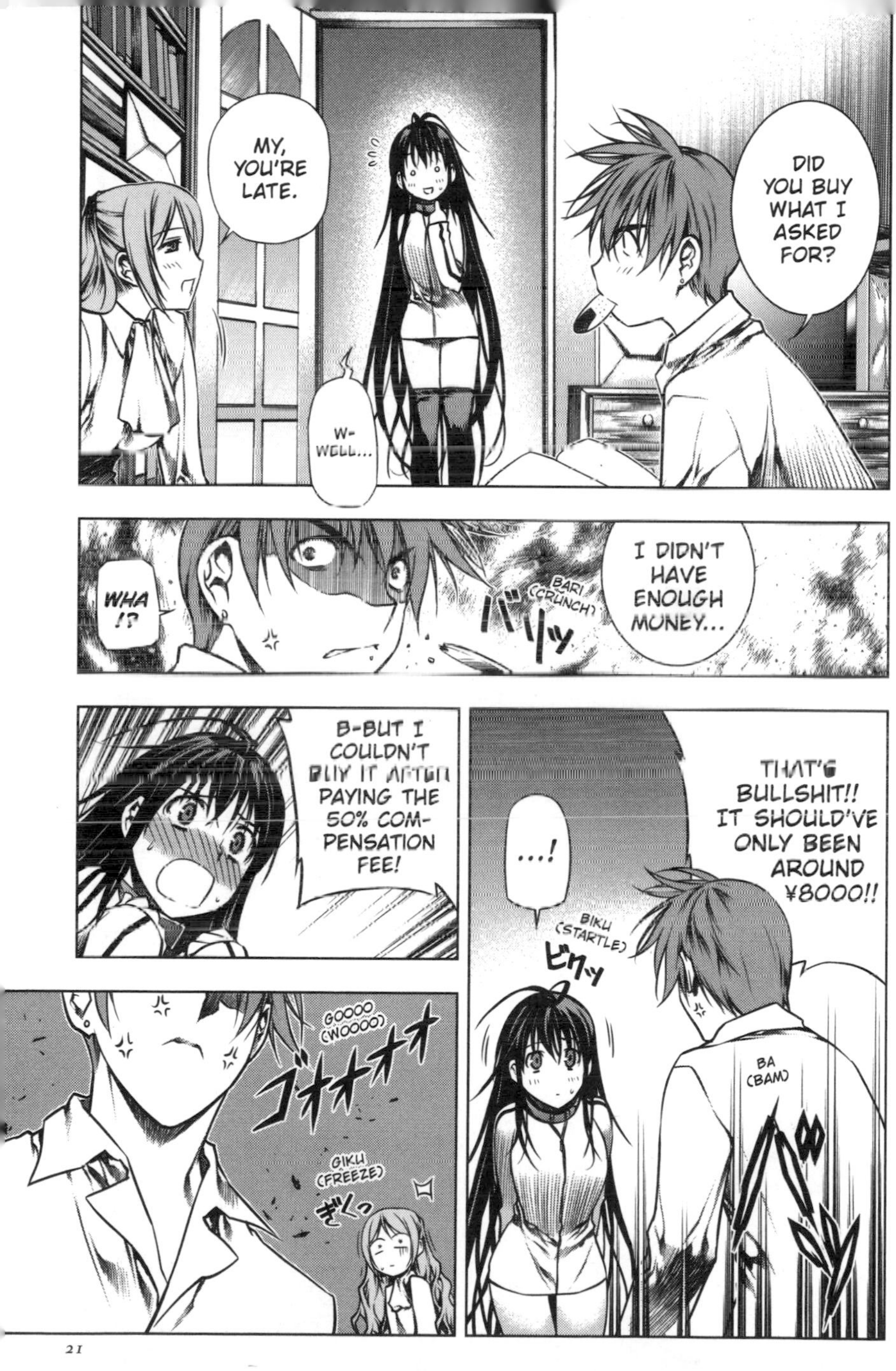
DID YOU BUY WHAT I ASKED FOR?
MY, YOU'RE LATE.
W-WELL...
I DIDN'T HAVE ENOUGH MONEY...
BARI (CRUNCH)
バリッ
WHA!?
THAT'S BULLSHIT!! IT SHOULD'VE ONLY BEEN AROUND ¥8000!!
...!
BIKU (STARTLE)
ビクッ
BA (BAM)
パッ
B-BUT I COULDN'T BUY IT AFTER PAYING THE 50% COMPENSATION FEE!
GOOOO (WOOOO)
ゴオオオ
GIKU (FREEZE)
ぎくっ

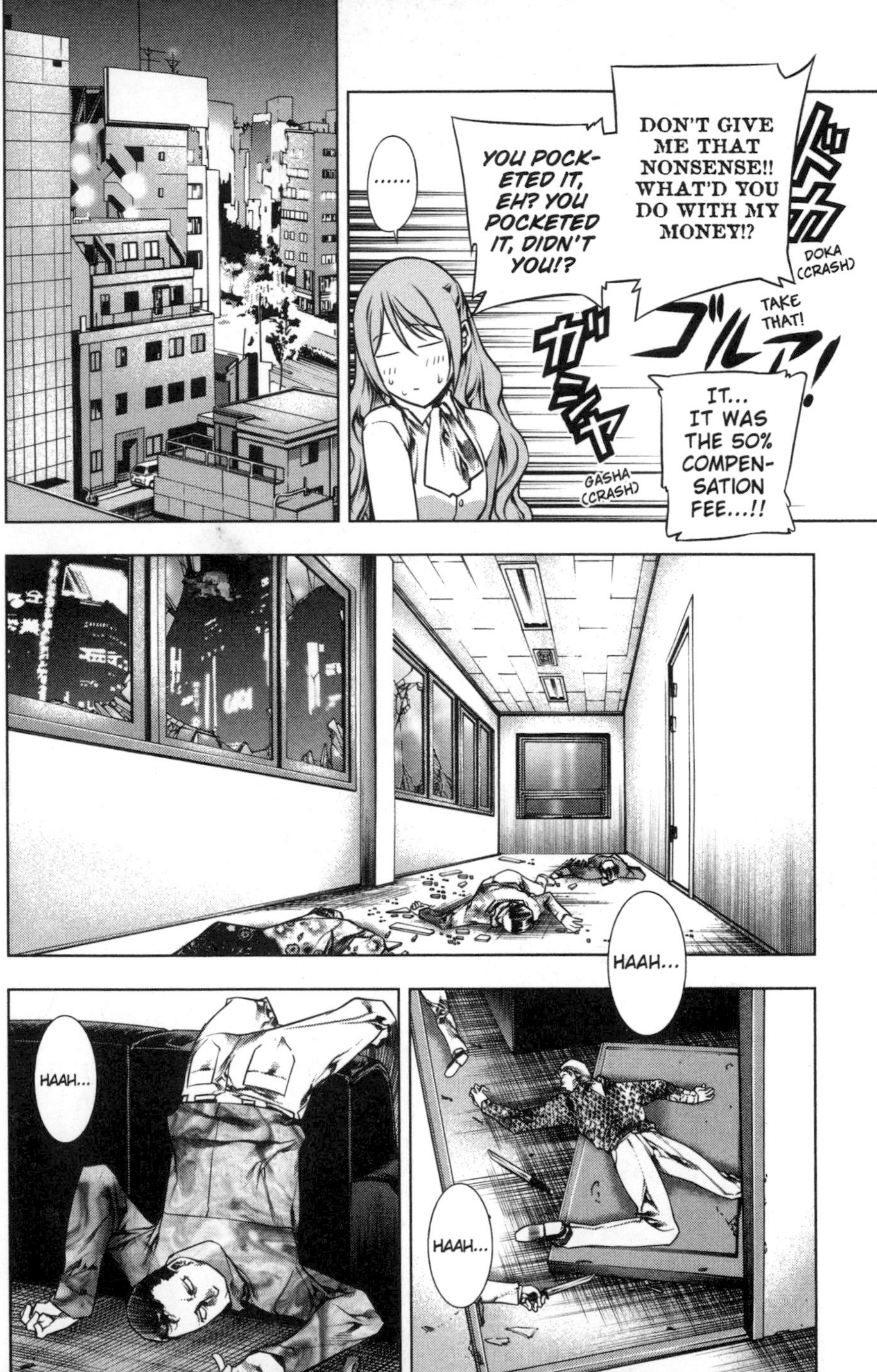
DON'T GIVE ME THAT NONSENSE!! WHAT'D YOU DO WITH MY MONEY!?
DOKA (CRASH)
YOU POCKETED IT, EH? YOU POCKETED IT, DIDN'T YOU!?
......
TAKE THAT!
IT... IT WAS THE 50% COMPENSATION FEE...!!
GASHA (CRASH)
HAAH...
HAAH...
HAAH...

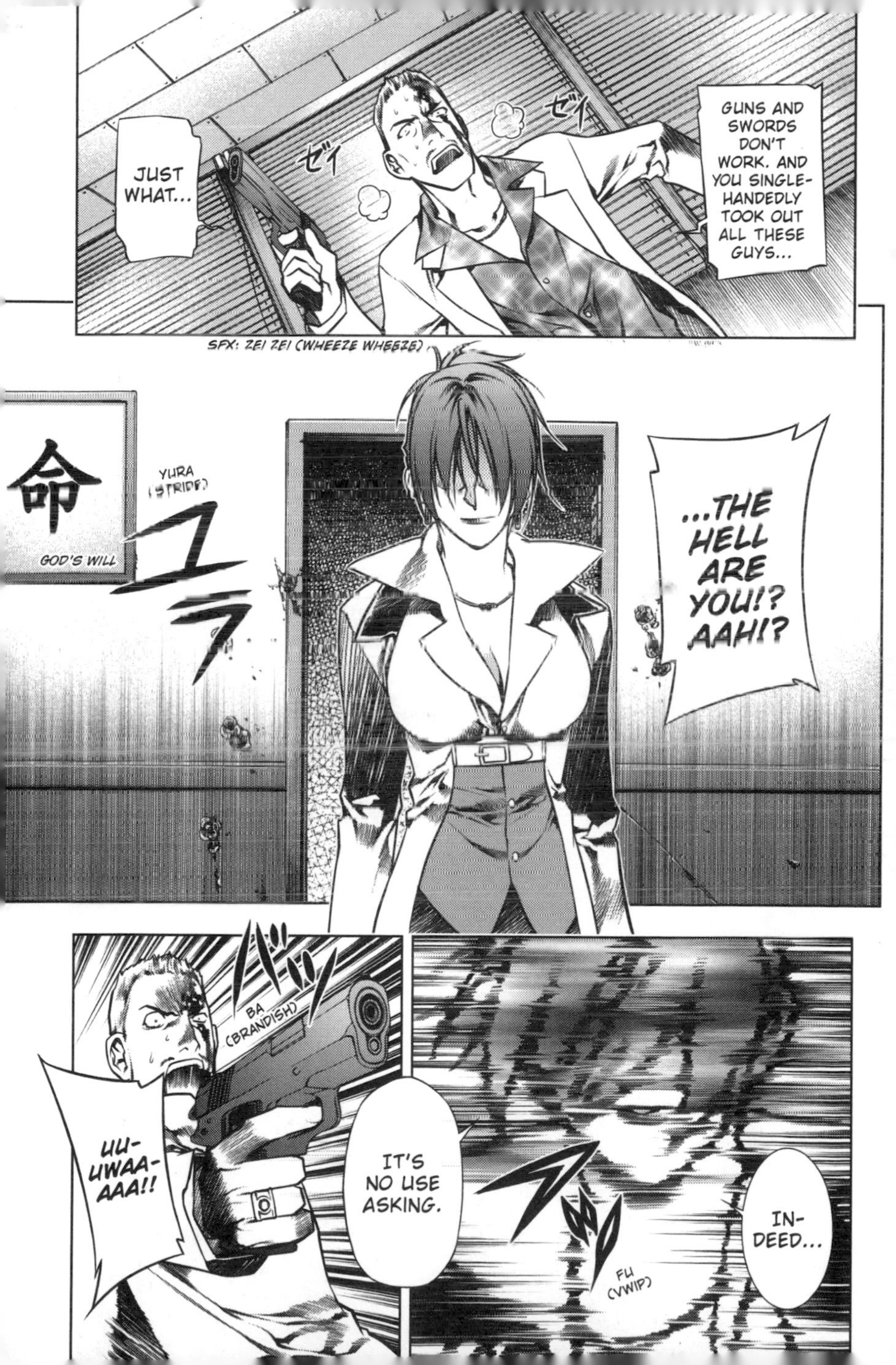
GUNS AND SWORDS DON'T WORK. AND YOU SINGLE-HANDEDLY TOOK OUT ALL THESE GUYS...
JUST WHAT...
SFX: ZEI ZEI (WHEEZE WHEEZE)
...THE HELL ARE YOU!? AAH!?
YURA (STRIDE)
GOD'S WILL
IN-DEED...
FU (VWIP)
IT'S NO USE ASKING.
BA (BRANDISH)
UU-UWAA-AAA!!

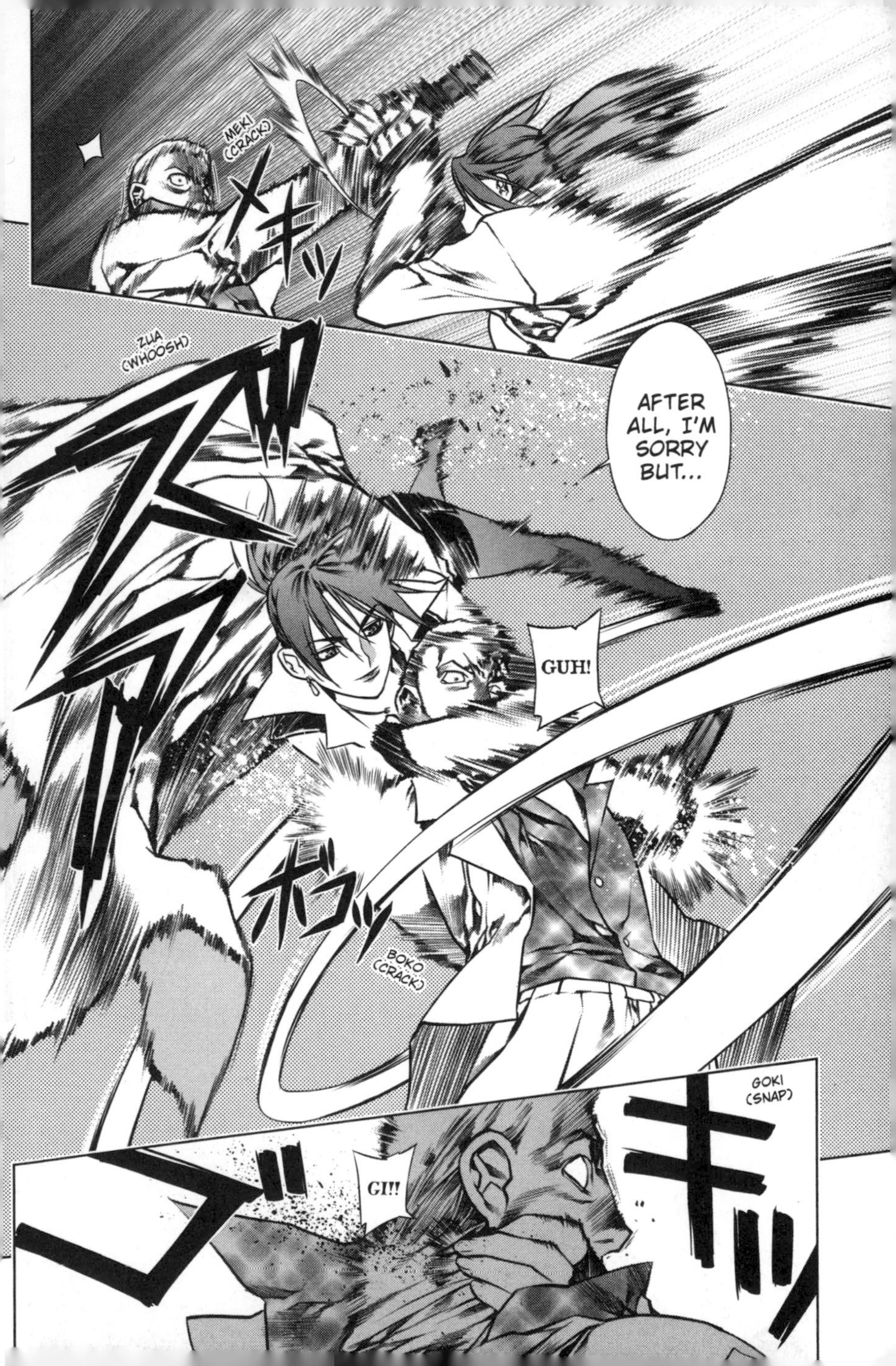
MEKI (CRACK)
AFTER ALL, I'M SORRY BUT...
ZUA (WHOOSH)
GUH!
BOKO (CRACK)
GOKI (SNAP)
GI!!

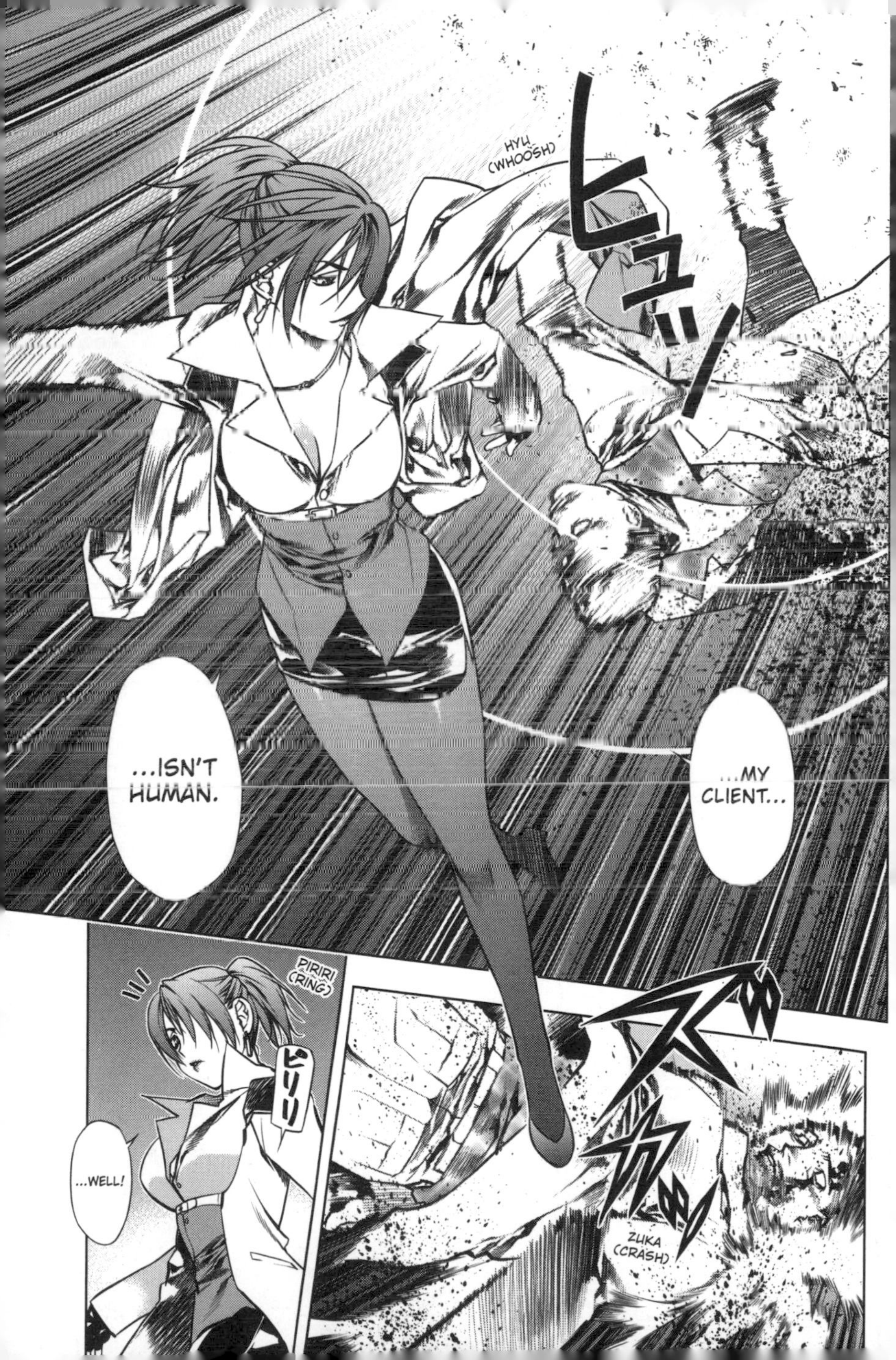
ヒュッ
HYU (WHOOSH)
...MY CLIENT...
...ISN'T HUMAN.
ズガッ
ZUKA (CRASH)
ピリリ
PIRIRI (RING)
...WELL!

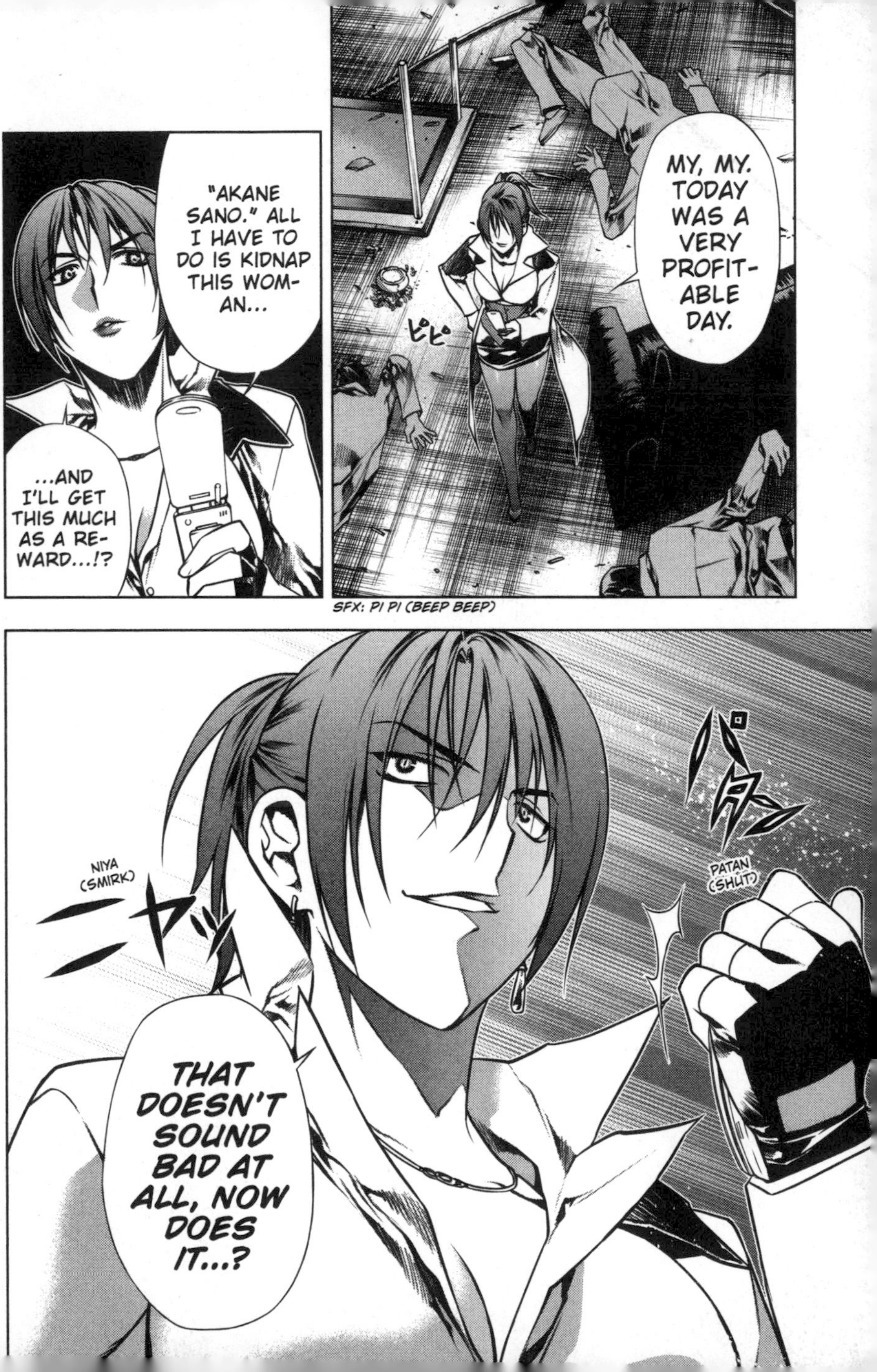
MY, MY. TODAY WAS A VERY PROFIT-ABLE DAY.
ピピ
"AKANE SANO." ALL I HAVE TO DO IS KIDNAP THIS WOM-AN...
...AND I'LL GET THIS MUCH AS A RE-WARD...!?
SFX: PI PI (BEEP BEEP)
PATAN (SHUT)
NIYA (SMIRK)
THAT DOESN'T SOUND BAD AT ALL, NOW DOES IT...?

FATE.7 Cross • Chance

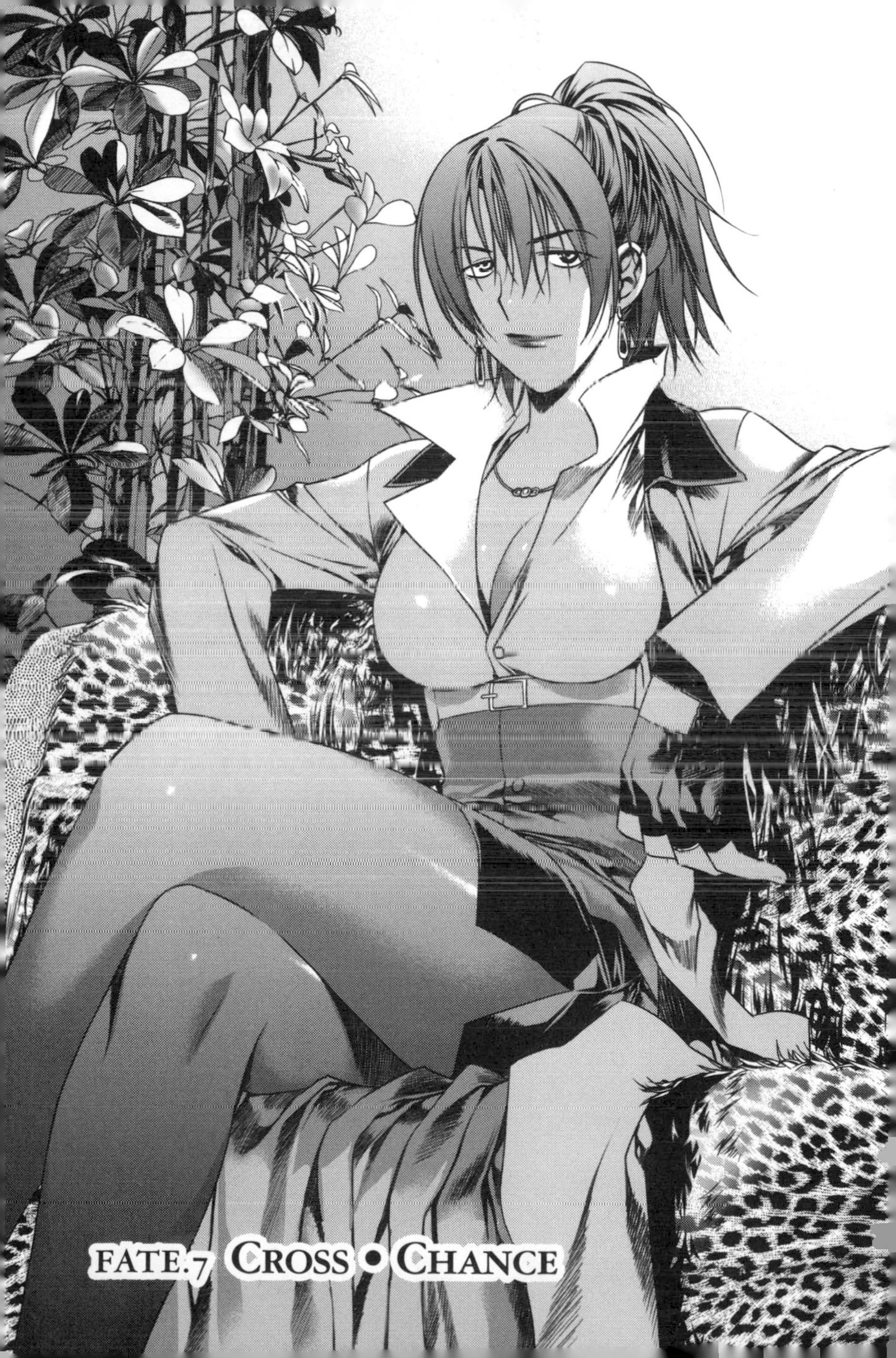

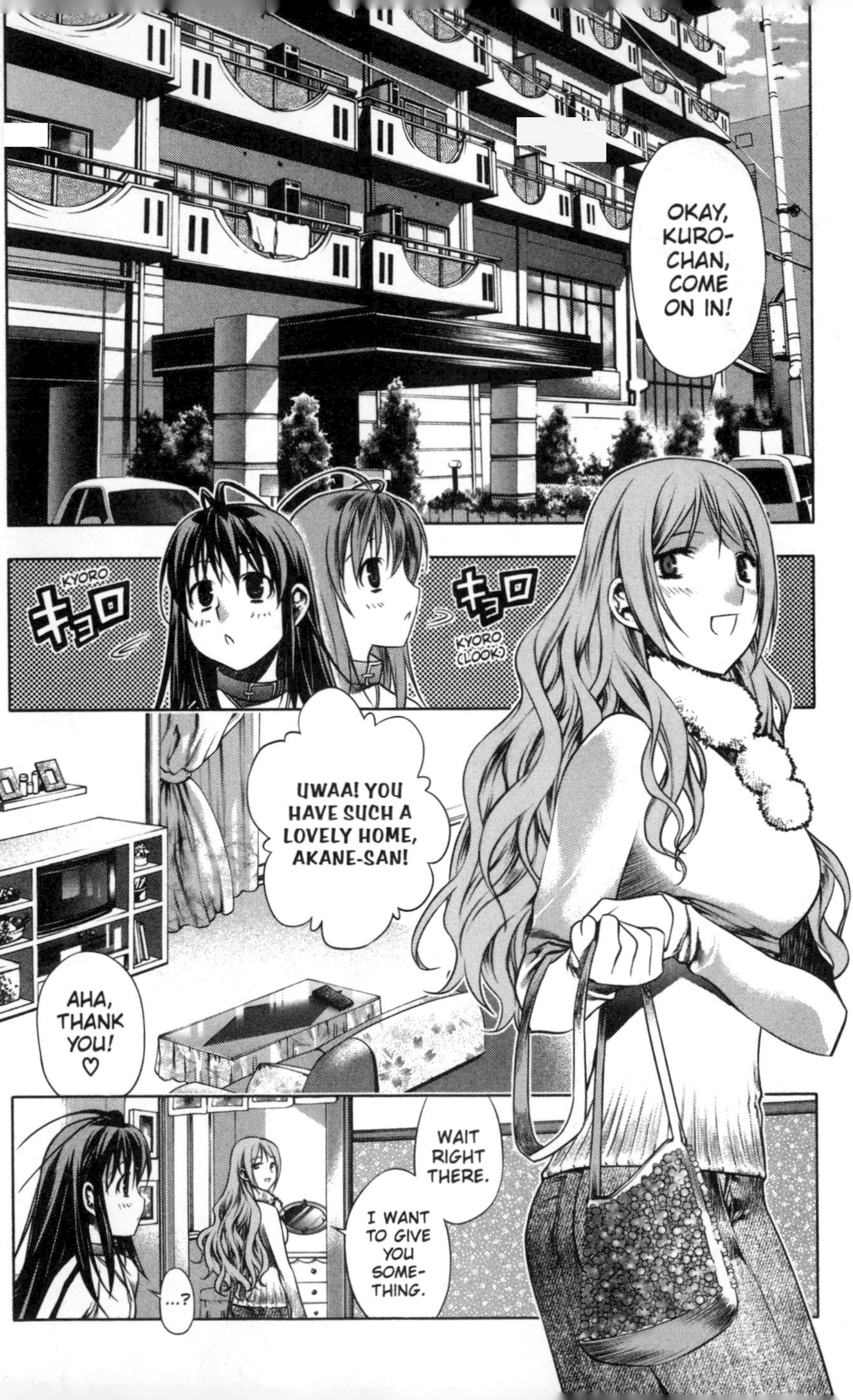
OKAY, KURO-CHAN, COME ON IN!
キョロ
KYORO (LOOK)
キョロ
KYORO
UWAA! YOU HAVE SUCH A LOVELY HOME, AKANE-SAN!
AHA, THANK YOU! ♡
WAIT RIGHT THERE.
I WANT TO GIVE YOU SOMETHING.
...?

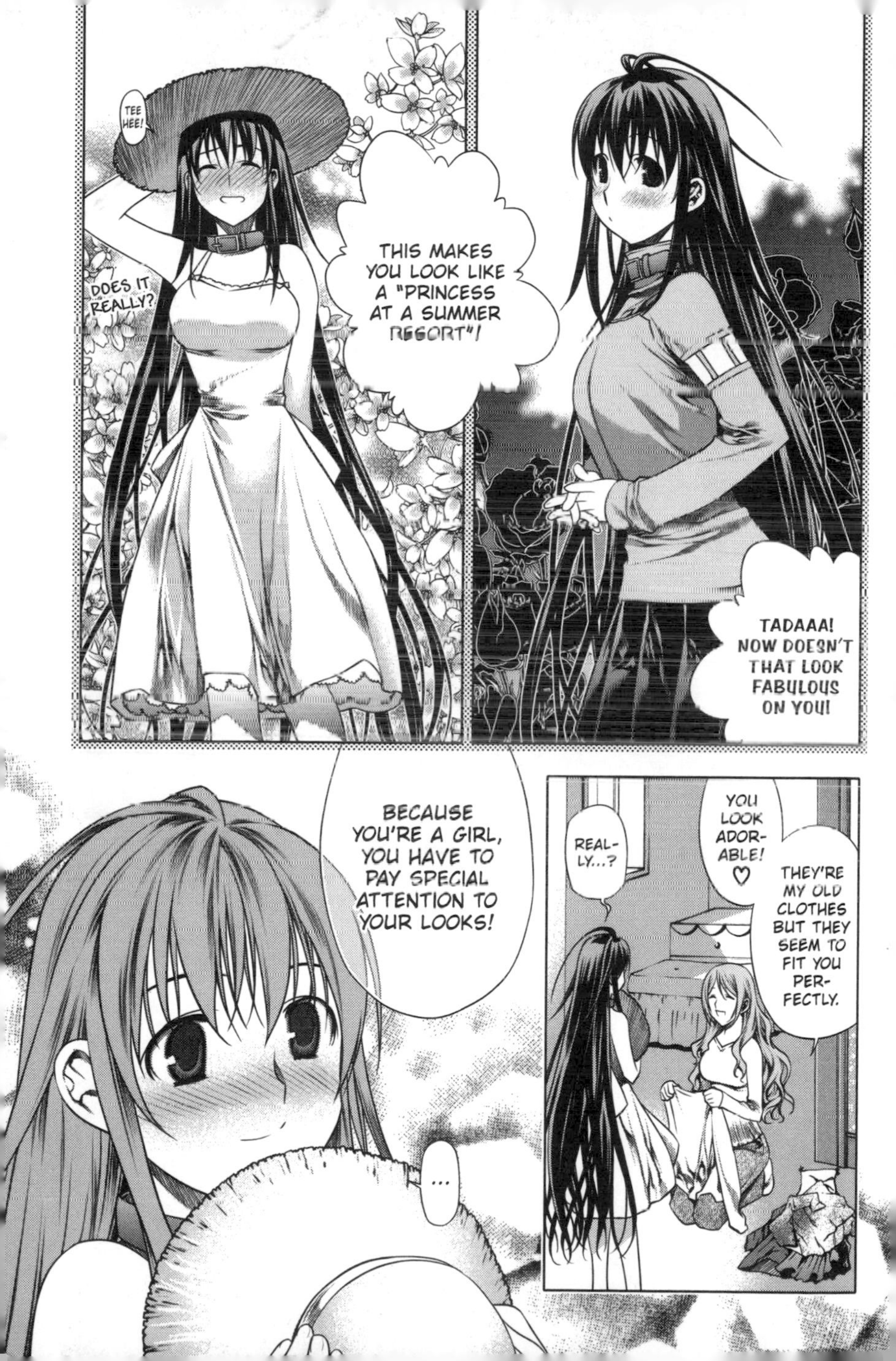
TADAAA! NOW DOESN'T THAT LOOK FABULOUS ON YOU!
THIS MAKES YOU LOOK LIKE A "PRINCESS AT A SUMMER RESORT"!
TEE HEE!
DOES IT REALLY?
YOU LOOK ADOR-ABLE! ♡
THEY'RE MY OLD CLOTHES BUT THEY SEEM TO FIT YOU PER-FECTLY.
REAL-LY...?
BECAUSE YOU'RE A GIRL, YOU HAVE TO PAY SPECIAL ATTENTION TO YOUR LOOKS!
...

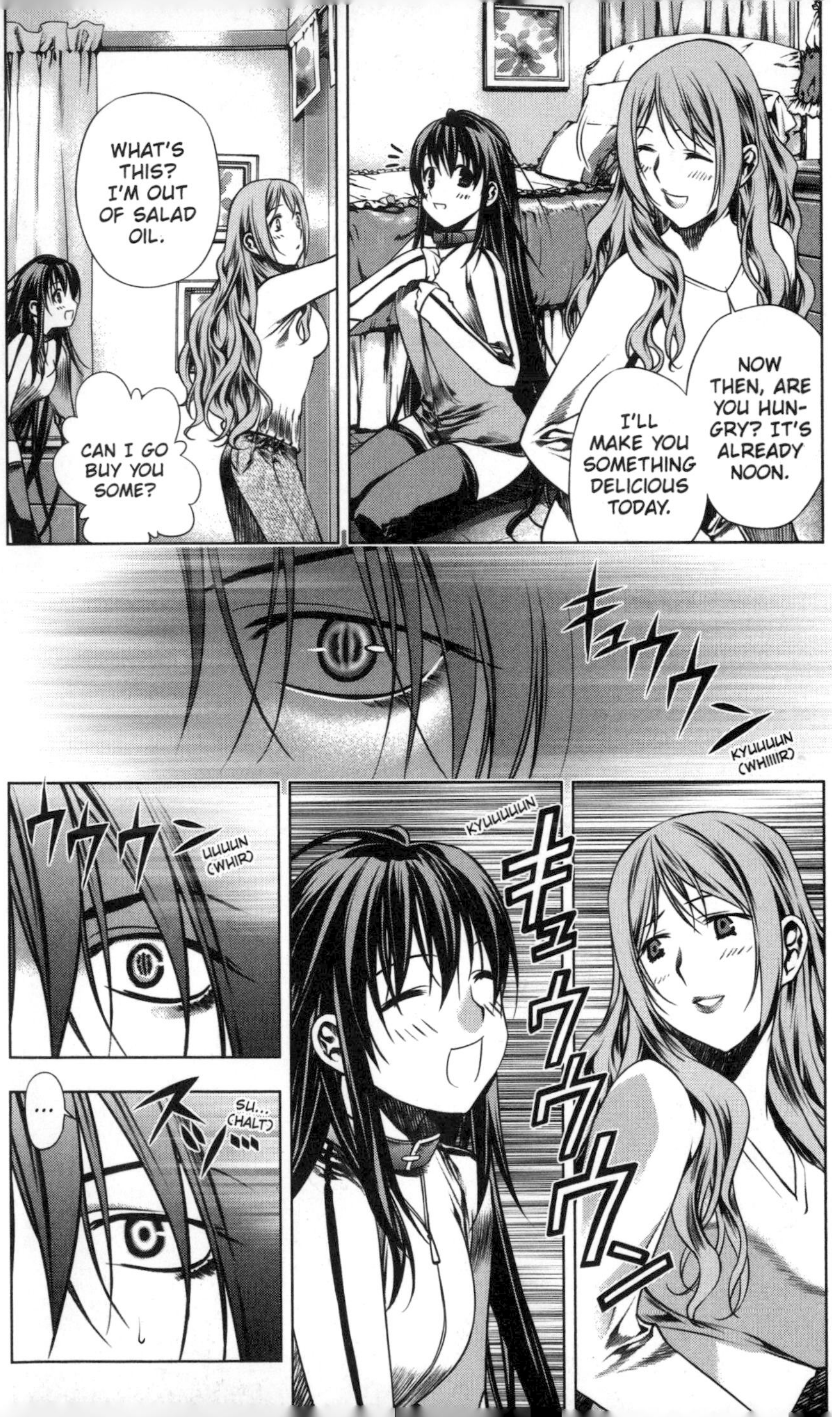
NOW THEN, ARE YOU HUNGRY? IT'S ALREADY NOON.
I'LL MAKE YOU SOMETHING DELICIOUS TODAY.
WHAT'S THIS? I'M OUT OF SALAD OIL.
CAN I GO BUY YOU SOME?
キュウウーン
KYUUUUN (WHIIIIR)
KYUUUUUN
キュウウウウウーン
ウウウーン
UUUUN (WHIR)
...
スッ...
SU... (HALT)

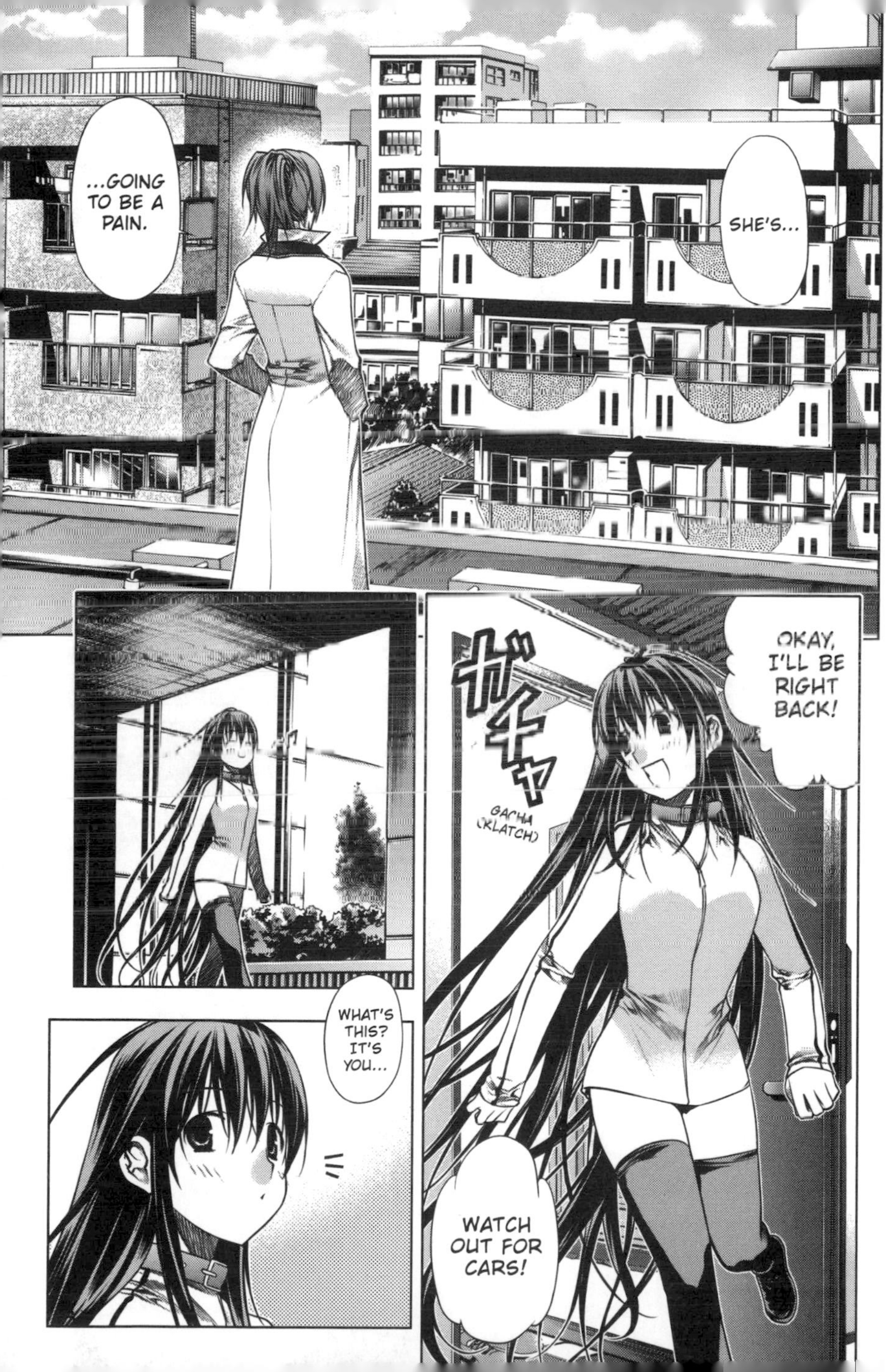
SHE'S...
...GOING TO BE A PAIN.
OKAY, I'LL BE RIGHT BACK!
GACHA (KLATCH)
WATCH OUT FOR CARS!
WHAT'S THIS? IT'S YOU...

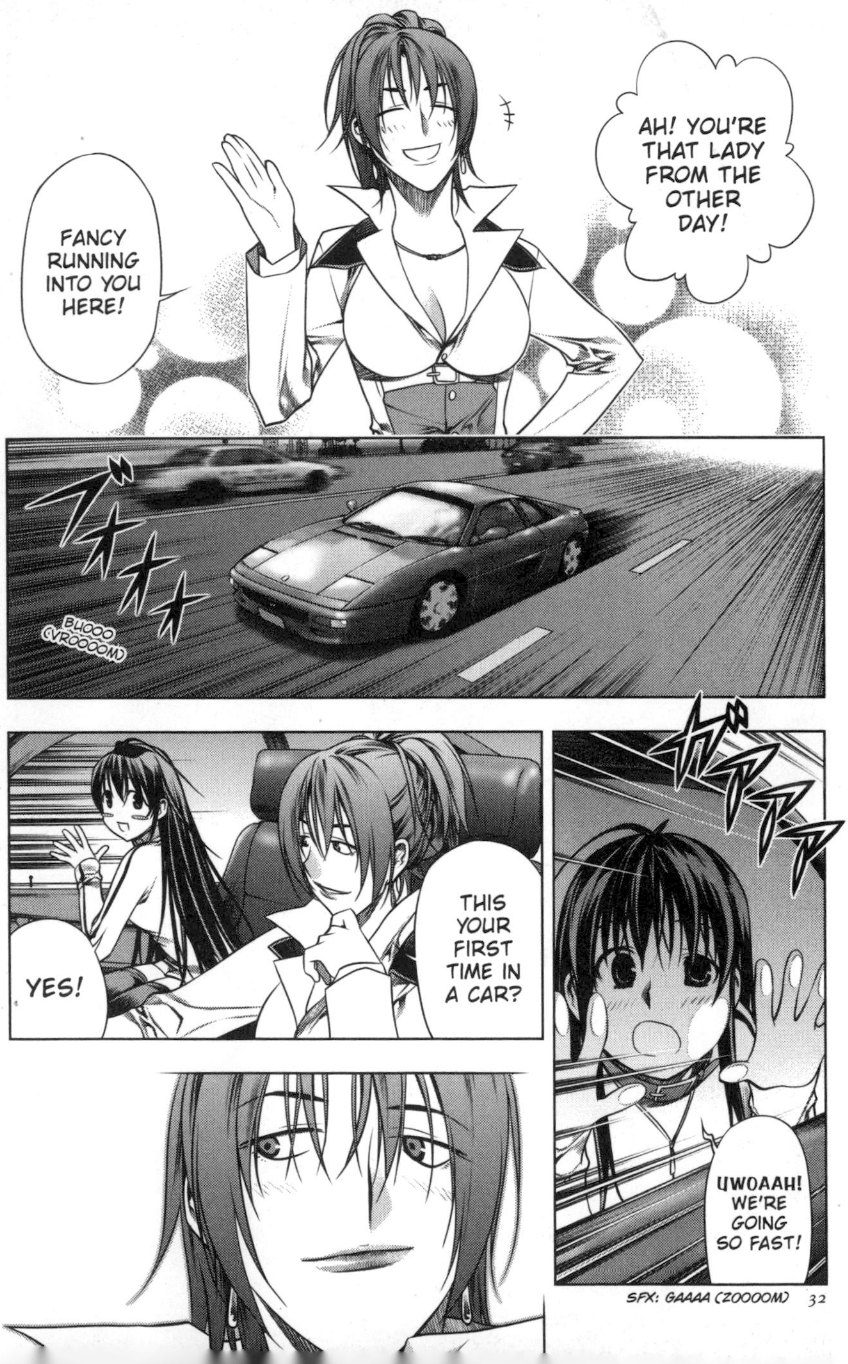
AH! YOU'RE THAT LADY FROM THE OTHER DAY!
FANCY RUNNING INTO YOU HERE!
BUOOO (VROOOOM)
UWOAAH! WE'RE GOING SO FAST!
THIS YOUR FIRST TIME IN A CAR?
YES!
SFX: GAAAA (ZOOOOM)

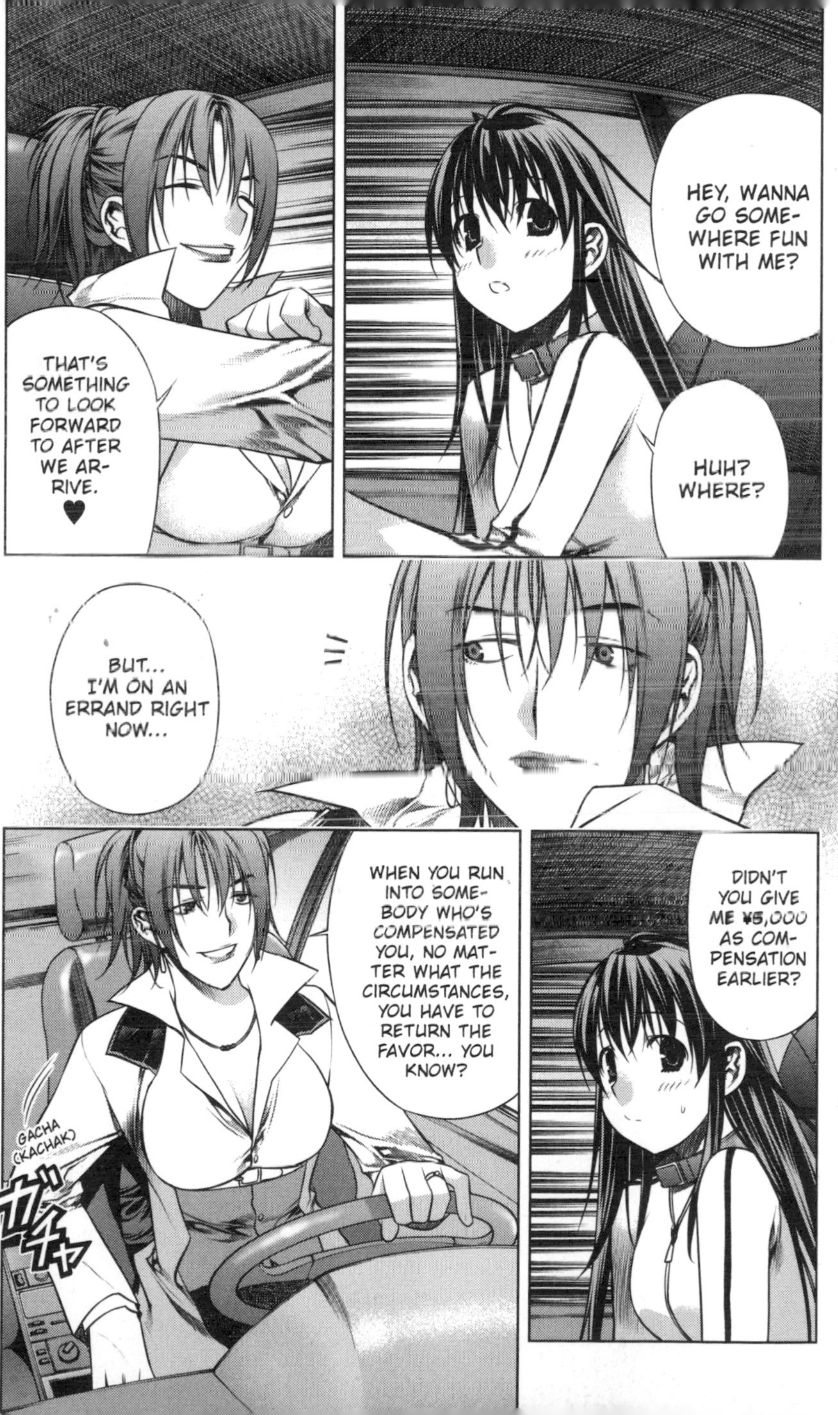
HEY, WANNA GO SOME-WHERE FUN WITH ME?
HUH? WHERE?
THAT'S SOMETHING TO LOOK FORWARD TO AFTER WE AR-RIVE. ♥
BUT... I'M ON AN ERRAND RIGHT NOW...
DIDN'T YOU GIVE ME ¥5,000 AS COM-PENSATION EARLIER?
WHEN YOU RUN INTO SOME-BODY WHO'S COMPENSATED YOU, NO MAT-TER WHAT THE CIRCUMSTANCES, YOU HAVE TO RETURN THE FAVOR... YOU KNOW?
GACHA (KACHAK)
ガチャ

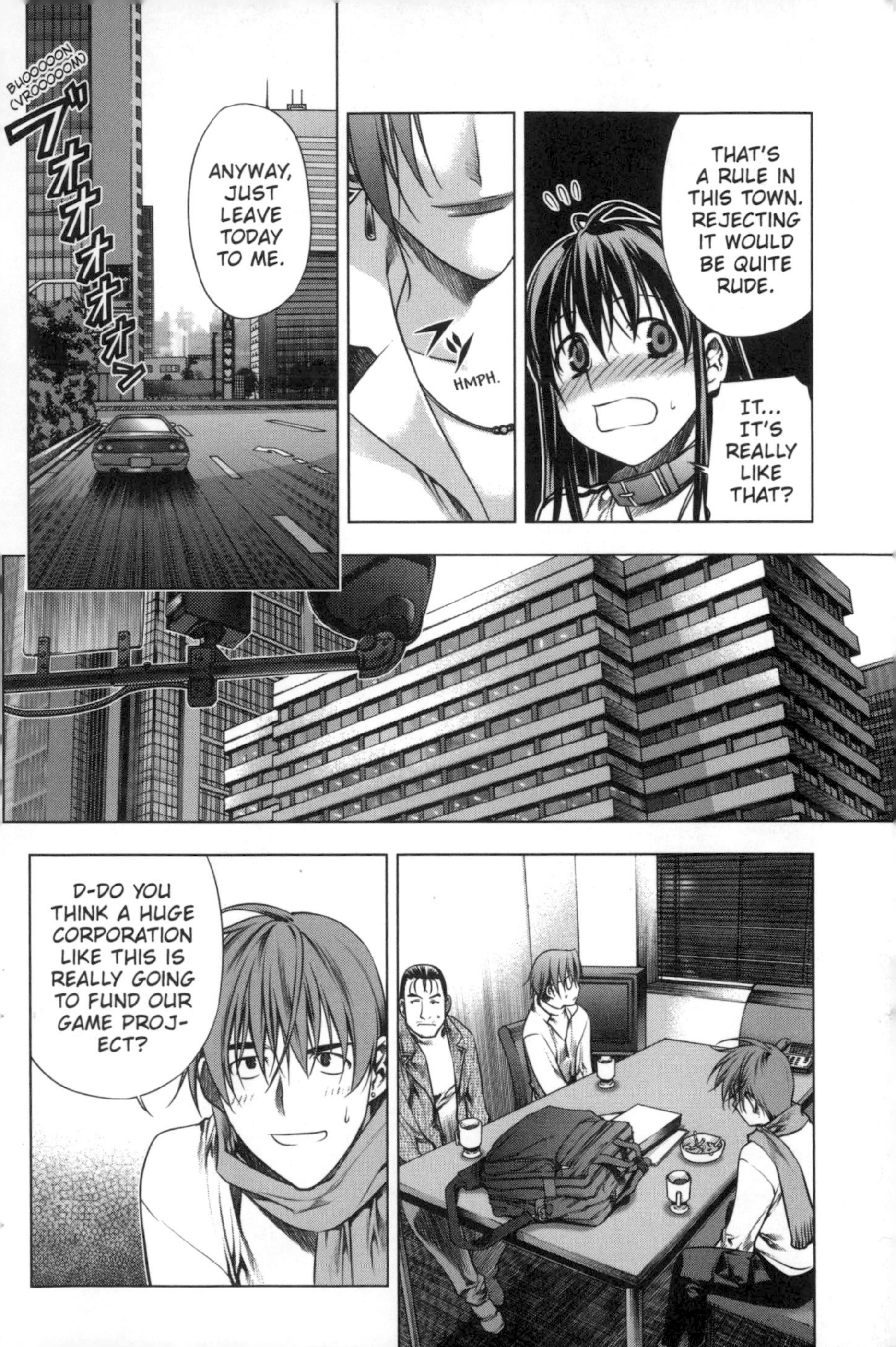
THAT'S A RULE IN THIS TOWN. REJECTING IT WOULD BE QUITE RUDE.
IT... IT'S REALLY LIKE THAT?
HMPH.
ANYWAY, JUST LEAVE TODAY TO ME.
BUOOOOON (VROOOOOOM)
D-DO YOU THINK A HUGE CORPORATION LIKE THIS IS REALLY GOING TO FUND OUR GAME PROJ-ECT?

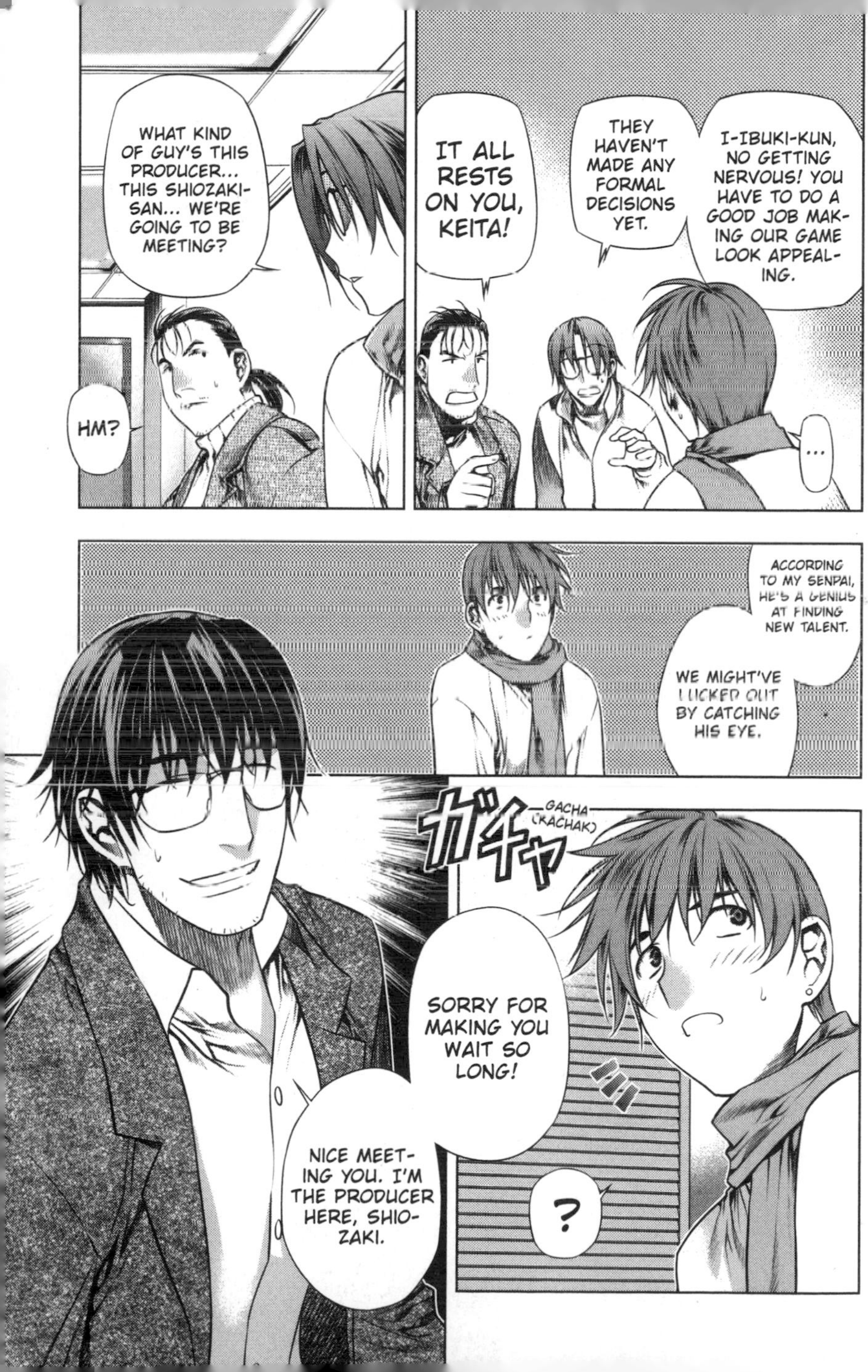
I-IBUKI-KUN, NO GETTING NERVOUS! YOU HAVE TO DO A GOOD JOB MAKING OUR GAME LOOK APPEALING.
THEY HAVEN'T MADE ANY FORMAL DECISIONS YET.
IT ALL RESTS ON YOU, KEITA!
...
WHAT KIND OF GUY'S THIS PRODUCER... THIS SHIOZAKI-SAN... WE'RE GOING TO BE MEETING?
HM?
ACCORDING TO MY SENPAI, HE'S A GENIUS AT FINDING NEW TALENT.
WE MIGHT'VE LUCKED OUT BY CATCHING HIS EYE.
ガチャ
GACHA (KACHAK)
?
SORRY FOR MAKING YOU WAIT SO LONG!
NICE MEETING YOU. I'M THE PRODUCER HERE, SHIOZAKI.

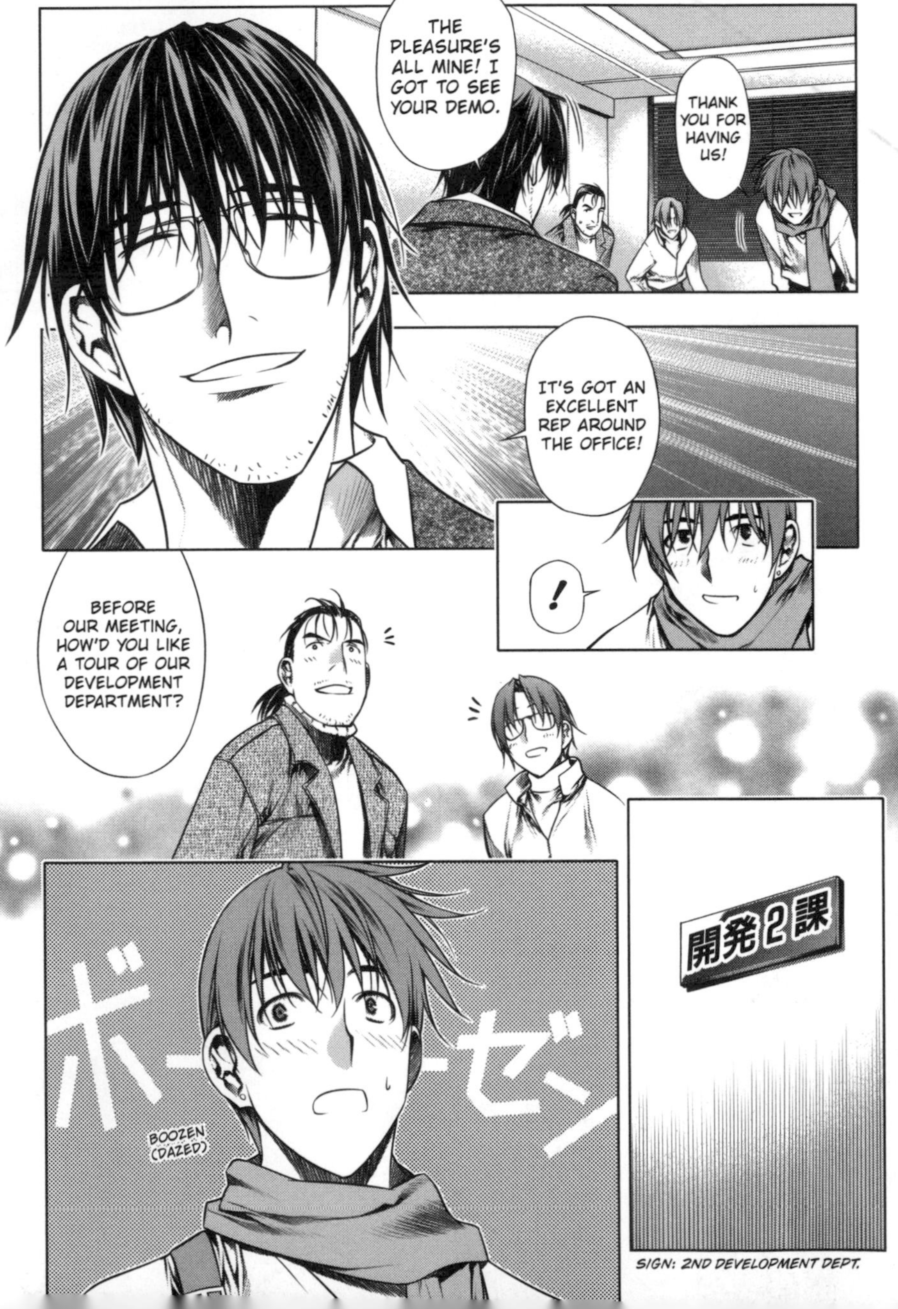
THANK YOU FOR HAVING US!
THE PLEASURE'S ALL MINE! I GOT TO SEE YOUR DEMO.
IT'S GOT AN EXCELLENT REP AROUND THE OFFICE!
!
BEFORE OUR MEETING, HOW'D YOU LIKE A TOUR OF OUR DEVELOPMENT DEPARTMENT?
開発2課
SIGN: 2ND DEVELOPMENT DEPT.
ボーーゼン
BOOZEN (DAZED)

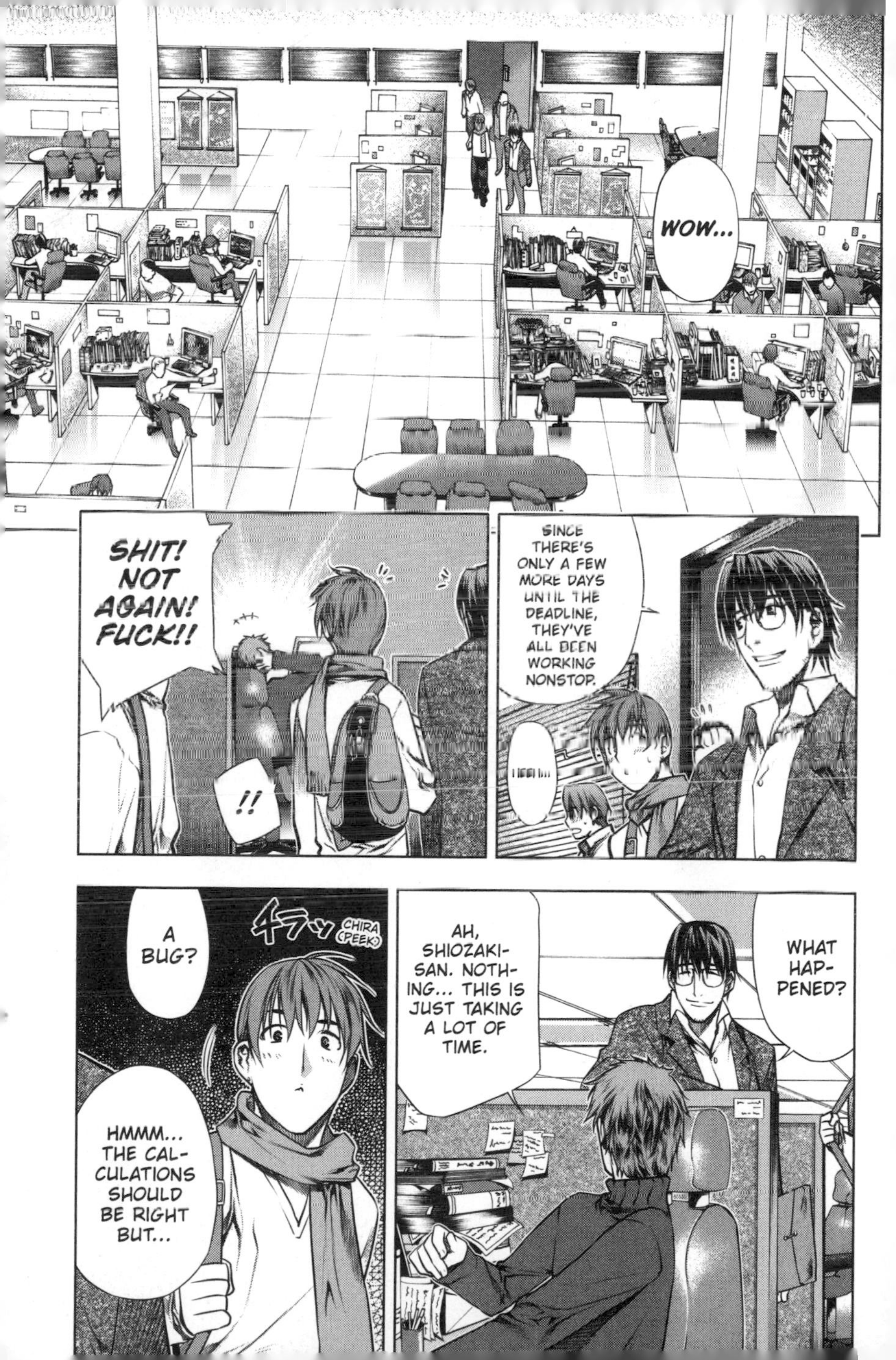
WOW...
SINCE THERE'S ONLY A FEW MORE DAYS UNTIL THE DEADLINE, THEY'VE ALL BEEN WORKING NONSTOP.
......
SHIT! NOT AGAIN! FUCK!!
!!
WHAT HAP-PENED?
AH, SHIOZAKI-SAN. NOTH-ING... THIS IS JUST TAKING A LOT OF TIME.
CHIRA (PEEK)
A BUG?
HMMM... THE CAL-CULATIONS SHOULD BE RIGHT BUT...

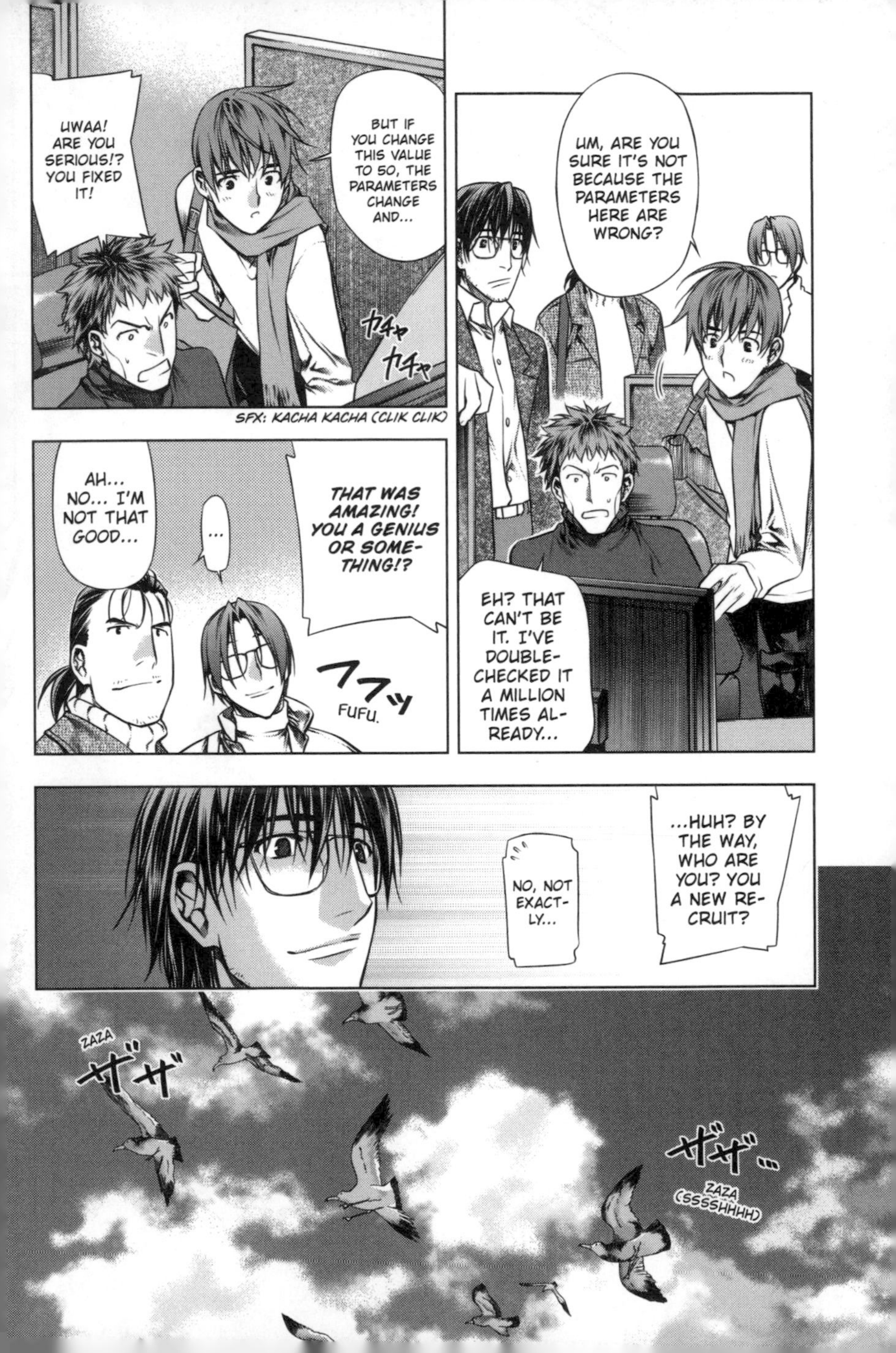
UM, ARE YOU SURE IT'S NOT BECAUSE THE PARAMETERS HERE ARE WRONG?
EH? THAT CAN'T BE IT. I'VE DOUBLE-CHECKED IT A MILLION TIMES AL-READY...
BUT IF YOU CHANGE THIS VALUE TO 50, THE PARAMETERS CHANGE AND...
UWAA! ARE YOU SERIOUS!? YOU FIXED IT!
カチャ カチャ
SFX: KACHA KACHA (CLIK CLIK)
THAT WAS AMAZING! YOU A GENIUS OR SOME-THING!?
...
AH... NO... I'M NOT THAT GOOD...
フフッ
FUFU.
...HUH? BY THE WAY, WHO ARE YOU? YOU A NEW RE-CRUIT?
NO, NOT EXACT-LY...
ザザ
ZAZA
ザザ
ZAZA (SSSSHHHH)

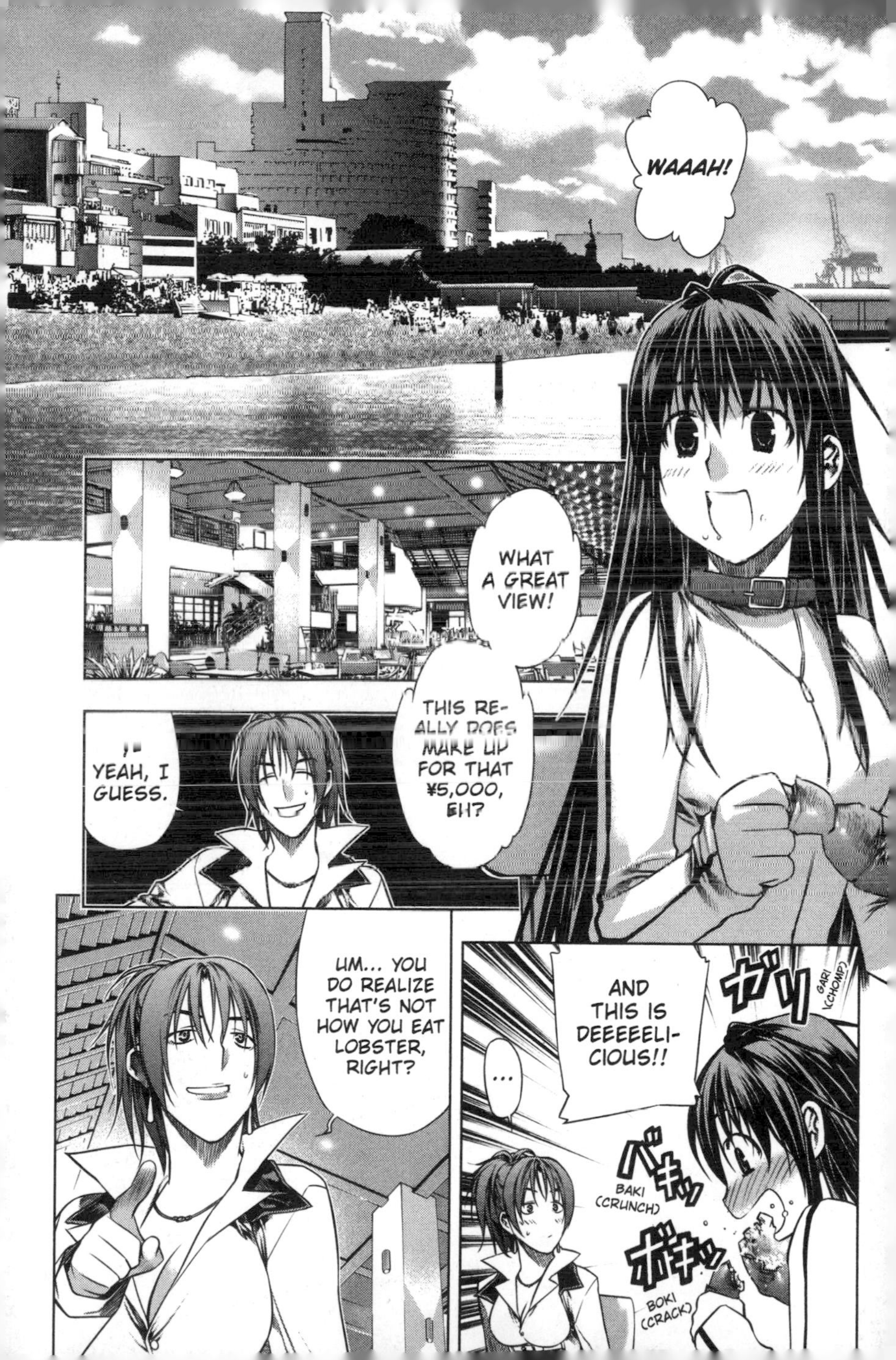
WAAAH!
WHAT A GREAT VIEW!
THIS REALLY DOES MAKE UP FOR THAT ¥5,000, EH?
YEAH, I GUESS.
AND THIS IS DEEEEELICIOUS!!
ガリ
GARI (CHOMP)
...
バキッ
BAKI (CRUNCH)
ボキッ
BOKI (CRACK)
UM... YOU DO REALIZE THAT'S NOT HOW YOU EAT LOBSTER, RIGHT?

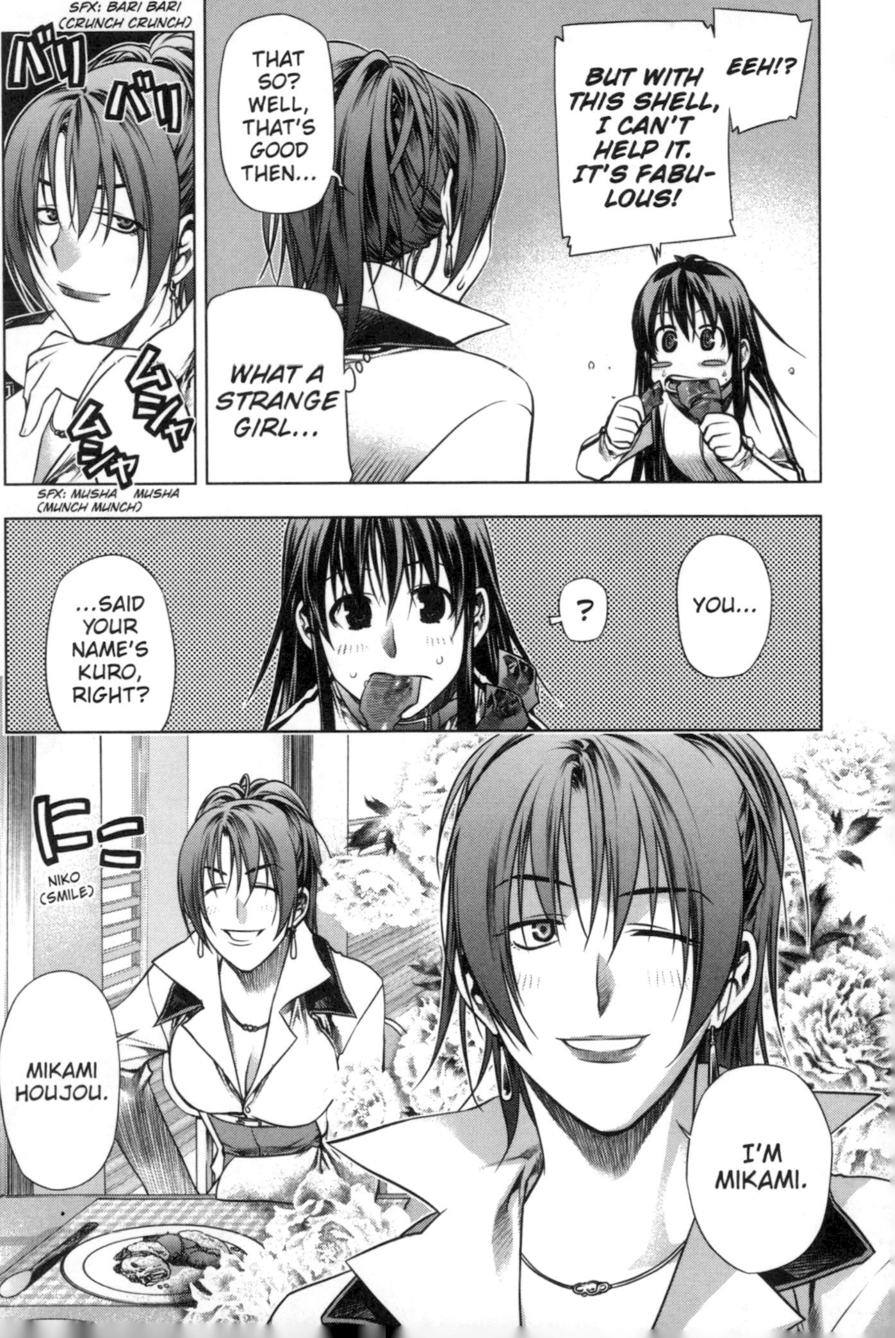
EEH!?
BUT WITH THIS SHELL, I CAN'T HELP IT. IT'S FABU-LOUS!
THAT SO? WELL, THAT'S GOOD THEN...
WHAT A STRANGE GIRL...
SFX: BARI BARI (CRUNCH CRUNCH)
SFX: MUSHA MUSHA (MUNCH MUNCH)
YOU...
?
...SAID YOUR NAME'S KURO, RIGHT?
I'M MIKAMI.
MIKAMI HOUJOU.
NIKO (SMILE)

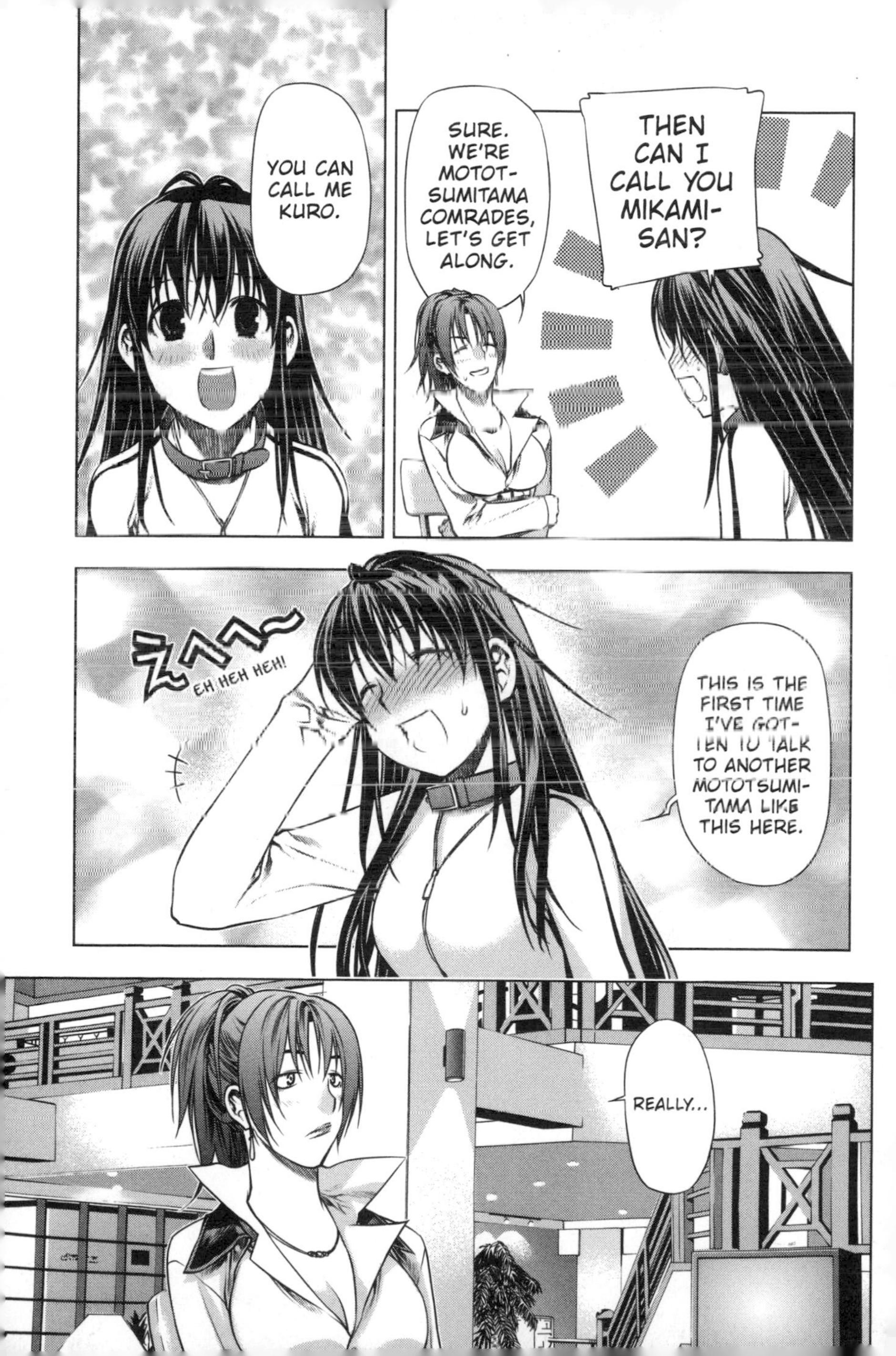

THEN CAN I CALL YOU MIKAMI-SAN?
SURE. WE'RE MOTOT-SUMITAMA COMRADES, LET'S GET ALONG.
YOU CAN CALL ME KURO.
THIS IS THE FIRST TIME I'VE GOT-TEN TO TALK TO ANOTHER MOTOTSUMI-TAMA LIKE THIS HERE.
EH HEH HEH!
REALLY...

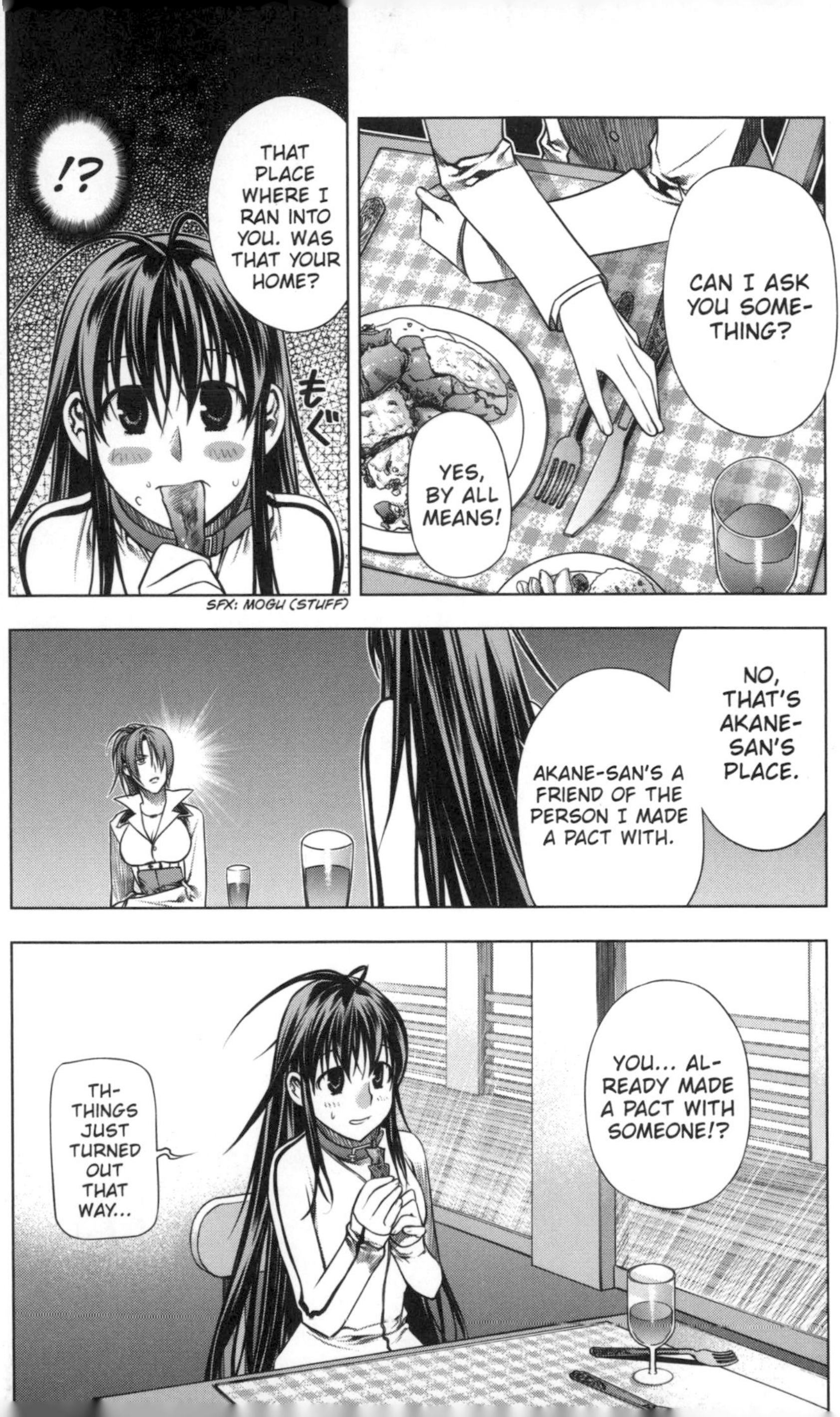
CAN I ASK YOU SOME-THING?
YES, BY ALL MEANS!
!?
THAT PLACE WHERE I RAN INTO YOU. WAS THAT YOUR HOME?
もぐ
SFX: MOGU (STUFF)
NO, THAT'S AKANE-SAN'S PLACE.
AKANE-SAN'S A FRIEND OF THE PERSON I MADE A PACT WITH.
YOU... AL-READY MADE A PACT WITH SOMEONE!?
TH-THINGS JUST TURNED OUT THAT WAY...

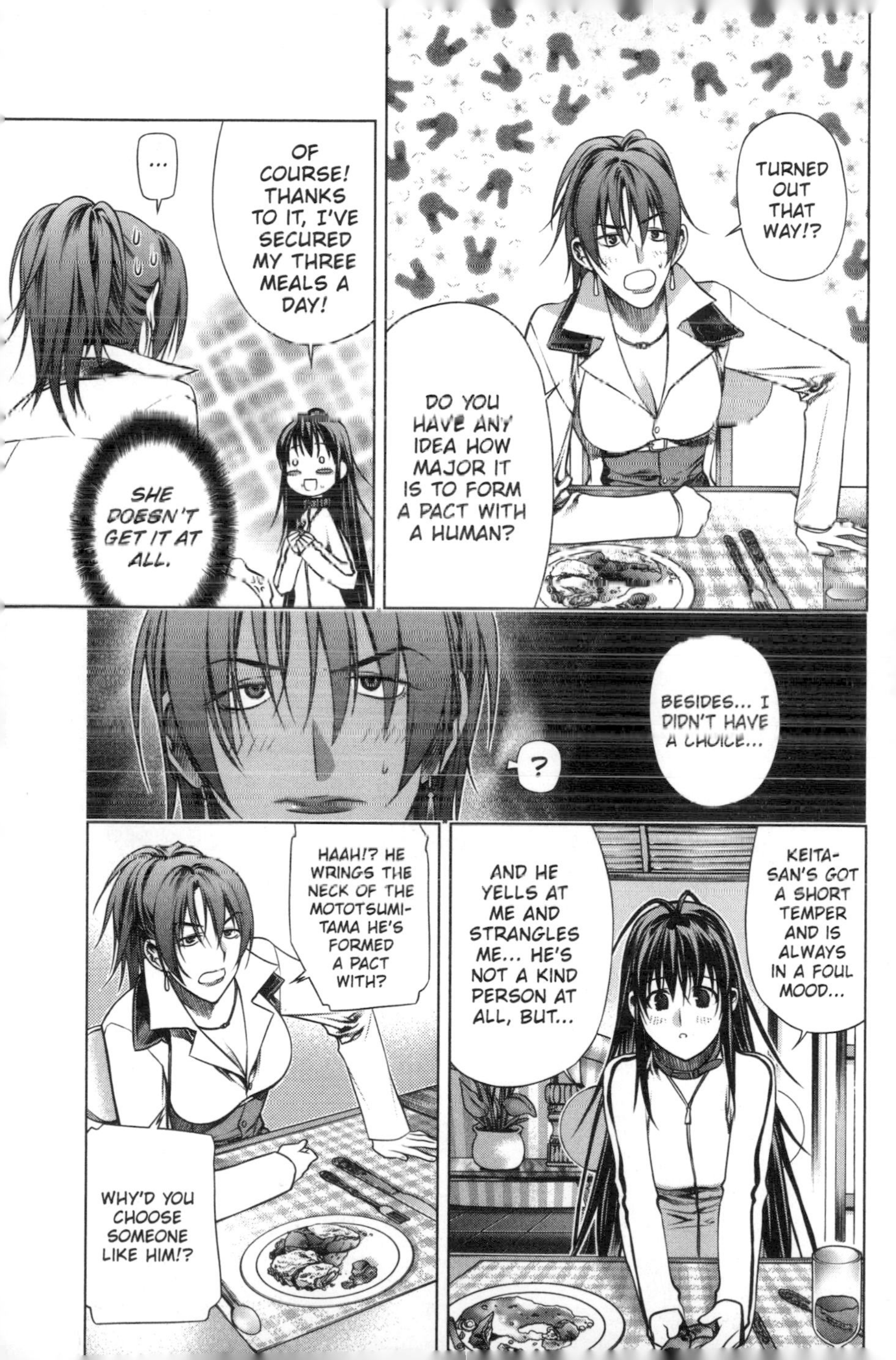
TURNED OUT THAT WAY!?
DO YOU HAVE ANY IDEA HOW MAJOR IT IS TO FORM A PACT WITH A HUMAN?
OF COURSE! THANKS TO IT, I'VE SECURED MY THREE MEALS A DAY!
...
SHE DOESN'T GET IT AT ALL.
BESIDES... I DIDN'T HAVE A CHOICE...
?
KEITA-SAN'S GOT A SHORT TEMPER AND IS ALWAYS IN A FOUL MOOD...
AND HE YELLS AT ME AND STRANGLES ME... HE'S NOT A KIND PERSON AT ALL, BUT...
HAAH!? HE WRINGS THE NECK OF THE MOTOTSUMI-TAMA HE'S FORMED A PACT WITH?
WHY'D YOU CHOOSE SOMEONE LIKE HIM!?

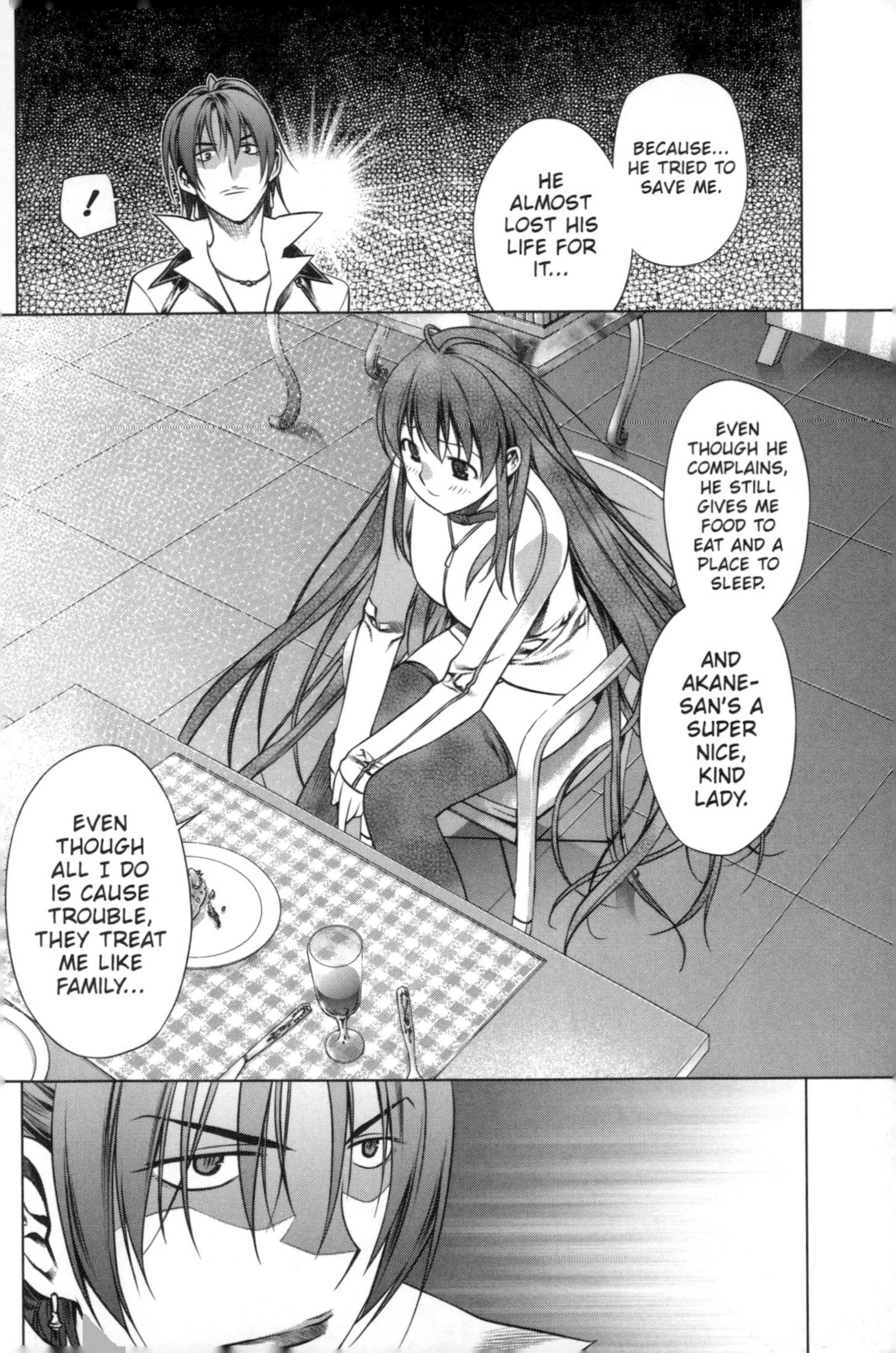
BECAUSE... HE TRIED TO SAVE ME.
HE ALMOST LOST HIS LIFE FOR IT...
!
EVEN THOUGH HE COMPLAINS, HE STILL GIVES ME FOOD TO EAT AND A PLACE TO SLEEP.
AND AKANE-SAN'S A SUPER NICE, KIND LADY.
EVEN THOUGH ALL I DO IS CAUSE TROUBLE, THEY TREAT ME LIKE FAMILY...

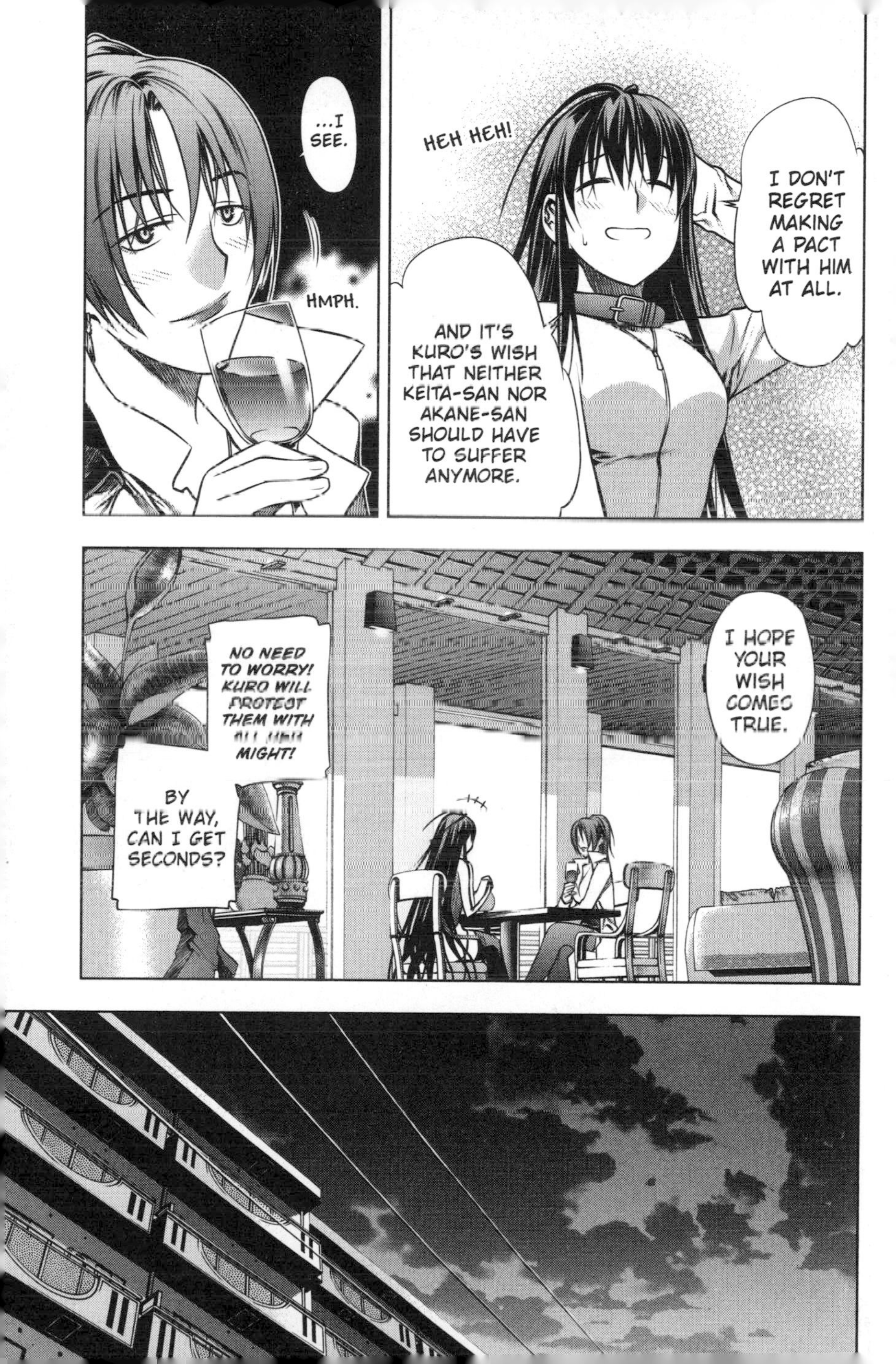
I DON'T REGRET MAKING A PACT WITH HIM AT ALL.
HEH HEH!
AND IT'S KURO'S WISH THAT NEITHER KEITA-SAN NOR AKANE-SAN SHOULD HAVE TO SUFFER ANYMORE.
...I SEE.
HMPH.
I HOPE YOUR WISH COMES TRUE.
NO NEED TO WORRY! KURO WILL PROTECT THEM WITH
MIGHT!
BY THE WAY, CAN I GET SECONDS?

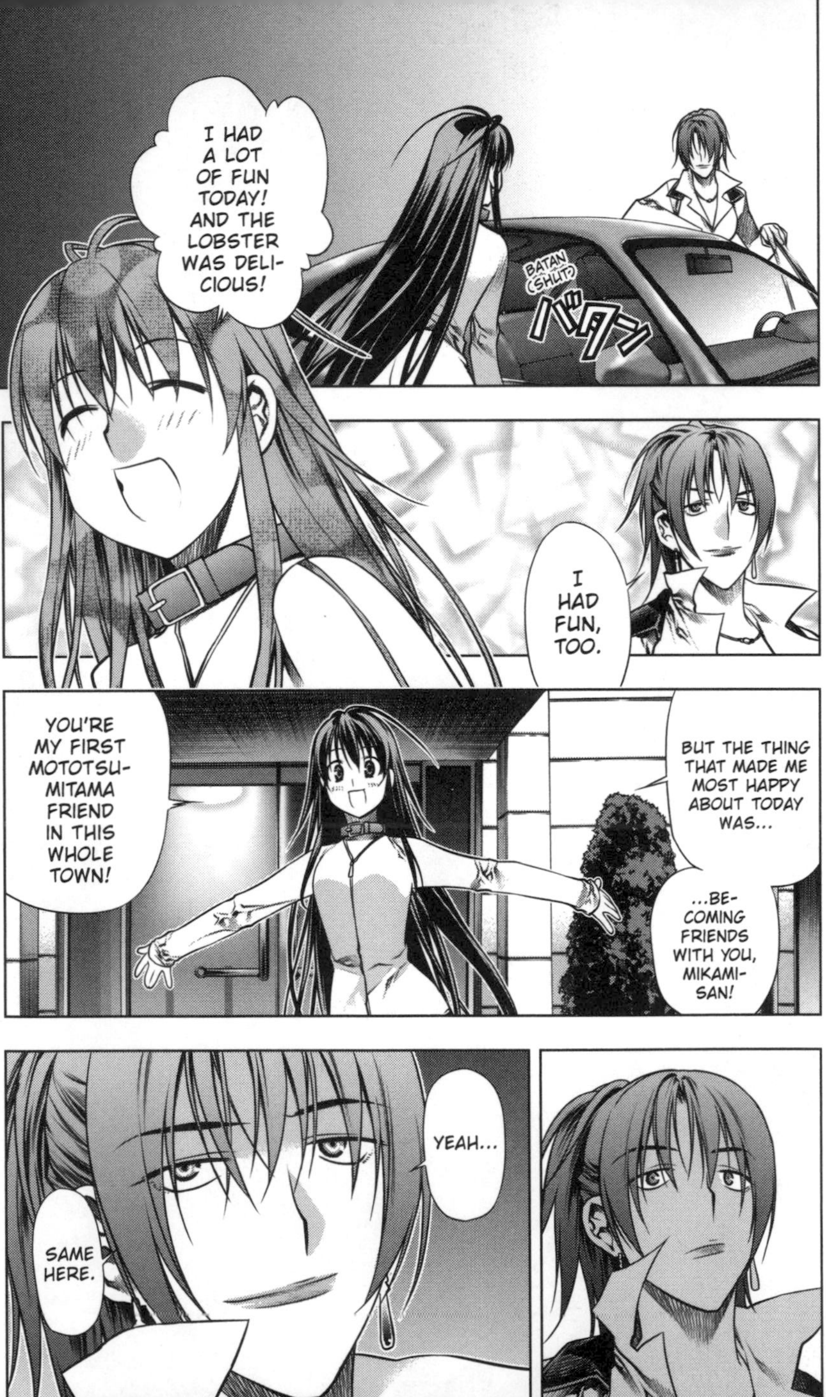
I HAD A LOT OF FUN TODAY! AND THE LOBSTER WAS DELICIOUS!
BATAN (SHUT)
バタン
I HAD FUN, TOO.
BUT THE THING THAT MADE ME MOST HAPPY ABOUT TODAY WAS...
...BE-COMING FRIENDS WITH YOU, MIKAMI-SAN!
YOU'RE MY FIRST MOTOTSU-MITAMA FRIEND IN THIS WHOLE TOWN!
YEAH...
SAME HERE.

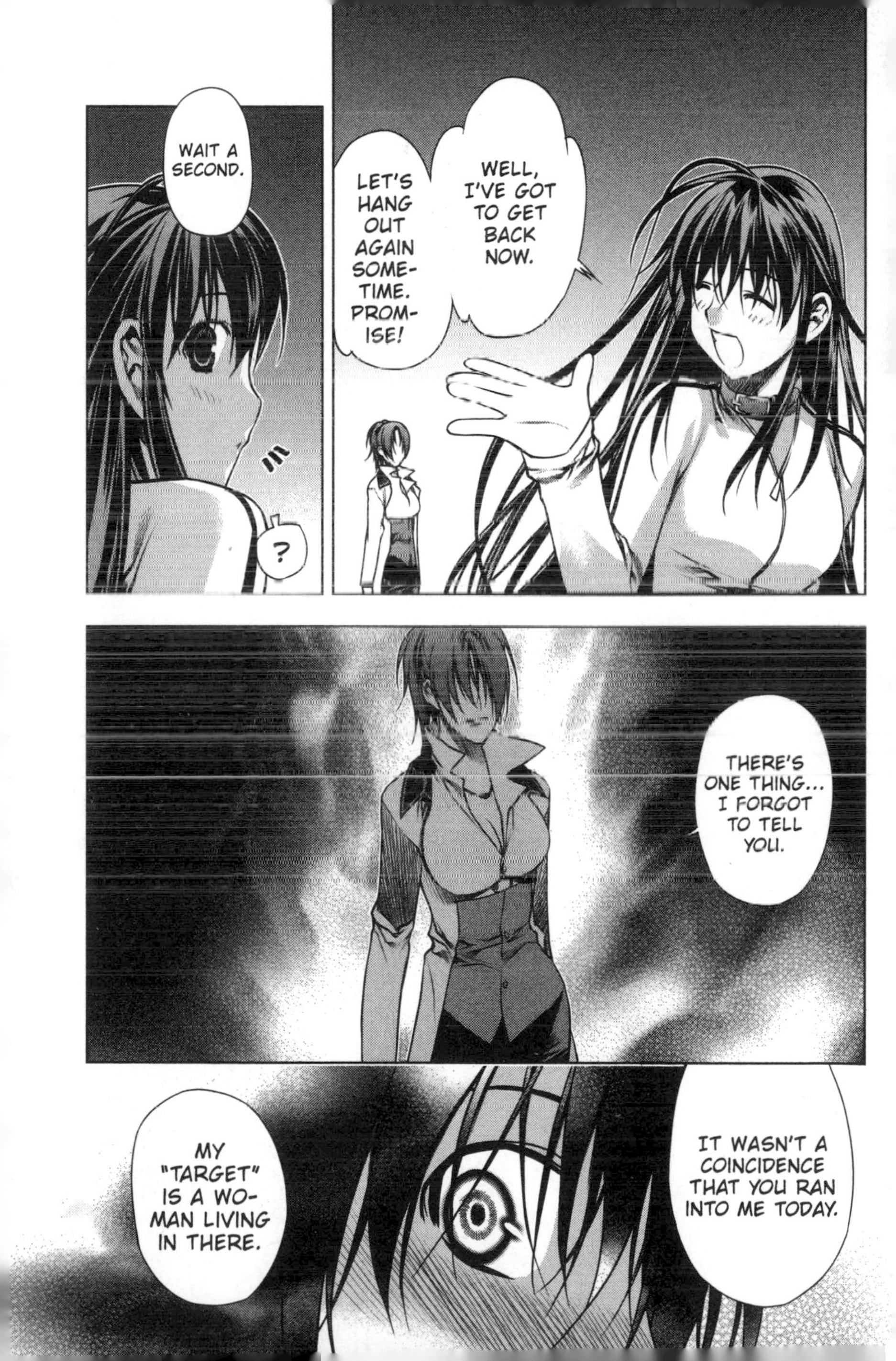
WELL, I'VE GOT TO GET BACK NOW.
LET'S HANG OUT AGAIN SOME-TIME. PROM-ISE!
WAIT A SECOND.
?
THERE'S ONE THING... I FORGOT TO TELL YOU.
IT WASN'T A COINCIDENCE THAT YOU RAN INTO ME TODAY.
MY "TARGET" IS A WO-MAN LIVING IN THERE.

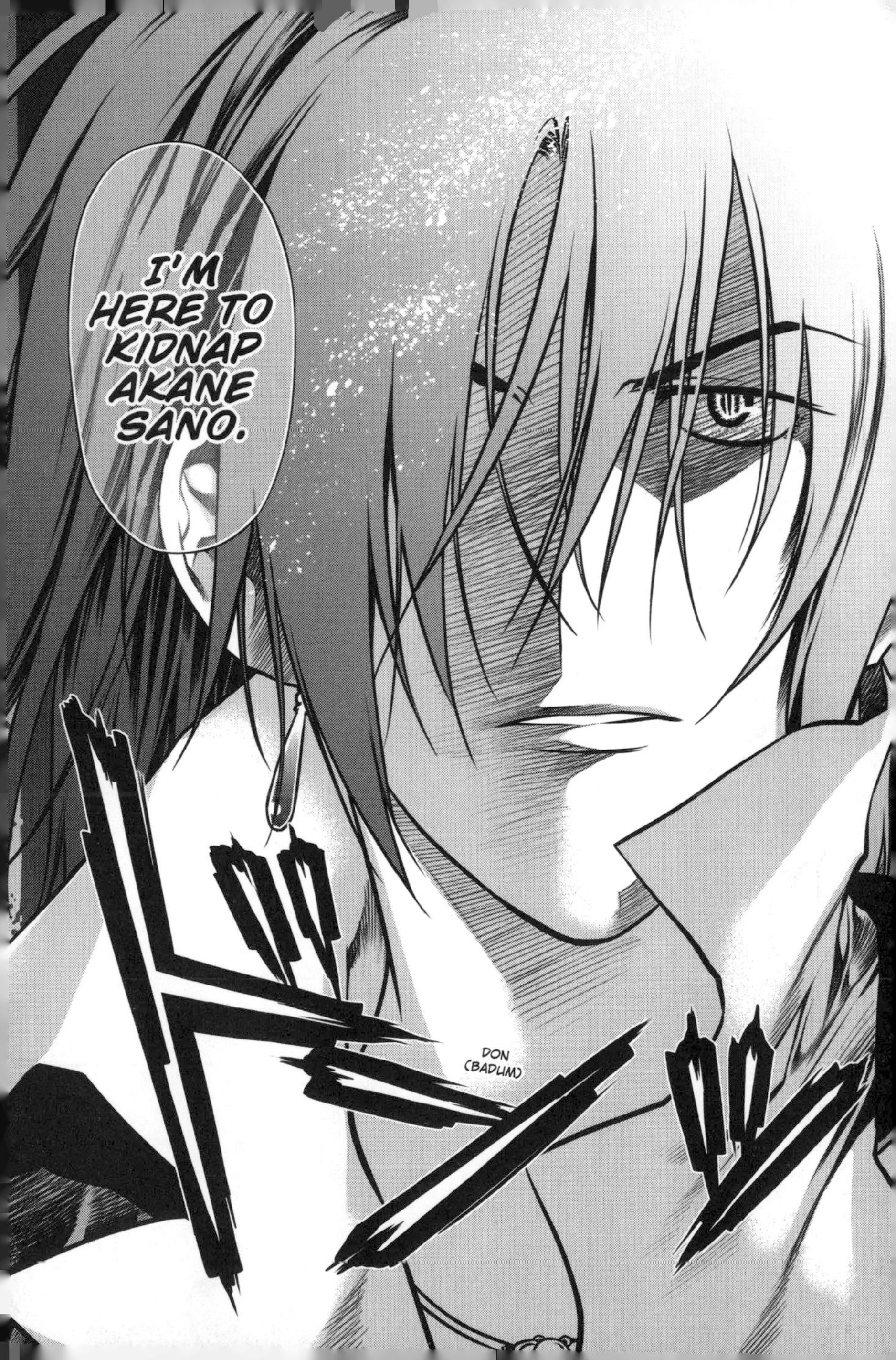
I'M HERE TO KIDNAP AKANE SANO.
DON (BADUM)

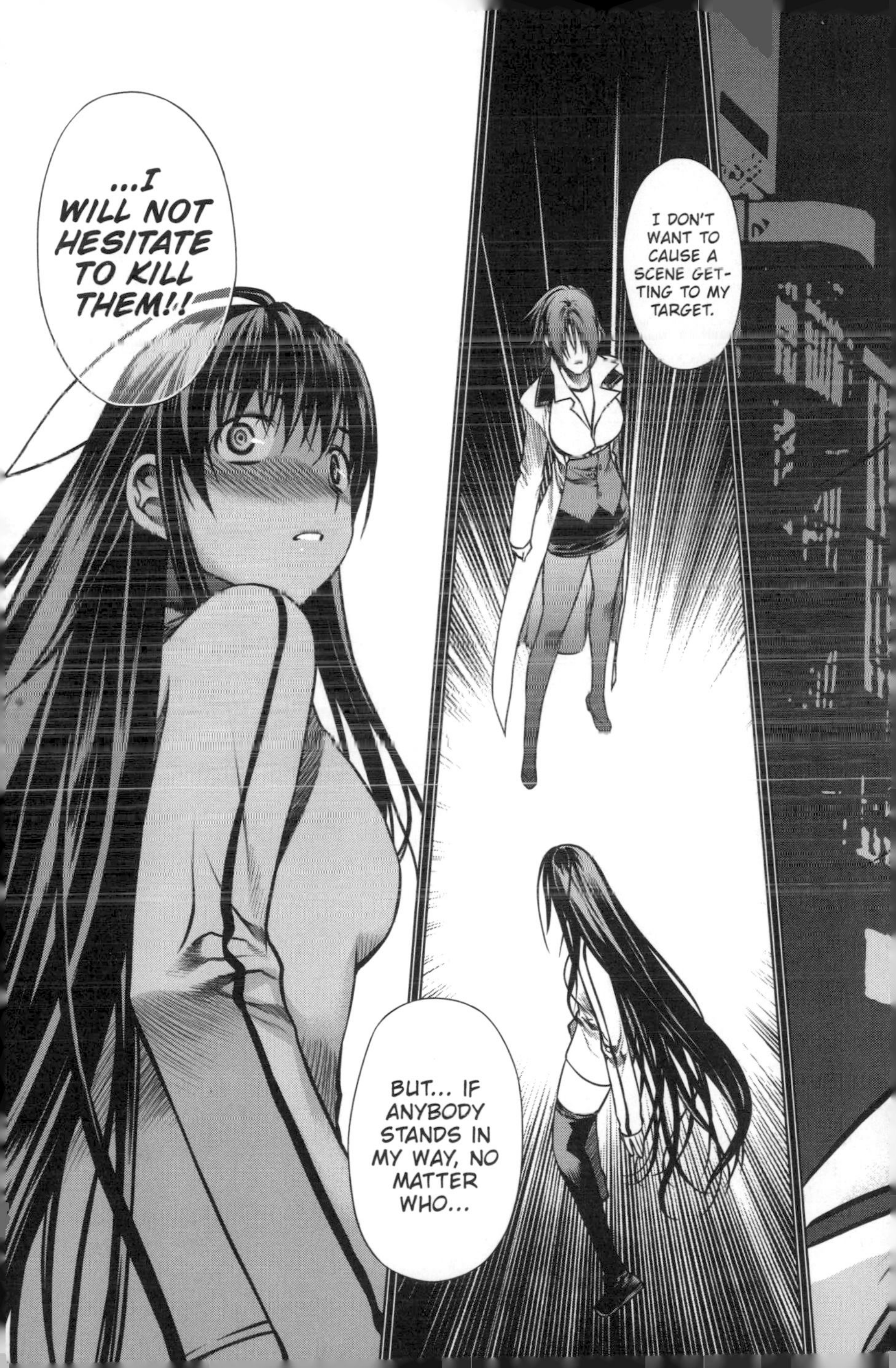
I DON'T WANT TO CAUSE A SCENE GETTING TO MY TARGET.
BUT... IF ANYBODY STANDS IN MY WAY, NO MATTER WHO...
...I WILL NOT HESITATE TO KILL THEM!!

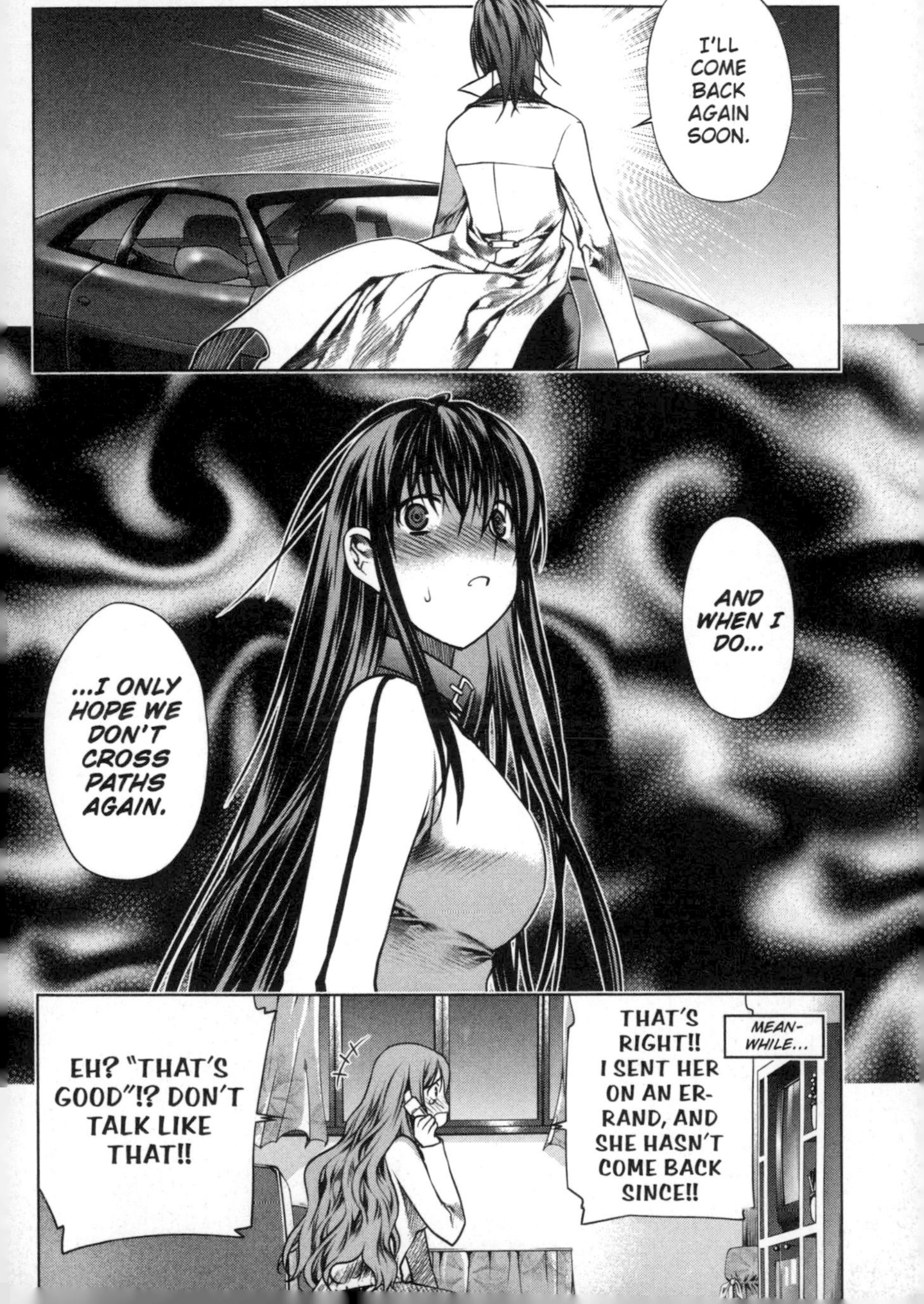
I'LL COME BACK AGAIN SOON.
AND WHEN I DO...
...I ONLY HOPE WE DON'T CROSS PATHS AGAIN.
MEAN-WHILE...
THAT'S RIGHT!! I SENT HER ON AN ER-RAND, AND SHE HASN'T COME BACK SINCE!!
EH? "THAT'S GOOD"!? DON'T TALK LIKE THAT!!

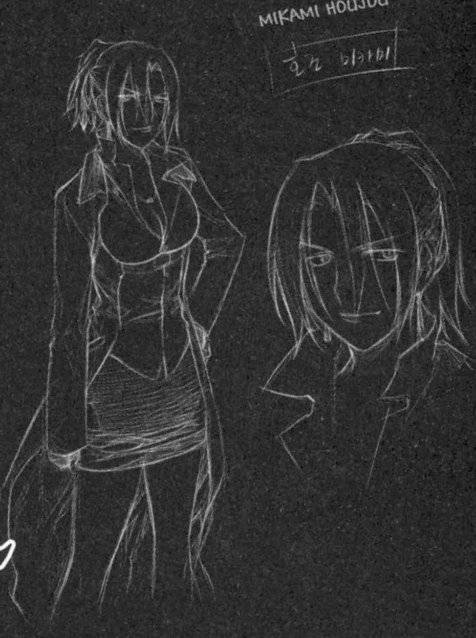
MIKAMI HOUJOU

黒神
BLACK GOD
which maintains balance in the world.

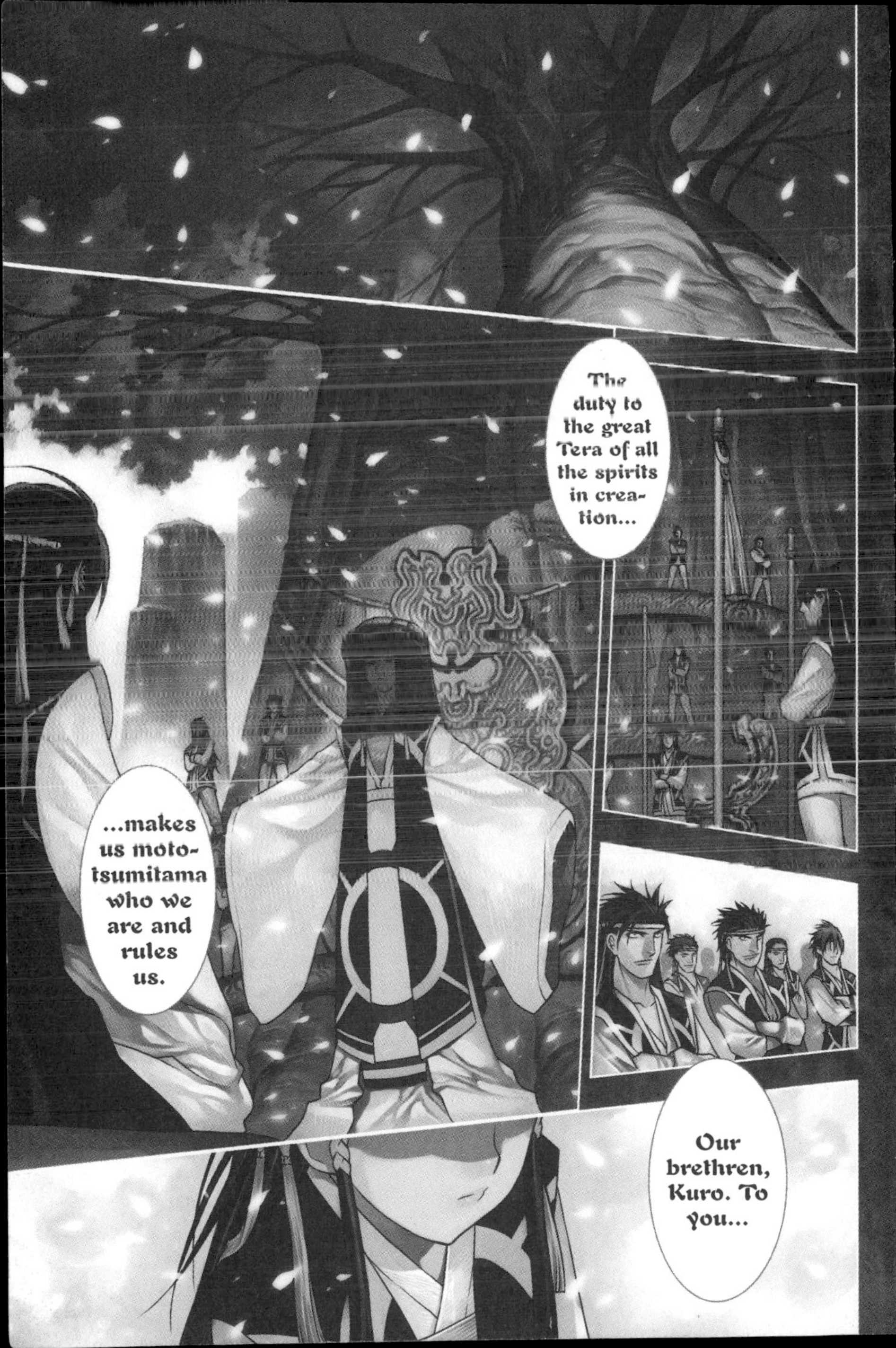
The duty to the great Tera of all the spirits in creation...
...makes us moto-tsumitama who we are and rules us.
Our brethren, Kuro. To you...

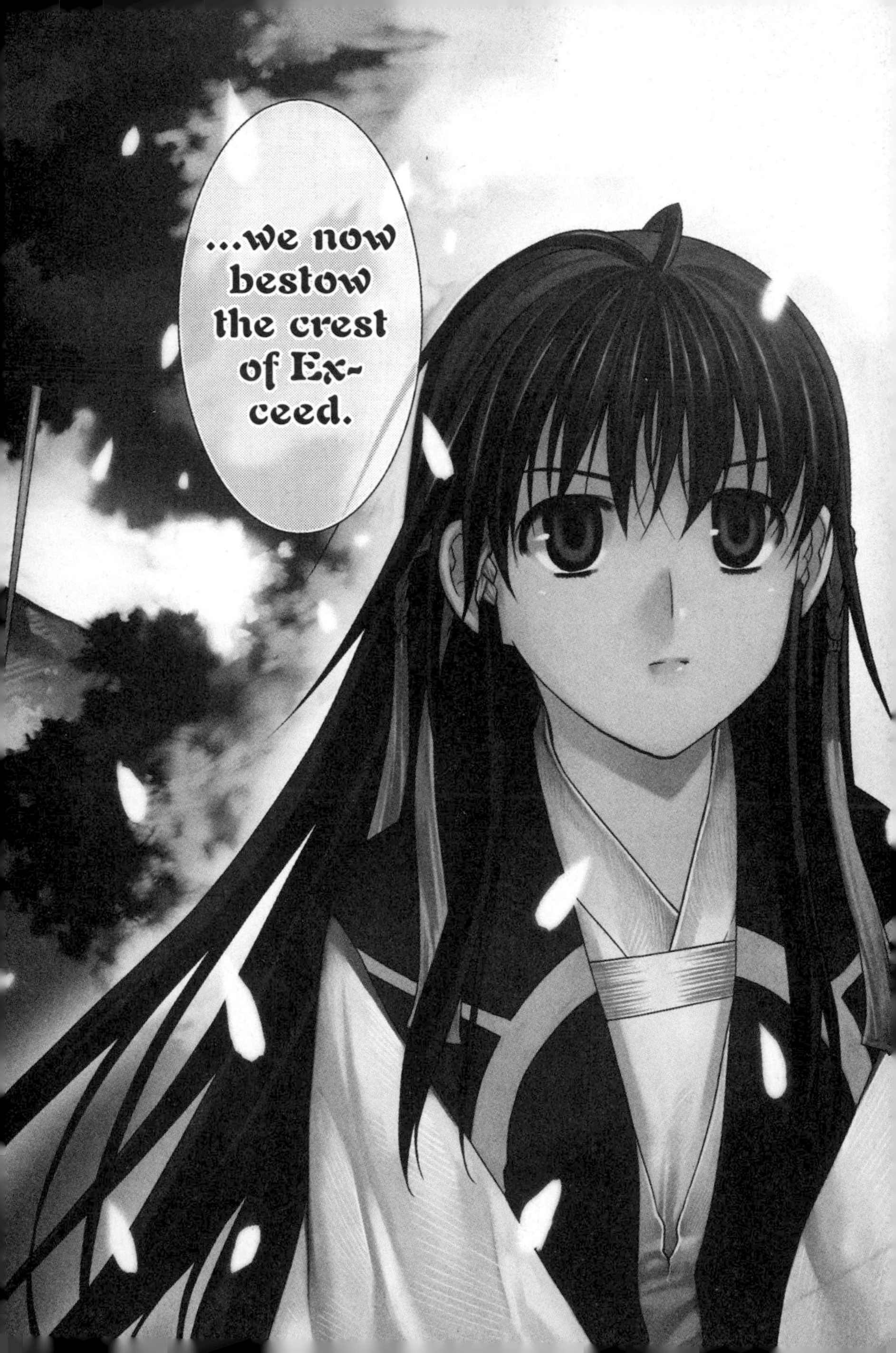
...we now bestow the crest of Ex-ceed.

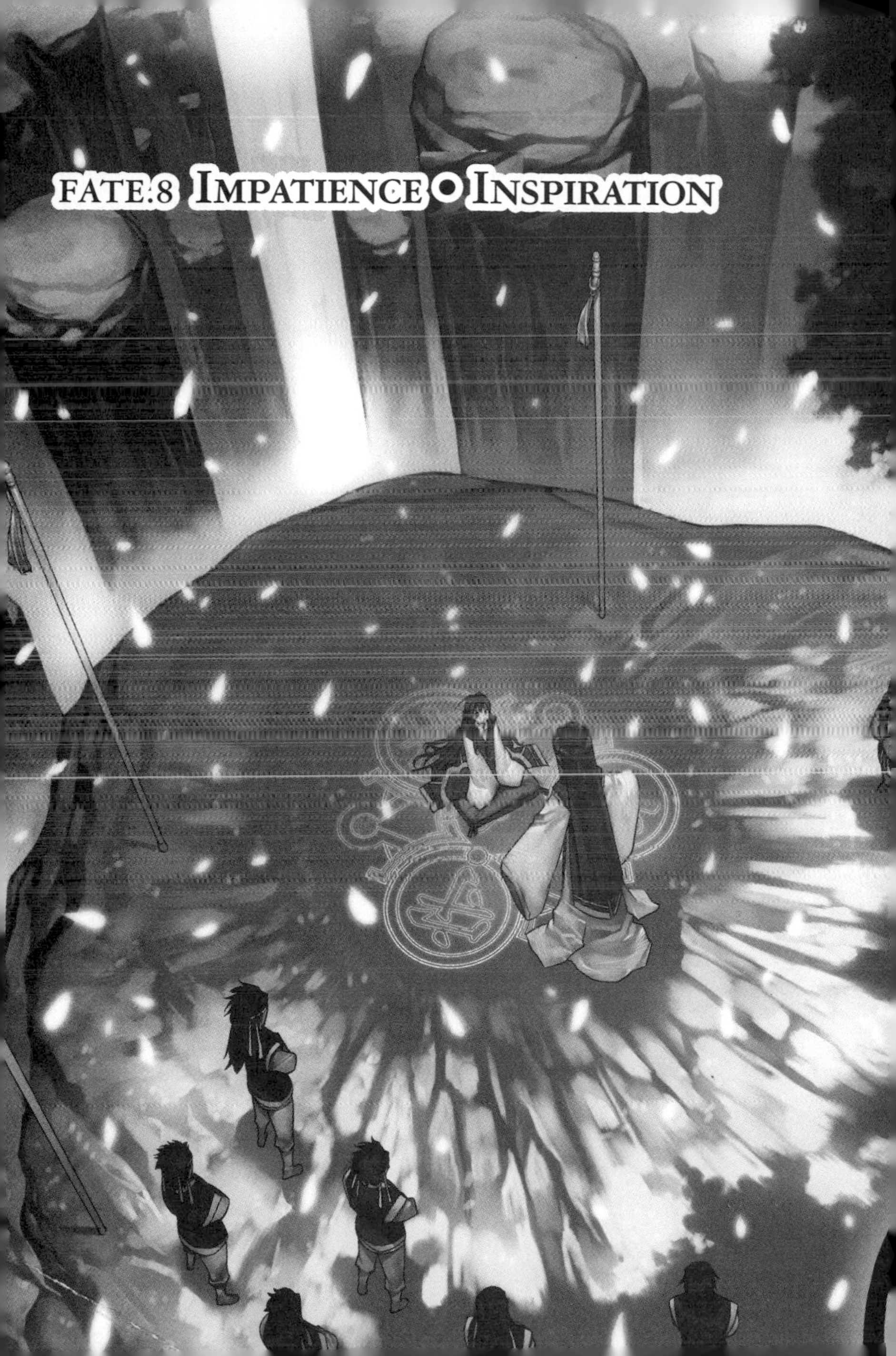
FATE.8 IMPATIENCE • INSPIRATION

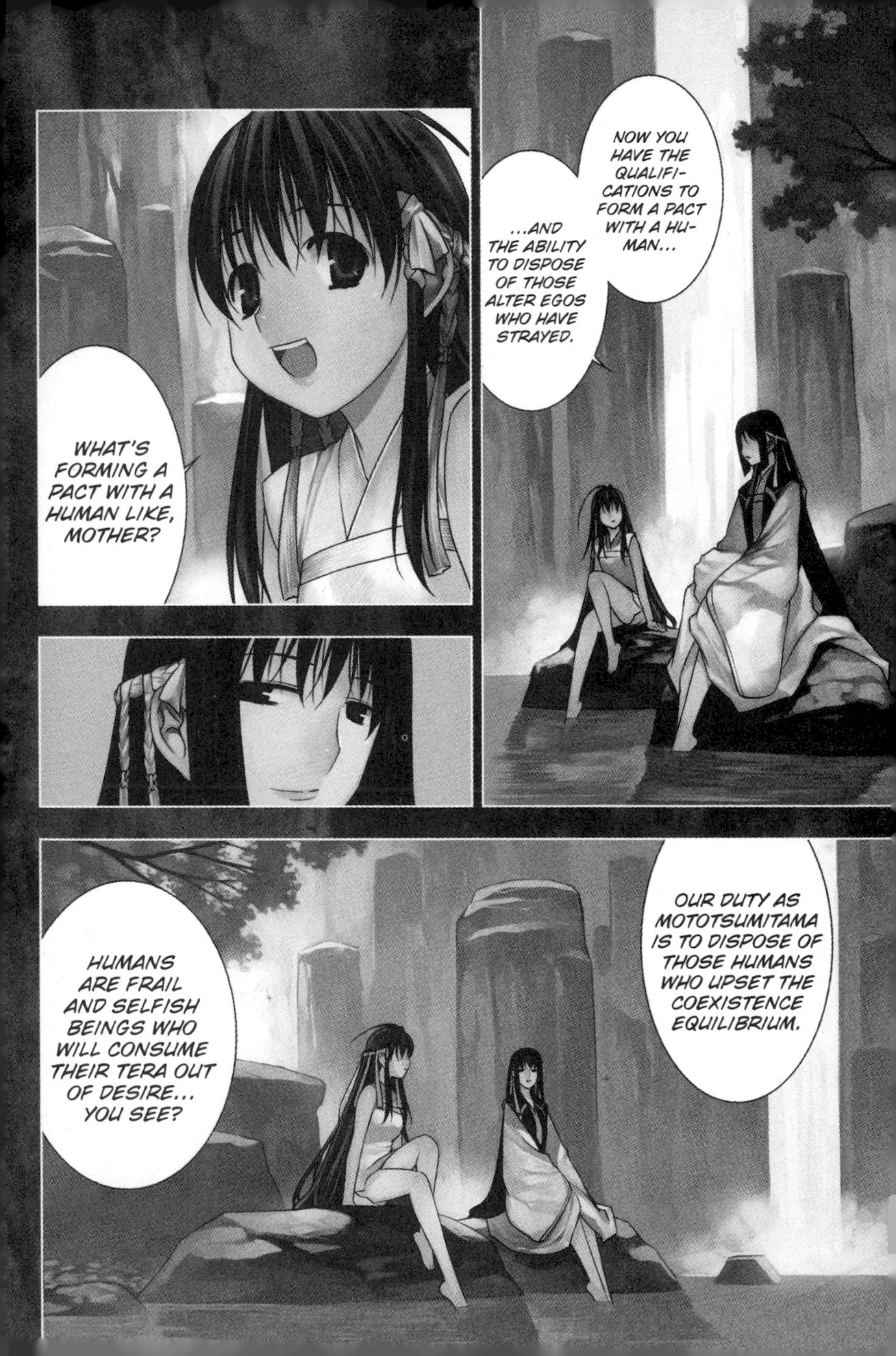
NOW YOU HAVE THE QUALIFI-CATIONS TO FORM A PACT WITH A HU-MAN...
...AND THE ABILITY TO DISPOSE OF THOSE ALTER EGOS WHO HAVE STRAYED.
WHAT'S FORMING A PACT WITH A HUMAN LIKE, MOTHER?
OUR DUTY AS MOTOTSUMITAMA IS TO DISPOSE OF THOSE HUMANS WHO UPSET THE COEXISTENCE EQUILIBRIUM.
HUMANS ARE FRAIL AND SELFISH BEINGS WHO WILL CONSUME THEIR TERA OUT OF DESIRE... YOU SEE?

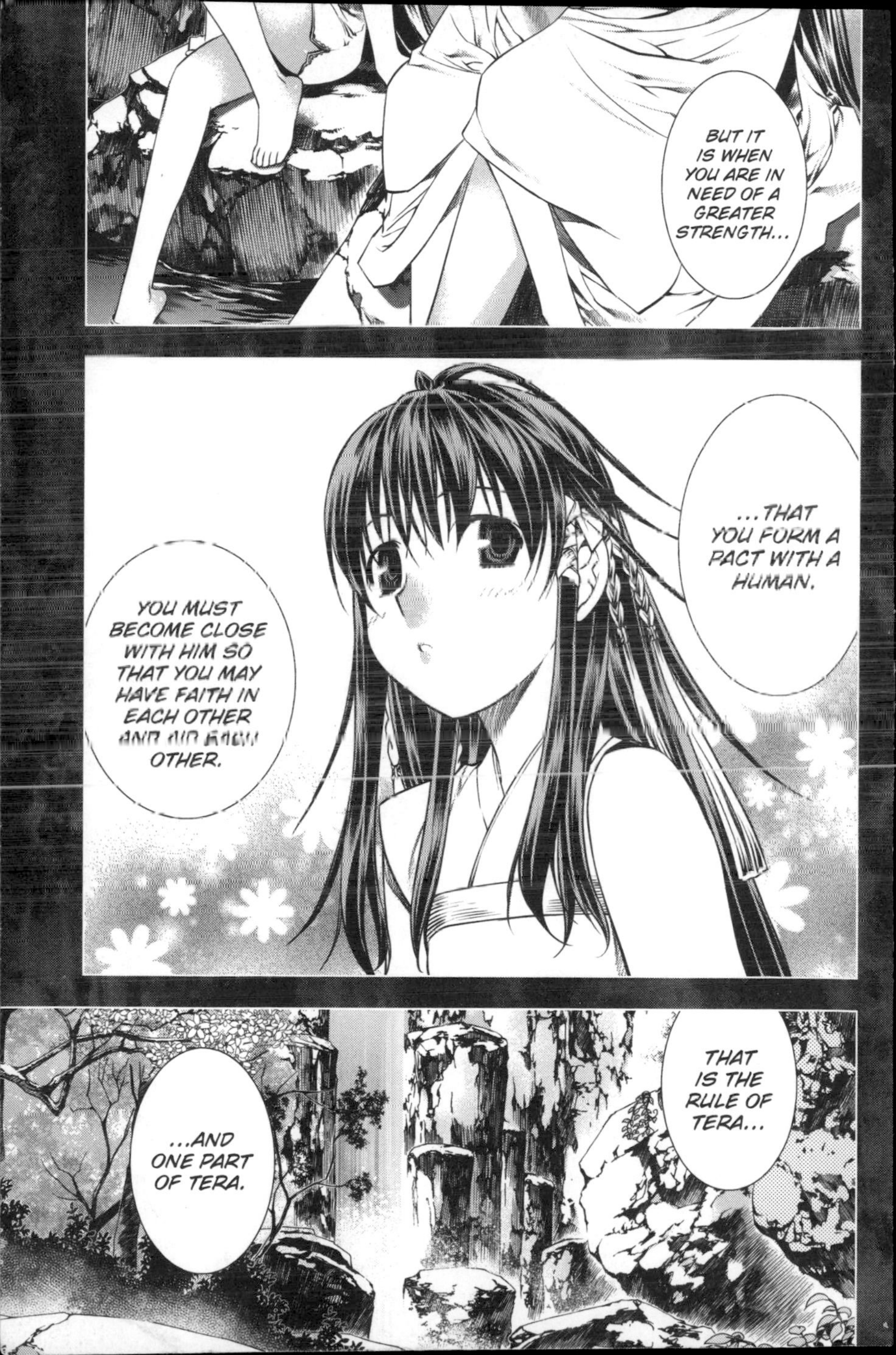
BUT IT IS WHEN YOU ARE IN NEED OF A GREATER STRENGTH...
...THAT YOU FORM A PACT WITH A HUMAN.
YOU MUST BECOME CLOSE WITH HIM SO THAT YOU MAY HAVE FAITH IN EACH OTHER AND AID EACH OTHER.
THAT IS THE RULE OF TERA...
...AND ONE PART OF TERA.

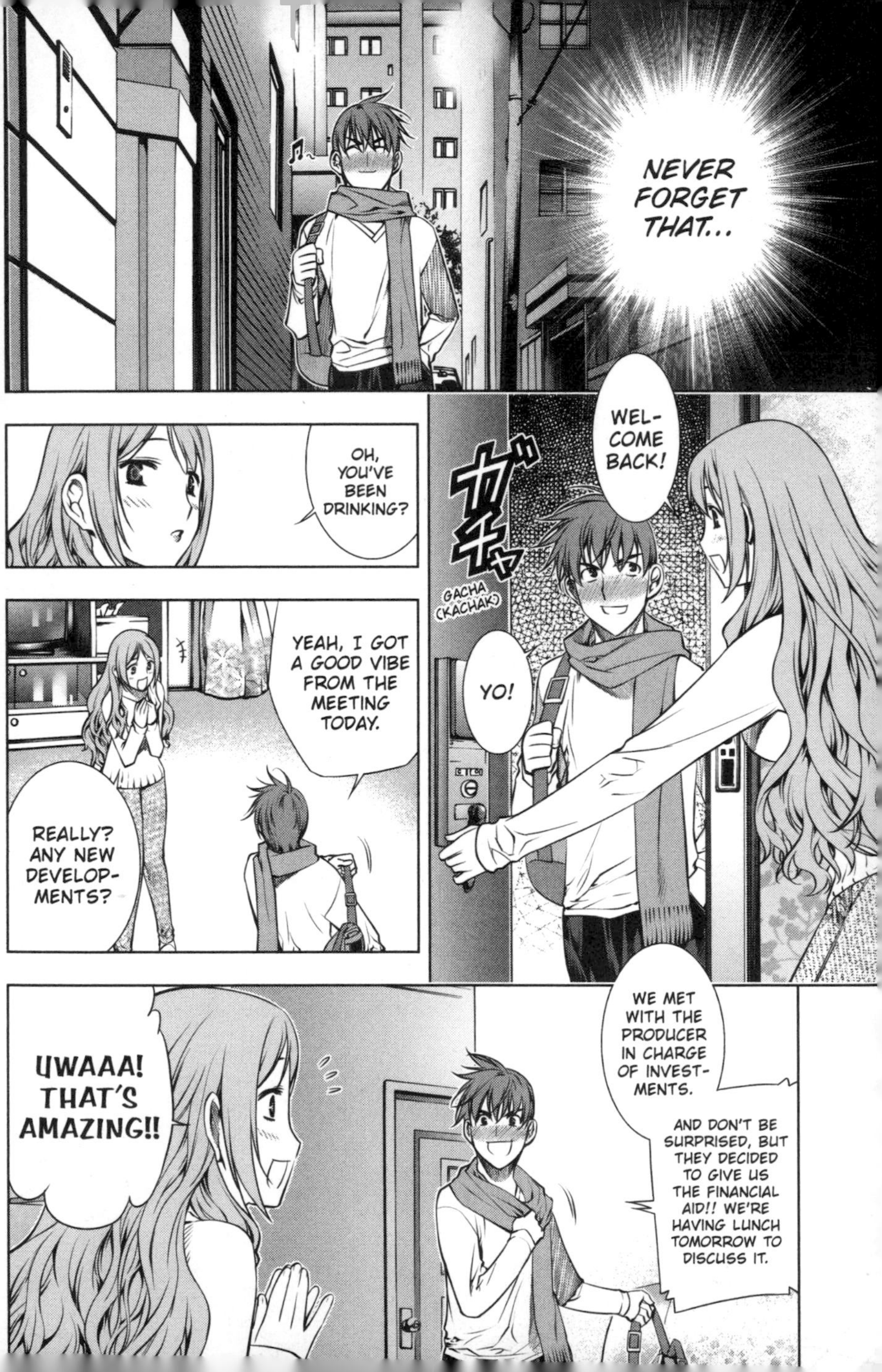
NEVER FORGET THAT...
WEL-COME BACK!
ガチャ
GACHA (KACHAK)
YO!
OH, YOU'VE BEEN DRINKING?
YEAH, I GOT A GOOD VIBE FROM THE MEETING TODAY.
REALLY? ANY NEW DEVELOP-MENTS?
WE MET WITH THE PRODUCER IN CHARGE OF INVEST-MENTS.
AND DON'T BE SURPRISED, BUT THEY DECIDED TO GIVE US THE FINANCIAL AID!! WE'RE HAVING LUNCH TOMORROW TO DISCUSS IT.
UWAAA! THAT'S AMAZING!!

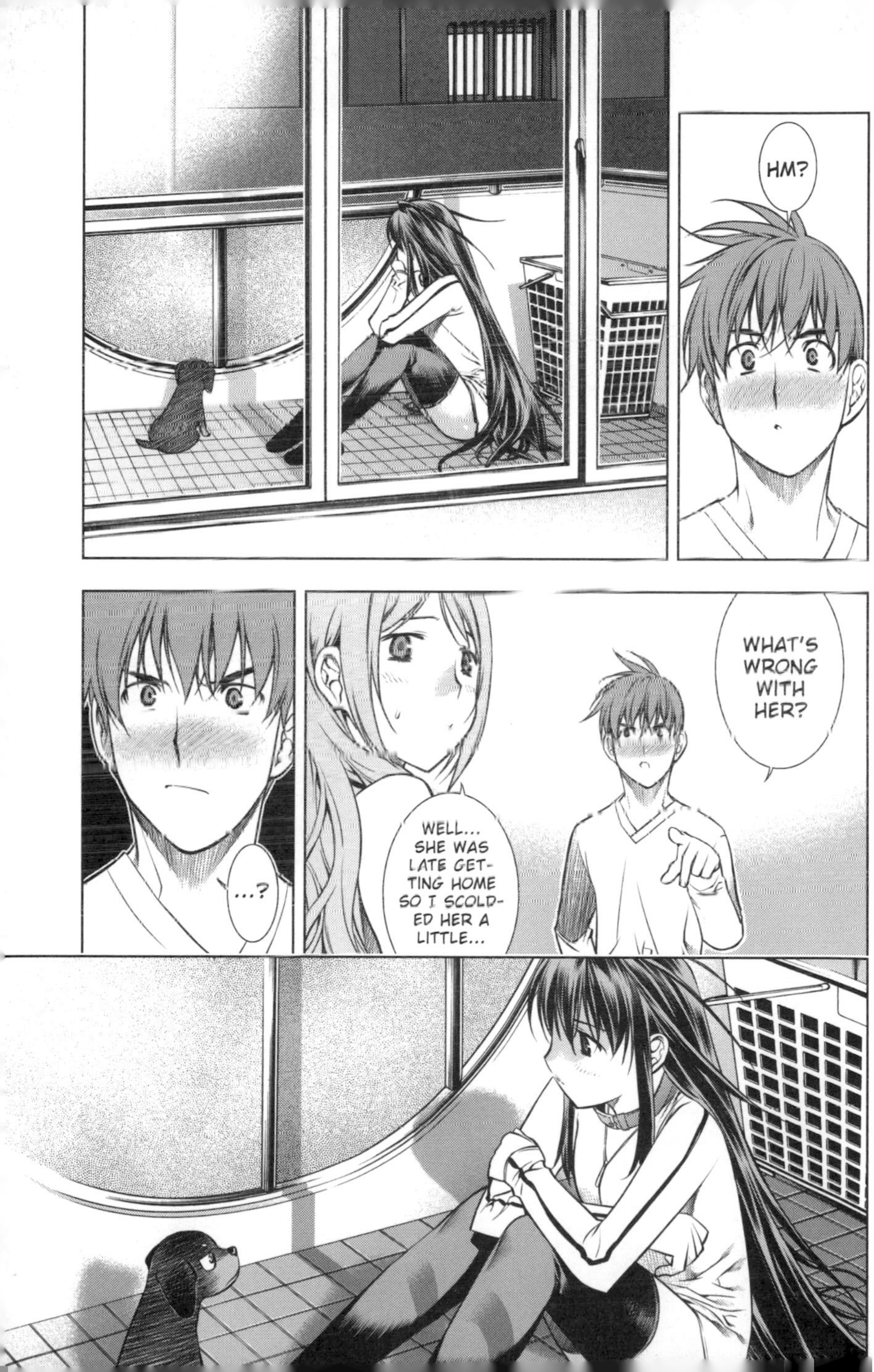
HM?
WHAT'S WRONG WITH HER?
WELL... SHE WAS LATE GET-TING HOME SO I SCOLD-ED HER A LITTLE...
...?

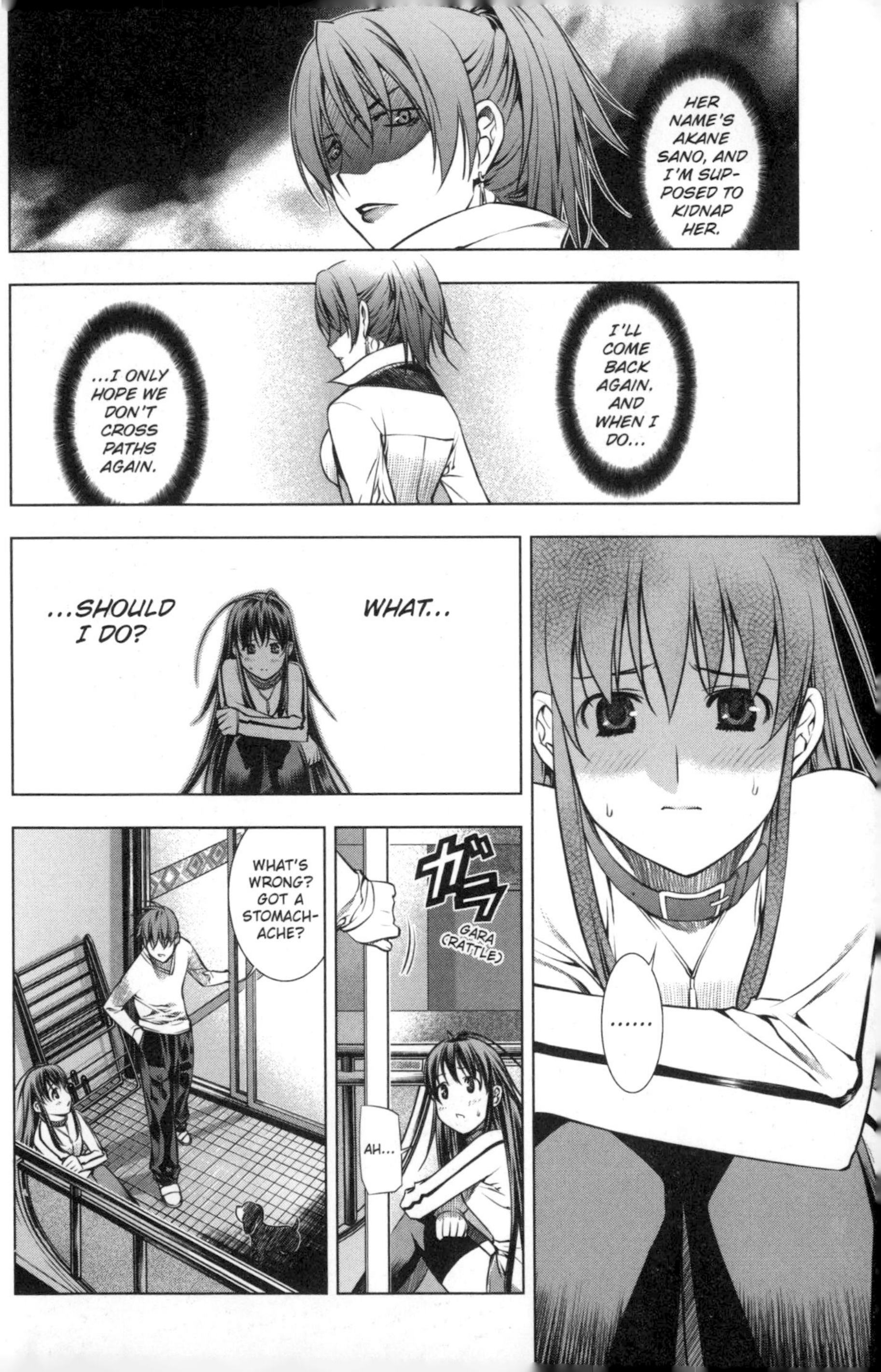
HER NAME'S AKANE SANO, AND I'M SUP-POSED TO KIDNAP HER.
I'LL COME BACK AGAIN. AND WHEN I DO...
...I ONLY HOPE WE DON'T CROSS PATHS AGAIN.
......
WHAT...
...SHOULD I DO?
GARA (RATTLE)
AH...
WHAT'S WRONG? GOT A STOMACH-ACHE?

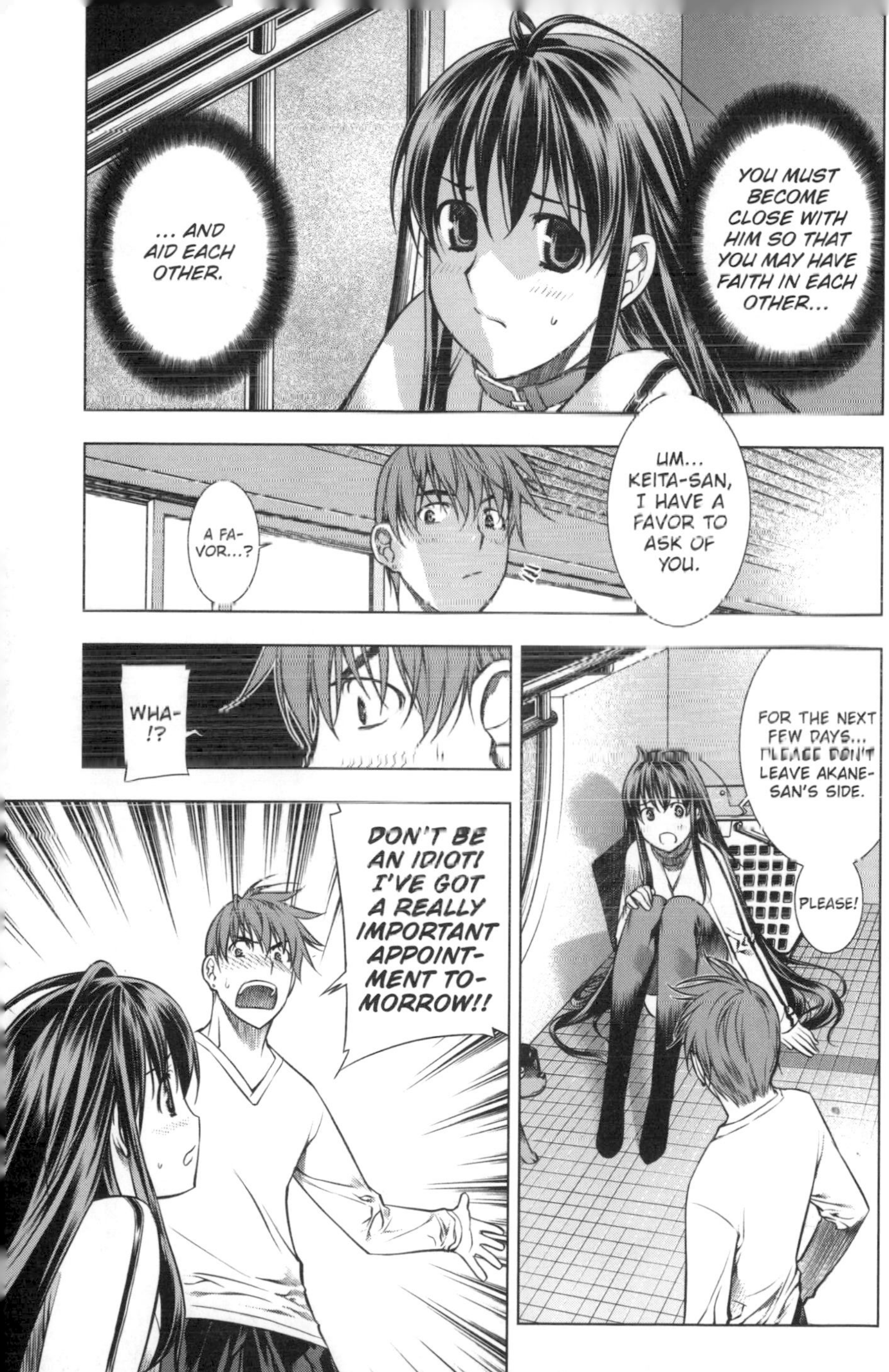
YOU MUST BECOME CLOSE WITH HIM SO THAT YOU MAY HAVE FAITH IN EACH OTHER...
... AND AID EACH OTHER.
UM... KEITA-SAN, I HAVE A FAVOR TO ASK OF YOU.
A FA-VOR...?
FOR THE NEXT FEW DAYS... PLEASE DON'T LEAVE AKANE-SAN'S SIDE.
PLEASE!
WHA-!?
DON'T BE AN IDIOT! I'VE GOT A REALLY IMPORTANT APPOINT-MENT TO-MORROW!!

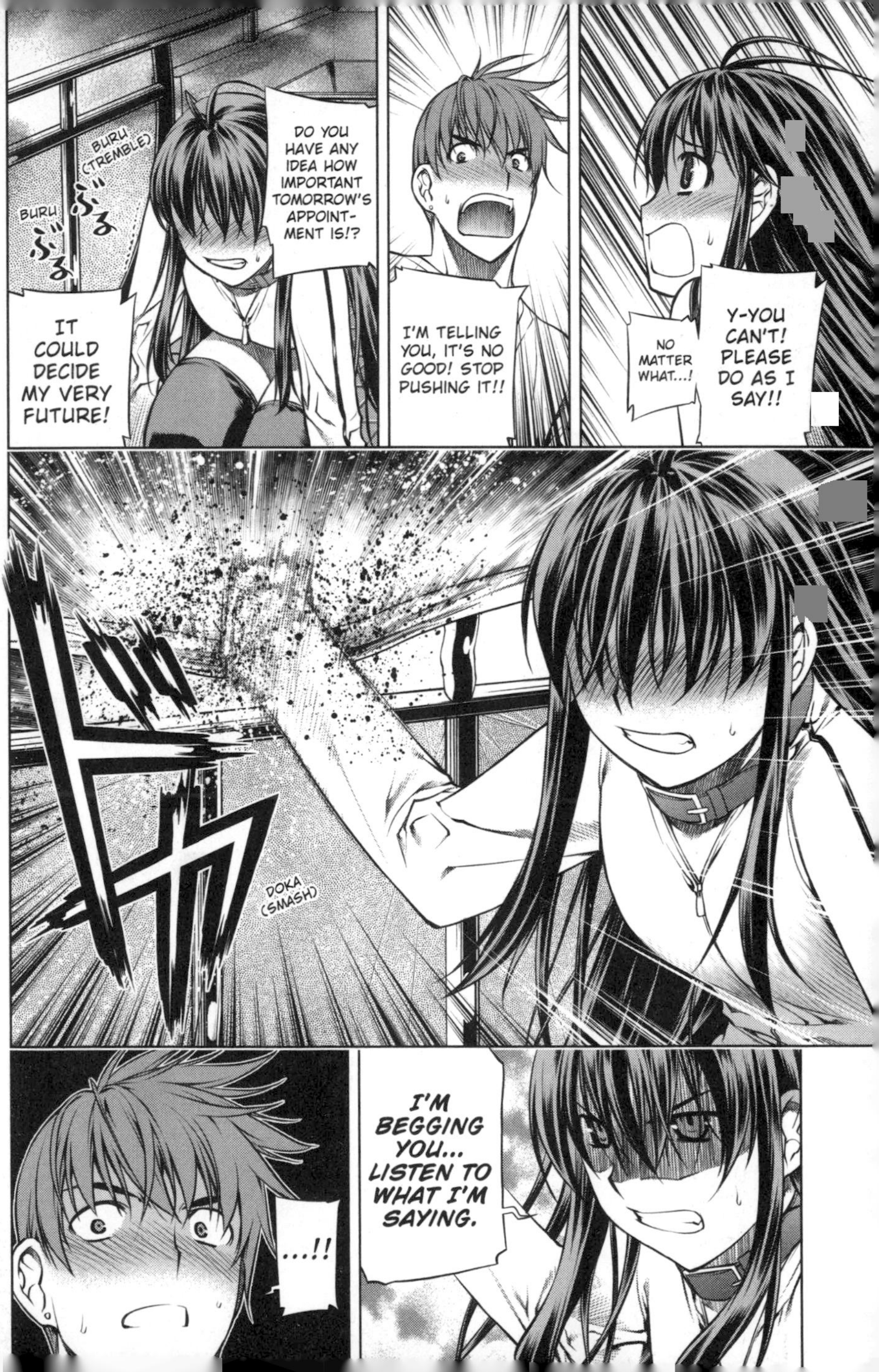
Y-YOU CAN'T! PLEASE DO AS I SAY!!
NO MATTER WHAT...!
I'M TELLING YOU, IT'S NO GOOD! STOP PUSHING IT!!
DO YOU HAVE ANY IDEA HOW IMPORTANT TOMORROW'S APPOINT-MENT IS!?
BURU (TREMBLE)
ぶる
BURU
ぶる
IT COULD DECIDE MY VERY FUTURE!
DOKA (SMASH)
I'M BEGGING YOU... LISTEN TO WHAT I'M SAYING.
...!!

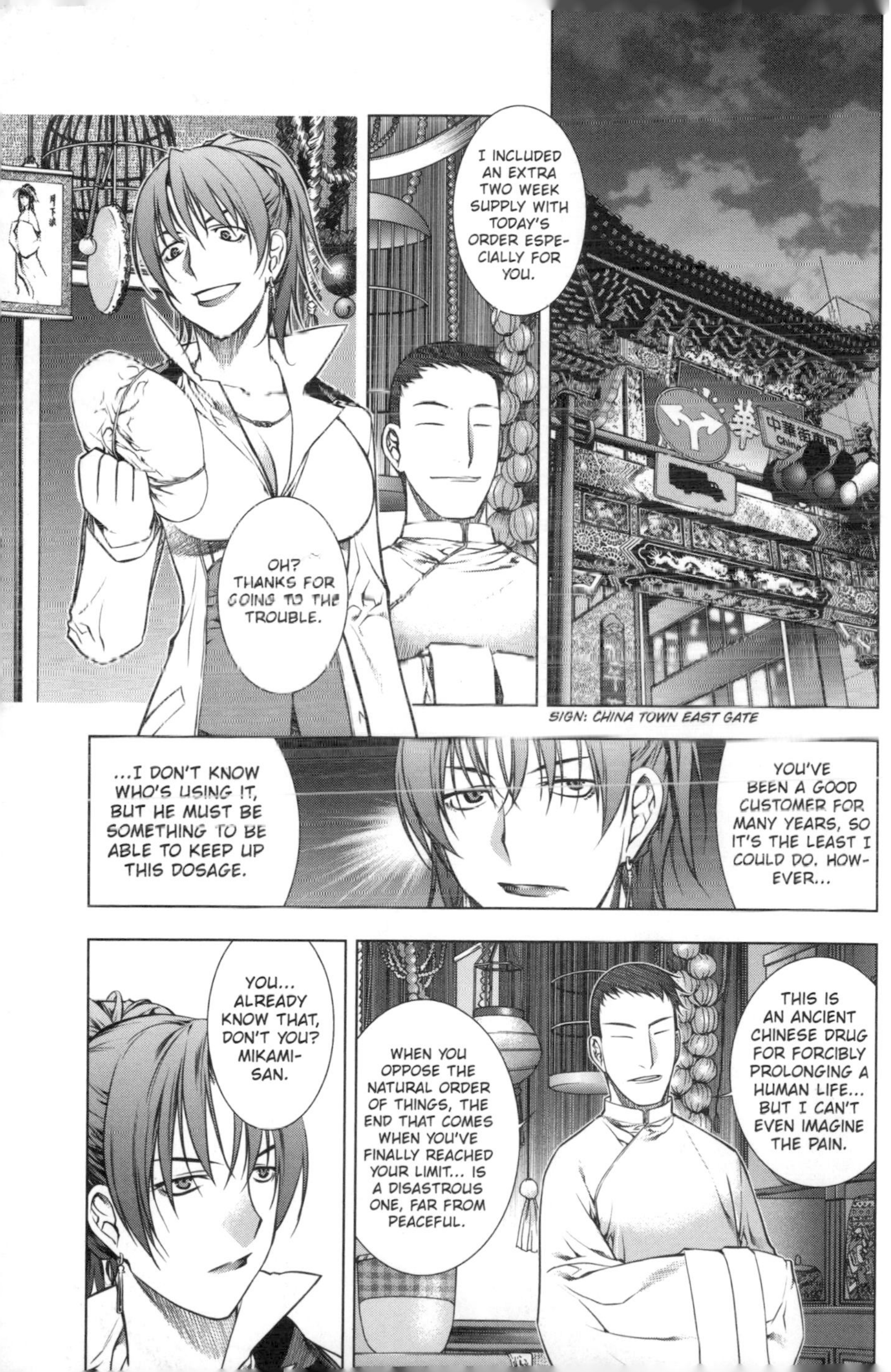
SIGN: CHINA TOWN EAST GATE
I INCLUDED AN EXTRA TWO WEEK SUPPLY WITH TODAY'S ORDER ESPE-CIALLY FOR YOU.
OH? THANKS FOR GOING TO THE TROUBLE.
YOU'VE BEEN A GOOD CUSTOMER FOR MANY YEARS, SO IT'S THE LEAST I COULD DO. HOW-EVER...
...I DON'T KNOW WHO'S USING IT, BUT HE MUST BE SOMETHING TO BE ABLE TO KEEP UP THIS DOSAGE.
THIS IS AN ANCIENT CHINESE DRUG FOR FORCIBLY PROLONGING A HUMAN LIFE... BUT I CAN'T EVEN IMAGINE THE PAIN.
WHEN YOU OPPOSE THE NATURAL ORDER OF THINGS, THE END THAT COMES WHEN YOU'VE FINALLY REACHED YOUR LIMIT... IS A DISASTROUS ONE, FAR FROM PEACEFUL.
YOU... ALREADY KNOW THAT, DON'T YOU? MIKAMI-SAN.

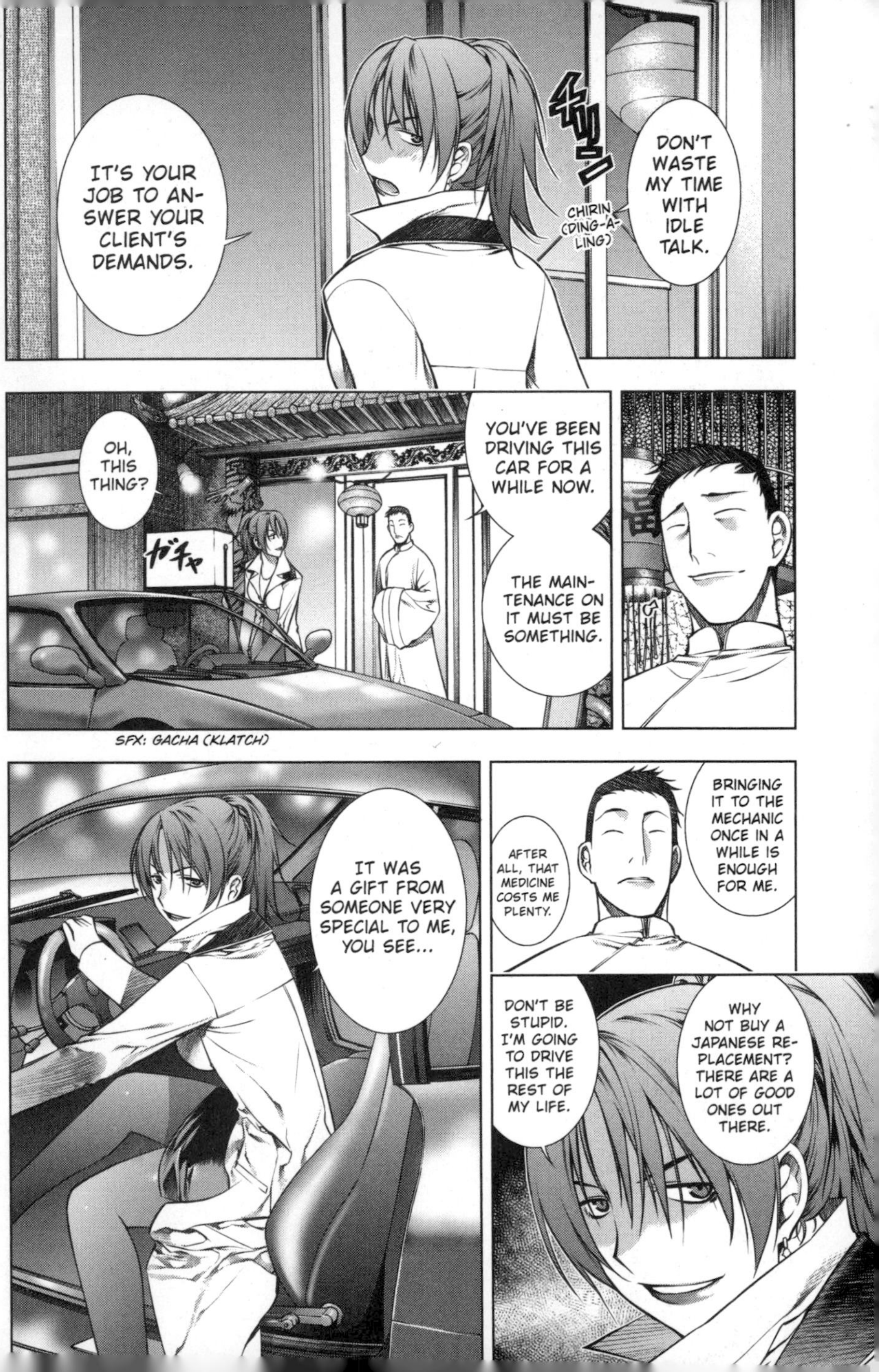
CHIRIN (DING-A-LING)
DON'T WASTE MY TIME WITH IDLE TALK.
IT'S YOUR JOB TO AN-SWER YOUR CLIENT'S DEMANDS.
YOU'VE BEEN DRIVING THIS CAR FOR A WHILE NOW.
THE MAIN-TENANCE ON IT MUST BE SOMETHING.
OH, THIS THING?
ガチャ
SFX: GACHA (KLATCH)
BRINGING IT TO THE MECHANIC ONCE IN A WHILE IS ENOUGH FOR ME.
AFTER ALL, THAT MEDICINE COSTS ME PLENTY.
WHY NOT BUY A JAPANESE RE-PLACEMENT? THERE ARE A LOT OF GOOD ONES OUT THERE.
DON'T BE STUPID. I'M GOING TO DRIVE THIS THE REST OF MY LIFE.
IT WAS A GIFT FROM SOMEONE VERY SPECIAL TO ME, YOU SEE...

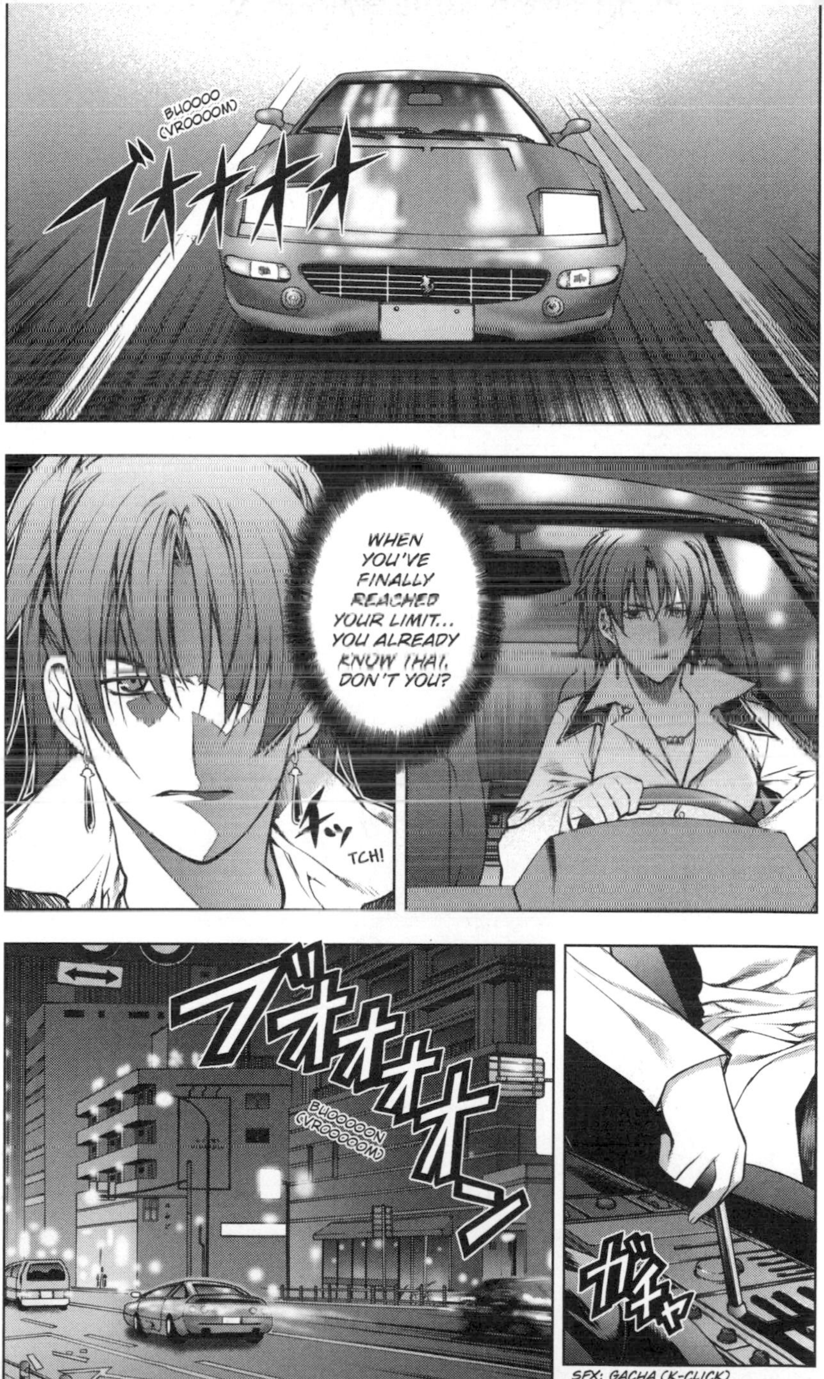
ブオオオオ
BUOOOO (VROOOOM)
WHEN YOU'VE FINALLY REACHED YOUR LIMIT... YOU ALREADY KNOW THAT, DON'T YOU?
チッ
TCH!
ガチャ
ブオオオオーン
BUOOOOON (VROOOOOM)
SFX: GACHA (K-CLICK)

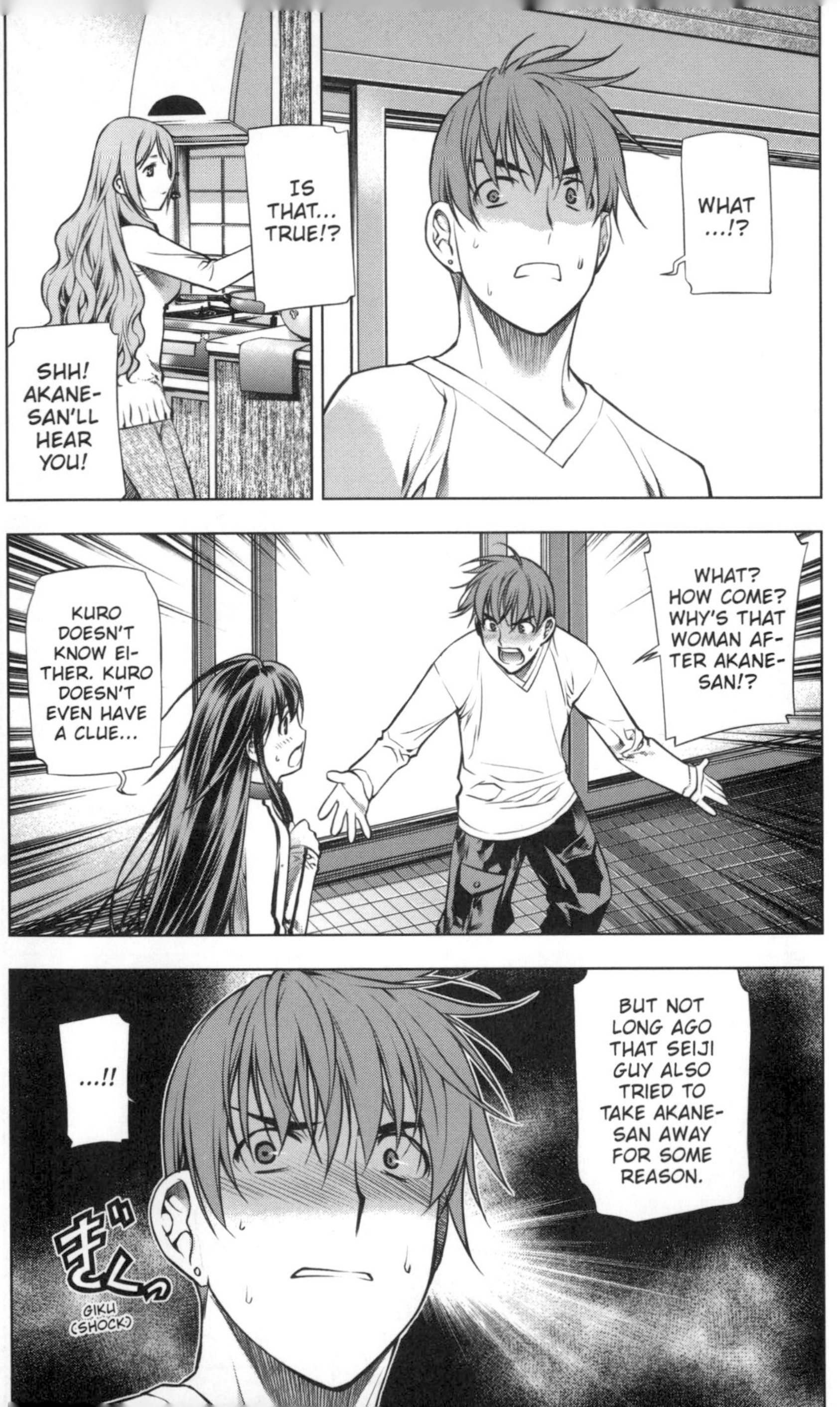
WHAT ...!?
IS THAT... TRUE!?
SHH! AKANE-SAN'LL HEAR YOU!
WHAT? HOW COME? WHY'S THAT WOMAN AFTER AKANE-SAN!?
KURO DOESN'T KNOW EITHER. KURO DOESN'T EVEN HAVE A CLUE...
BUT NOT LONG AGO THAT SEIJI GUY ALSO TRIED TO TAKE AKANE-SAN AWAY FOR SOME REASON.
...!!
ぎくっ
GIKU (SHOCK)

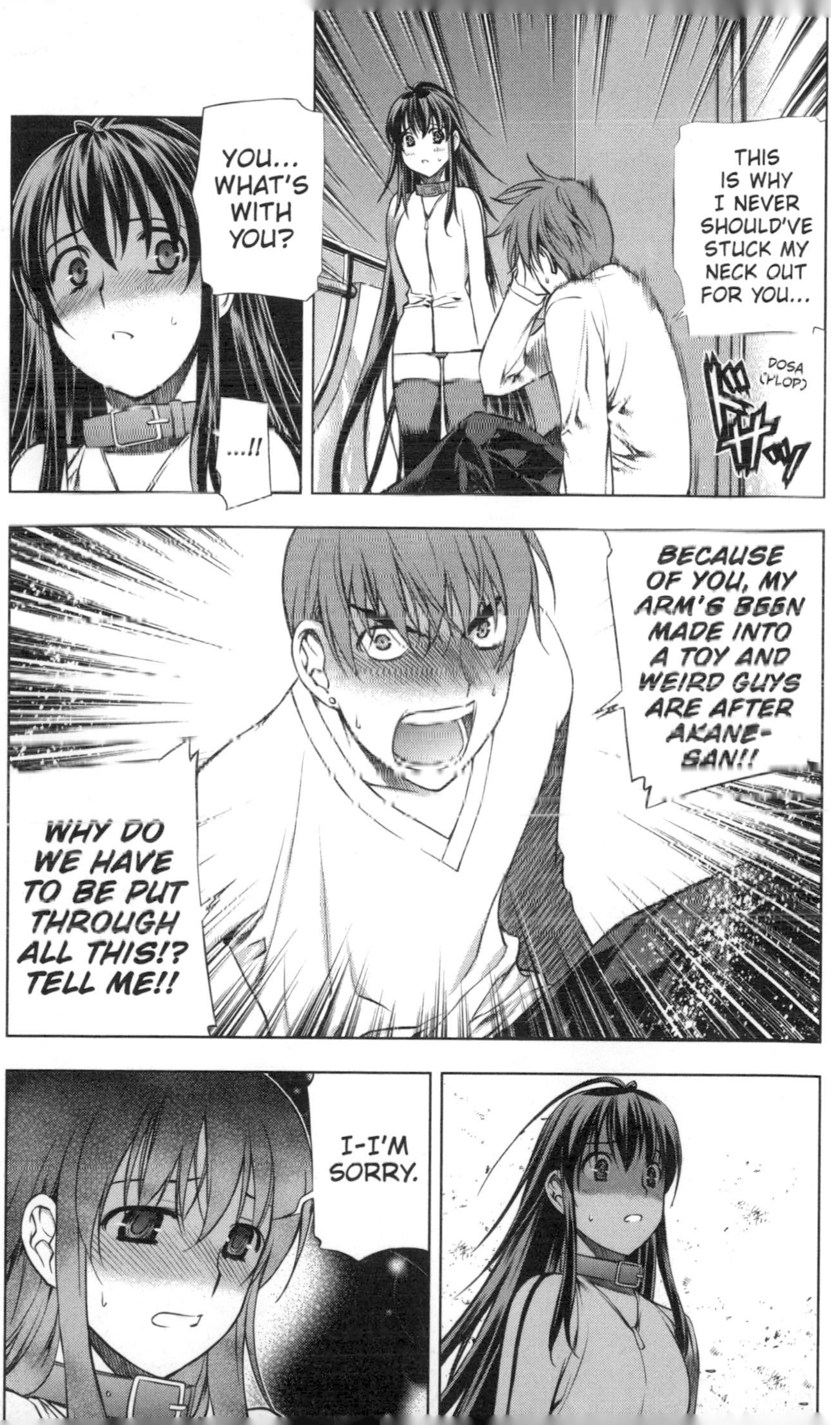
THIS IS WHY I NEVER SHOULD'VE STUCK MY NECK OUT FOR YOU...
DOSA (FLOP)
YOU... WHAT'S WITH YOU?
...!!
BECAUSE OF YOU, MY ARM'S BEEN MADE INTO A TOY AND WEIRD GUYS ARE AFTER AKANE-SAN!!
WHY DO WE HAVE TO BE PUT THROUGH ALL THIS!? TELL ME!!
I-I'M SORRY.

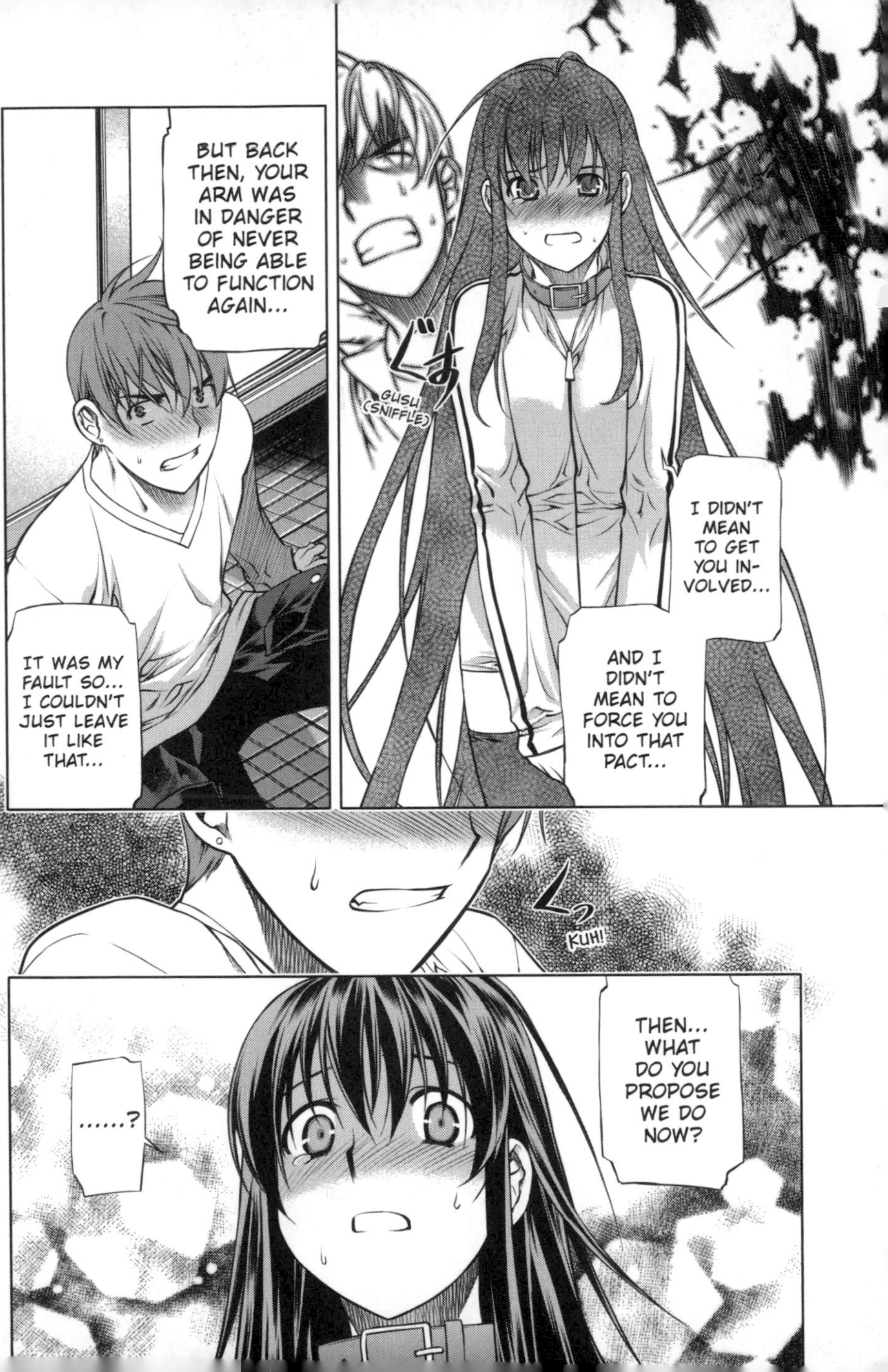
GUSU (SNIFFLE)
I DIDN'T MEAN TO GET YOU IN-VOLVED...
AND I DIDN'T MEAN TO FORCE YOU INTO THAT PACT...
BUT BACK THEN, YOUR ARM WAS IN DANGER OF NEVER BEING ABLE TO FUNCTION AGAIN...
IT WAS MY FAULT SO... I COULDN'T JUST LEAVE IT LIKE THAT...
KUH!
THEN... WHAT DO YOU PROPOSE WE DO NOW?
......?

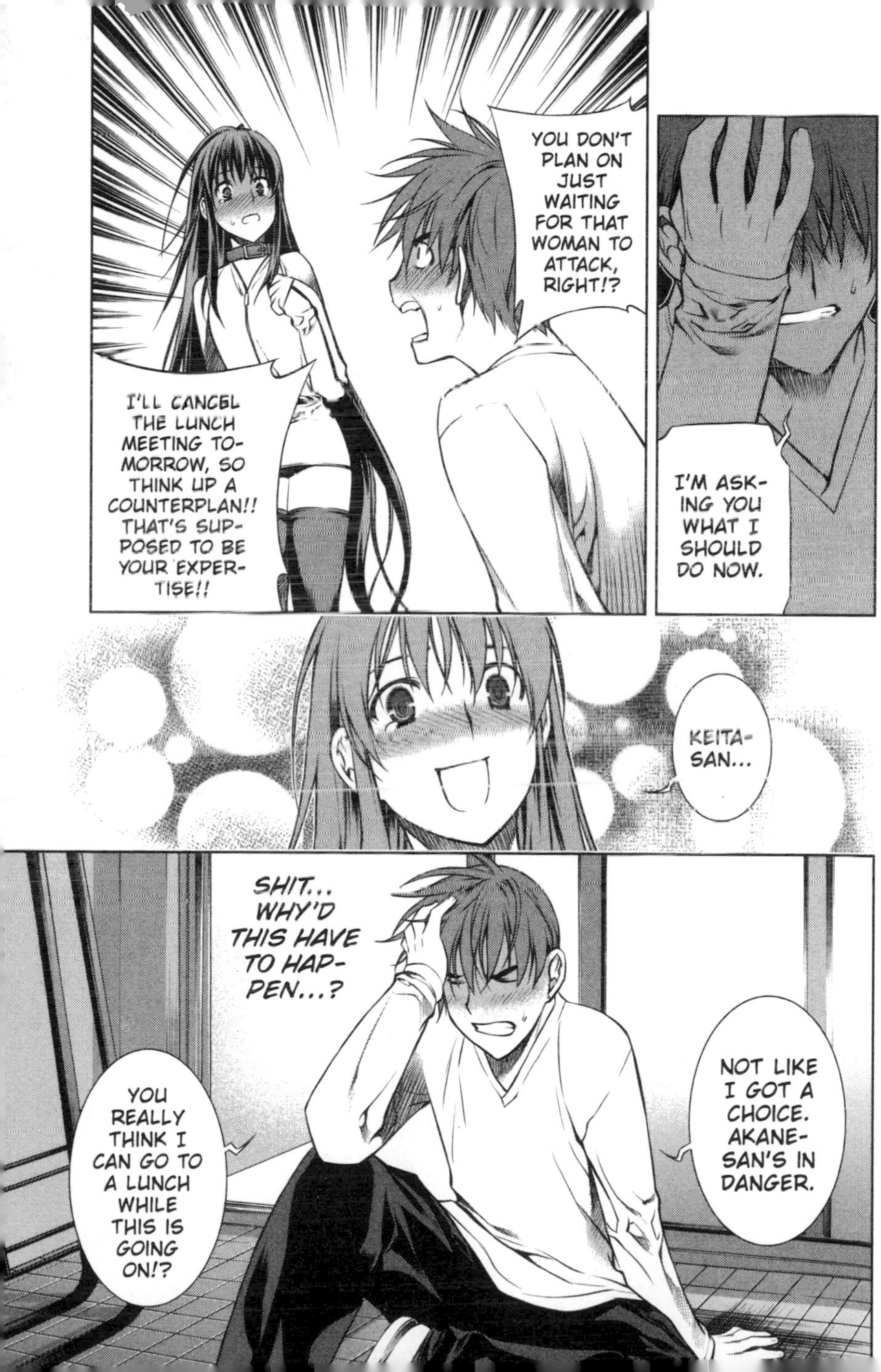
I'M ASKING YOU WHAT I SHOULD DO NOW.
YOU DON'T PLAN ON JUST WAITING FOR THAT WOMAN TO ATTACK, RIGHT!?
I'LL CANCEL THE LUNCH MEETING TOMORROW, SO THINK UP A COUNTERPLAN!! THAT'S SUPPOSED TO BE YOUR EXPERTISE!!
KEITA-SAN...
SHIT... WHY'D THIS HAVE TO HAPPEN...?
NOT LIKE I GOT A CHOICE. AKANE-SAN'S IN DANGER.
YOU REALLY THINK I CAN GO TO A LUNCH WHILE THIS IS GOING ON!?

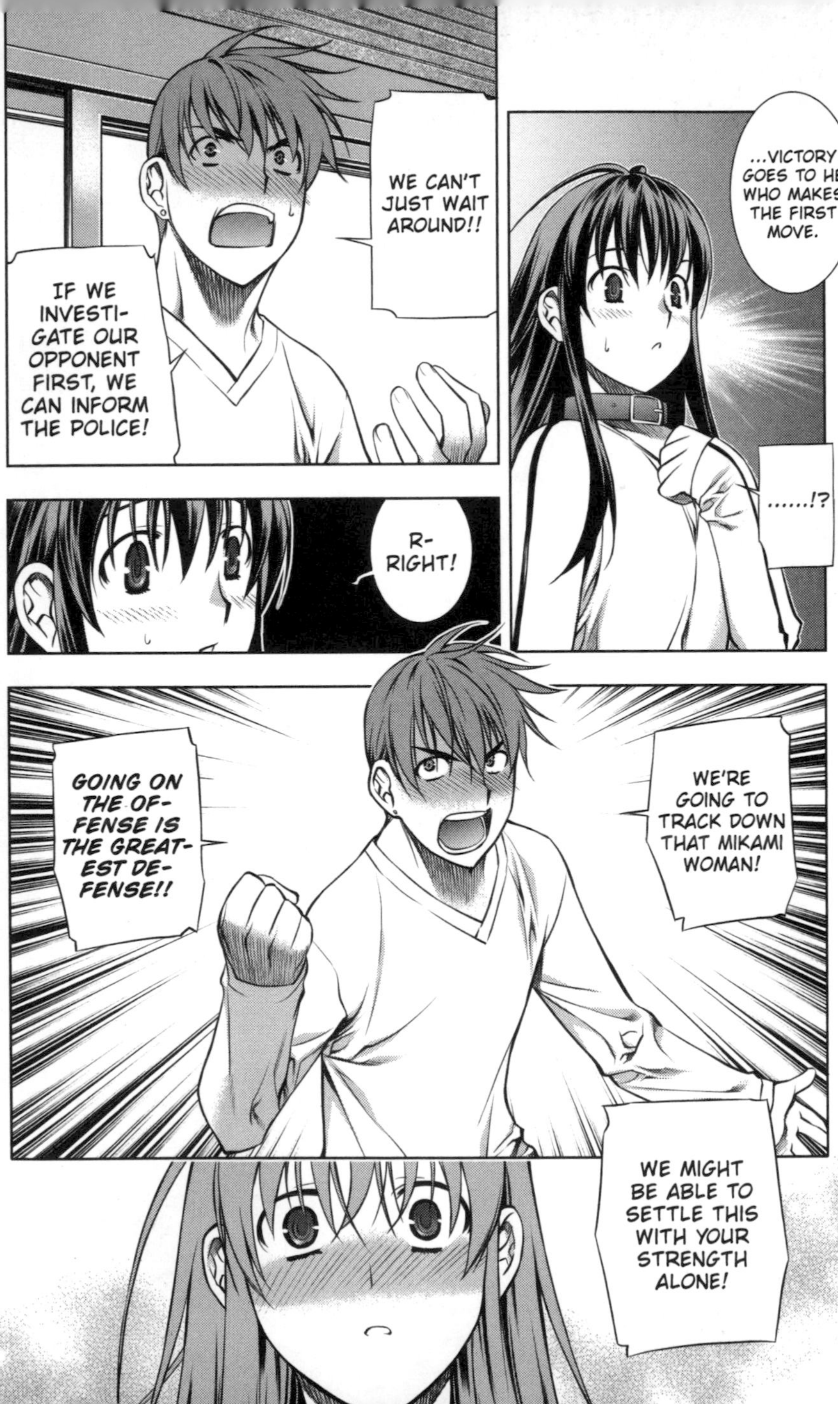
...VICTORY GOES TO HE WHO MAKES THE FIRST MOVE.
......!?
WE CAN'T JUST WAIT AROUND!!
IF WE INVESTI-GATE OUR OPPONENT FIRST, WE CAN INFORM THE POLICE!
R-RIGHT!
WE'RE GOING TO TRACK DOWN THAT MIKAMI WOMAN!
GOING ON THE OF-FENSE IS THE GREAT-EST DE-FENSE!!
WE MIGHT BE ABLE TO SETTLE THIS WITH YOUR STRENGTH ALONE!

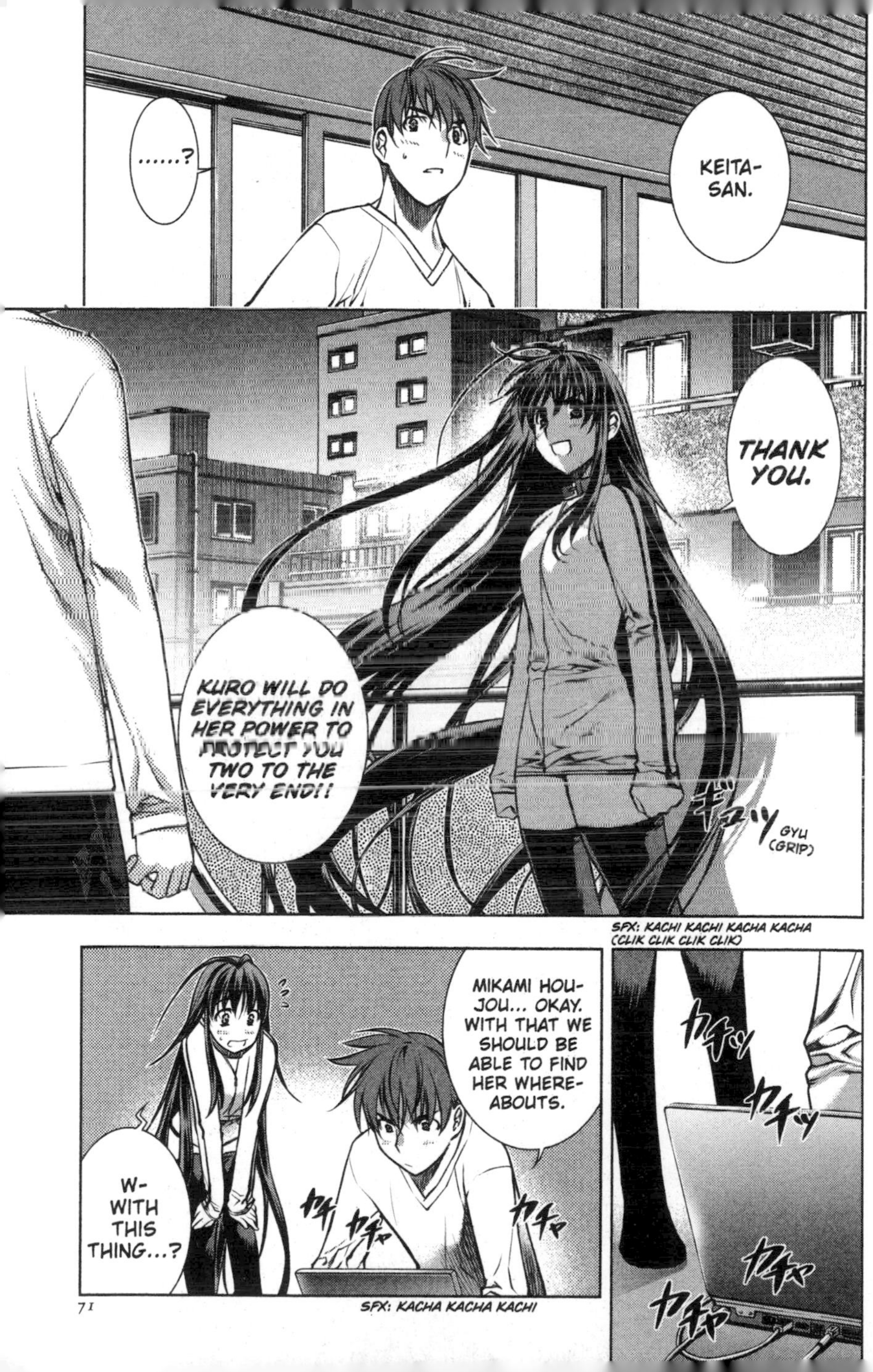
KEITA-SAN.
......?
THANK YOU.
KURO WILL DO EVERYTHING IN HER POWER TO PROTECT YOU TWO TO THE VERY END!!
GYU (GRIP)
SFX: KACHI KACHI KACHA KACHA (CLIK CLIK CLIK CLIK)
MIKAMI HOU-JOU... OKAY. WITH THAT WE SHOULD BE ABLE TO FIND HER WHERE-ABOUTS.
W-WITH THIS THING...?
SFX: KACHA KACHA KACHI

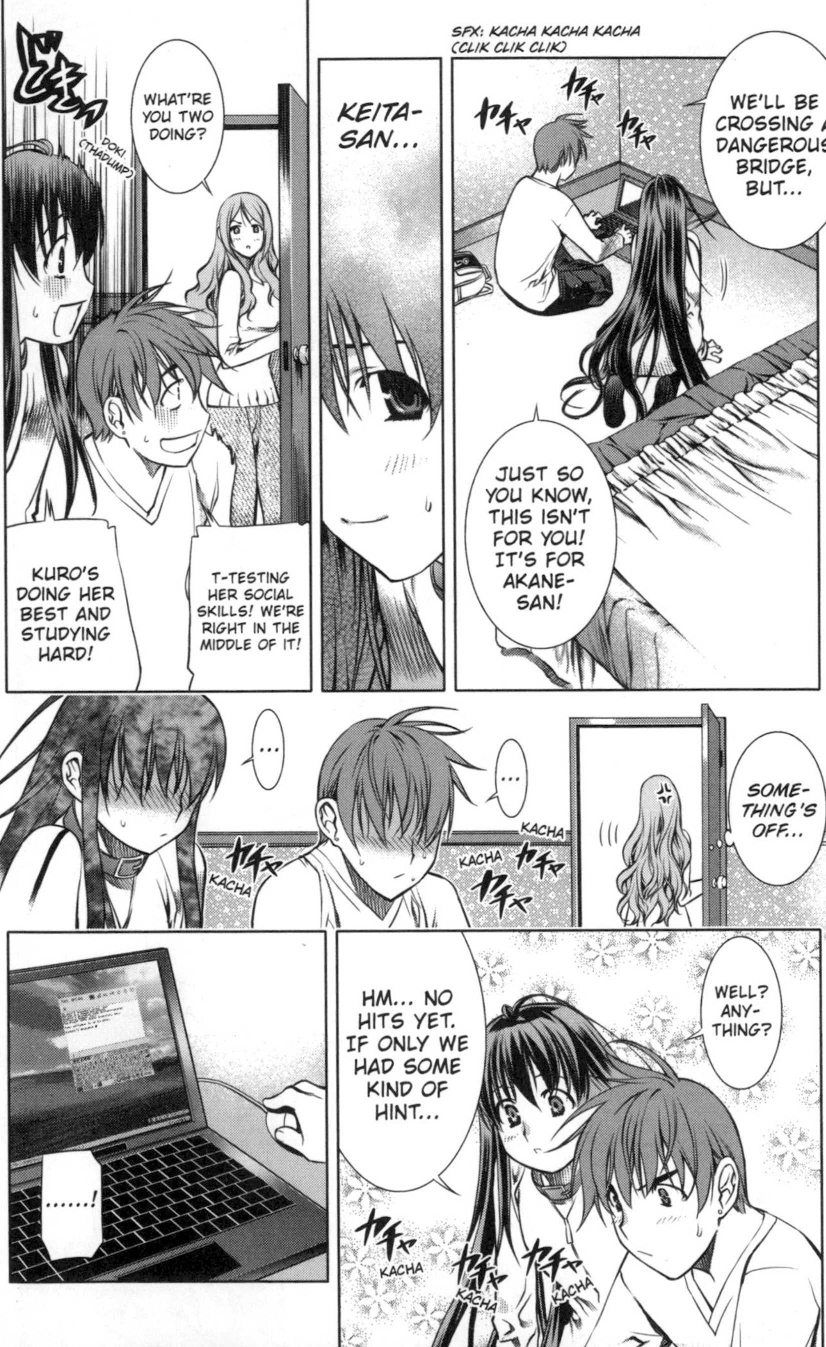
SFX: KACHA KACHA KACHA (CLIK CLIK CLIK)
WE'LL BE CROSSING A DANGEROUS BRIDGE, BUT...
JUST SO YOU KNOW, THIS ISN'T FOR YOU! IT'S FOR AKANE-SAN!
KEITA-SAN...
WHAT'RE YOU TWO DOING?
DOKI (THADUMP)
T-TESTING HER SOCIAL SKILLS! WE'RE RIGHT IN THE MIDDLE OF IT!
KURO'S DOING HER BEST AND STUDYING HARD!
SOME-THING'S OFF...
KACHA
...
KACHA
KACHA
...
WELL? ANY-THING?
HM... NO HITS YET. IF ONLY WE HAD SOME KIND OF HINT...
KACHA
KACHA
KACHA
......!

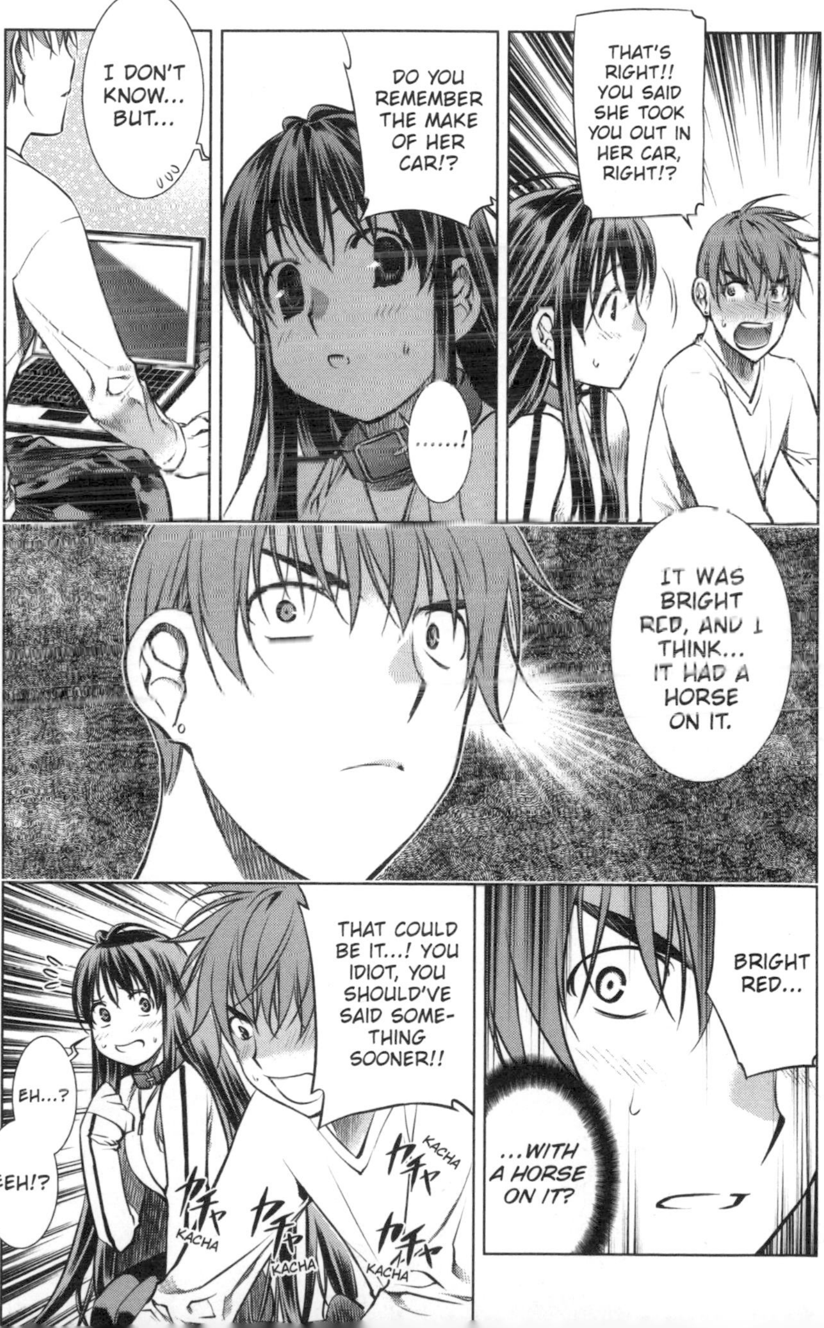
THAT'S RIGHT!! YOU SAID SHE TOOK YOU OUT IN HER CAR, RIGHT!?
DO YOU REMEMBER THE MAKE OF HER CAR!?
......!
I DON'T KNOW... BUT...
IT WAS BRIGHT RED, AND I THINK... IT HAD A HORSE ON IT.
BRIGHT RED...
...WITH A HORSE ON IT?
THAT COULD BE IT...! YOU IDIOT, YOU SHOULD'VE SAID SOME-THING SOONER!!
EH...?
EEH!?
カチャ KACHA
カチャ KACHA
カチャ KACHA
カチャ KACHA

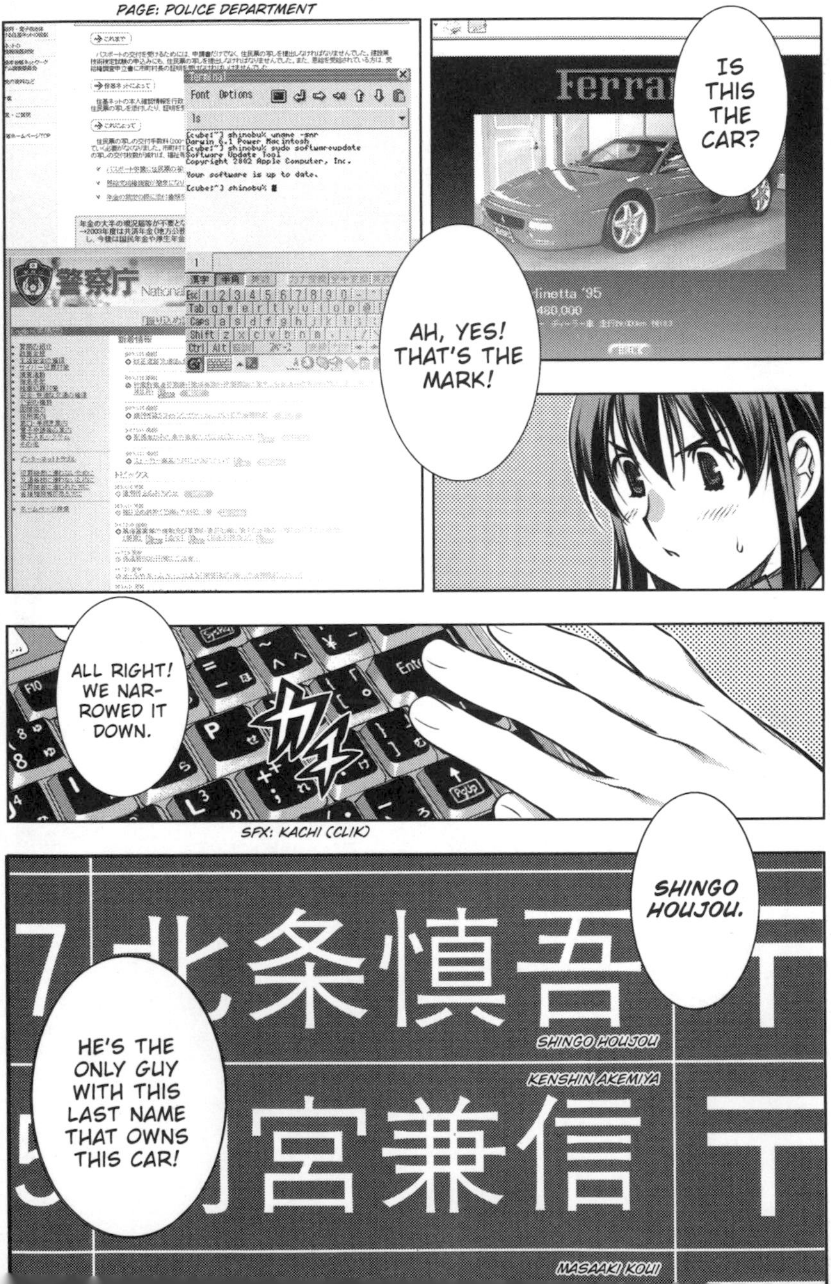
IS THIS THE CAR?
AH, YES! THAT'S THE MARK!
PAGE: POLICE DEPARTMENT
ALL RIGHT! WE NAR-ROWED IT DOWN.
SFX: KACHI (CLIK)
SHINGO HOUJOU.
北条慎吾
SHINGO HOUJOU
KENSHIN AKEMIYA
宮兼信
MASAAKI KOUI
HE'S THE ONLY GUY WITH THIS LAST NAME THAT OWNS THIS CAR!

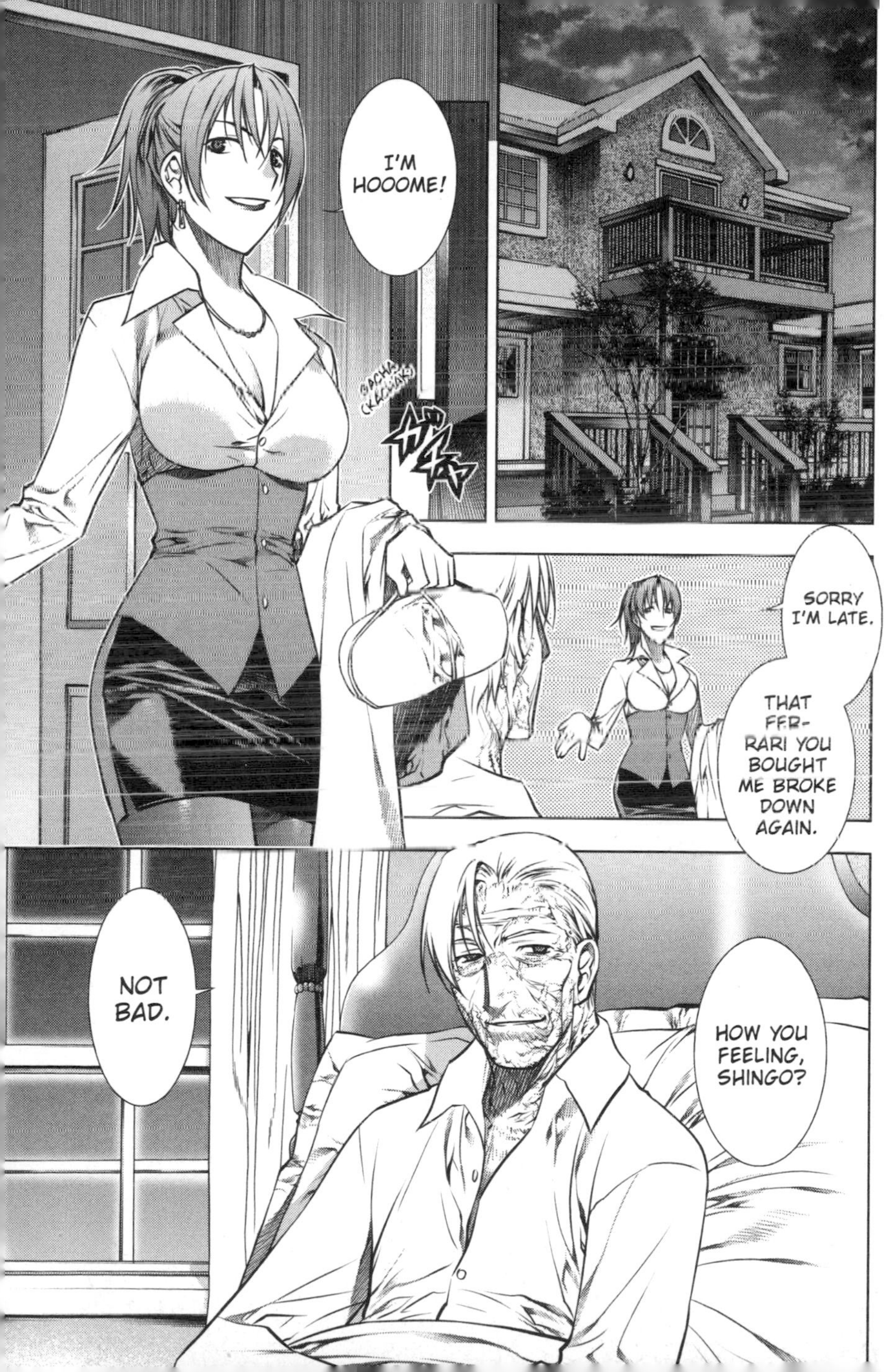
GACHA (KACHAK)
I'M HOOOME!
SORRY I'M LATE.
THAT FER-RARI YOU BOUGHT ME BROKE DOWN AGAIN.
HOW YOU FEELING, SHINGO?
NOT BAD.

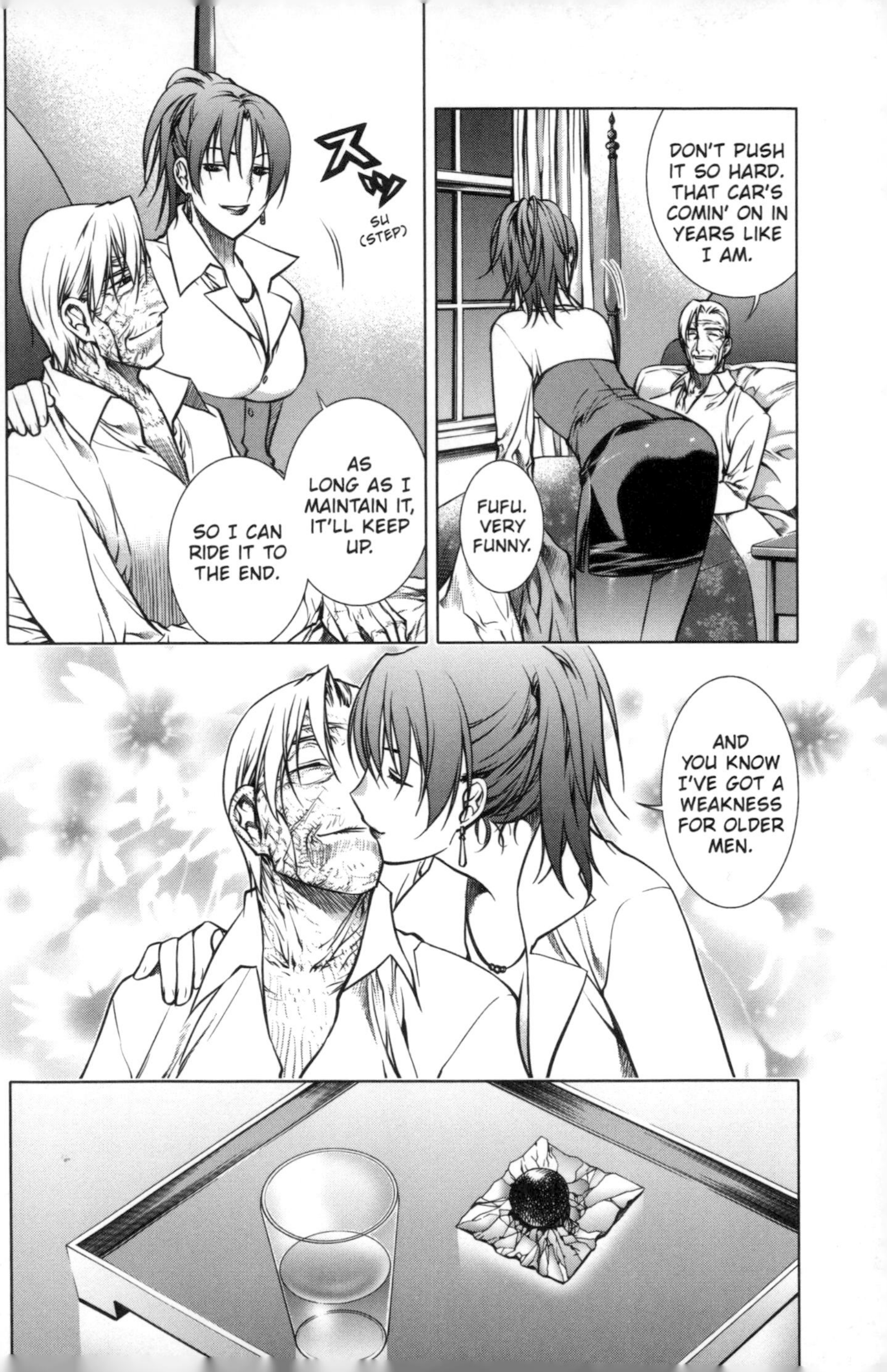
DON'T PUSH IT SO HARD. THAT CAR'S COMIN' ON IN YEARS LIKE I AM.
FUFU. VERY FUNNY.
スッ
SU (STEP)
AS LONG AS I MAINTAIN IT, IT'LL KEEP UP.
SO I CAN RIDE IT TO THE END.
AND YOU KNOW I'VE GOT A WEAKNESS FOR OLDER MEN.

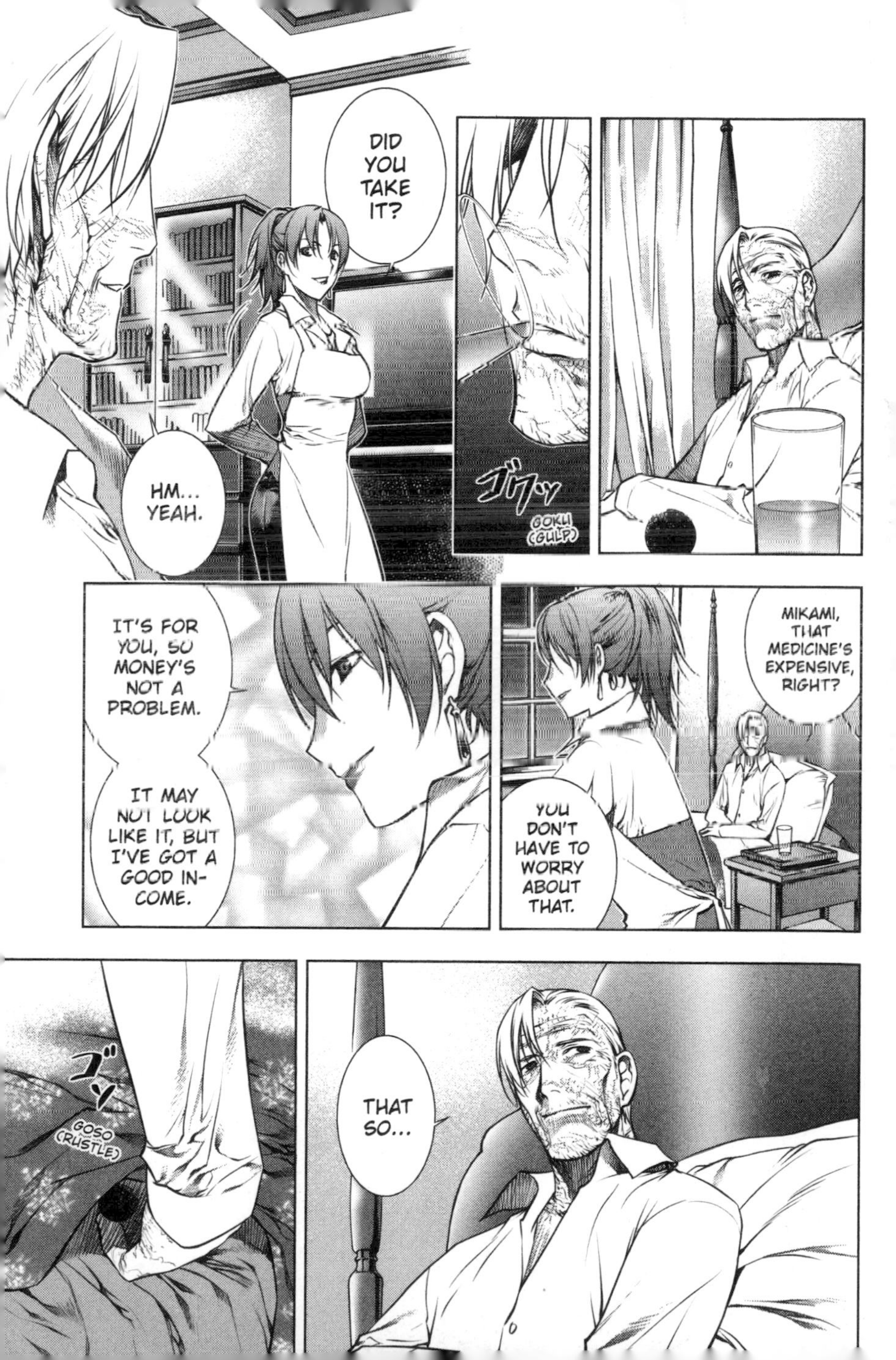
ゴクッ
GOKU (GULP)
DID YOU TAKE IT?
HM... YEAH.
MIKAMI, THAT MEDICINE'S EXPENSIVE, RIGHT?
YOU DON'T HAVE TO WORRY ABOUT THAT.
IT'S FOR YOU, SO MONEY'S NOT A PROBLEM.
IT MAY NOT LOOK LIKE IT, BUT I'VE GOT A GOOD IN-COME.
THAT SO...
ゴソ
GOSO (RUSTLE)

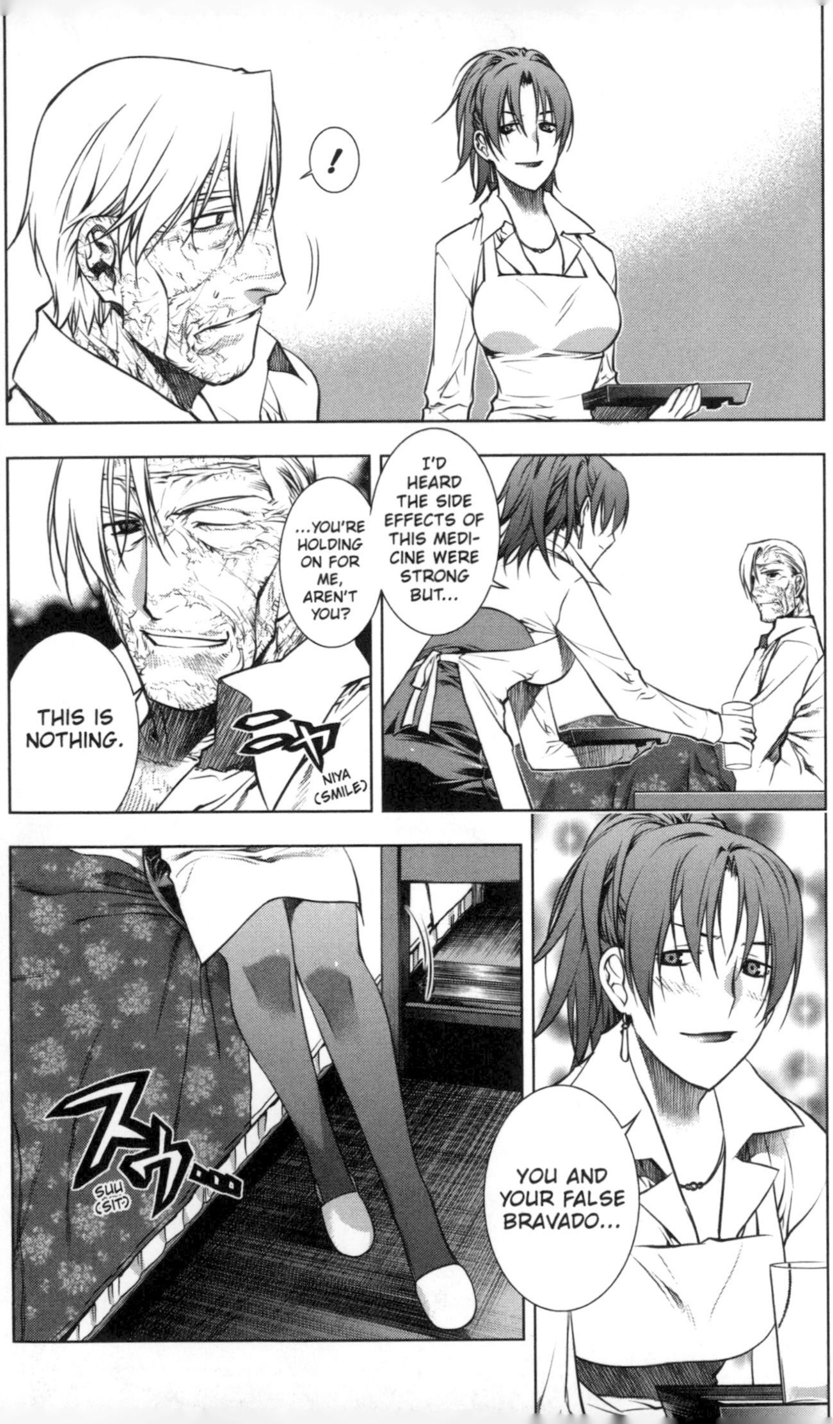
!
I'D HEARD THE SIDE EFFECTS OF THIS MEDICINE WERE STRONG BUT...
...YOU'RE HOLDING ON FOR ME, AREN'T YOU?
ニヤ
NIYA (SMILE)
THIS IS NOTHING.
YOU AND YOUR FALSE BRAVADO...
スウ…
SUU (SIT)

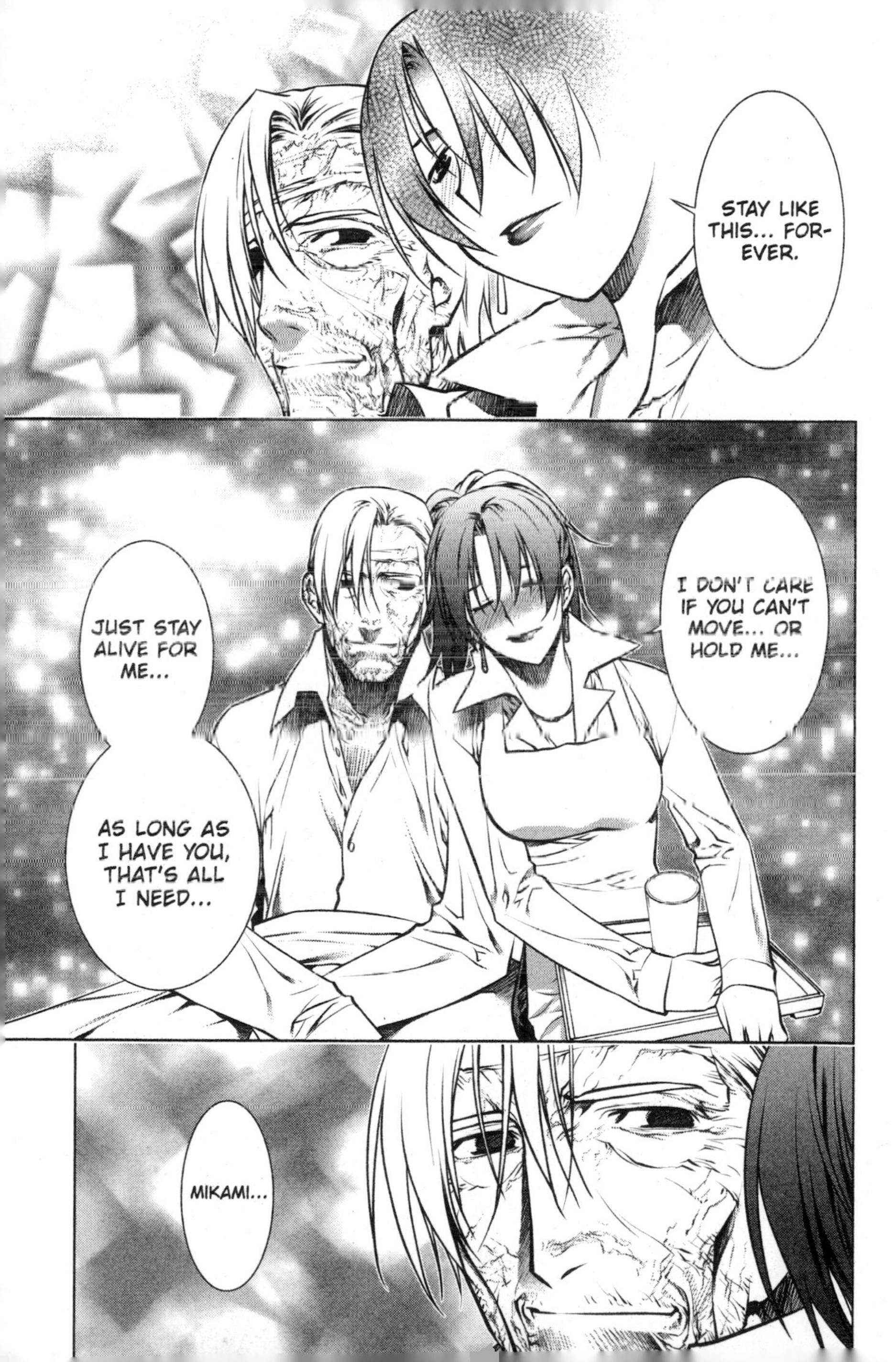
STAY LIKE THIS... FOR-EVER.
I DON'T CARE IF YOU CAN'T MOVE... OR HOLD ME...
JUST STAY ALIVE FOR ME...
AS LONG AS I HAVE YOU, THAT'S ALL I NEED...
MIKAMI...

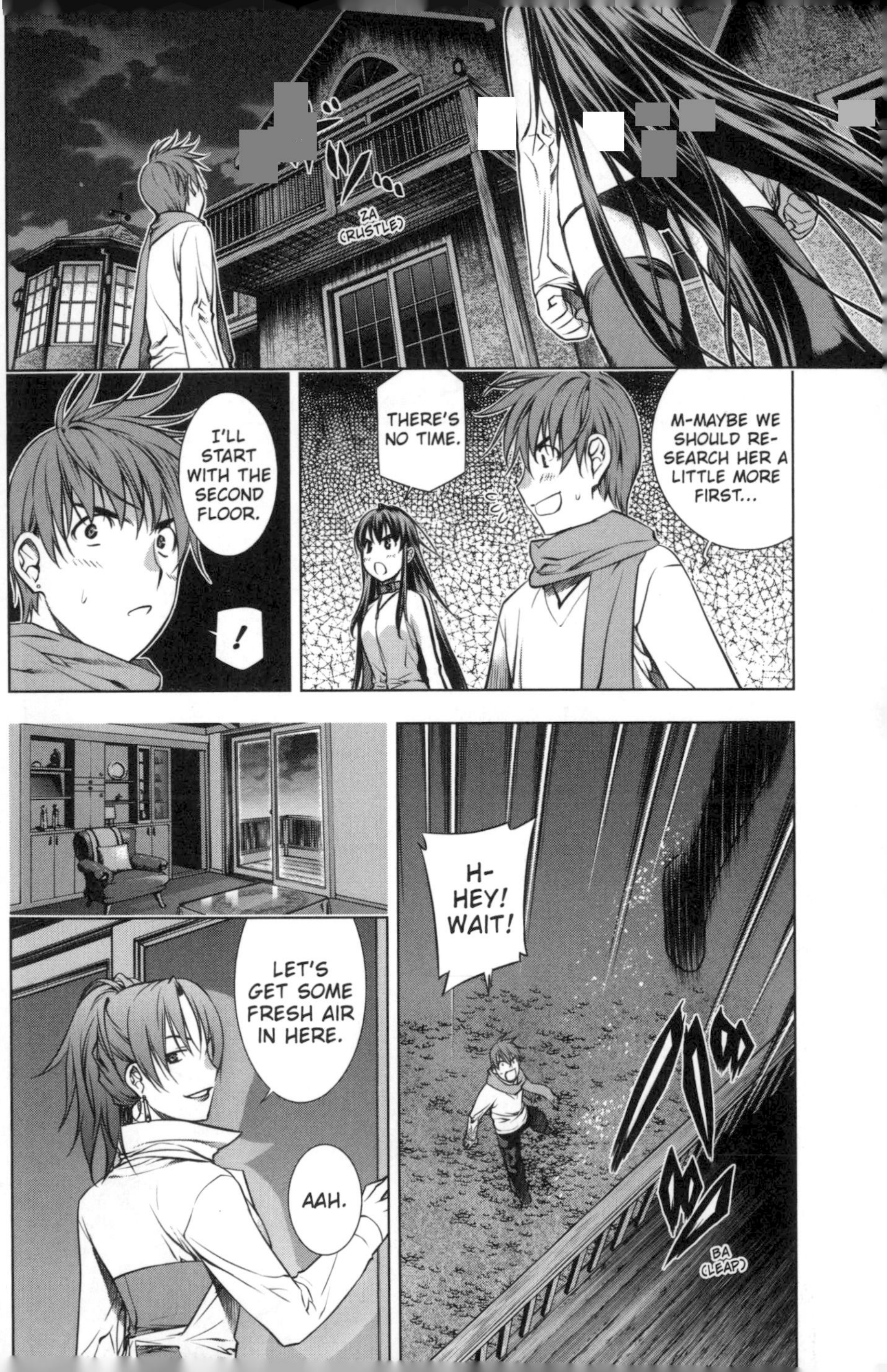
ZA (RUSTLE)
M-MAYBE WE SHOULD RE-SEARCH HER A LITTLE MORE FIRST...
THERE'S NO TIME.
!
I'LL START WITH THE SECOND FLOOR.
H- HEY! WAIT!
BA (LEAP)
LET'S GET SOME FRESH AIR IN HERE.
AAH.

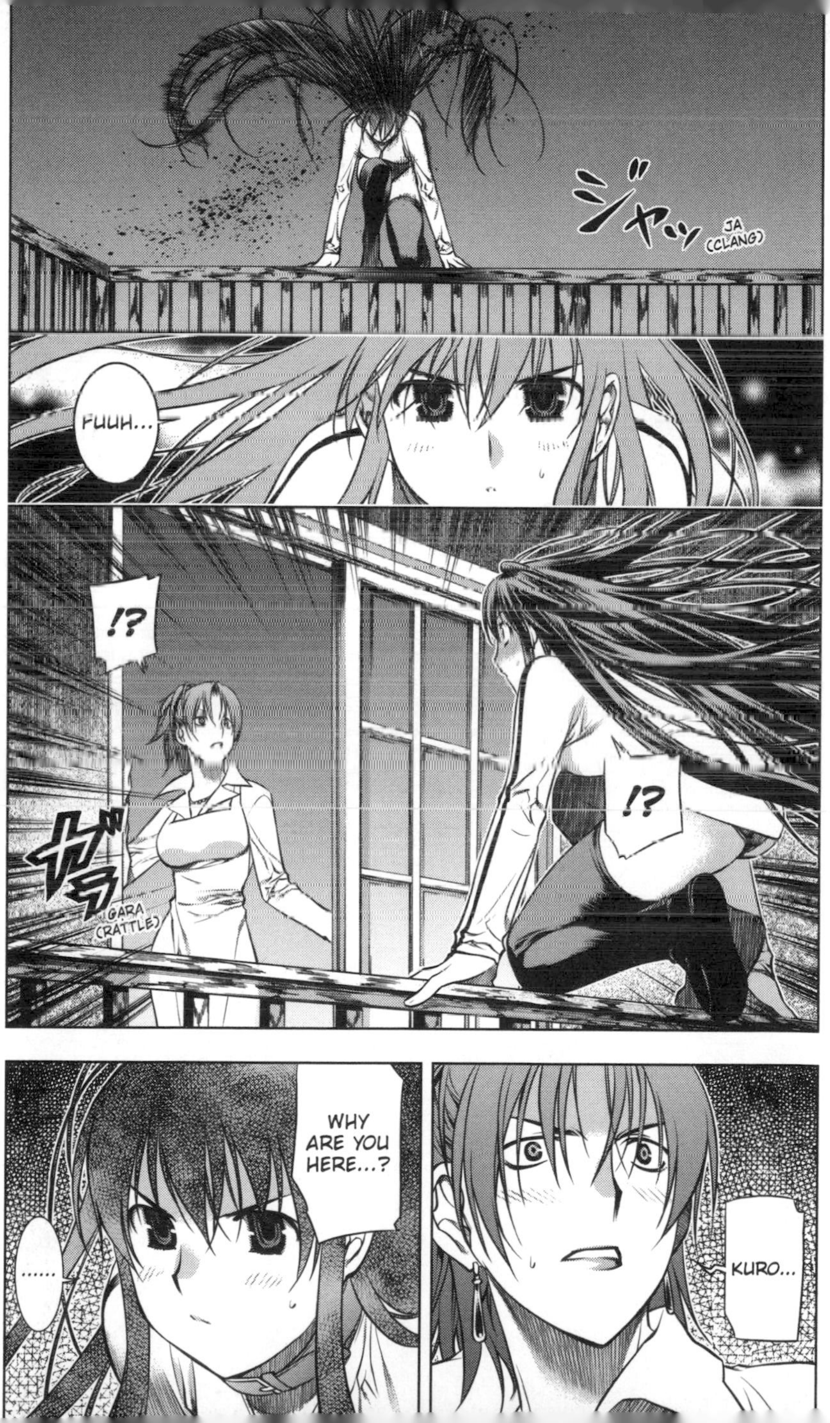
ジャッ
JA (CLANG)
FUUH...
!?
!?
ガラ
GARA (RATTLE)
KURO...
WHY ARE YOU HERE...?
......

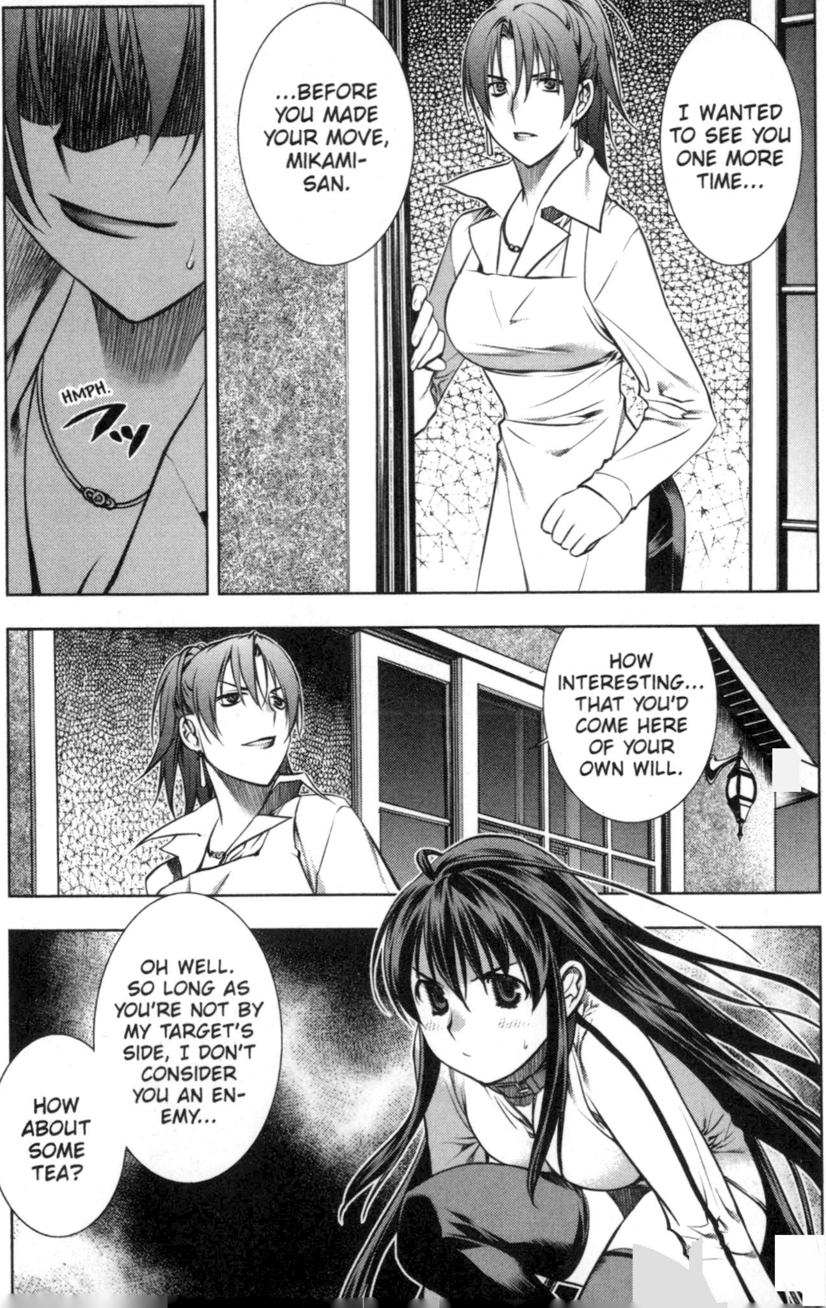
I WANTED TO SEE YOU ONE MORE TIME...
...BEFORE YOU MADE YOUR MOVE, MIKAMI-SAN.
HMPH.
HOW INTERESTING... THAT YOU'D COME HERE OF YOUR OWN WILL.
OH WELL. SO LONG AS YOU'RE NOT BY MY TARGET'S SIDE, I DON'T CONSIDER YOU AN EN-EMY...
HOW ABOUT SOME TEA?

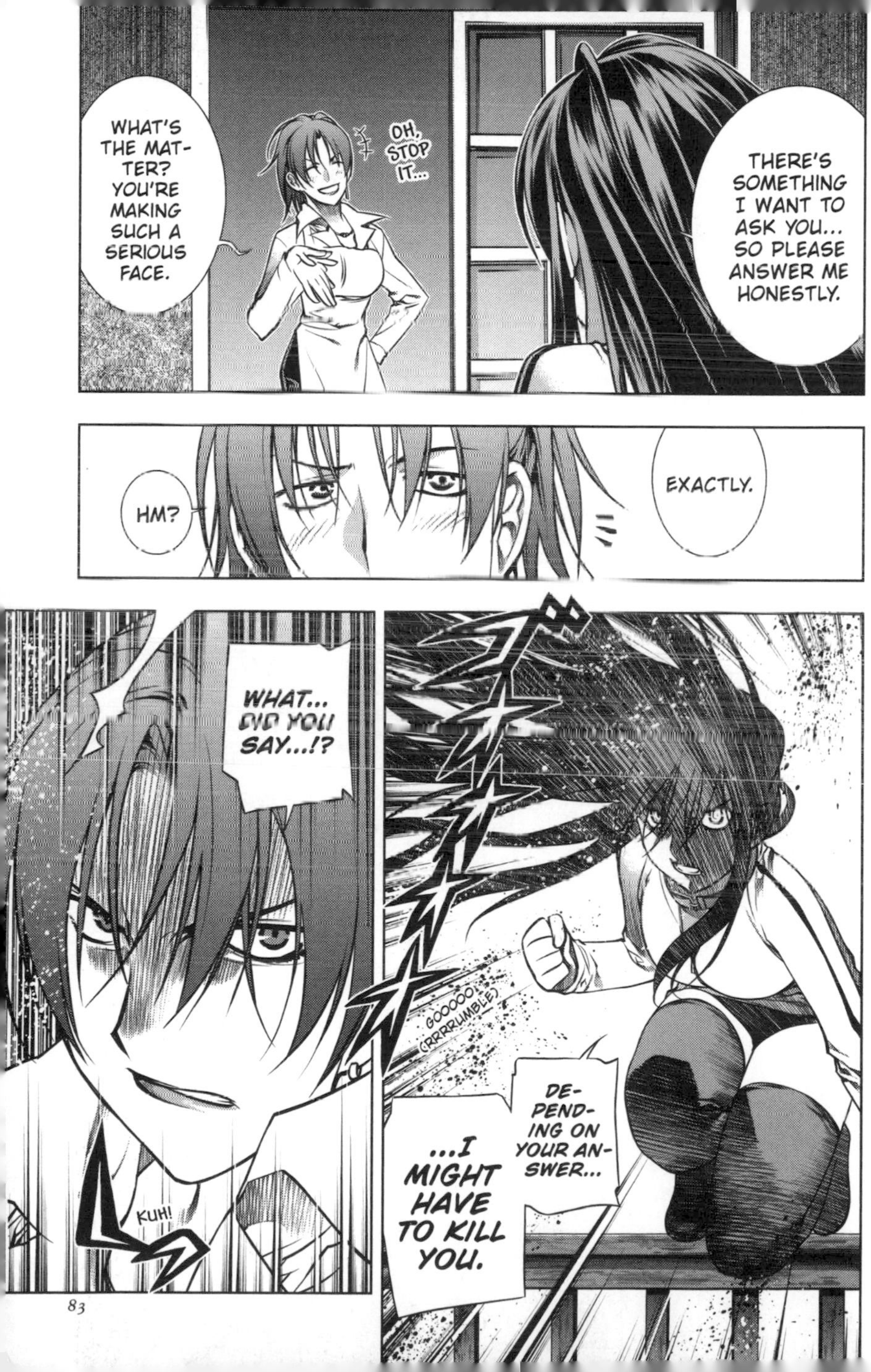
THERE'S SOMETHING I WANT TO ASK YOU... SO PLEASE ANSWER ME HONESTLY.
OH, STOP IT...
WHAT'S THE MAT-TER? YOU'RE MAKING SUCH A SERIOUS FACE.
EXACTLY.
HM?
GOOOOO (RRRRUMBLE)
DE-PEND-ING ON YOUR AN-SWER...
...I MIGHT HAVE TO KILL YOU.
WHAT... DID YOU SAY...!?
KUH!

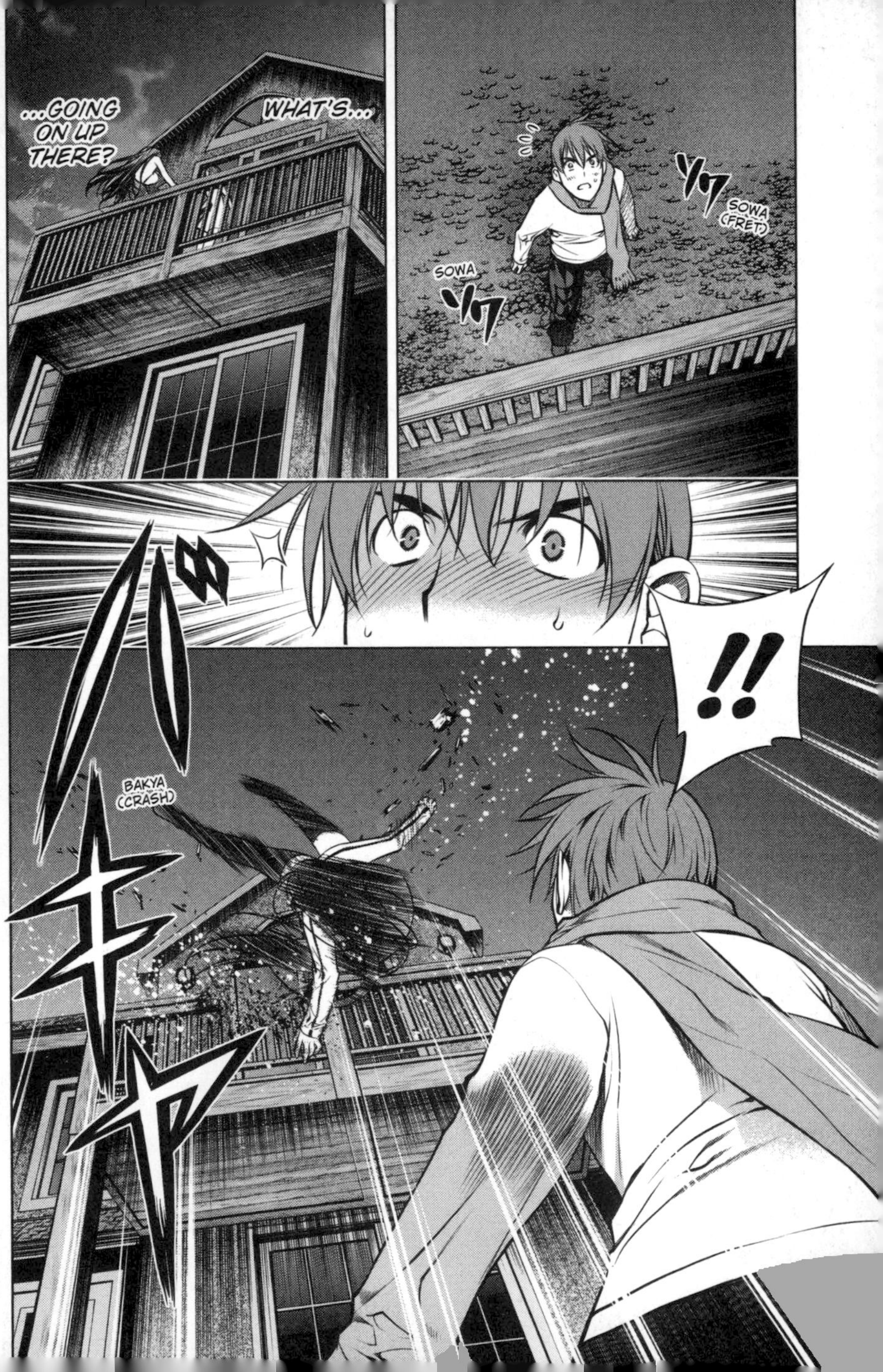
ソワ
SOWA (FRET)
SOWA
ソワ
WHAT'S...
...GOING ON UP THERE?
!!
BAKYA (CRASH)

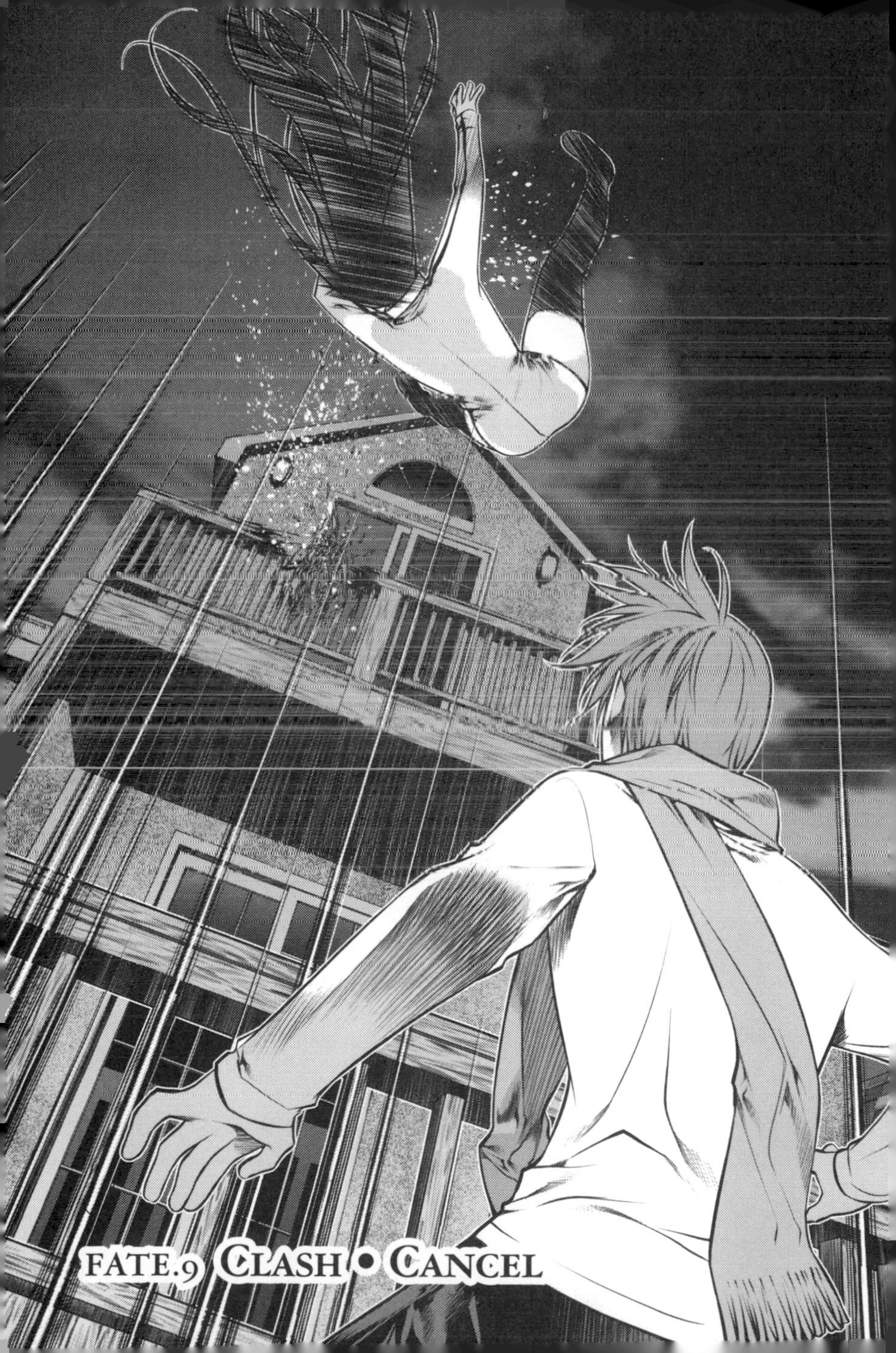
FATE.9 CLASH • CANCEL

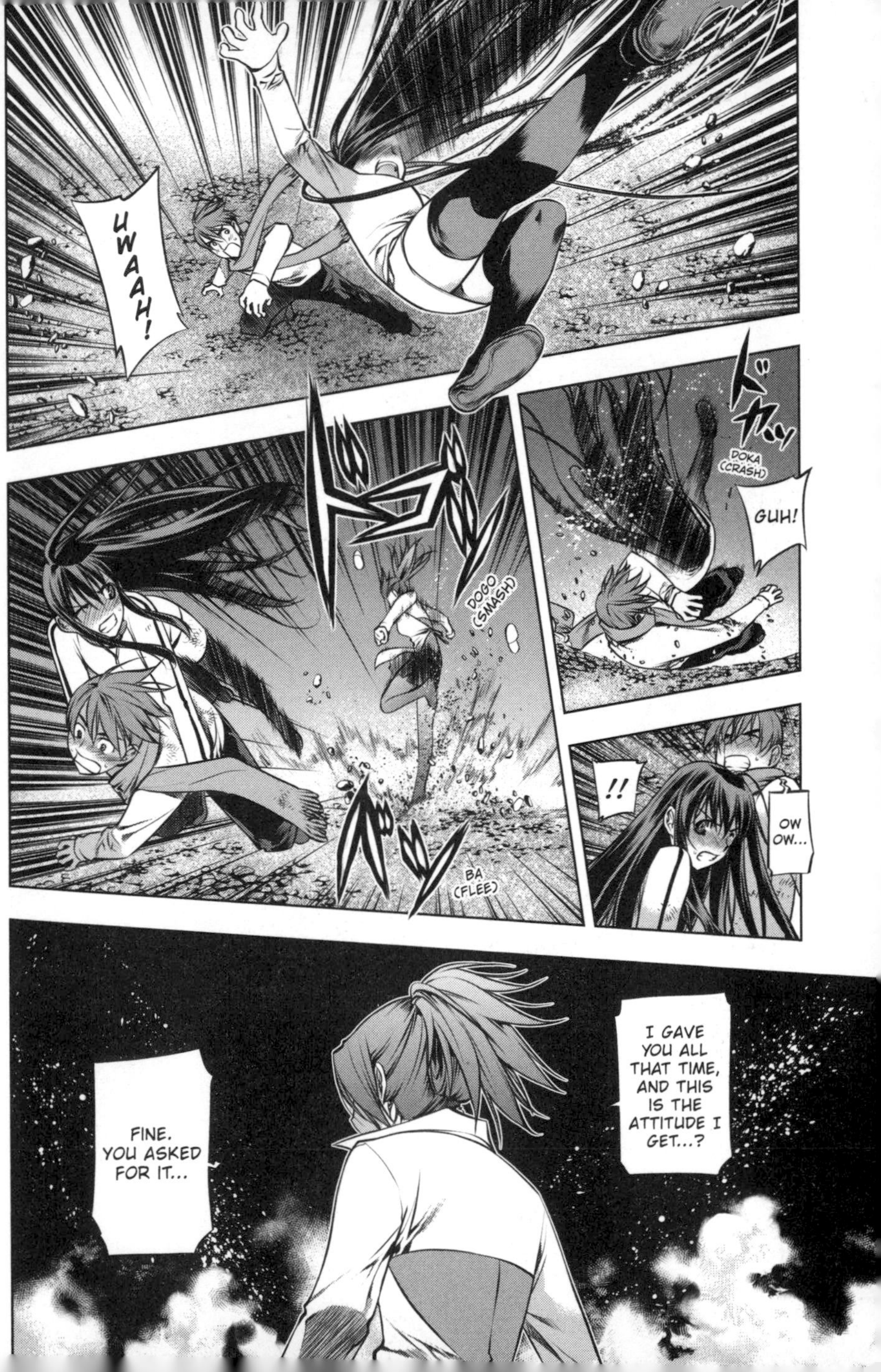
UWAAH!
DOKA (CRASH)
GUH!
OW OW...
!!
DOGO (SMASH)
BA (FLEE)
I GAVE YOU ALL THAT TIME, AND THIS IS THE ATTITUDE I GET...?
FINE. YOU ASKED FOR IT...

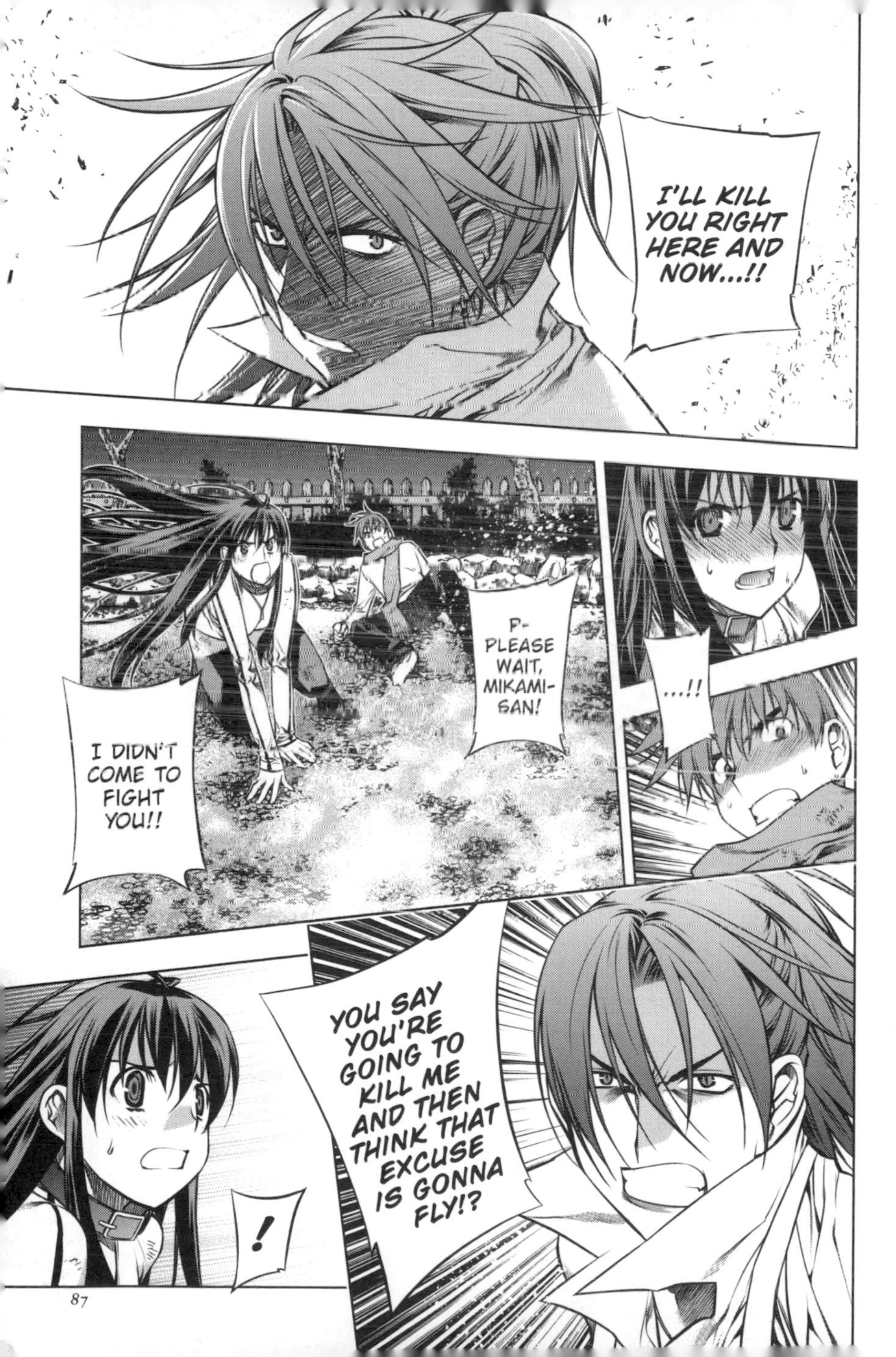
I'LL KILL YOU RIGHT HERE AND NOW...!!
...!!
P-PLEASE WAIT, MIKAMI-SAN!
I DIDN'T COME TO FIGHT YOU!!
YOU SAY YOU'RE GOING TO KILL ME AND THEN THINK THAT EXCUSE IS GONNA FLY!?
!

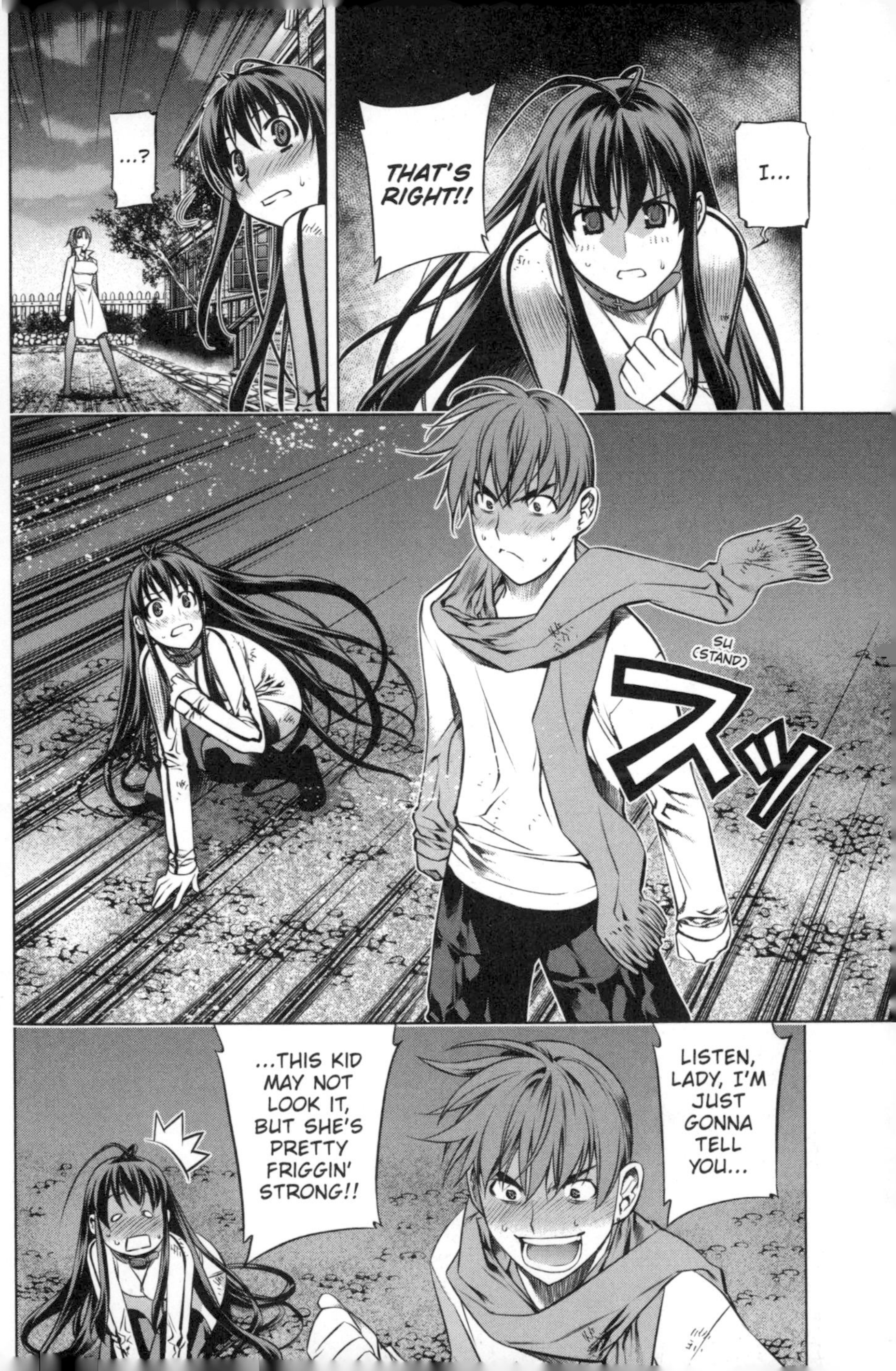
I...
THAT'S RIGHT!!
...?
SU (STAND)
スッ
LISTEN, LADY, I'M JUST GONNA TELL YOU...
...THIS KID MAY NOT LOOK IT, BUT SHE'S PRETTY FRIGGIN' STRONG!!

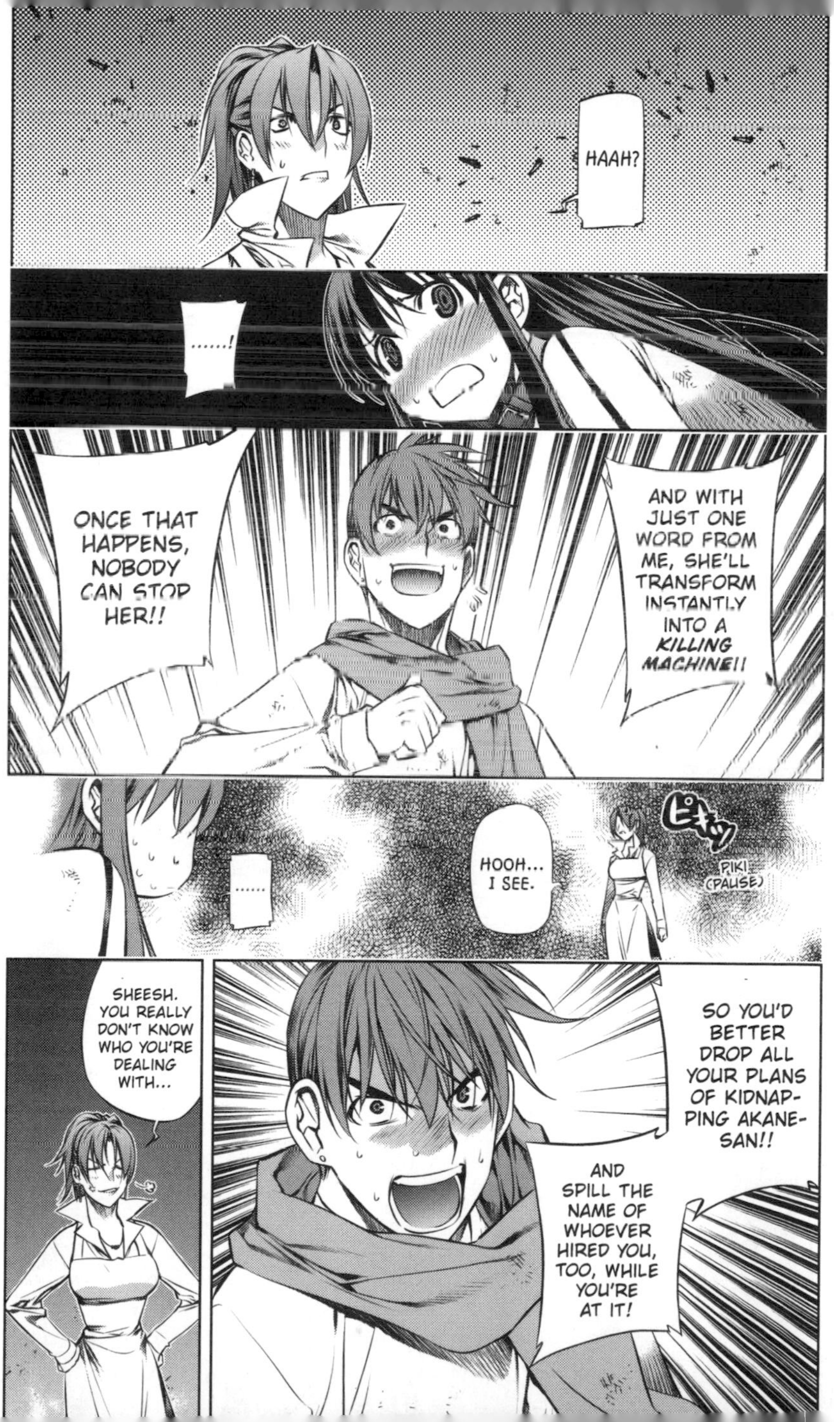
HAAH?
......!
AND WITH JUST ONE WORD FROM ME, SHE'LL TRANSFORM INSTANTLY INTO A KILLING MACHINE!!
ONCE THAT HAPPENS, NOBODY CAN STOP HER!!
PIKI (PAUSE)
HOOH... I SEE.
......
SO YOU'D BETTER DROP ALL YOUR PLANS OF KIDNAP-PING AKANE-SAN!!
AND SPILL THE NAME OF WHOEVER HIRED YOU, TOO, WHILE YOU'RE AT IT!
SHEESH. YOU REALLY DON'T KNOW WHO YOU'RE DEALING WITH...

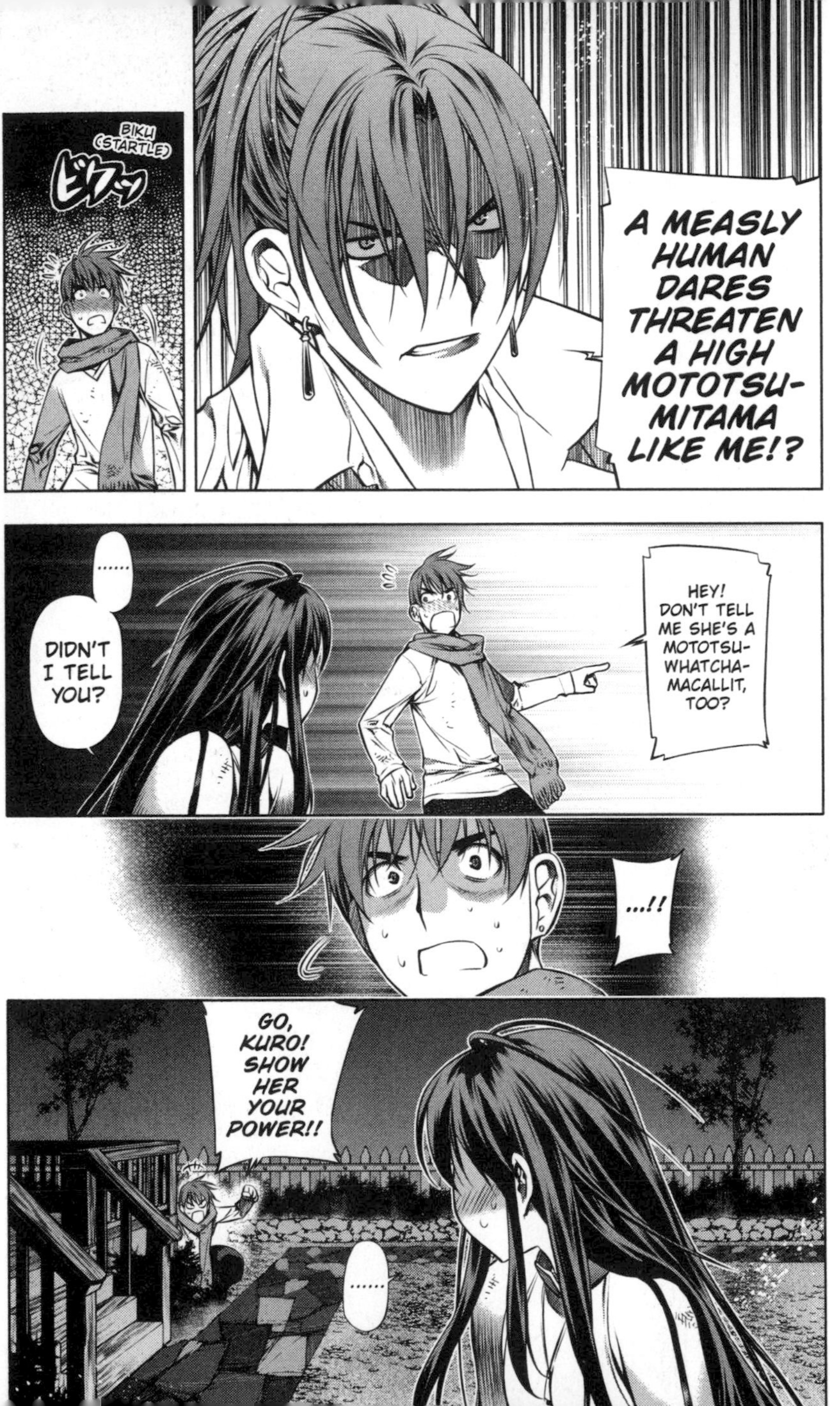
A MEASLY HUMAN DARES THREATEN A HIGH MOTOTSU-MITAMA LIKE ME!?
BIKU (STARTLE)
ビクッ
HEY! DON'T TELL ME SHE'S A MOTOTSU-WHATCHA-MACALLIT, TOO?
......
DIDN'T I TELL YOU?
...!!
GO, KURO! SHOW HER YOUR POWER!!
......

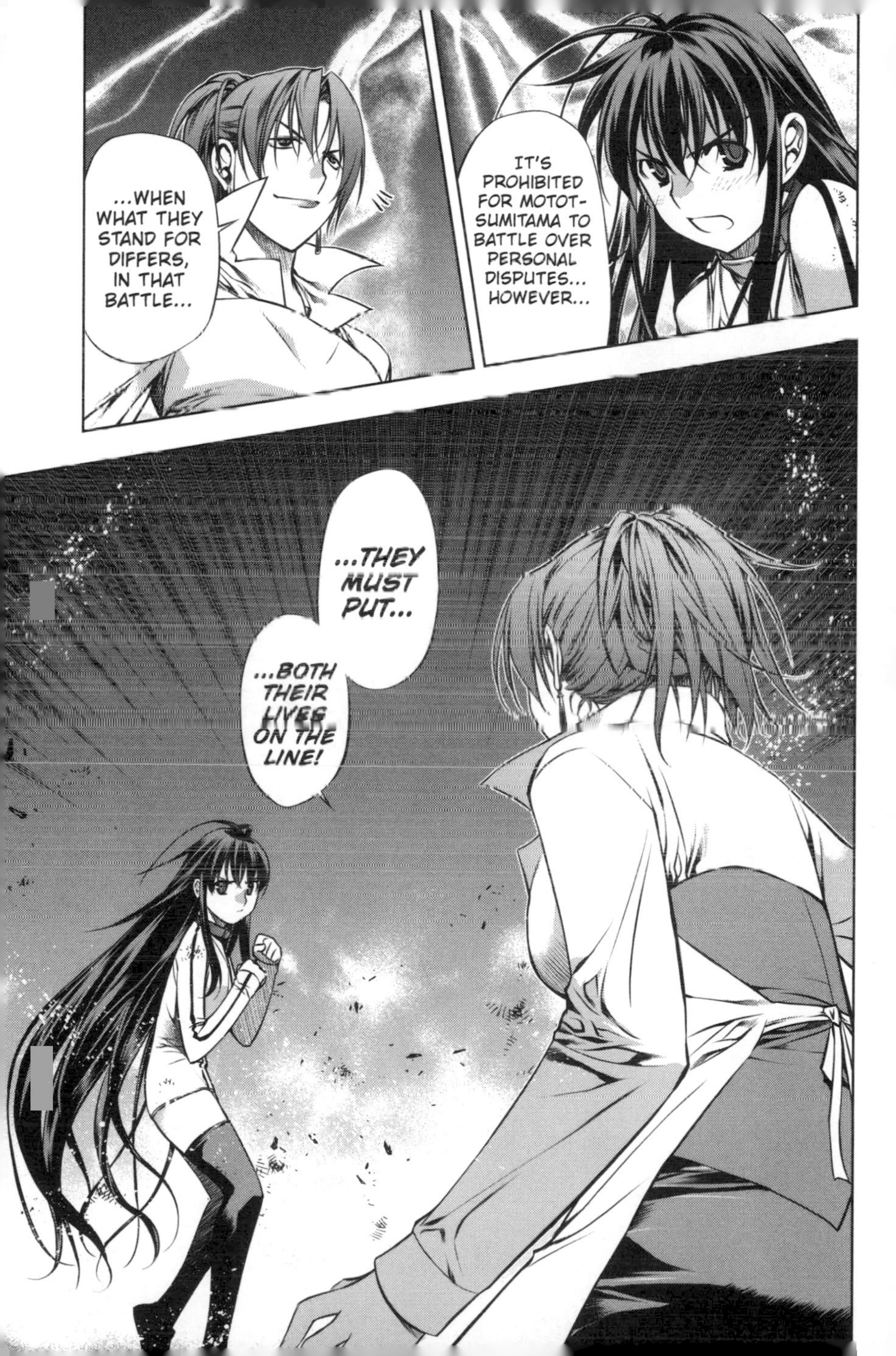
IT'S PROHIBITED FOR MOTOT-SUMITAMA TO BATTLE OVER PERSONAL DISPUTES... HOWEVER...
...WHEN WHAT THEY STAND FOR DIFFERS, IN THAT BATTLE...
...THEY MUST PUT...
...BOTH THEIR LIVES ON THE LINE!

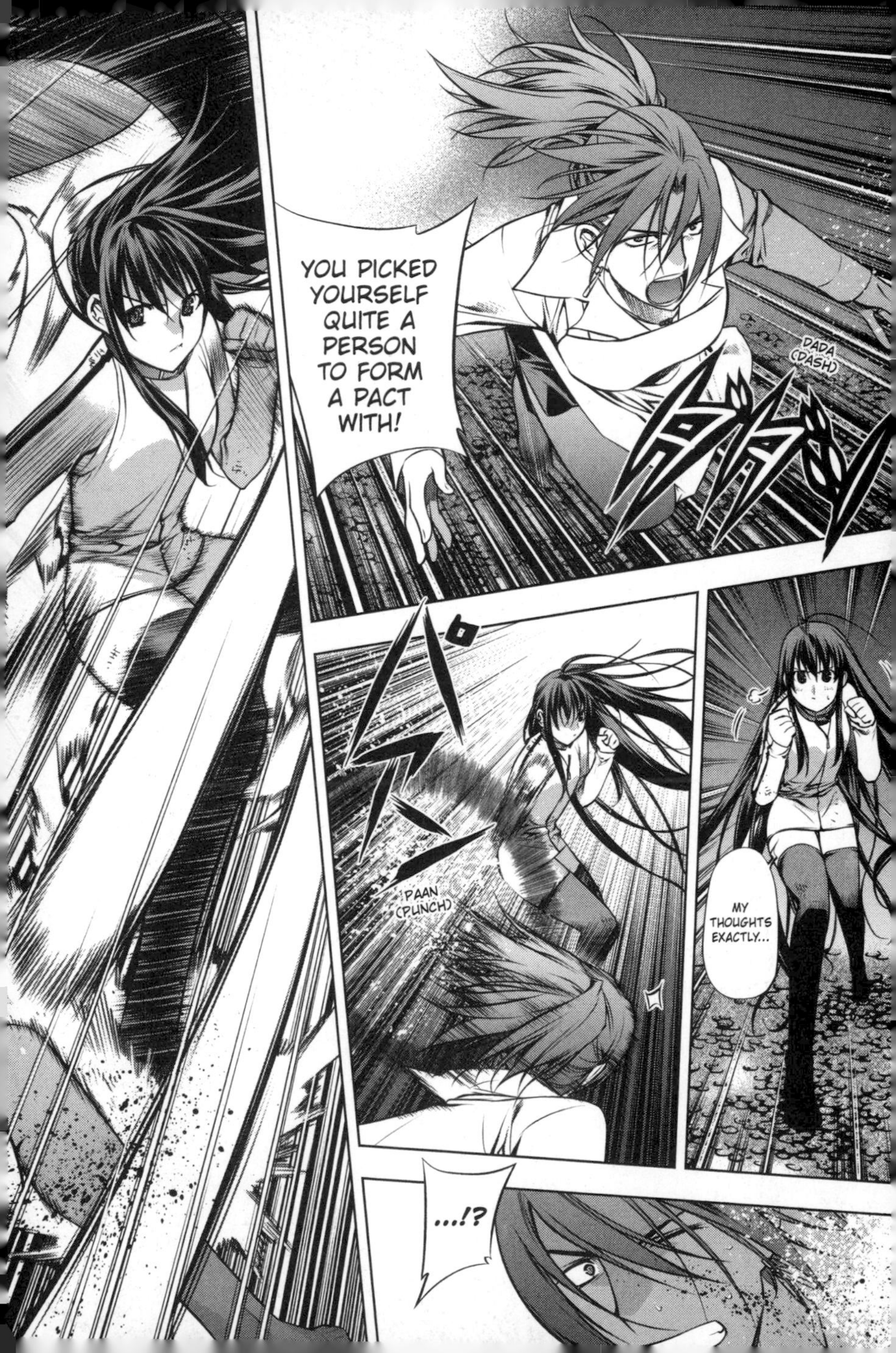
YOU PICKED YOURSELF QUITE A PERSON TO FORM A PACT WITH!
DADA (DASH)
MY THOUGHTS EXACTLY...
PAAN (PUNCH)
...!?

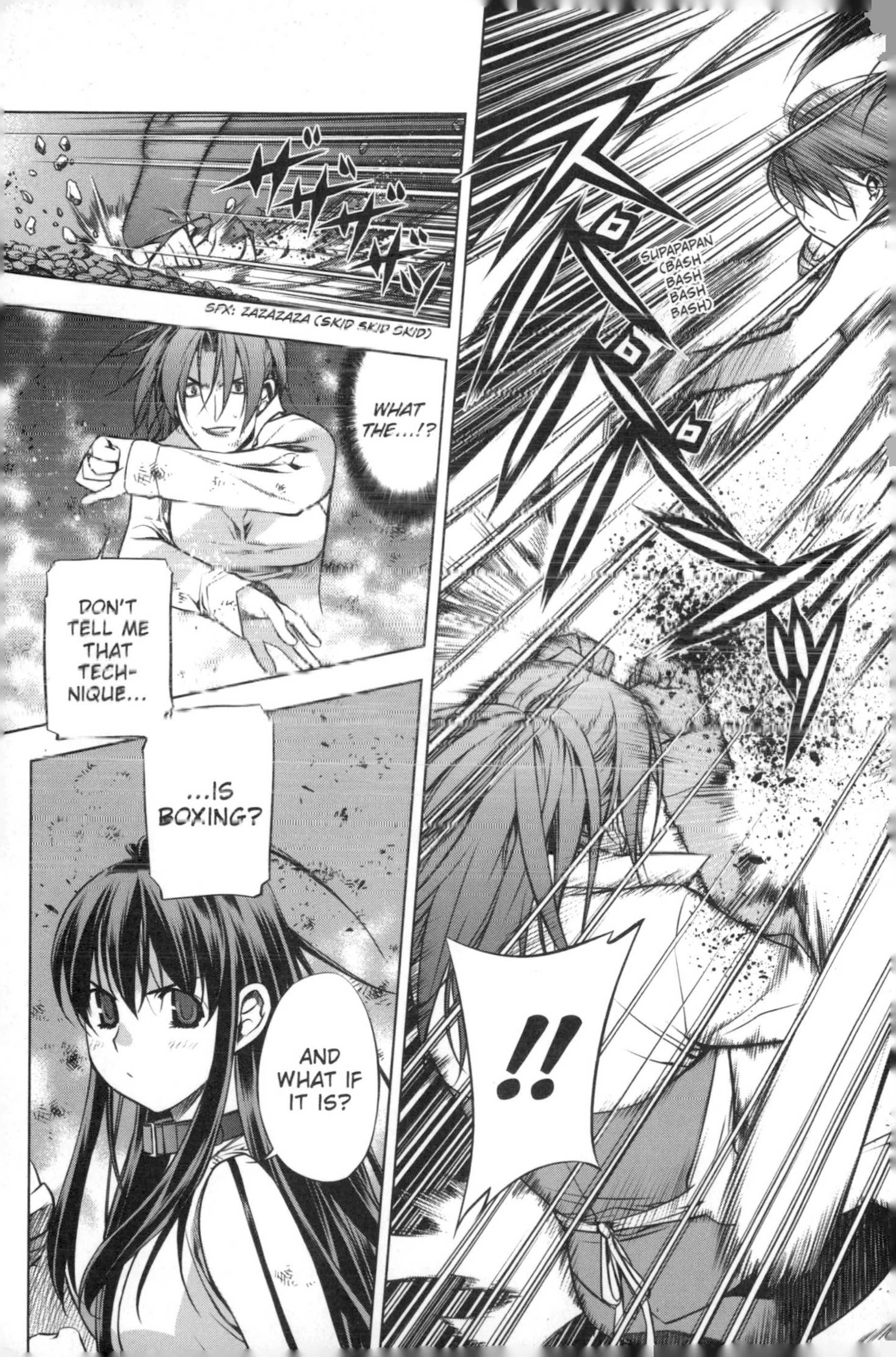
SUPAPAPAN (BASH BASH BASH BASH)
!!
SFX: ZAZAZAZA (SKID SKID SKID)
WHAT THE...!?
DON'T TELL ME THAT TECH-NIQUE...
...IS BOXING?
AND WHAT IF IT IS?

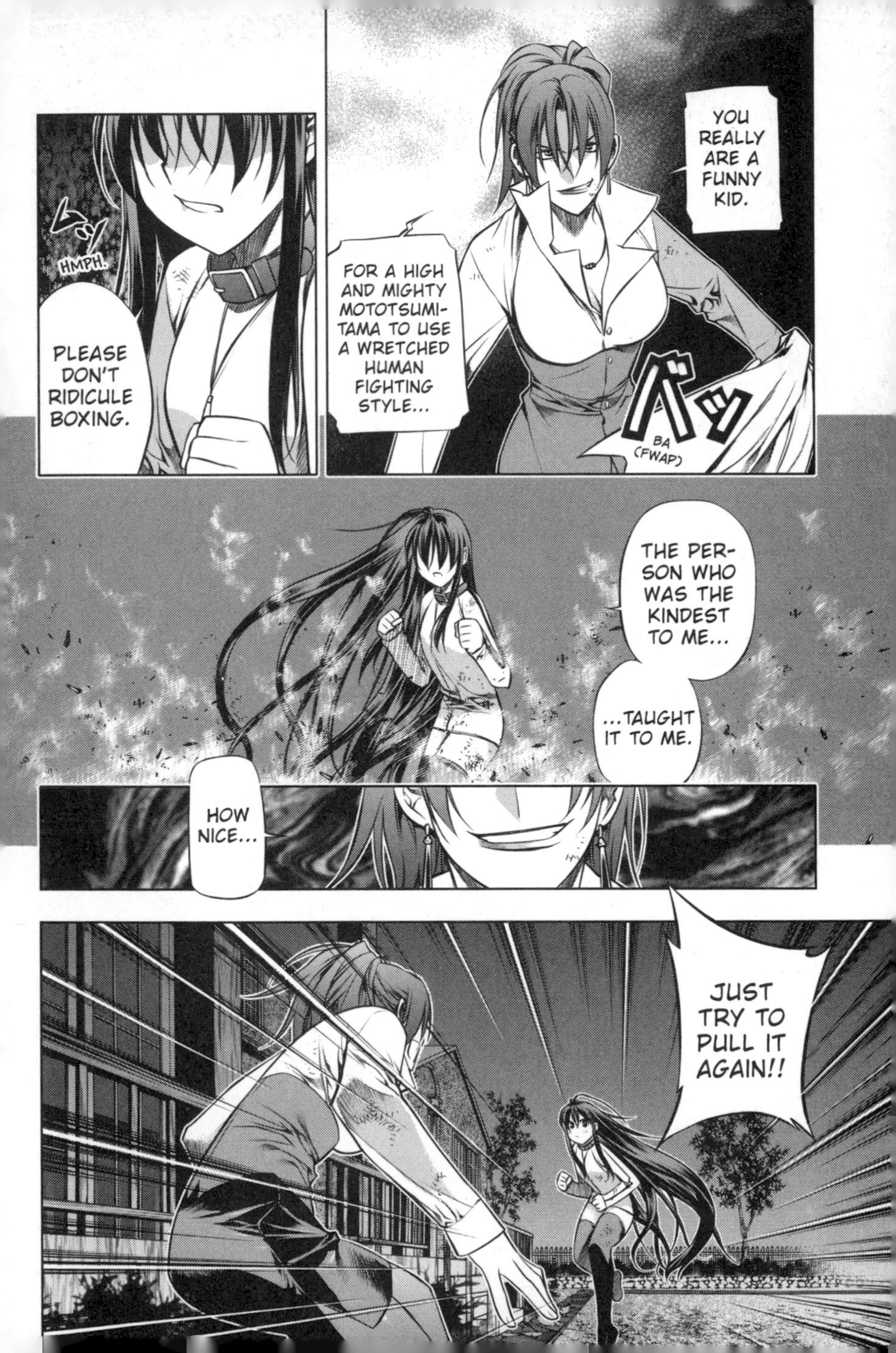
YOU REALLY ARE A FUNNY KID.
FOR A HIGH AND MIGHTY MOTOTSUMI-TAMA TO USE A WRETCHED HUMAN FIGHTING STYLE...
BA (FWAP)
HMPH.
PLEASE DON'T RIDICULE BOXING.
THE PER-SON WHO WAS THE KINDEST TO ME...
...TAUGHT IT TO ME.
HOW NICE...
JUST TRY TO PULL IT AGAIN!!

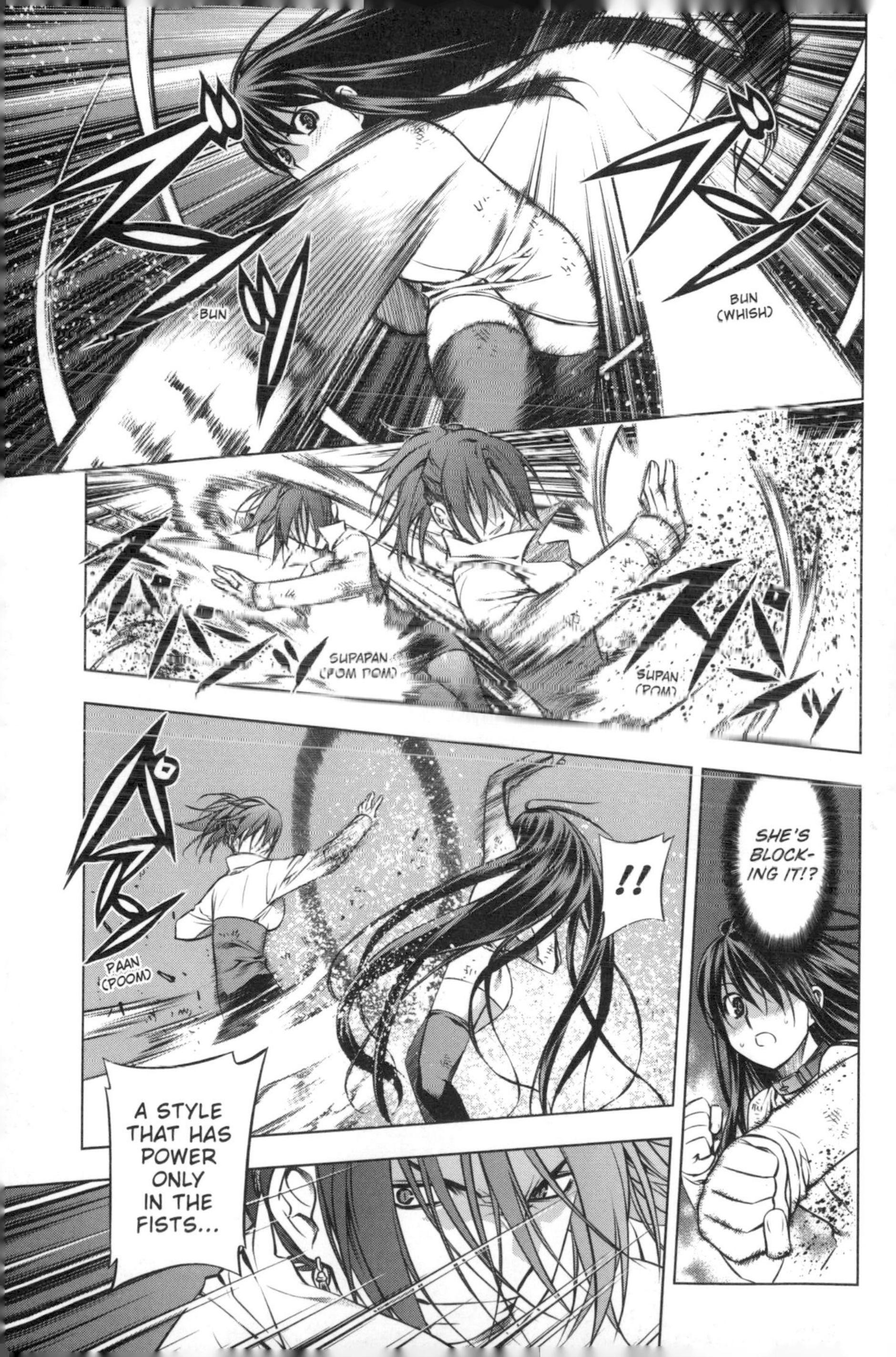
BUN (WHISH)
BUN
SUPAN (POM)
SUPAPAN (POM POM)
SHE'S BLOCKING IT!?
!!
PAAN (POOM)
A STYLE THAT HAS POWER ONLY IN THE FISTS...

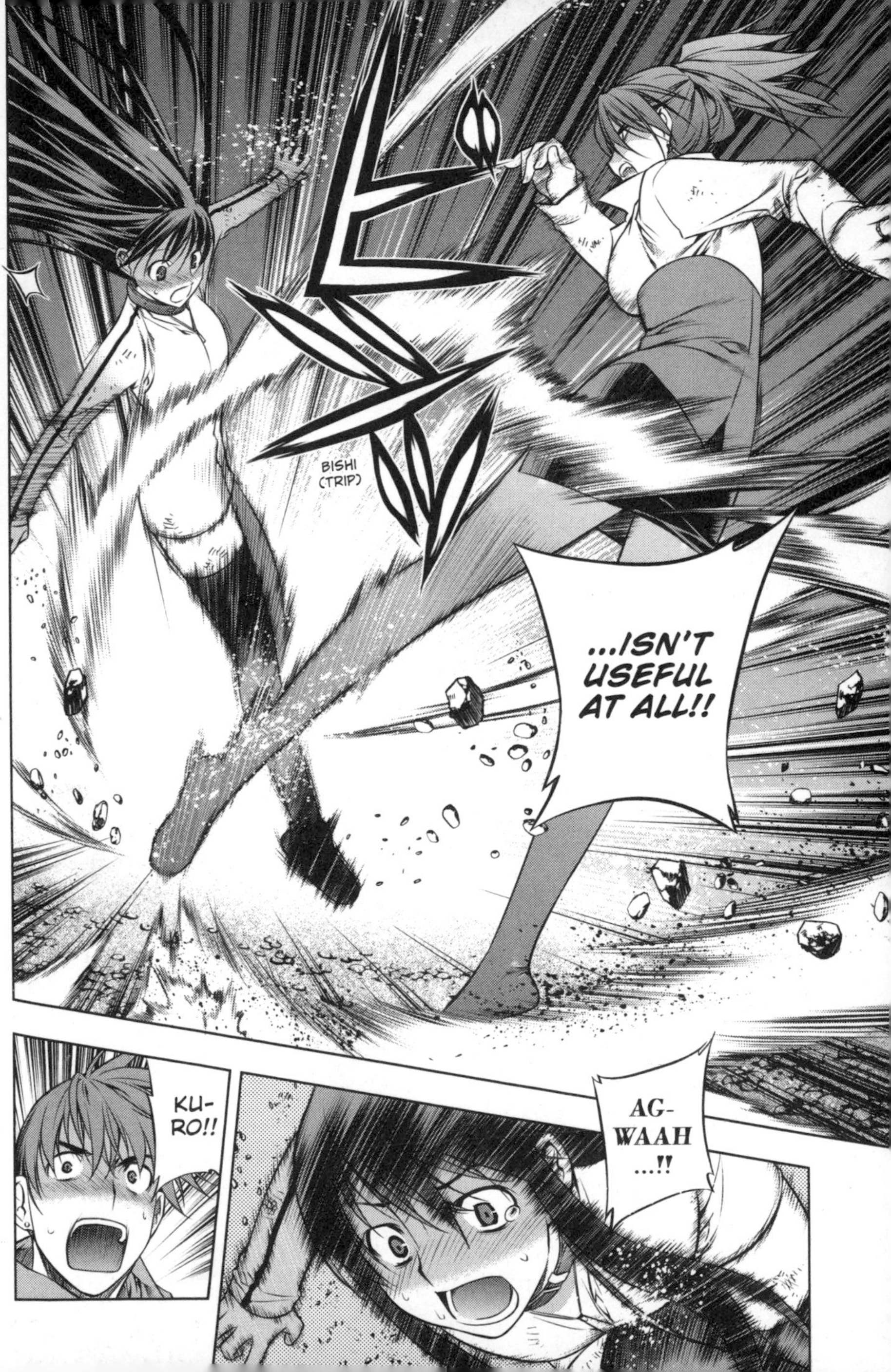
BISHI
(TRIP)
...ISN'T USEFUL AT ALL!!
AG-WAAH ...!!
KU-RO!!

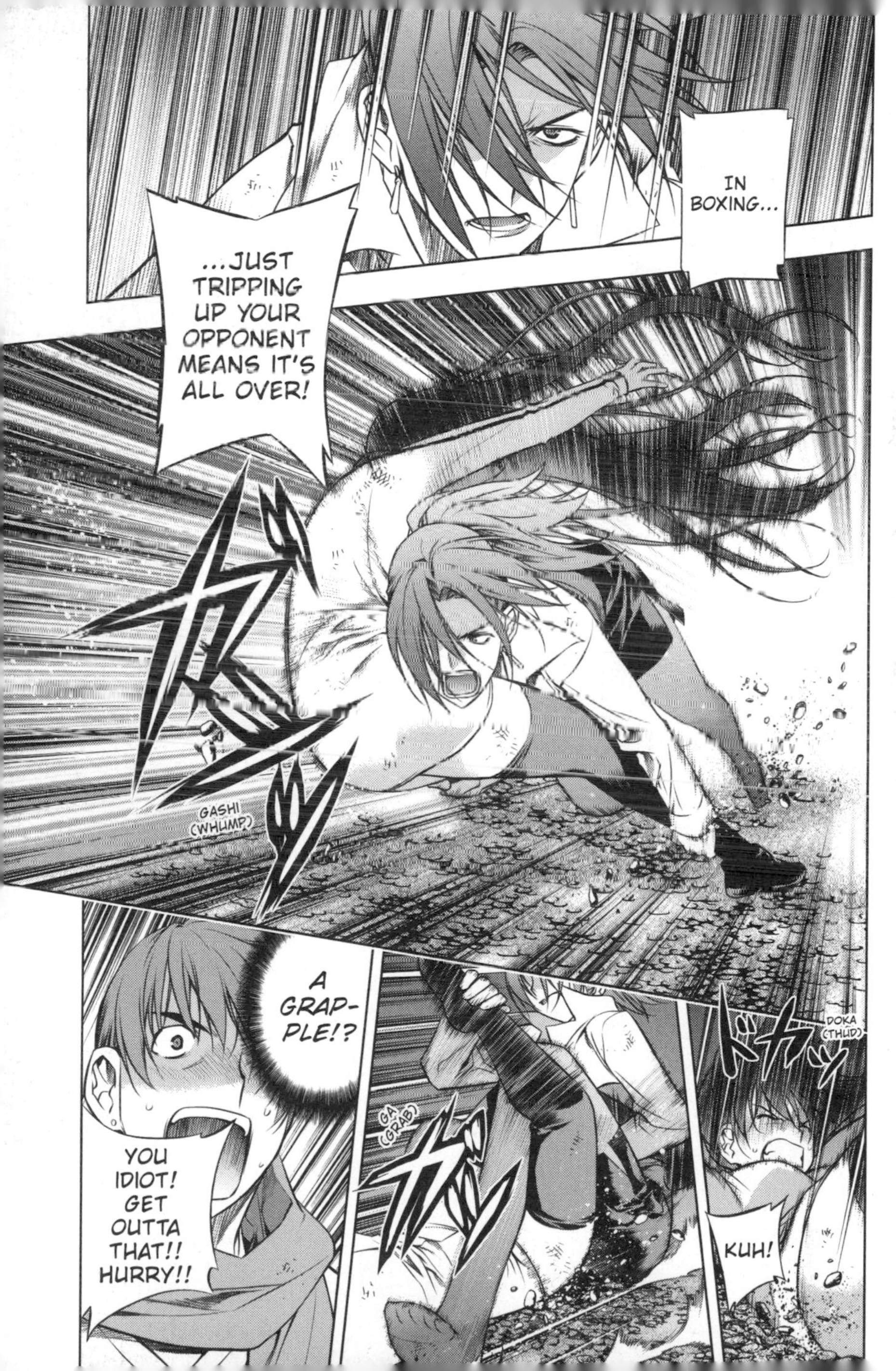
IN BOXING...
...JUST TRIPPING UP YOUR OPPONENT MEANS IT'S ALL OVER!
GASHI (WHUMP)
DOKA (THUD)
KUH!
GA (GRAB)
A GRAP-PLE!?
YOU IDIOT! GET OUTTA THAT!! HURRY!!

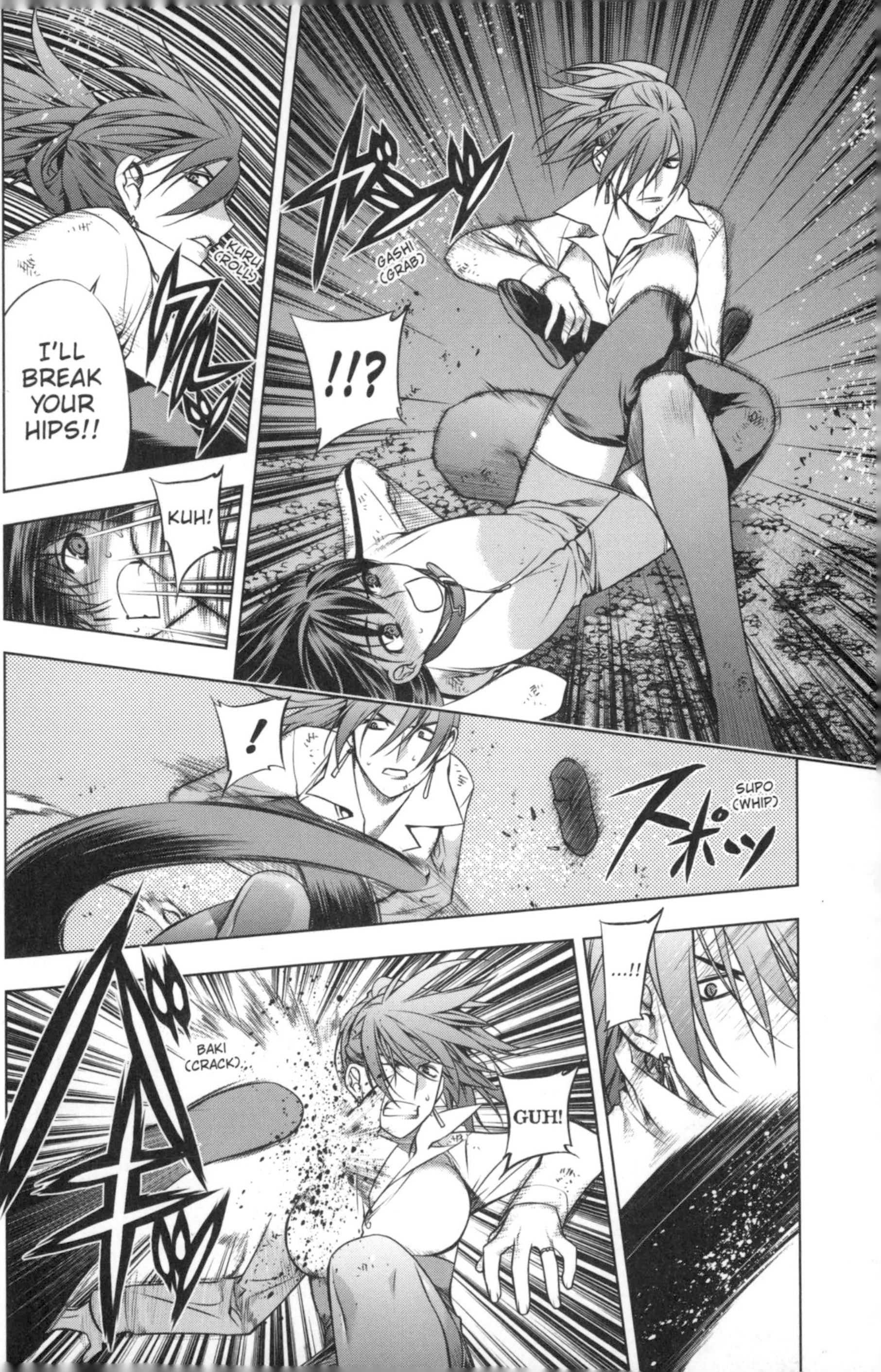
GASHI (GRAB)
!!?
KURU (ROLL)
I'LL BREAK YOUR HIPS!!
KUH!
SUPO (WHIP)
!
...!!
GUH!
BAKI (CRACK)

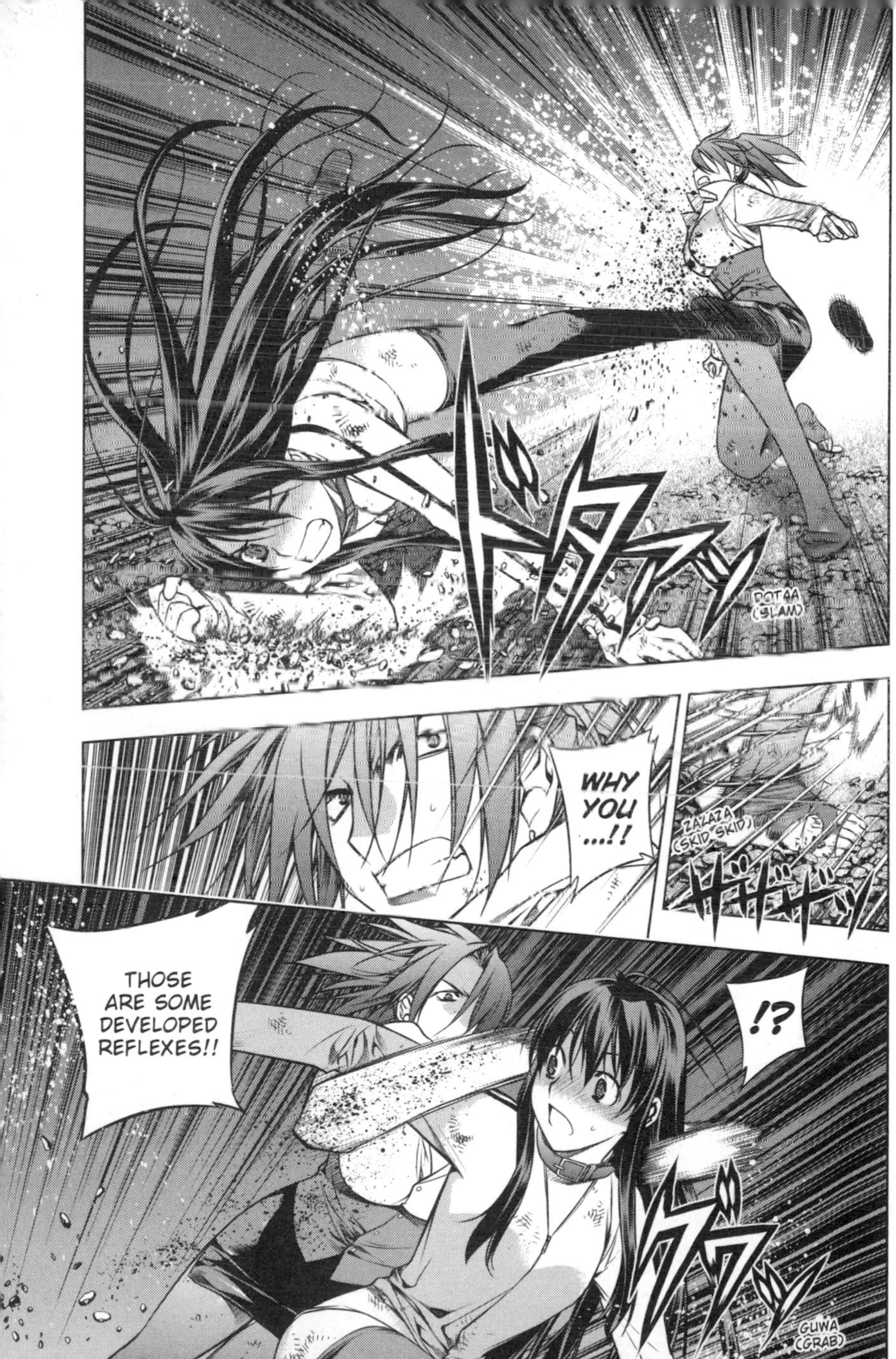
DOTAA (SLAM)
ZAZAZA (SKID SKID)
WHY YOU ...!!
!?
THOSE ARE SOME DEVELOPED REFLEXES!!
GUWA (GRAB)

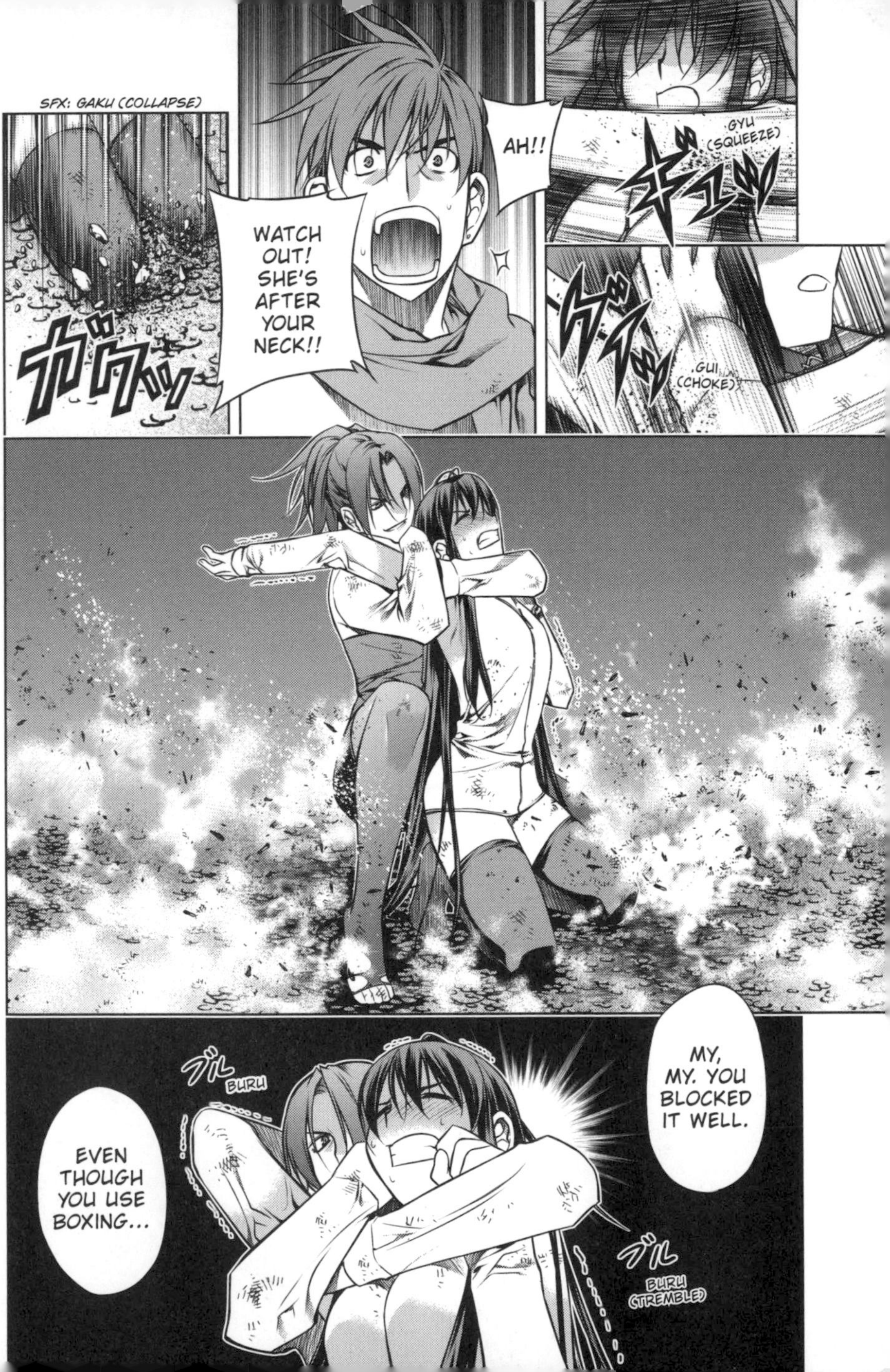
GYU (SQUEEZE)
GUI (CHOKE)
AH!!
WATCH OUT! SHE'S AFTER YOUR NECK!!
SFX: GAKU (COLLAPSE)
MY, MY. YOU BLOCKED IT WELL.
ブル BURU
EVEN THOUGH YOU USE BOXING...
ブル BURU (TREMBLE)

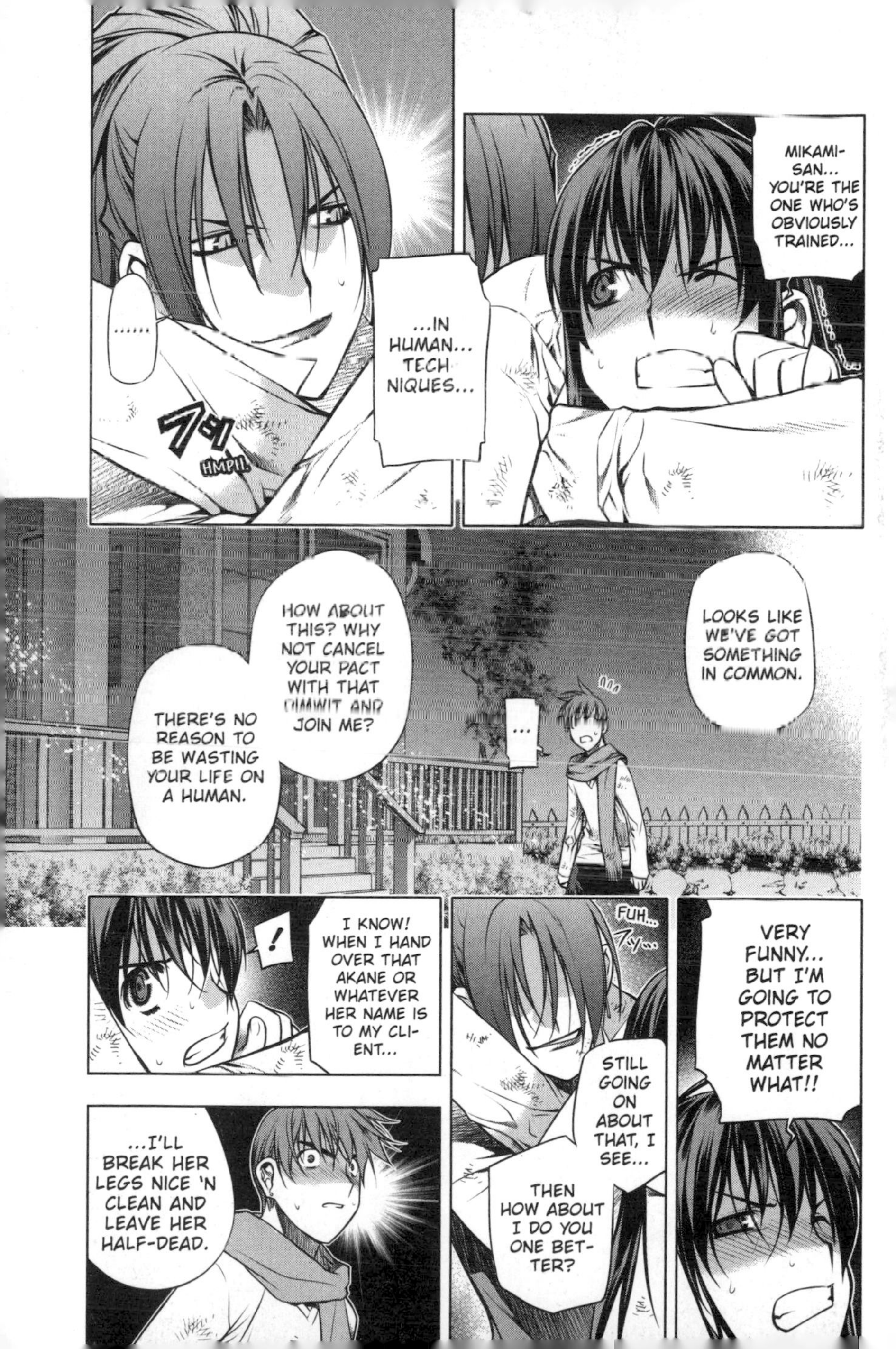
MIKAMI-SAN... YOU'RE THE ONE WHO'S OBVIOUSLY TRAINED...
...IN HUMAN... TECHNIQUES...
......
HMPH!
LOOKS LIKE WE'VE GOT SOMETHING IN COMMON.
...
HOW ABOUT THIS? WHY NOT CANCEL YOUR PACT WITH THAT DIMWIT AND JOIN ME?
THERE'S NO REASON TO BE WASTING YOUR LIFE ON A HUMAN.
VERY FUNNY... BUT I'M GOING TO PROTECT THEM NO MATTER WHAT!!
FUH...
STILL GOING ON ABOUT THAT, I SEE...
THEN HOW ABOUT I DO YOU ONE BETTER?
!
I KNOW! WHEN I HAND OVER THAT AKANE OR WHATEVER HER NAME IS TO MY CLIENT...
...I'LL BREAK HER LEGS NICE 'N CLEAN AND LEAVE HER HALF-DEAD.

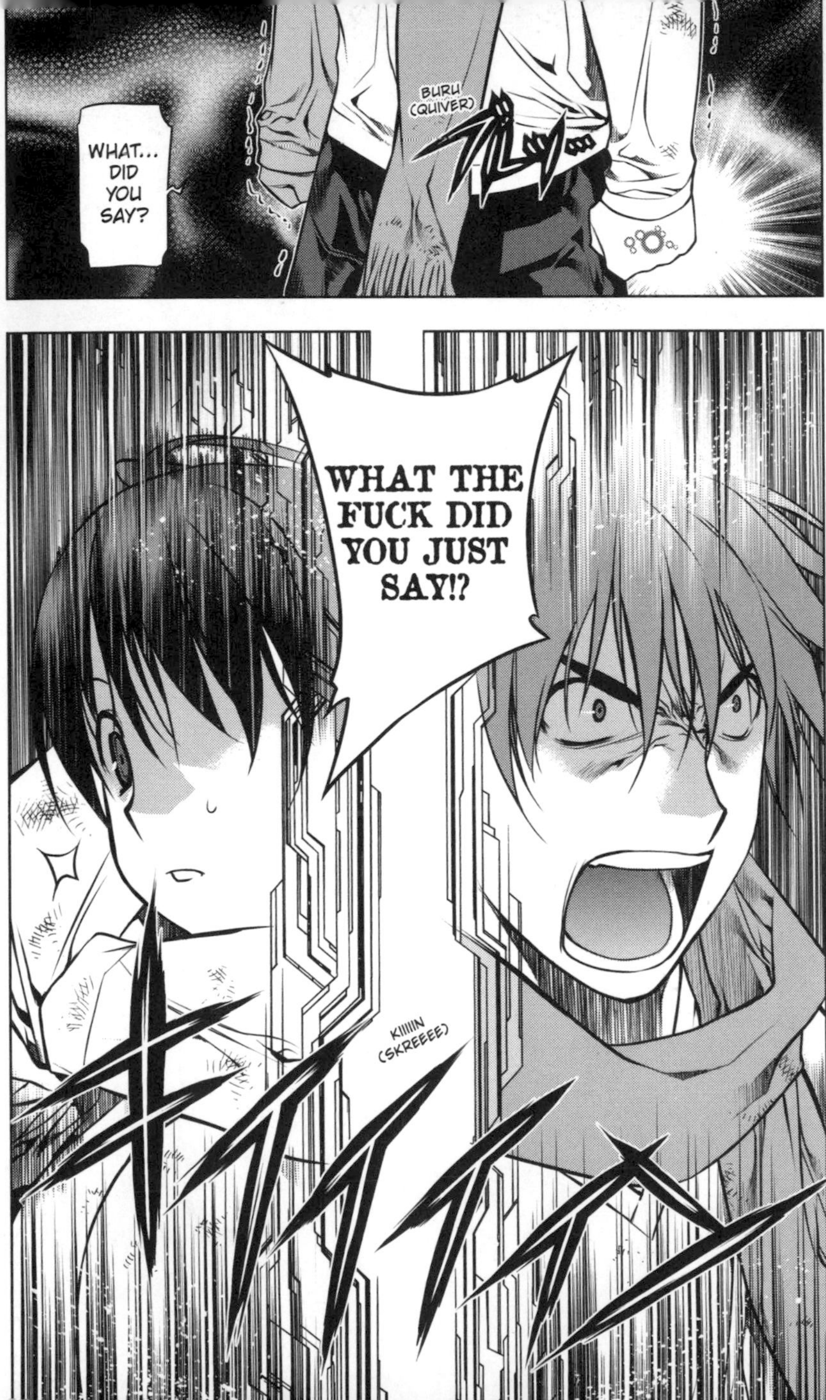
BURU (QUIVER)
WHAT... DID YOU SAY?
WHAT THE FUCK DID YOU JUST SAY!?
KIIIIIN (SKREEEE)

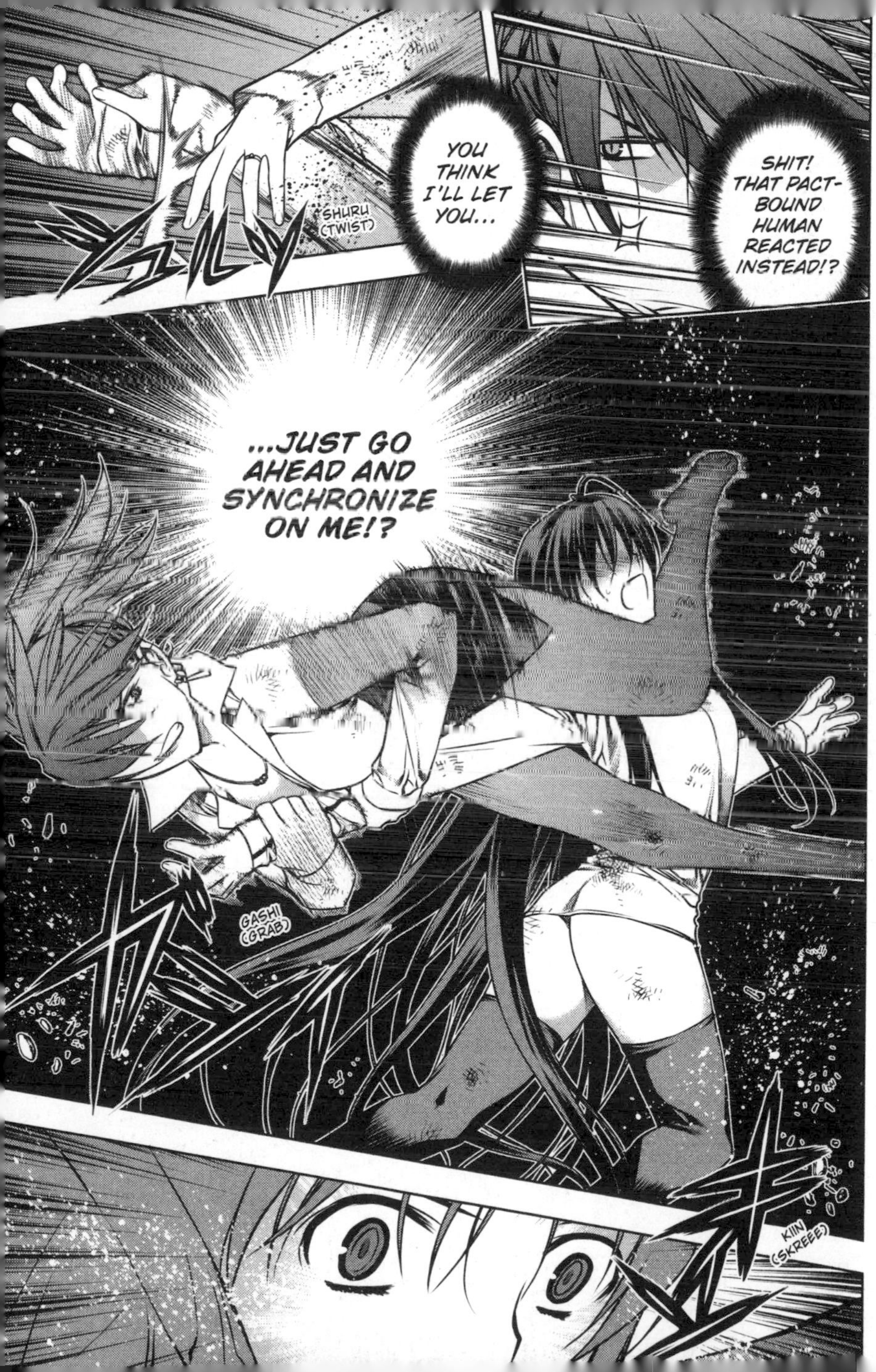
SHIT! THAT PACT-BOUND HUMAN REACTED INSTEAD!?
YOU THINK I'LL LET YOU...
SHURU (TWIST)
...JUST GO AHEAD AND SYNCHRONIZE ON ME!?
GASHI (GRAB)
KIIN (SKREEE)

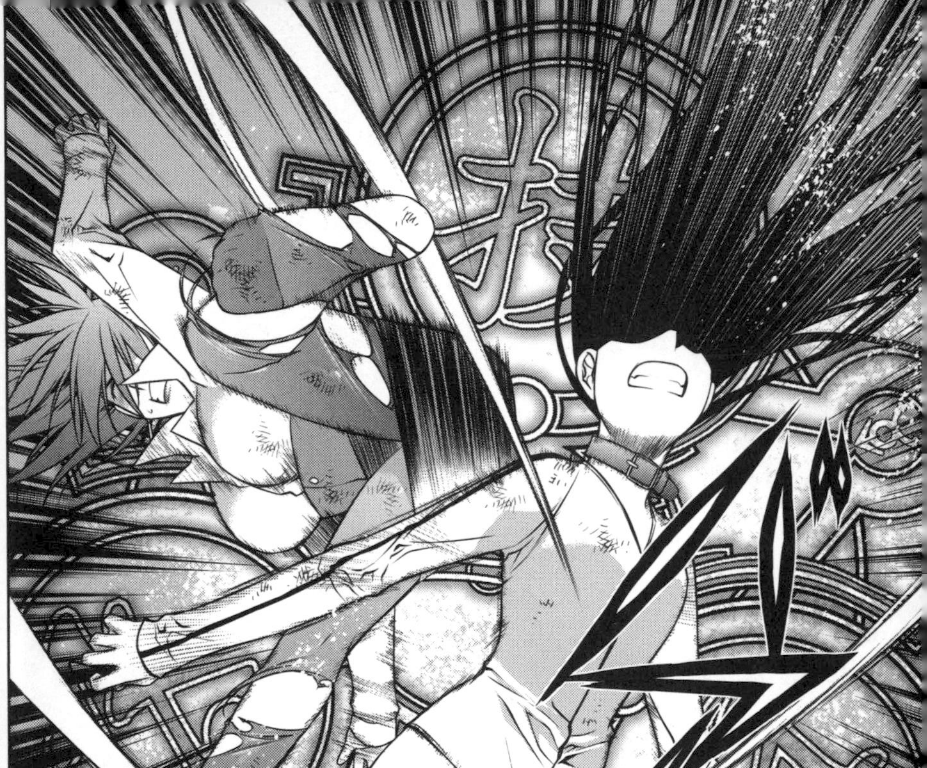
BAA
(BASH)
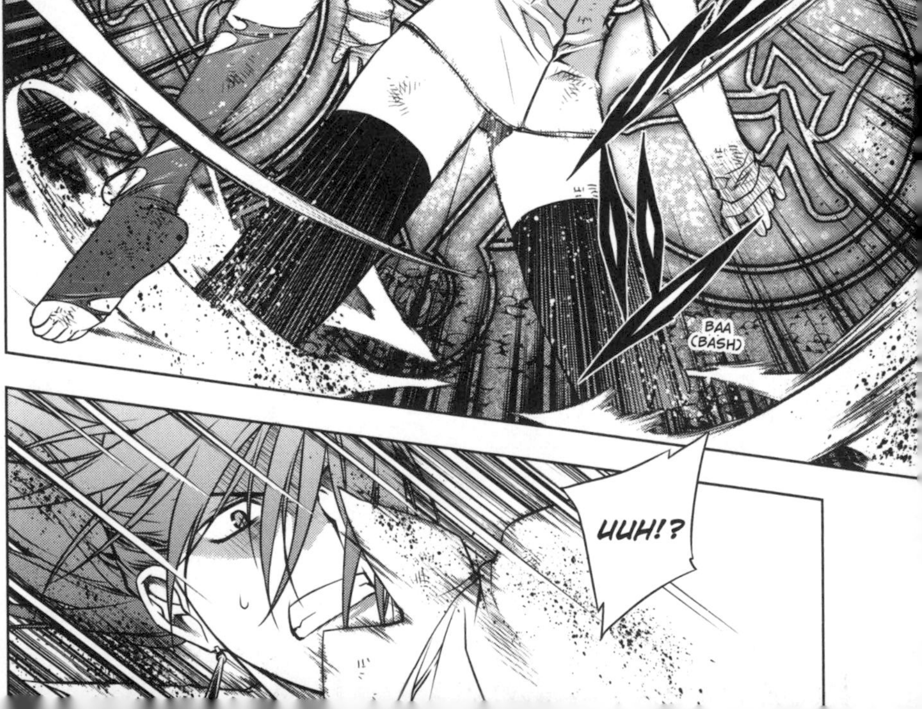
UUH!?

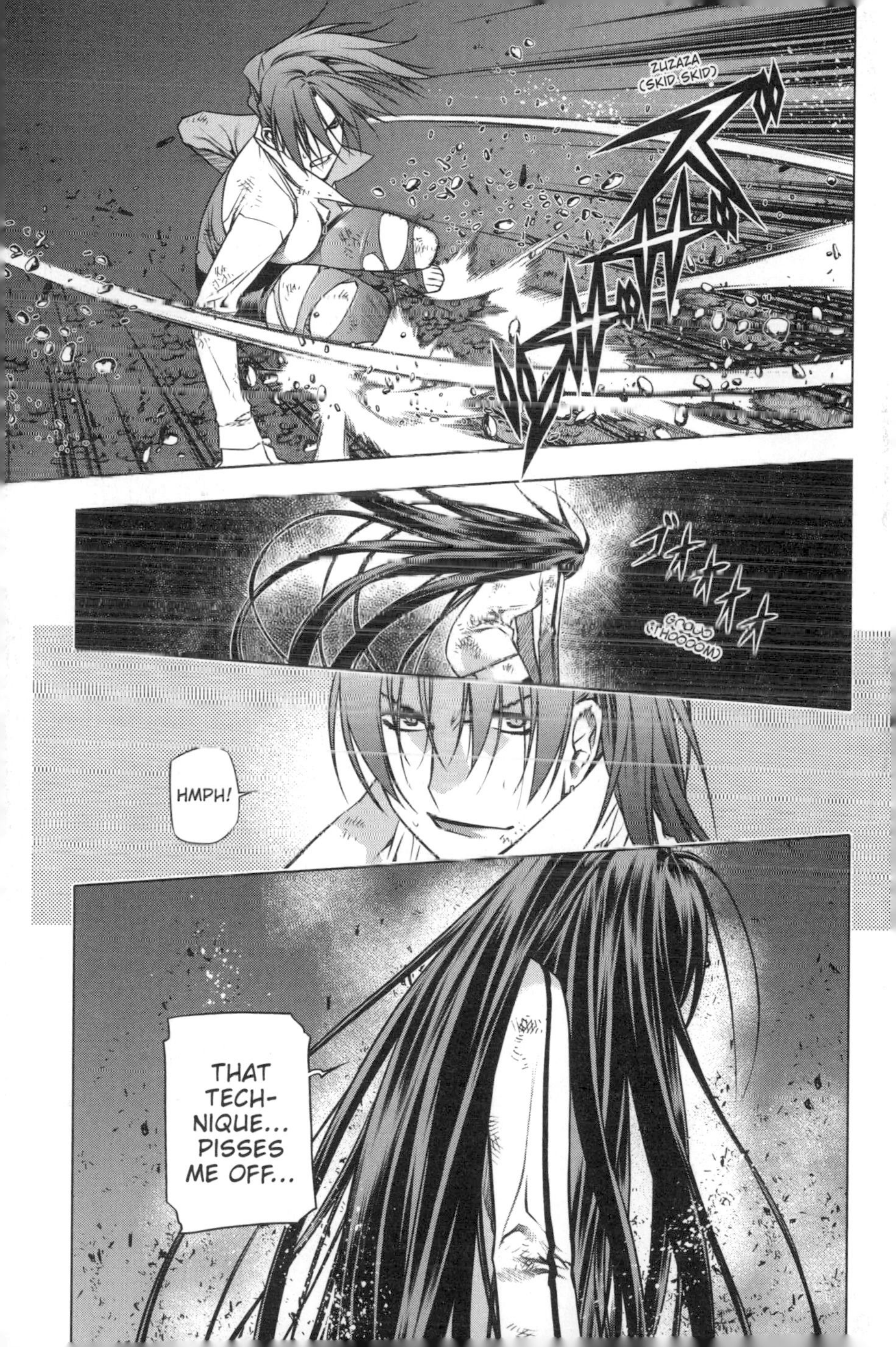
ZUZAZA
(SKID SKID)
GOOOO
(WHOOOOM)
HMPH!
THAT TECH-NIQUE... PISSES ME OFF...

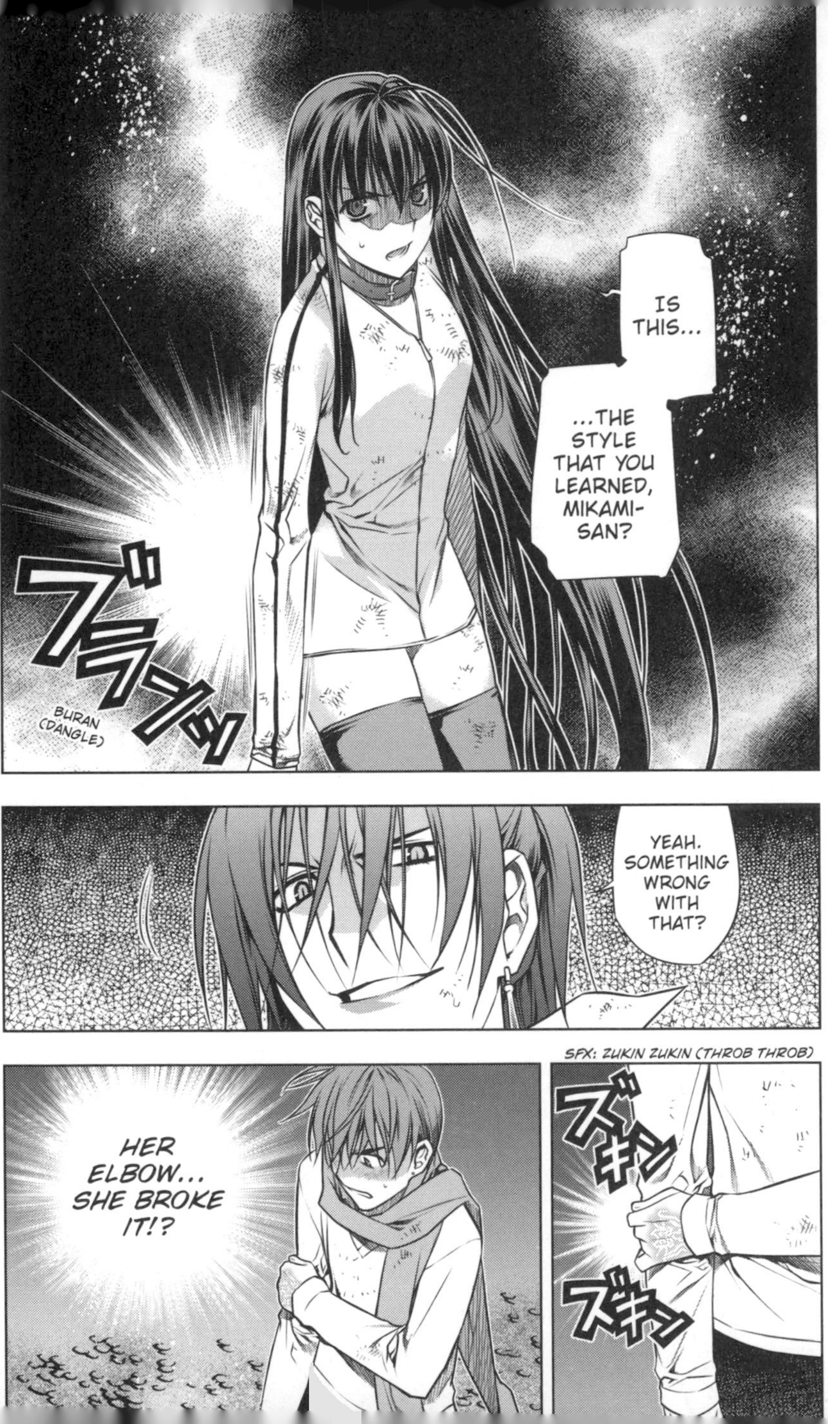
IS THIS...
...THE STYLE THAT YOU LEARNED, MIKAMI-SAN?
BURAN (DANGLE)
YEAH. SOMETHING WRONG WITH THAT?
SFX: ZUKIN ZUKIN (THROB THROB)
ズキン
ズキン
HER ELBOW... SHE BROKE IT!?

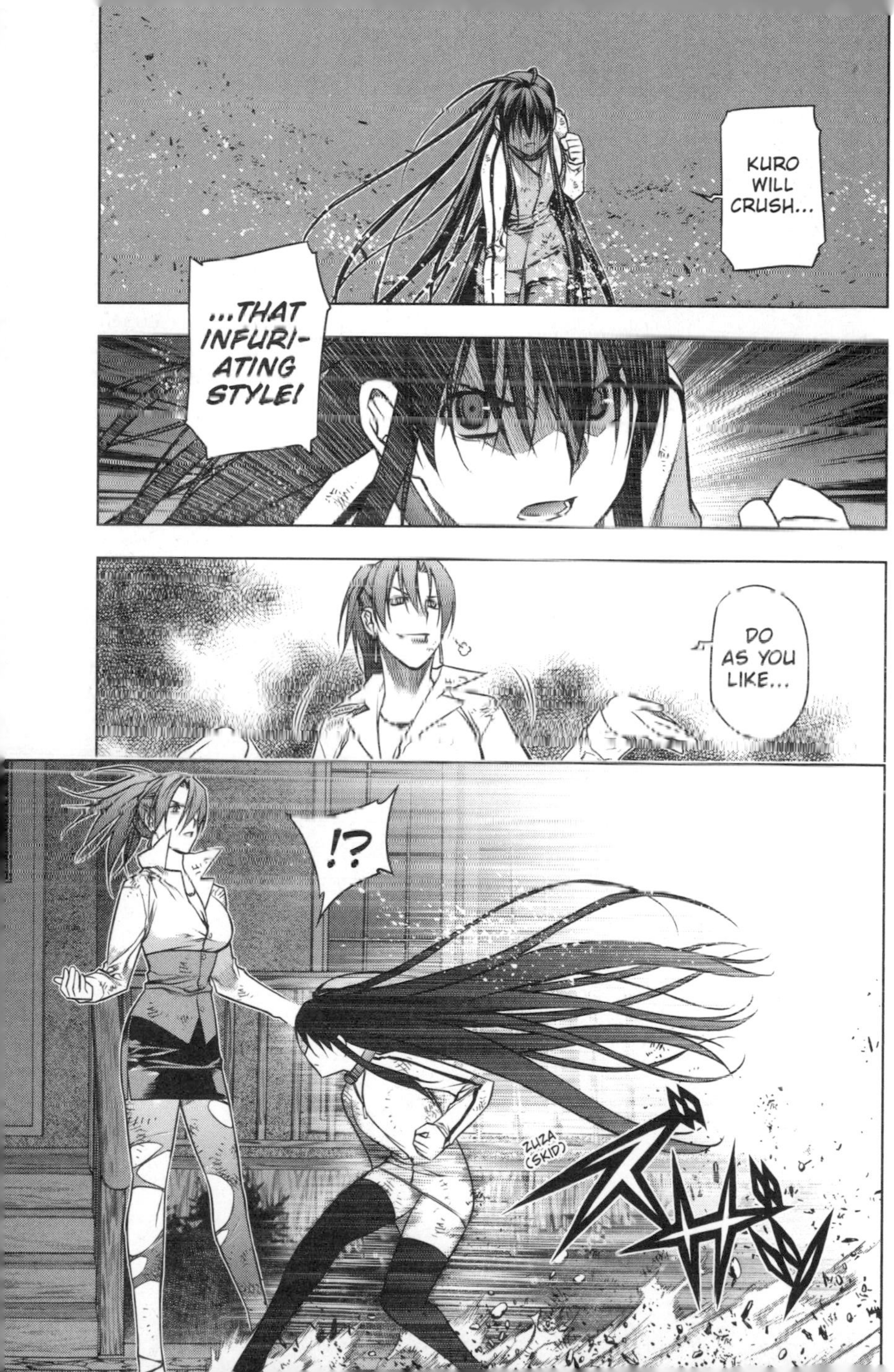
KURO WILL CRUSH...
...THAT INFURI-ATING STYLE!
DO AS YOU LIKE...
!?
ZUZA (SKID)

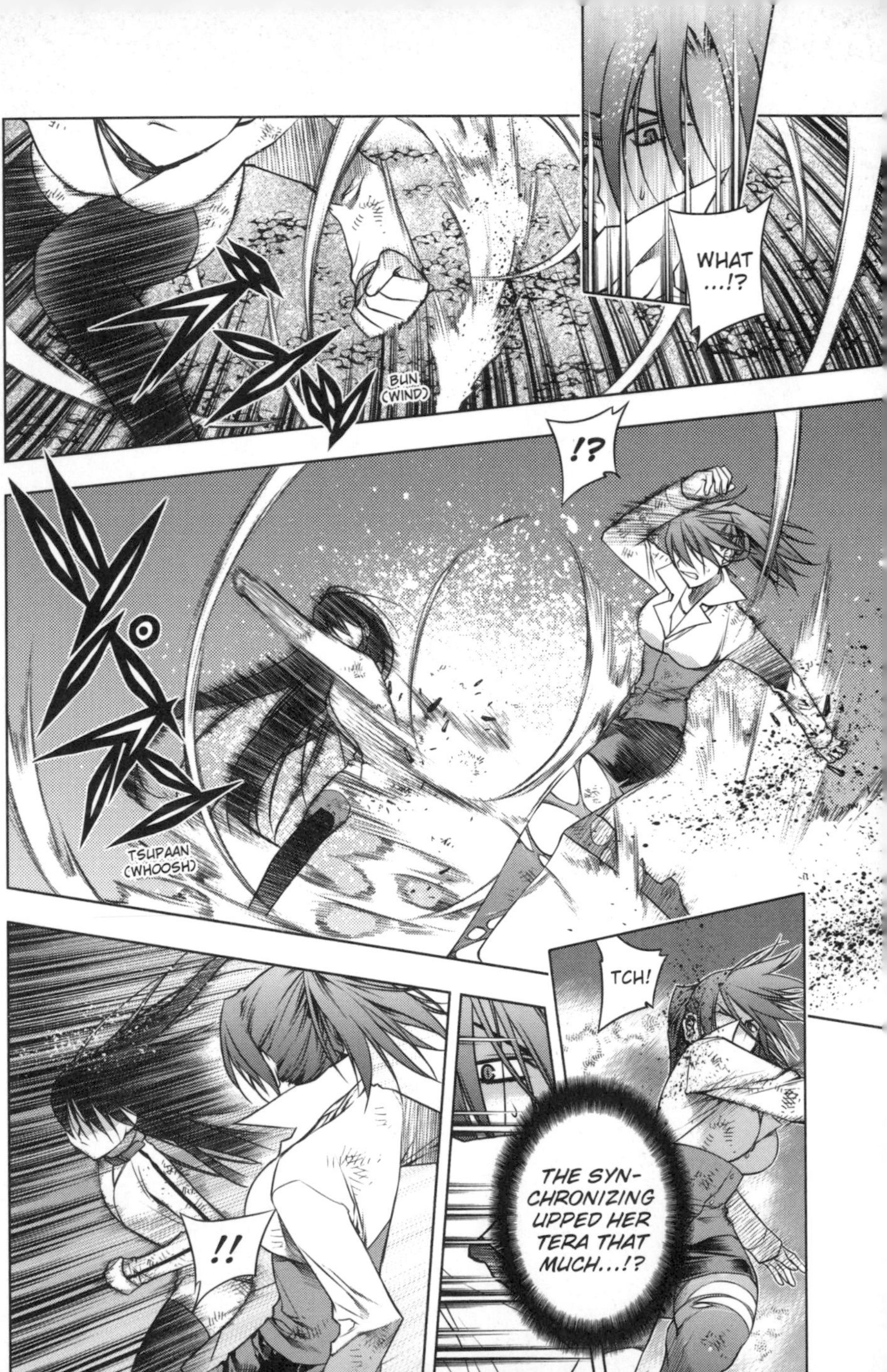
WHAT …!?
BUN (WIND)
!?
TSUPAAN (WHOOSH)
TCH!
THE SYN-CHRONIZING UPPED HER TERA THAT MUCH…!?
!!

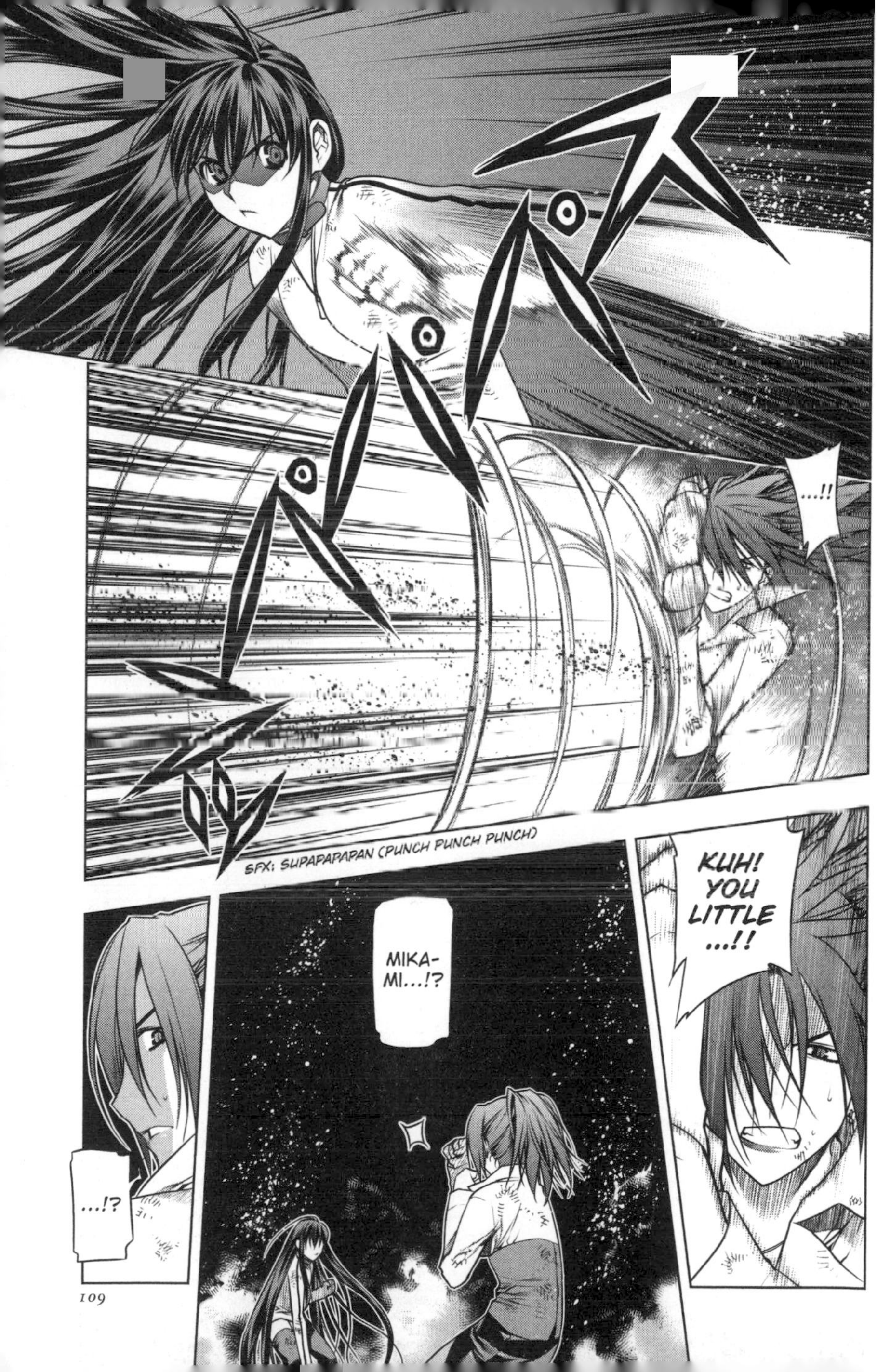
...!!
SFX: SUPAPAPAPAN (PUNCH PUNCH PUNCH)
KUH! YOU LITTLE ...!!
MIKA-MI...!?
...!?

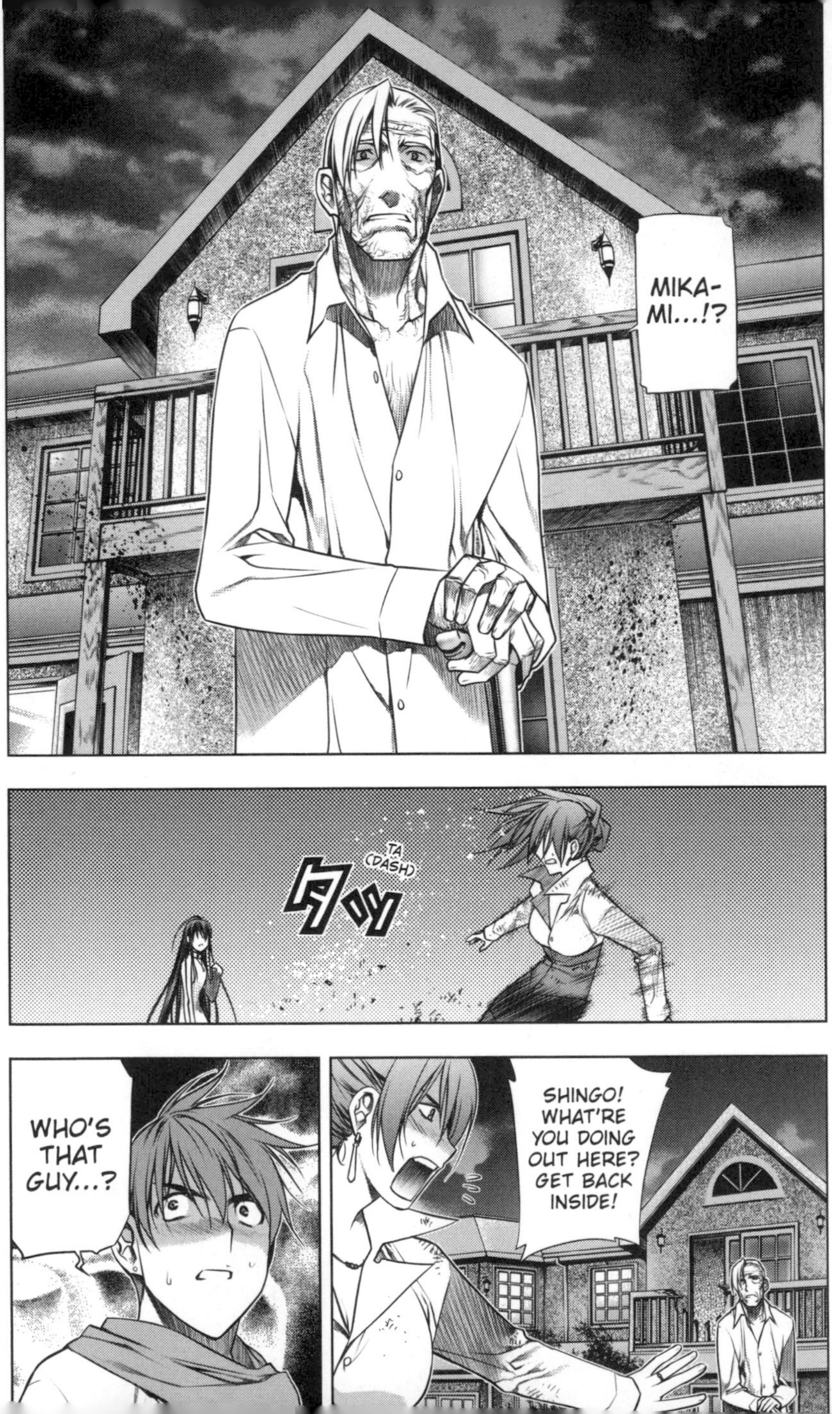
MIKA-MI...!?
TA (DASH)
SHINGO! WHAT'RE YOU DOING OUT HERE? GET BACK INSIDE!
WHO'S THAT GUY...?

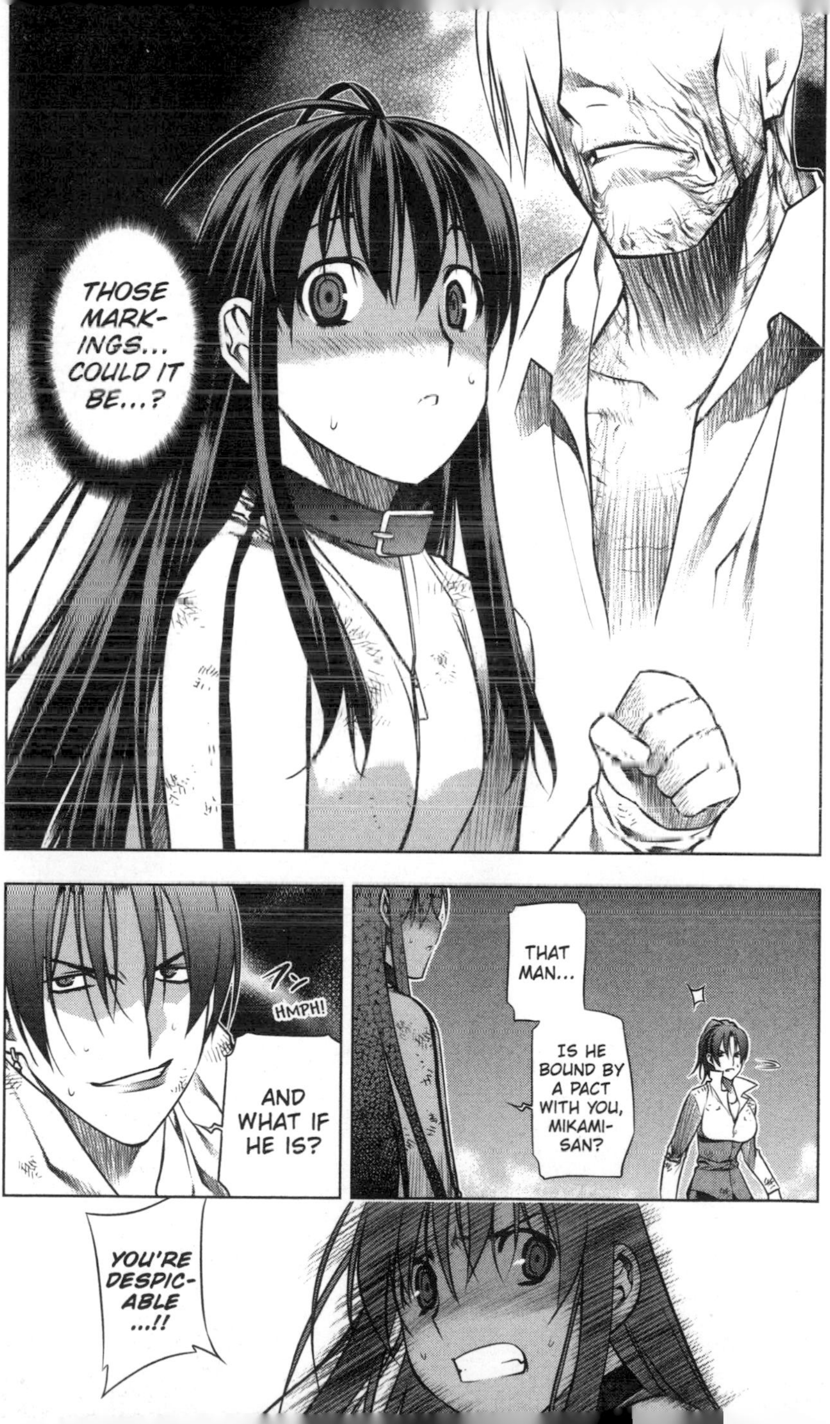
THOSE MARKINGS... COULD IT BE...?
THAT MAN...
IS HE BOUND BY A PACT WITH YOU, MIKAMI-SAN?
HMPH!
AND WHAT IF HE IS?
YOU'RE DESPICABLE...!!

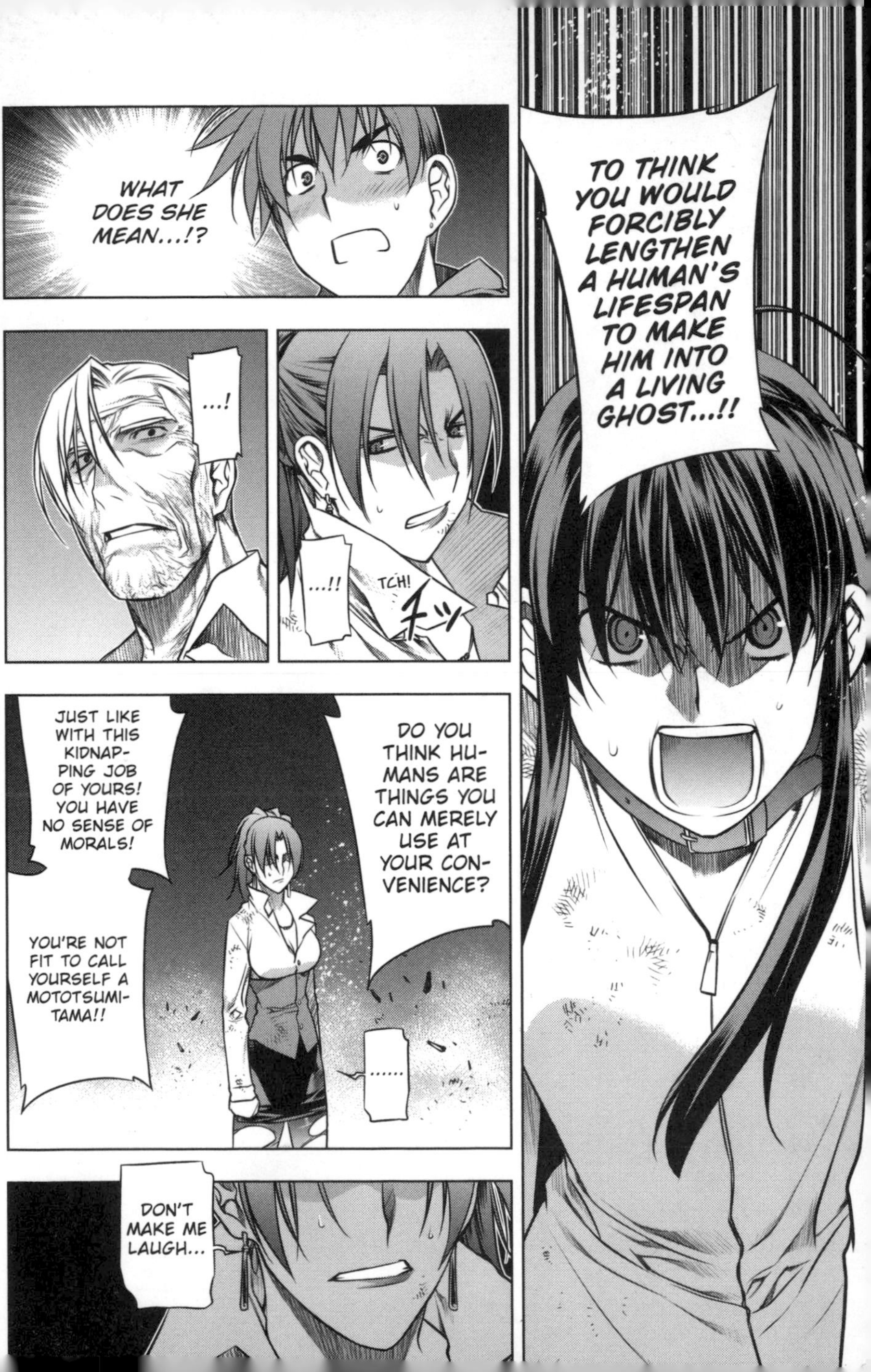

TO THINK YOU WOULD FORCIBLY LENGTHEN A HUMAN'S LIFESPAN TO MAKE HIM INTO A LIVING GHOST...!!
WHAT DOES SHE MEAN...!?
...!!
TCH!
チッ
...!
DO YOU THINK HU-MANS ARE THINGS YOU CAN MERELY USE AT YOUR CON-VENIENCE?
JUST LIKE WITH THIS KIDNAP-PING JOB OF YOURS! YOU HAVE NO SENSE OF MORALS!
YOU'RE NOT FIT TO CALL YOURSELF A MOTOTSUMI-TAMA!!
......
DON'T MAKE ME LAUGH...

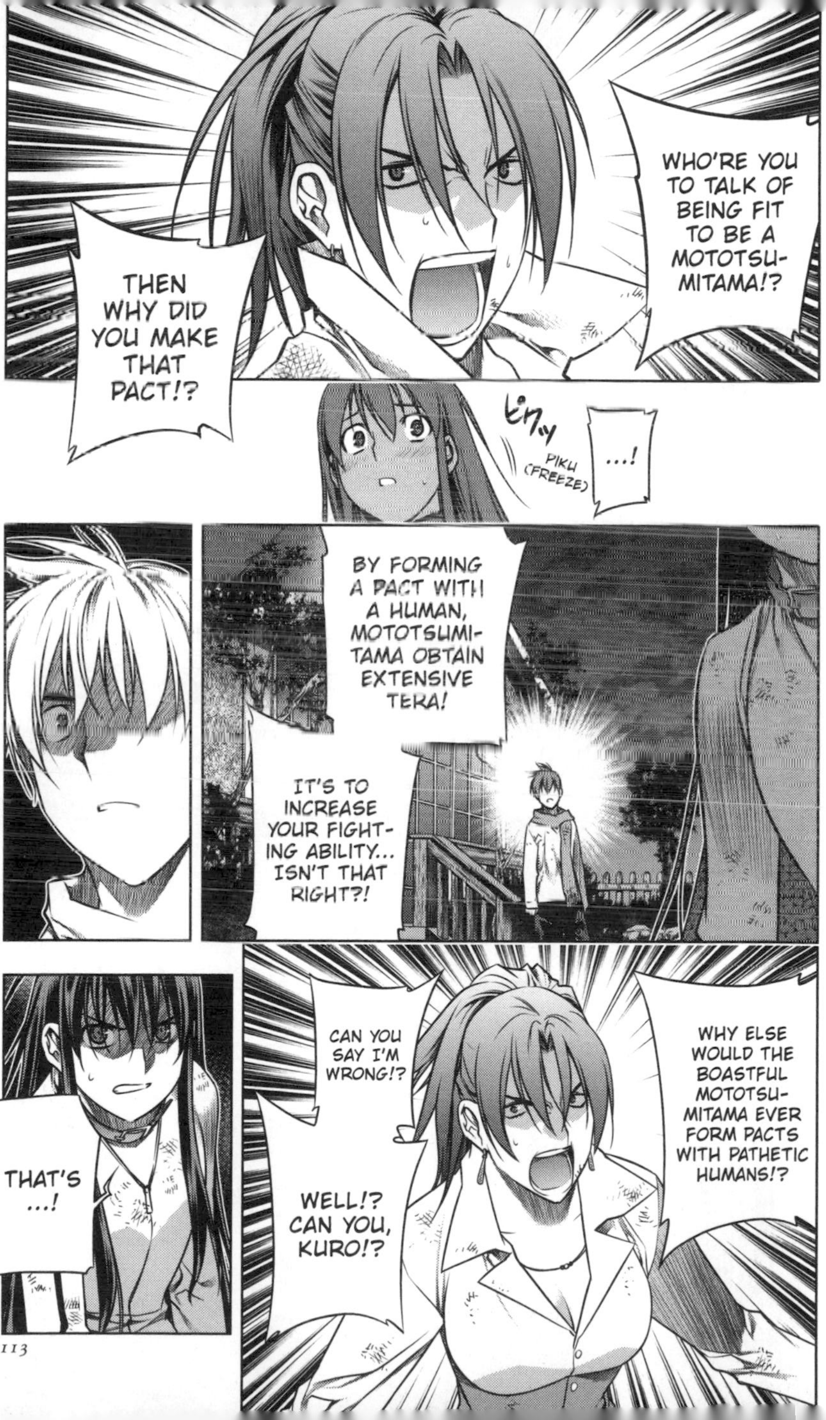
WHO'RE YOU TO TALK OF BEING FIT TO BE A MOTOTSUMITAMA!?
THEN WHY DID YOU MAKE THAT PACT!?
ピクッ
PIKU (FREEZE)
...!
BY FORMING A PACT WITH A HUMAN, MOTOTSUMITAMA OBTAIN EXTENSIVE TERA!
IT'S TO INCREASE YOUR FIGHTING ABILITY... ISN'T THAT RIGHT?!
WHY ELSE WOULD THE BOASTFUL MOTOTSUMITAMA EVER FORM PACTS WITH PATHETIC HUMANS!?
CAN YOU SAY I'M WRONG!?
WELL!? CAN YOU, KURO!?
THAT'S ...!

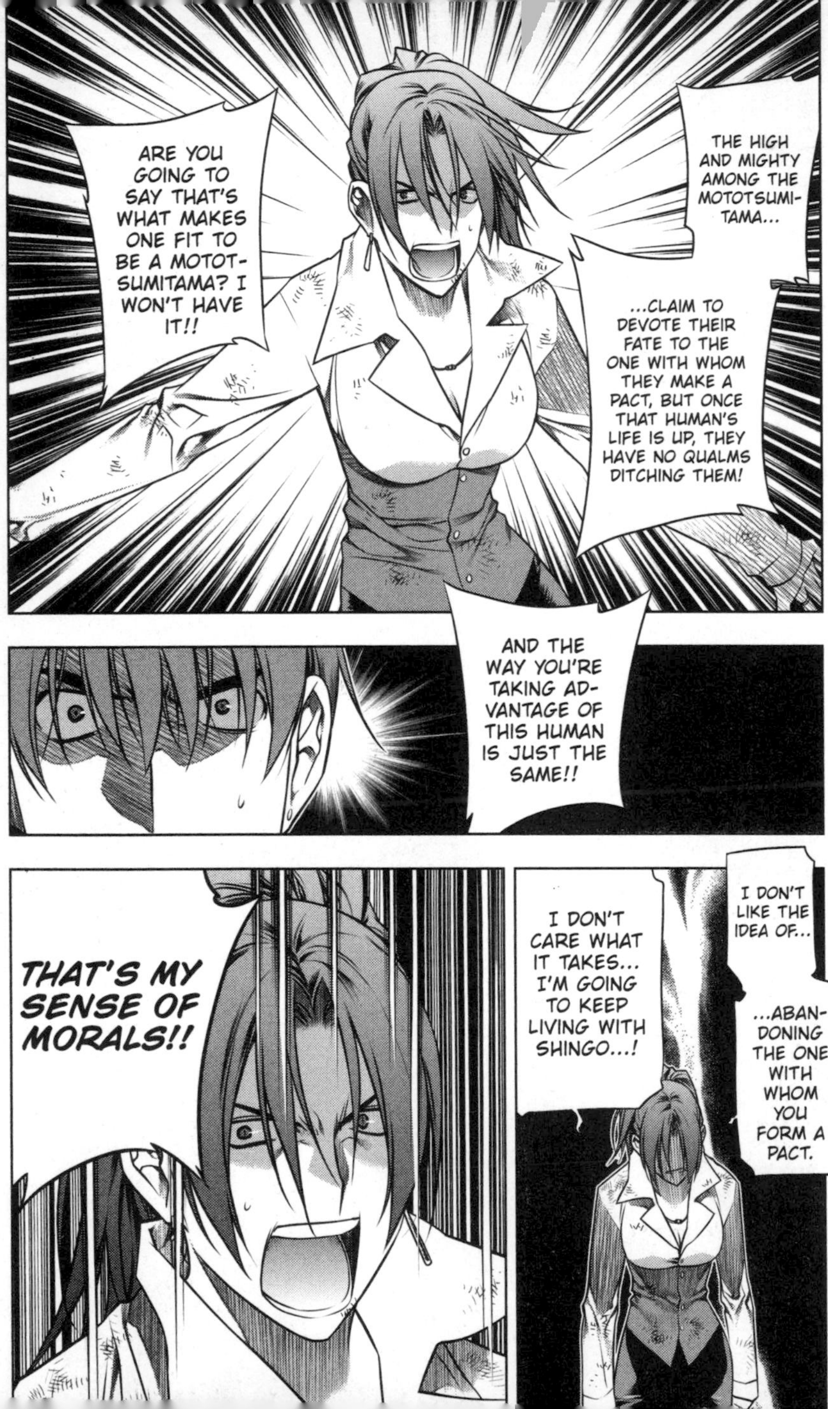
THE HIGH AND MIGHTY AMONG THE MOTOTSUMI-TAMA...
...CLAIM TO DEVOTE THEIR FATE TO THE ONE WITH WHOM THEY MAKE A PACT, BUT ONCE THAT HUMAN'S LIFE IS UP, THEY HAVE NO QUALMS DITCHING THEM!
ARE YOU GOING TO SAY THAT'S WHAT MAKES ONE FIT TO BE A MOTOT-SUMITAMA? I WON'T HAVE IT!!
AND THE WAY YOU'RE TAKING AD-VANTAGE OF THIS HUMAN IS JUST THE SAME!!
I DON'T LIKE THE IDEA OF...
...ABAN-DONING THE ONE WITH WHOM YOU FORM A PACT.
I DON'T CARE WHAT IT TAKES... I'M GOING TO KEEP LIVING WITH SHINGO...!
THAT'S MY SENSE OF MORALS!!

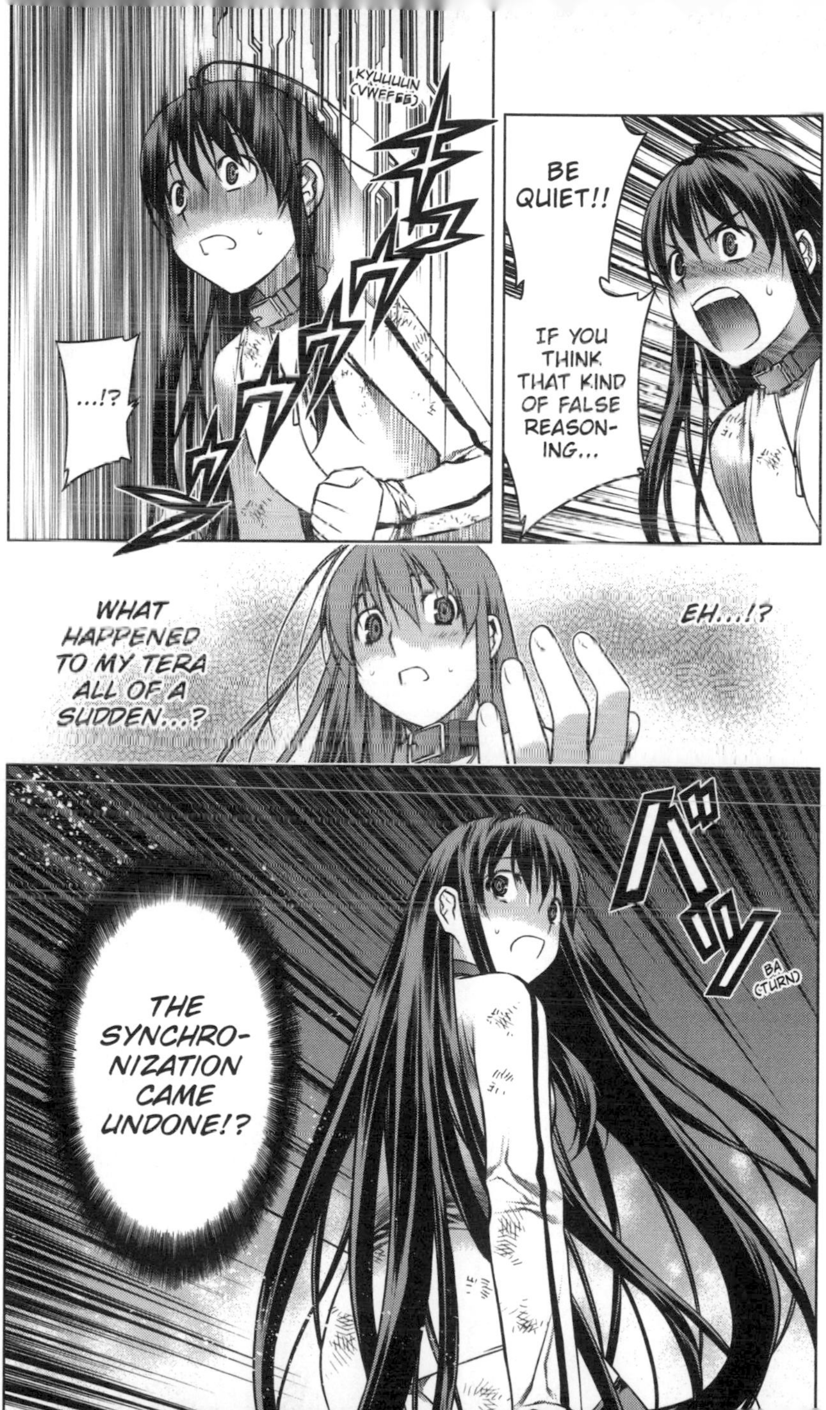
BE QUIET!!
IF YOU THINK THAT KIND OF FALSE REASON-ING...
KYUUUUN (VWEEEE)
...!?
EH...!?
WHAT HAPPENED TO MY TERA ALL OF A SUDDEN...?
BA (TURN)
THE SYNCHRO-NIZATION CAME UNDONE!?

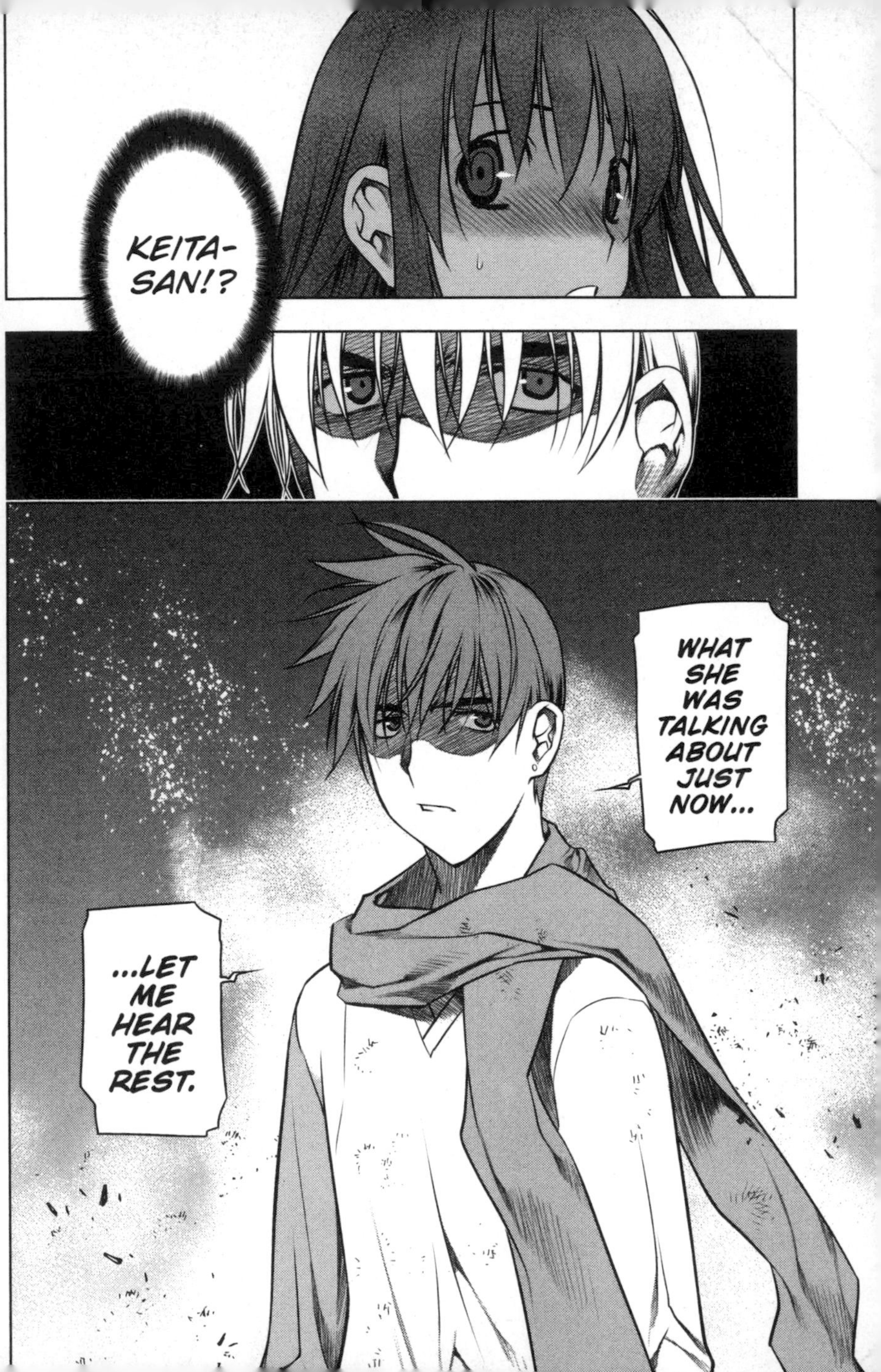
KEITA-SAN!?
WHAT SHE WAS TALKING ABOUT JUST NOW...
...LET ME HEAR THE REST.

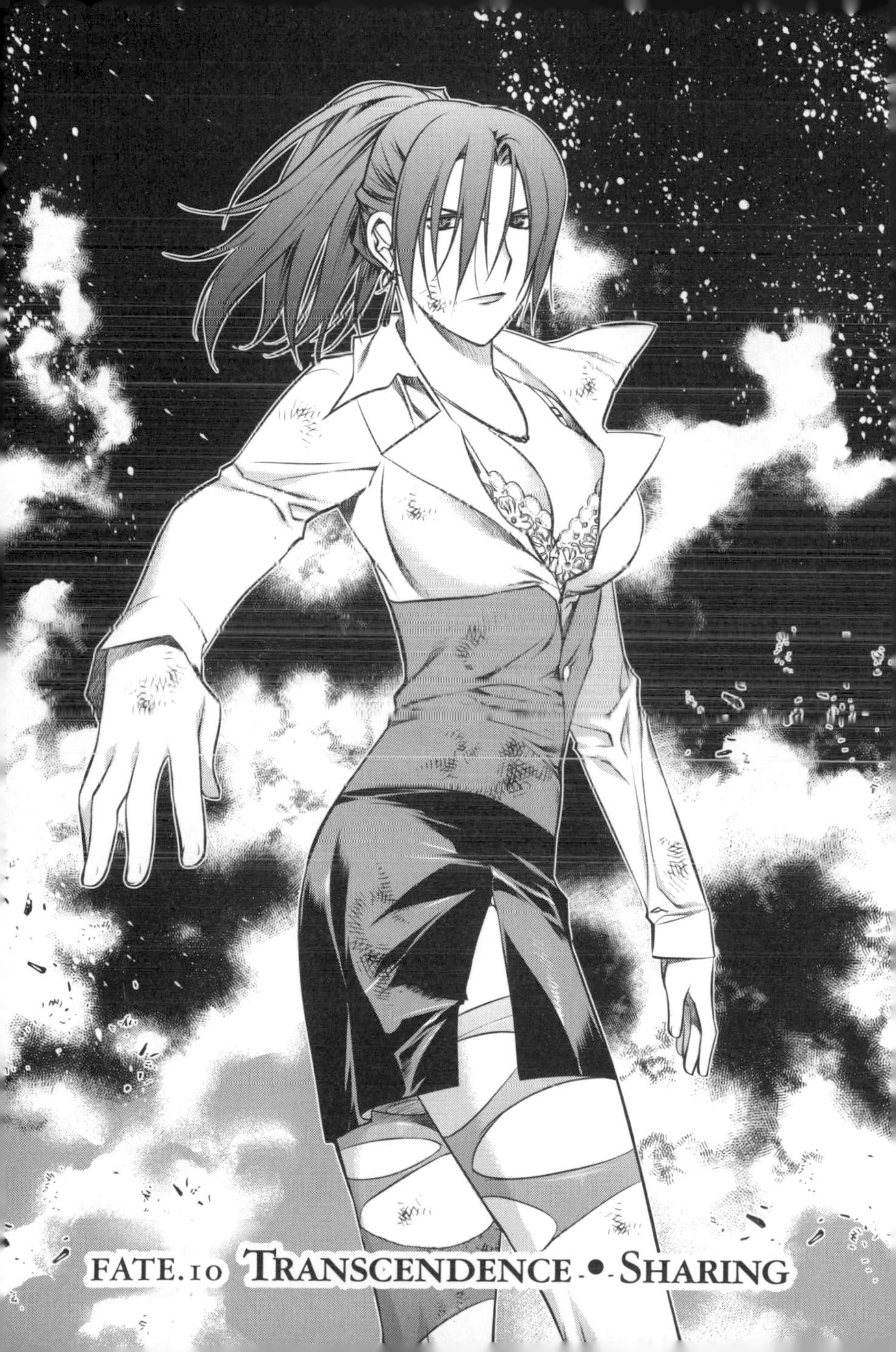

FATE.10 Transcendence • Sharing

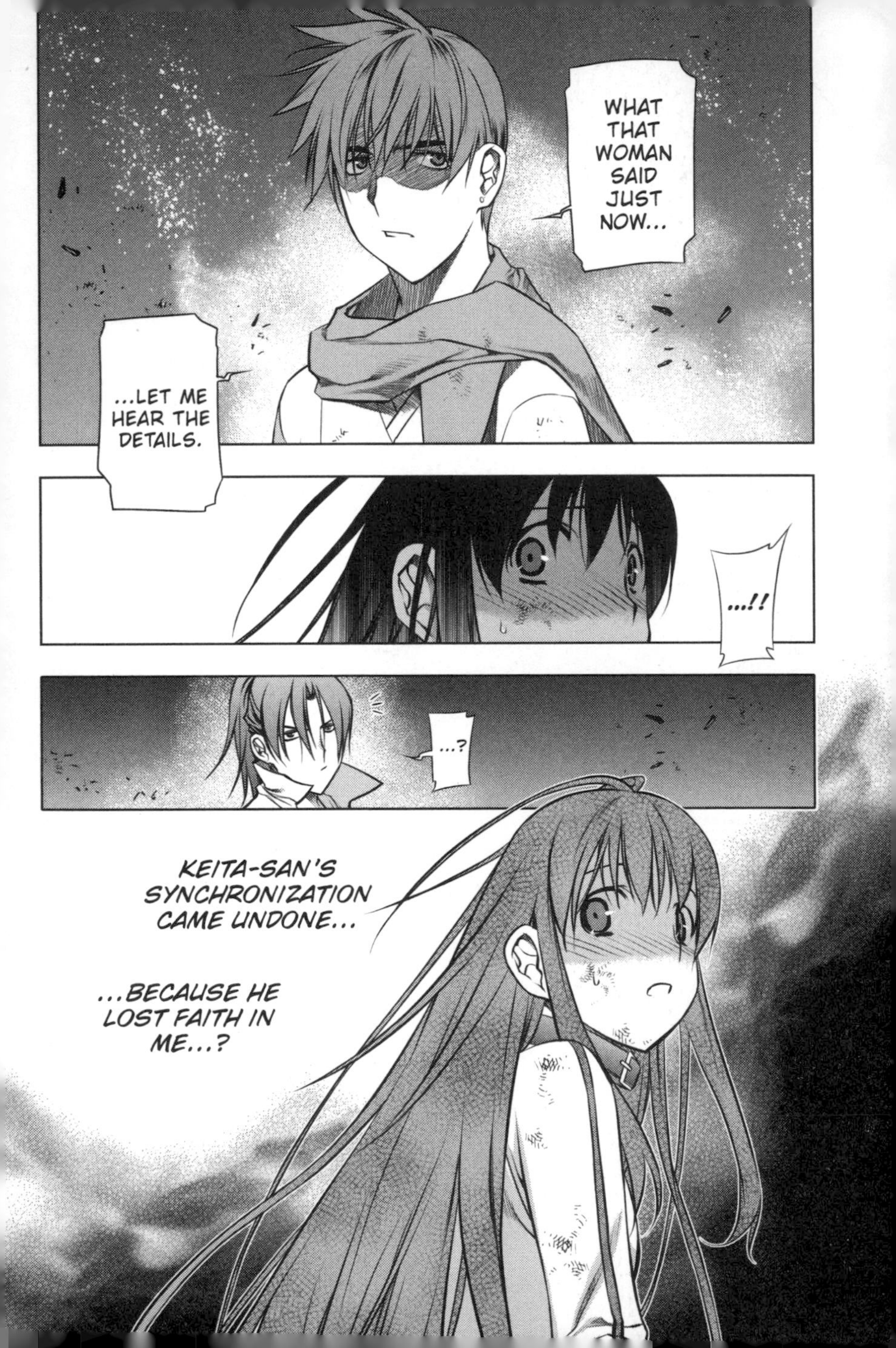
WHAT THAT WOMAN SAID JUST NOW...
...LET ME HEAR THE DETAILS.
...!!
...?
KEITA-SAN'S SYNCHRONIZATION CAME UNDONE...
...BECAUSE HE LOST FAITH IN ME...?

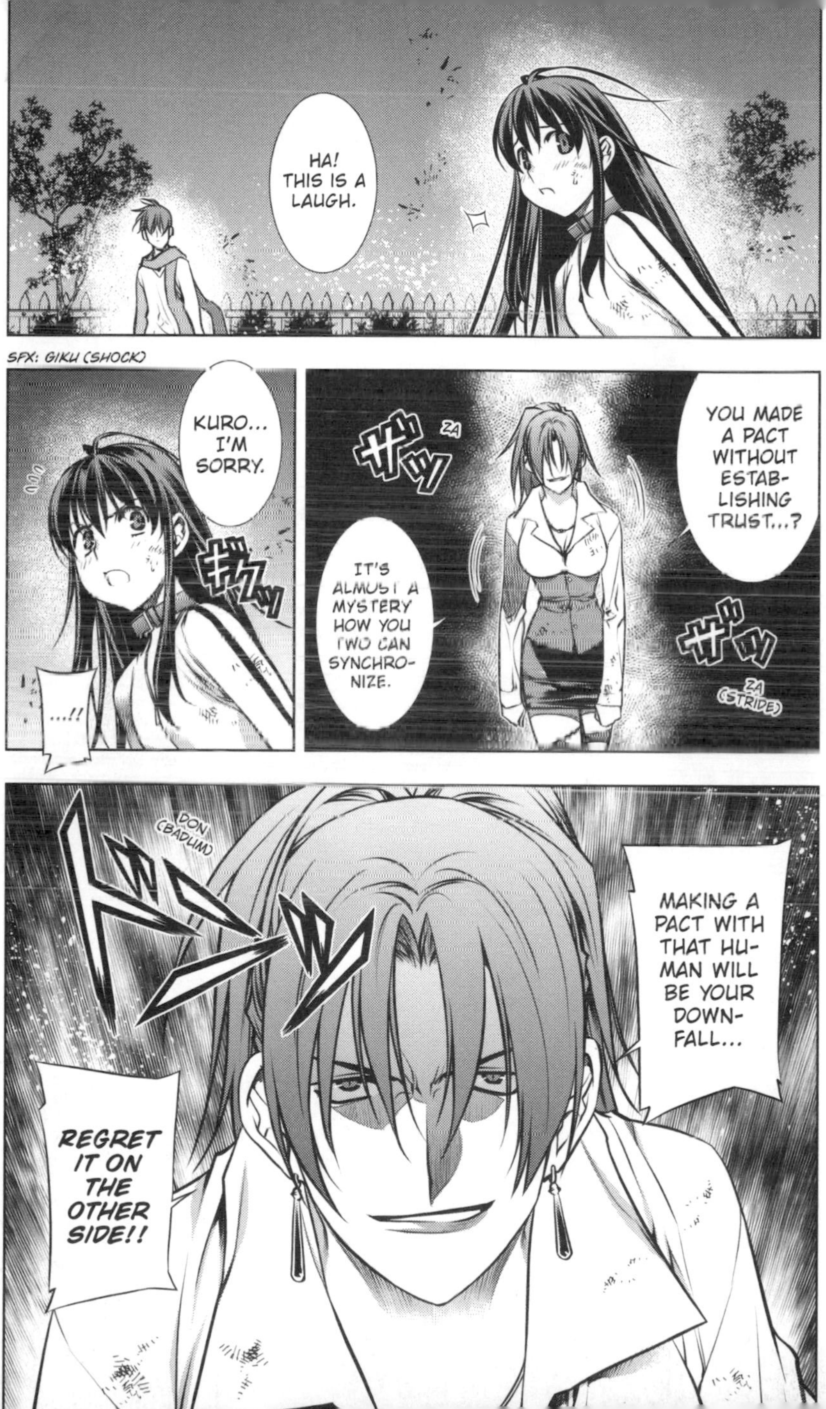
HA! THIS IS A LAUGH.
SFX: GIKU (SHOCK)
ZA
YOU MADE A PACT WITHOUT ESTAB-LISHING TRUST...?
IT'S ALMOST A MYSTERY HOW YOU TWO CAN SYNCHRO-NIZE.
ZA (STRIDE)
KURO... I'M SORRY.
...!!
DON (BADUM)
MAKING A PACT WITH THAT HU-MAN WILL BE YOUR DOWN-FALL...
REGRET IT ON THE OTHER SIDE!!

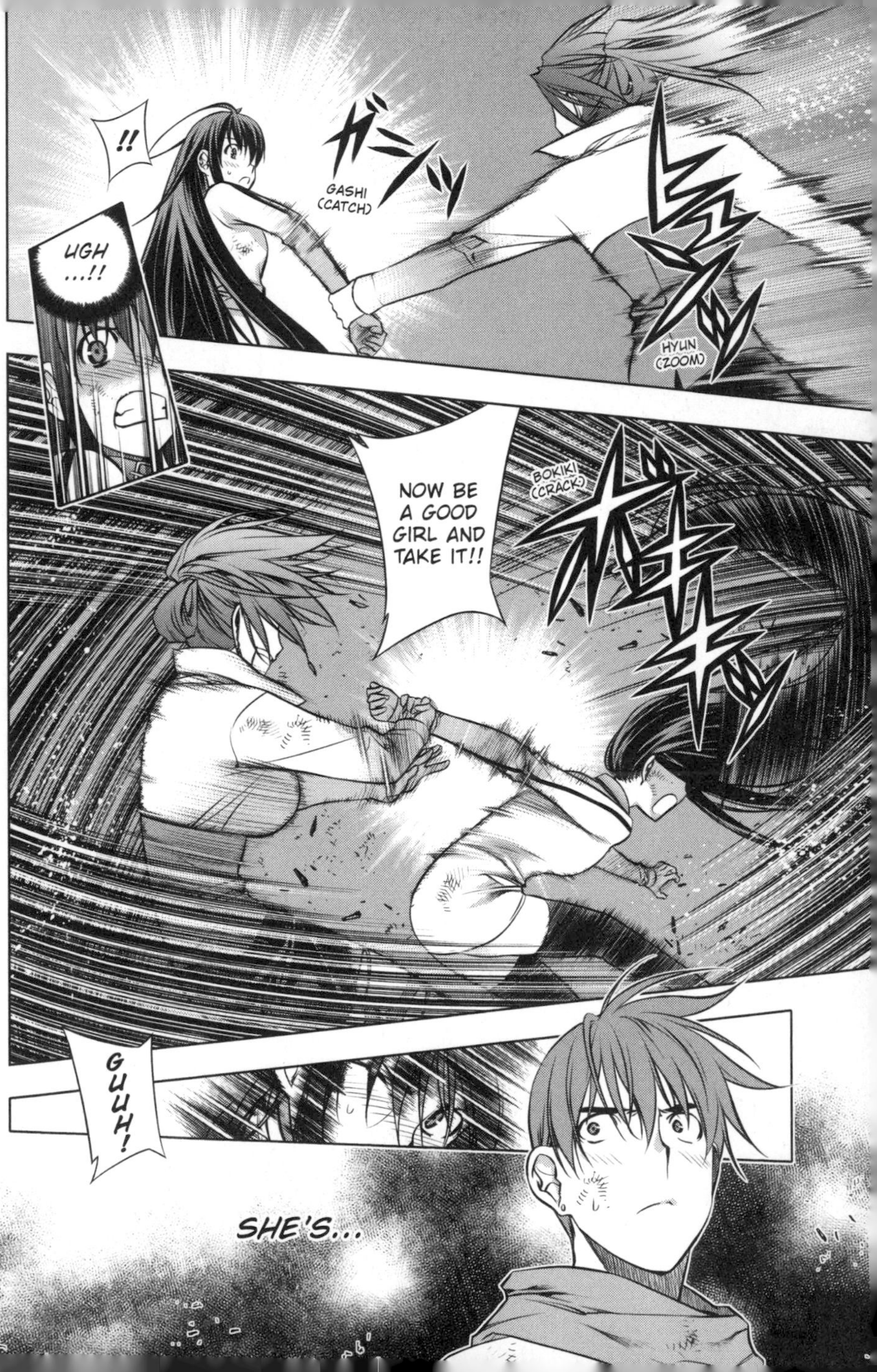

HYUN (ZOOM)
GASHI (CATCH)
!!
UGH ...!!
BOKIKI (CRACK)
NOW BE A GOOD GIRL AND TAKE IT!!
SHE'S...
GUUH!

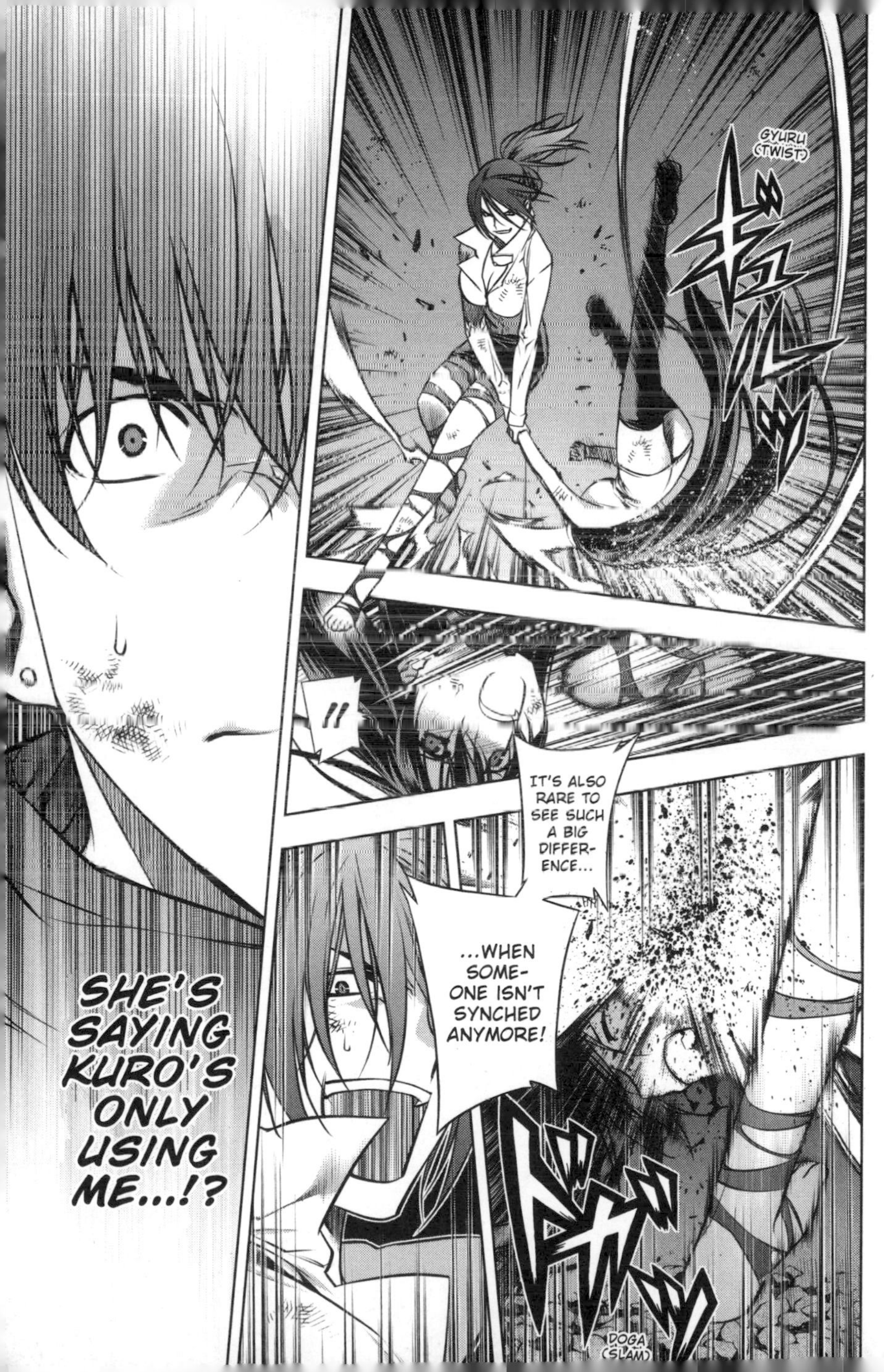
GYURU (TWIST)
!!
IT'S ALSO RARE TO SEE SUCH A BIG DIFFER-ENCE...
...WHEN SOME-ONE ISN'T SYNCHED ANYMORE!
DOGA (SLAM)
SHE'S SAYING KURO'S ONLY USING ME...!?

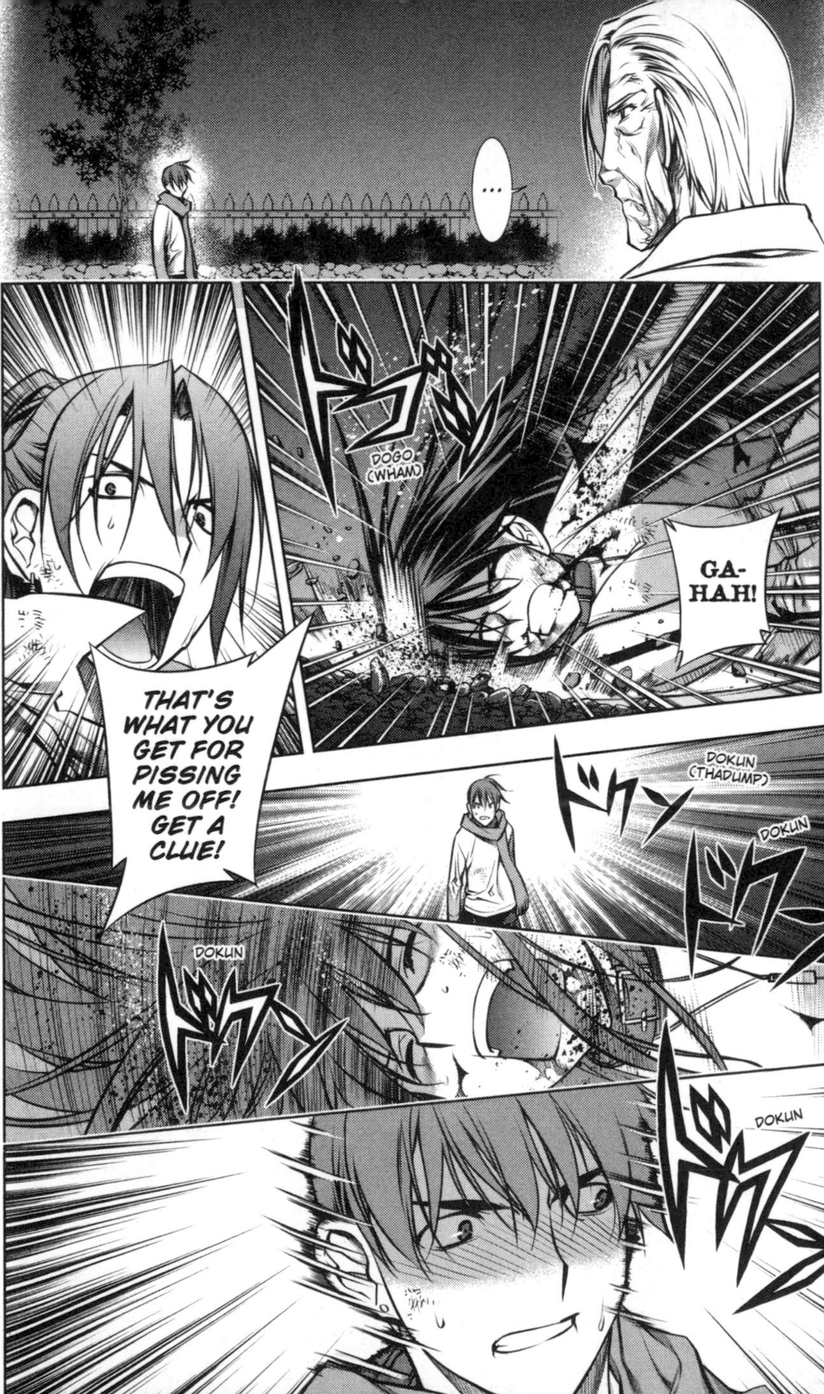
...
DOGO (WHAM)
GA-HAH!
THAT'S WHAT YOU GET FOR PISSING ME OFF! GET A CLUE!
DOKUN (THADUMP)
DOKUN
DOKUN
DOKUN

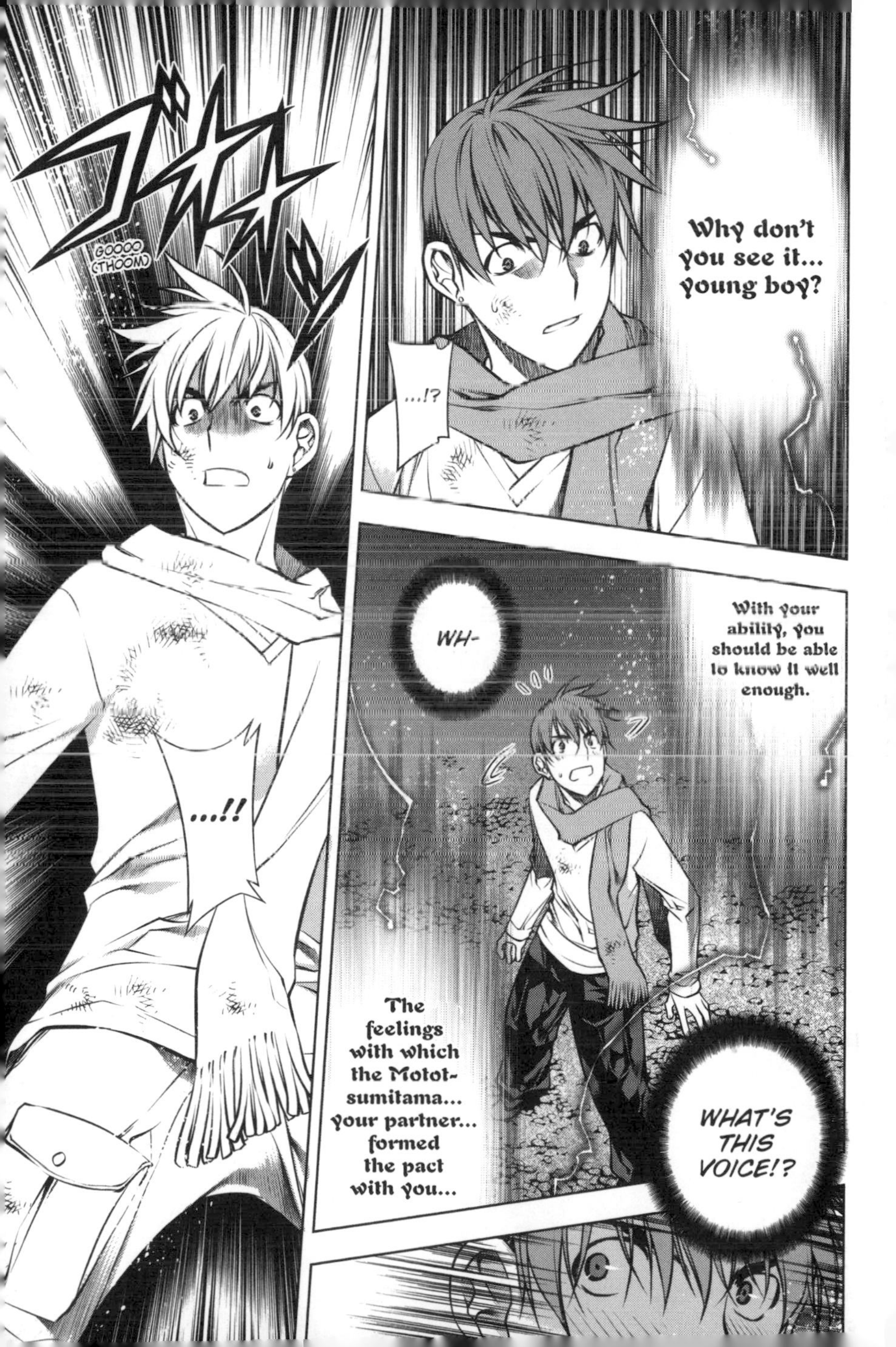
Why don't you see it... young boy?
...!?
With your ability, you should be able to know it well enough.
WH-
The feelings with which the Motot-sumitama... your partner... formed the pact with you...
WHAT'S THIS VOICE!?
GOOOO (THOOM)
...!!

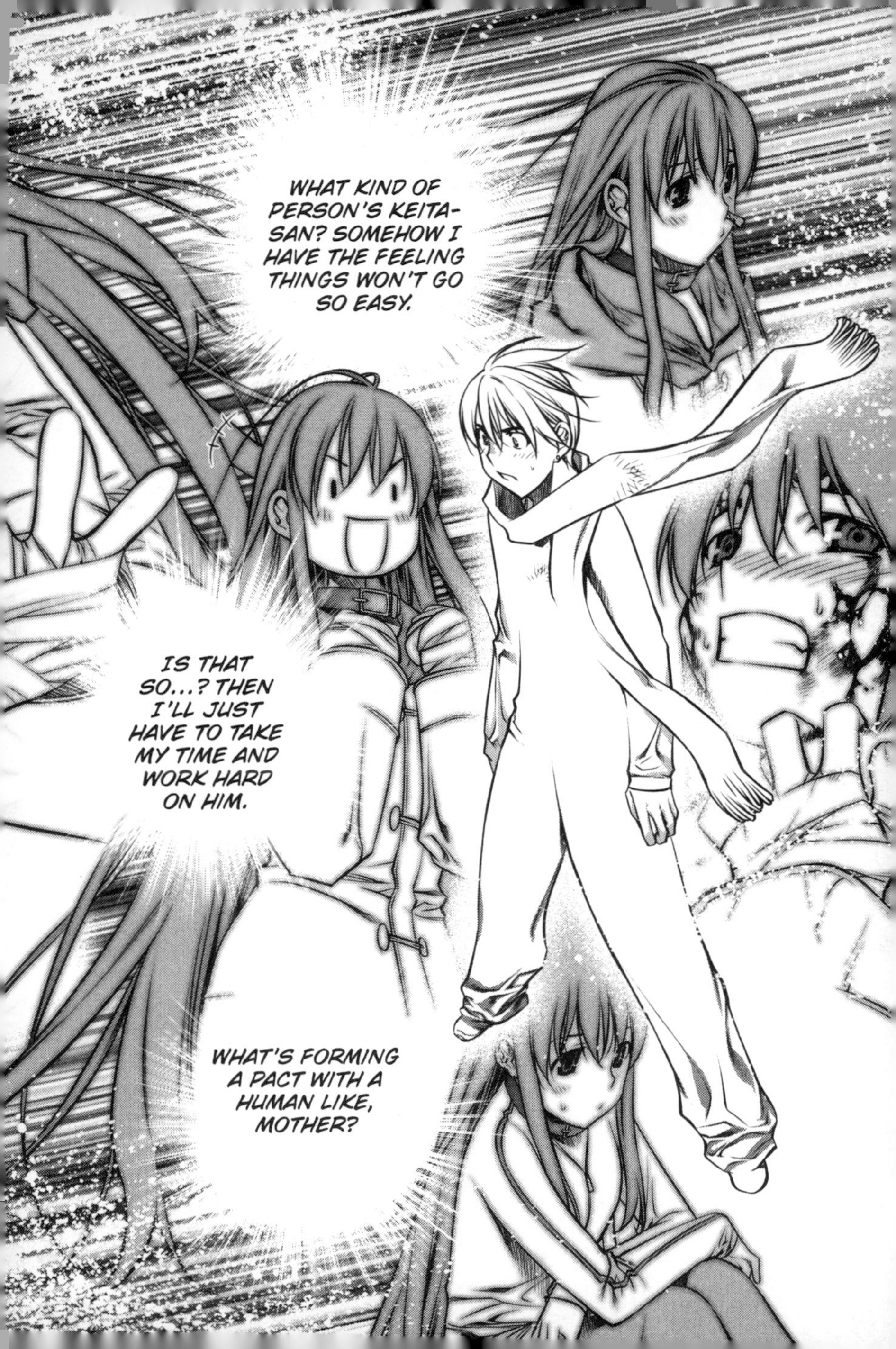
WHAT KIND OF PERSON'S KEITA-SAN? SOMEHOW I HAVE THE FEELING THINGS WON'T GO SO EASY.
IS THAT SO...? THEN I'LL JUST HAVE TO TAKE MY TIME AND WORK HARD ON HIM.
WHAT'S FORMING A PACT WITH A HUMAN LIKE, MOTHER?

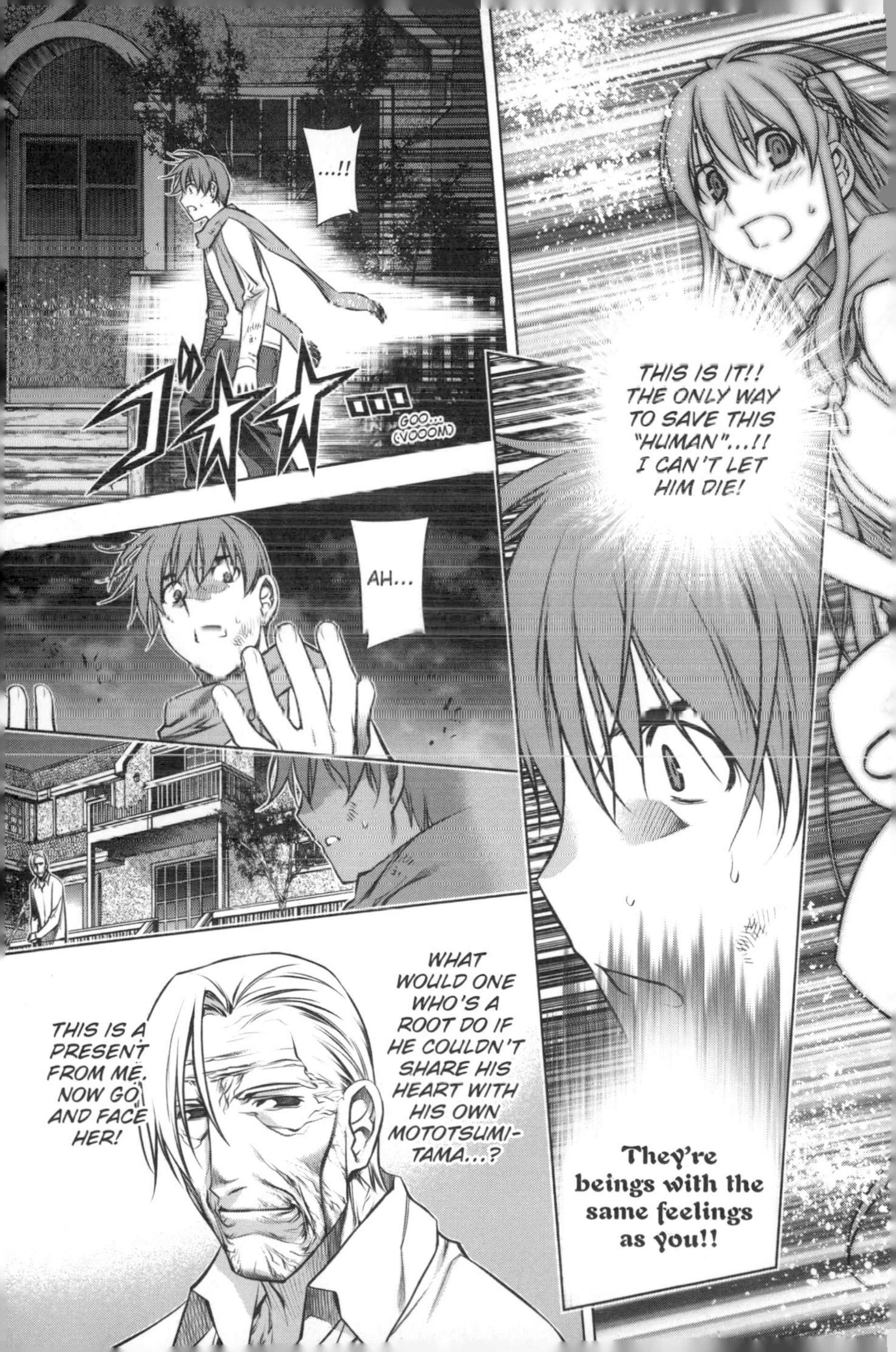
THIS IS IT!! THE ONLY WAY TO SAVE THIS "HUMAN"...!! I CAN'T LET HIM DIE!
They're beings with the same feelings as you!!
...!!
GOO... (VOOOM)
AH...
WHAT WOULD ONE WHO'S A ROOT DO IF HE COULDN'T SHARE HIS HEART WITH HIS OWN MOTOTSUMITAMA...?
THIS IS A PRESENT FROM ME. NOW GO AND FACE HER!

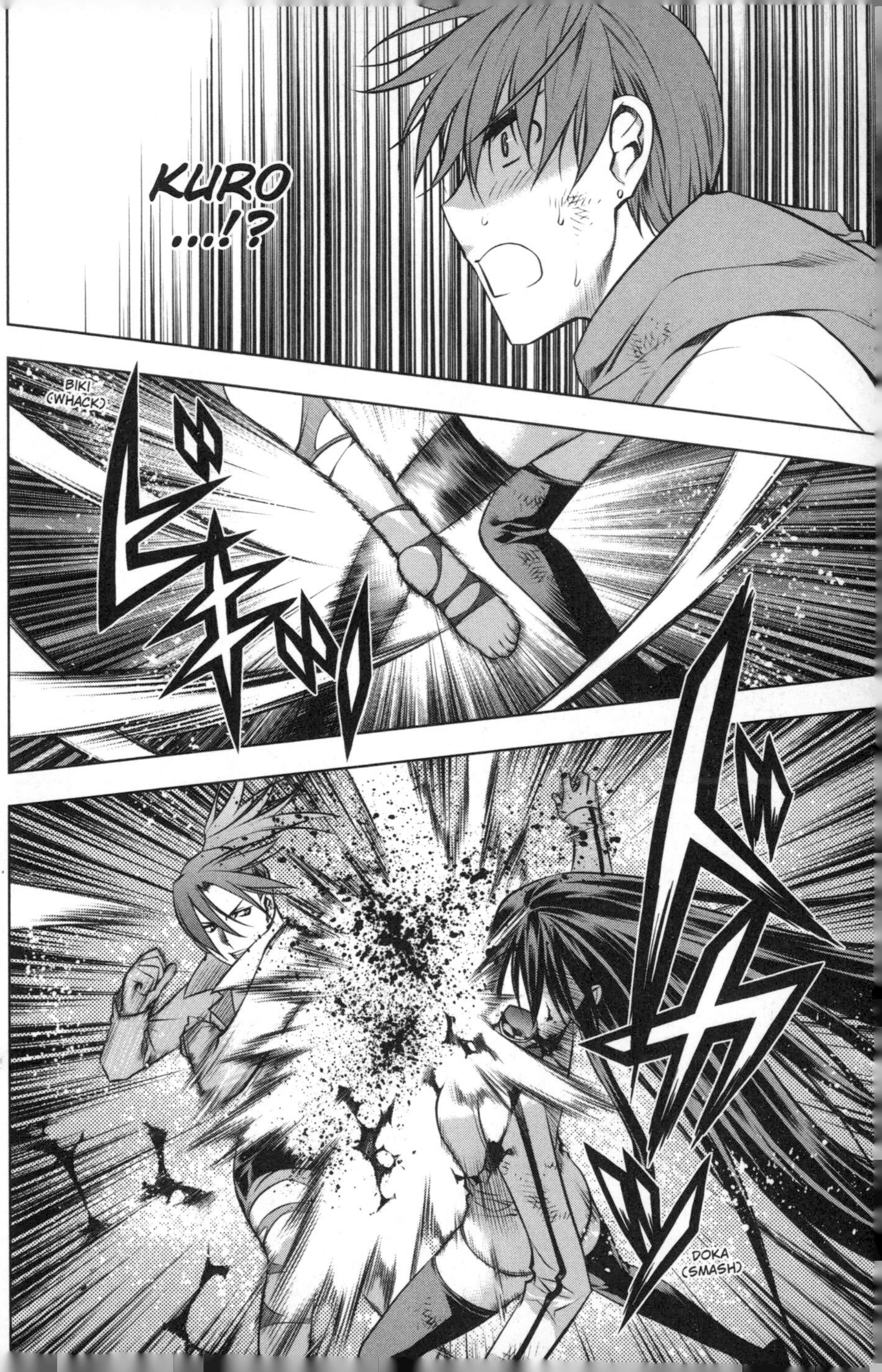
KURO ...!?
BIKI (WHACK)
DOKA (SMASH)

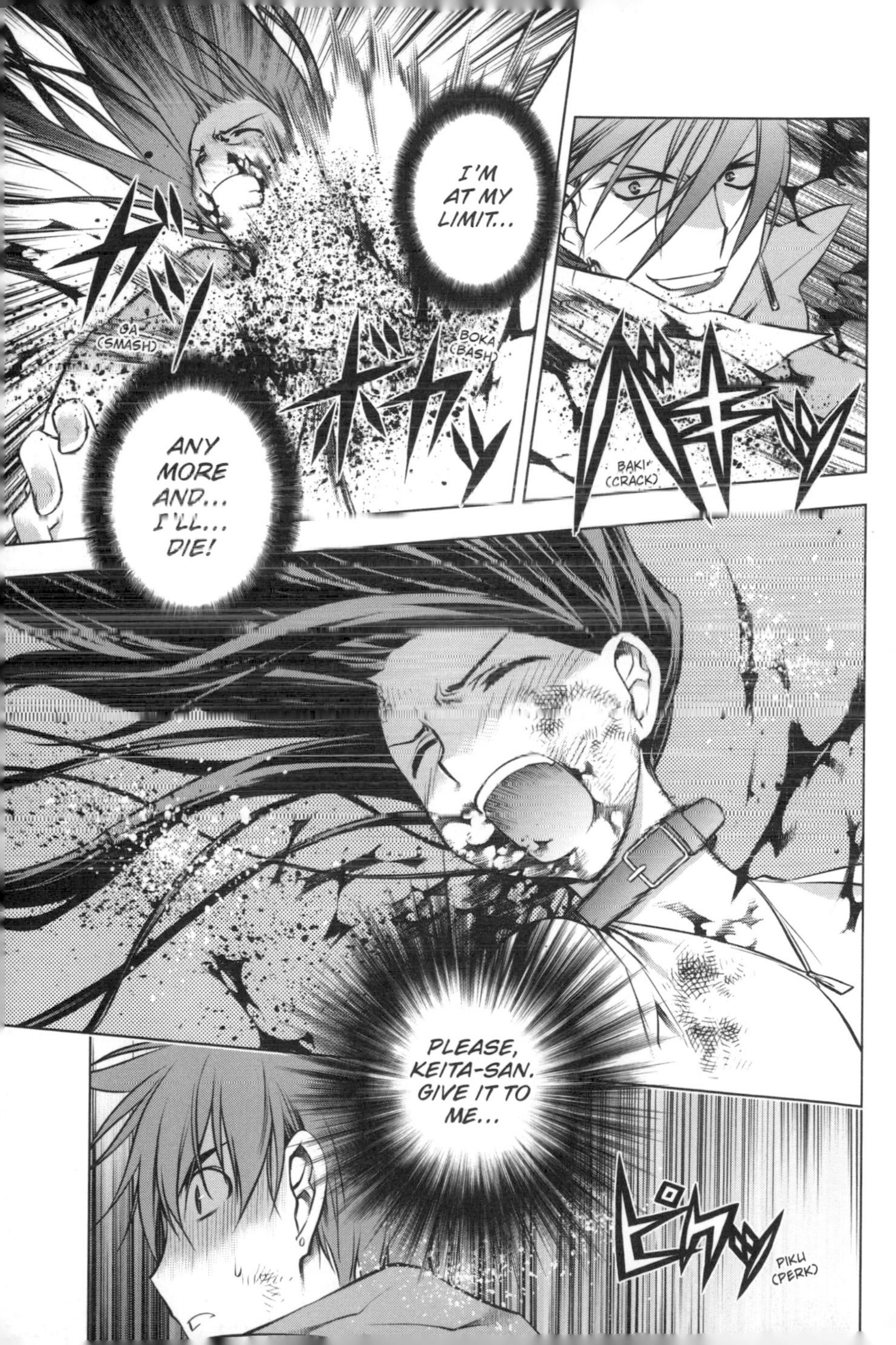
BAKI (CRACK)
I'M AT MY LIMIT...
BOKA (BASH)
GA (SMASH)
ANY MORE AND... I'LL... DIE!
PLEASE, KEITA-SAN. GIVE IT TO ME...
PIKU (PERK)

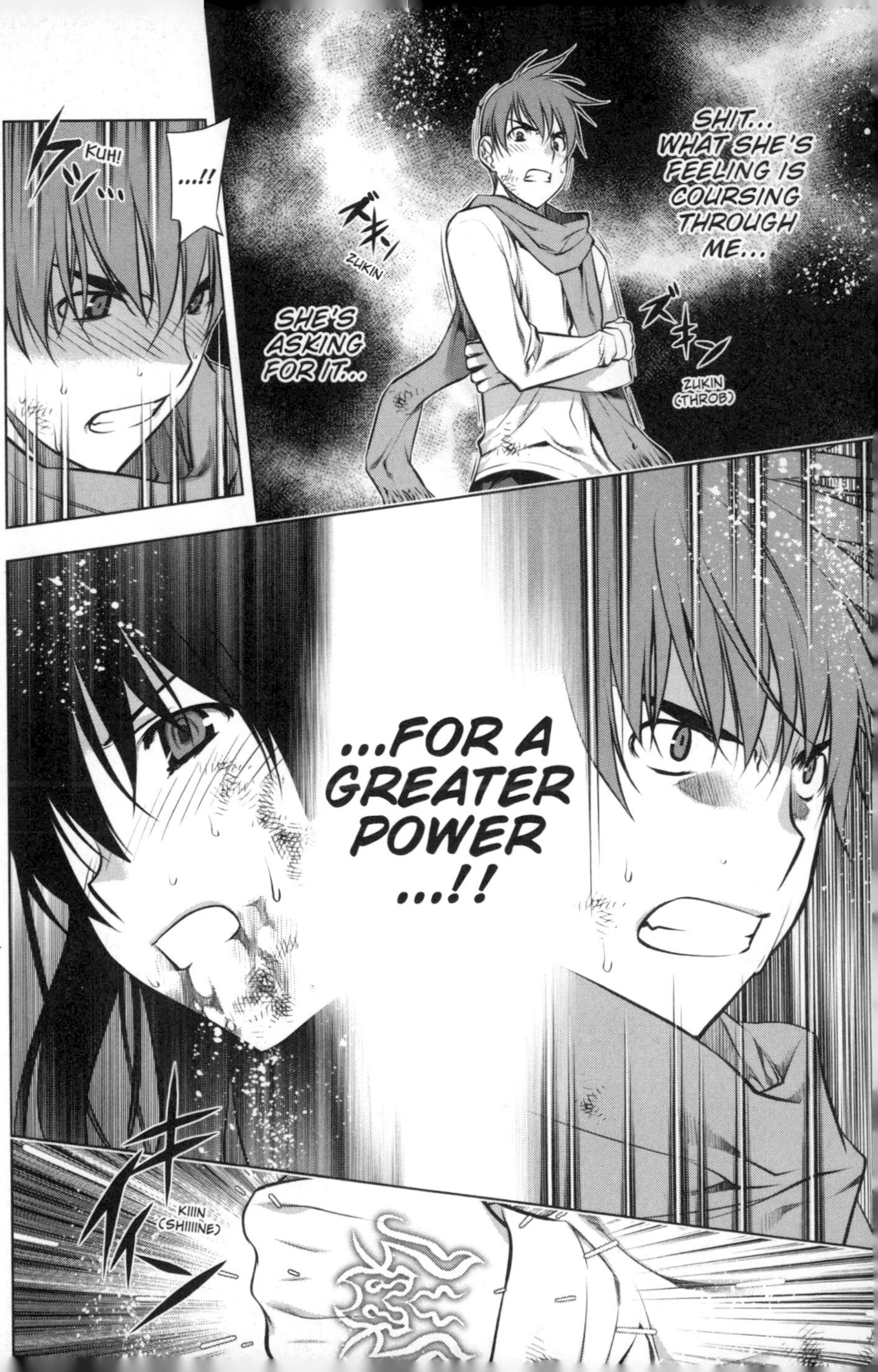
SHIT... WHAT SHE'S FEELING IS COURSING THROUGH ME...
ZUKIN
SHE'S ASKING FOR IT...
ZUKIN (THROB)
...!!
KUH!
...FOR A GREATER POWER ...!!
KIIN (SHIIIINE)

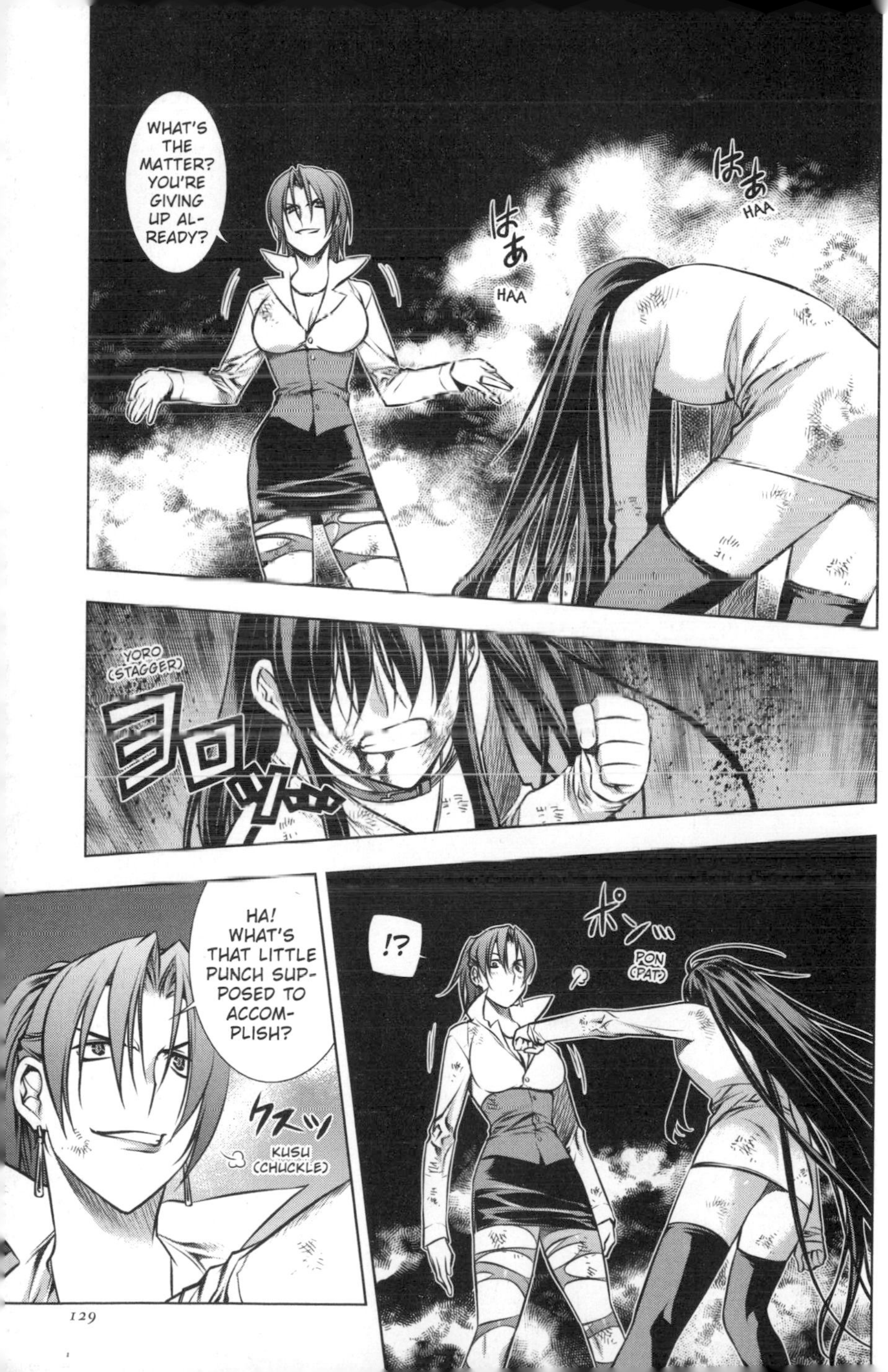
はぁ
HAA
はぁ
HAA
WHAT'S THE MATTER? YOU'RE GIVING UP AL-READY?
ヨロッ
YORO (STAGGER)
ポンッ
PON (PAT)
!?
HA! WHAT'S THAT LITTLE PUNCH SUP-POSED TO ACCOM-PLISH?
クスッ
KUSU (CHUCKLE)

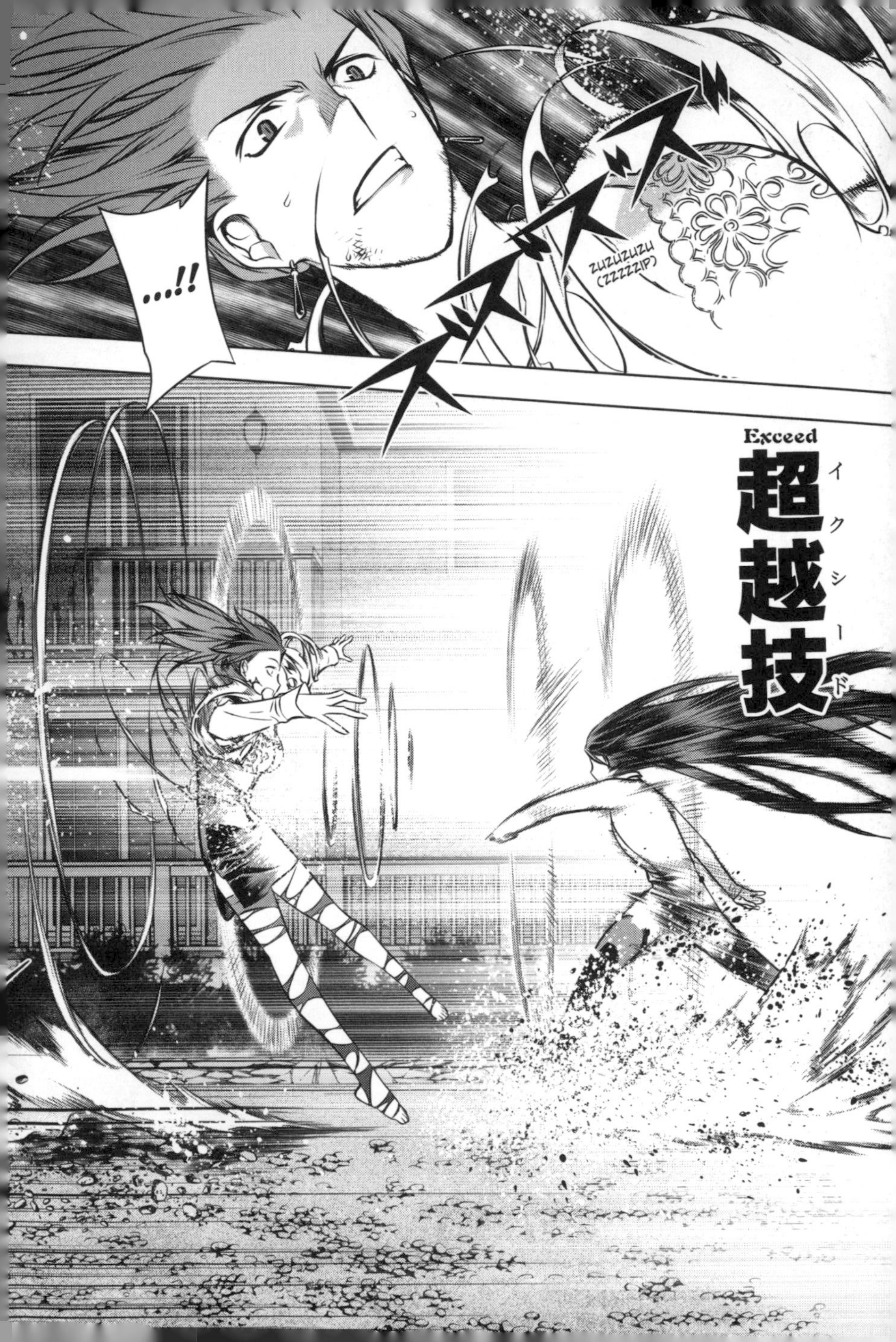
ZUZUZUZU (ZZZZZIP)
...!!
Exceed
超越技(イクシード)

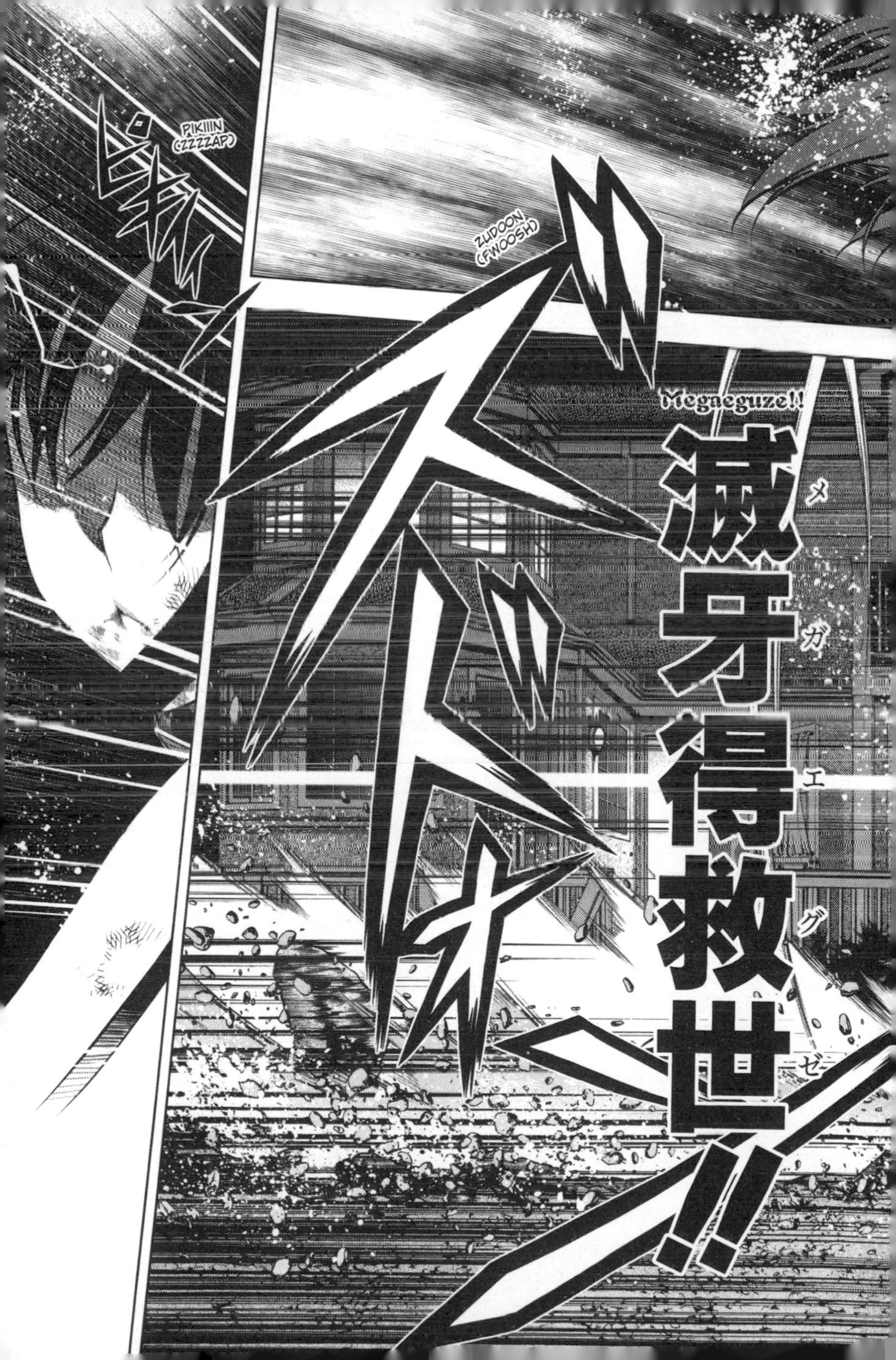

ZUDOON (FWOOSH)
Megaeguze!!
滅牙得救世!!
メガエグゼ
PIKIIIN (ZZZZAP)

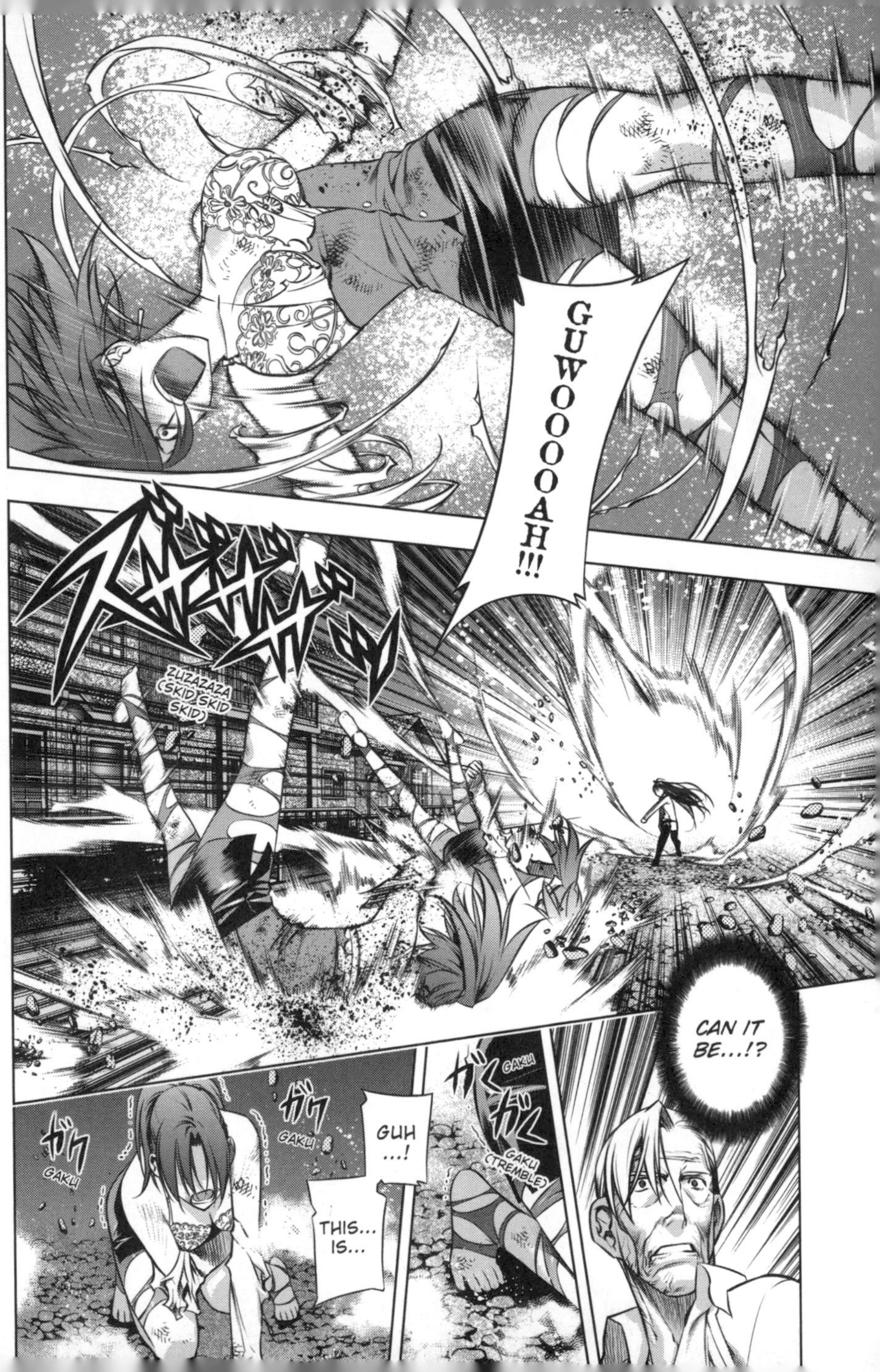
GUWOOOOOAH!!!
ZUZAZAZA (SKID SKID SKID)
CAN IT BE...!?
GAKU
GAKU (TREMBLE)
GUH ...!
THIS... IS...
GAKU
GAKU

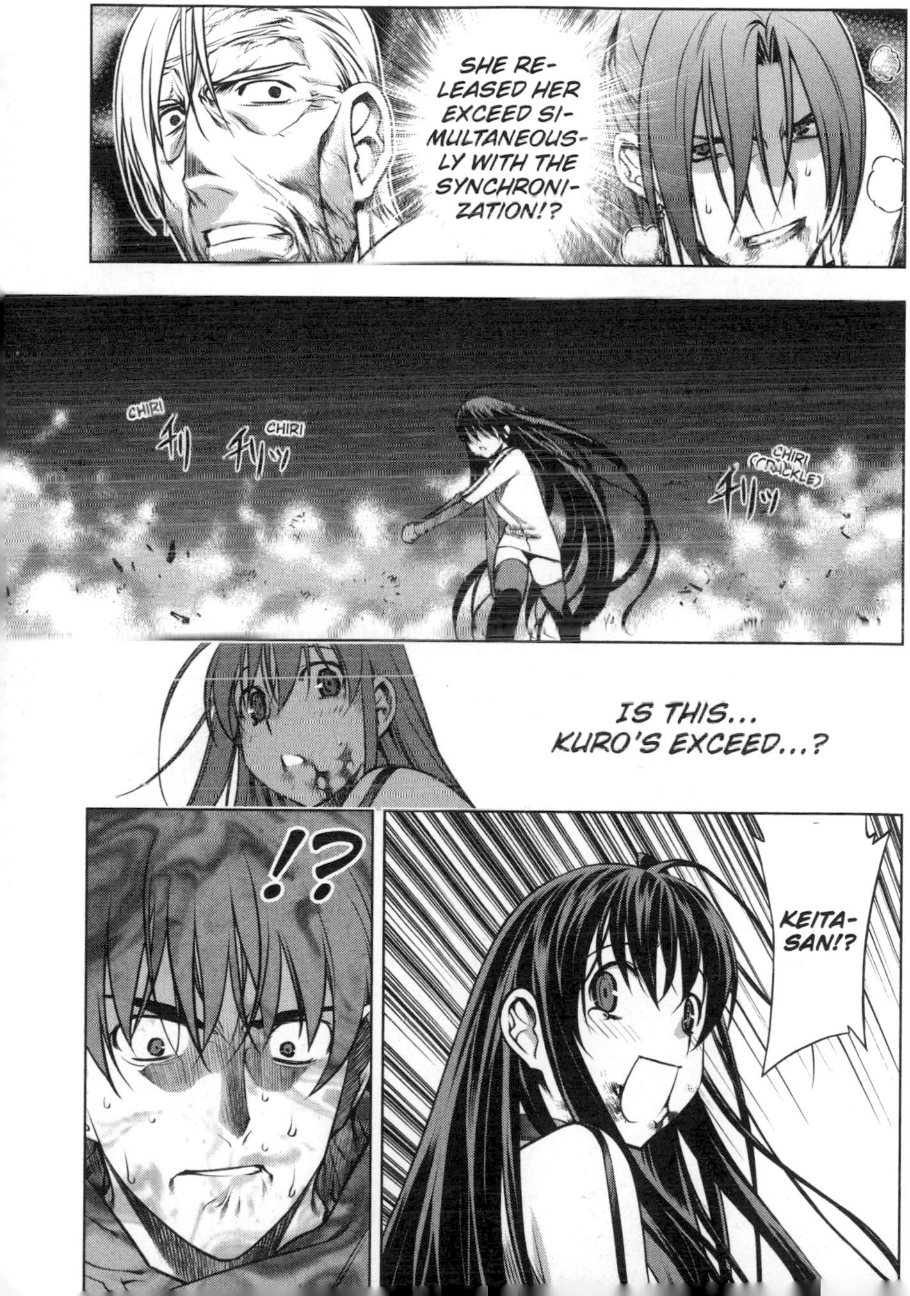
SHE RE-LEASED HER EXCEED SI-MULTANEOUS-LY WITH THE SYNCHRONI-ZATION!?
CHIRI (CRACKLE)
CHIRI
CHIRI
IS THIS... KURO'S EXCEED...?
KEITA-SAN!?
!?

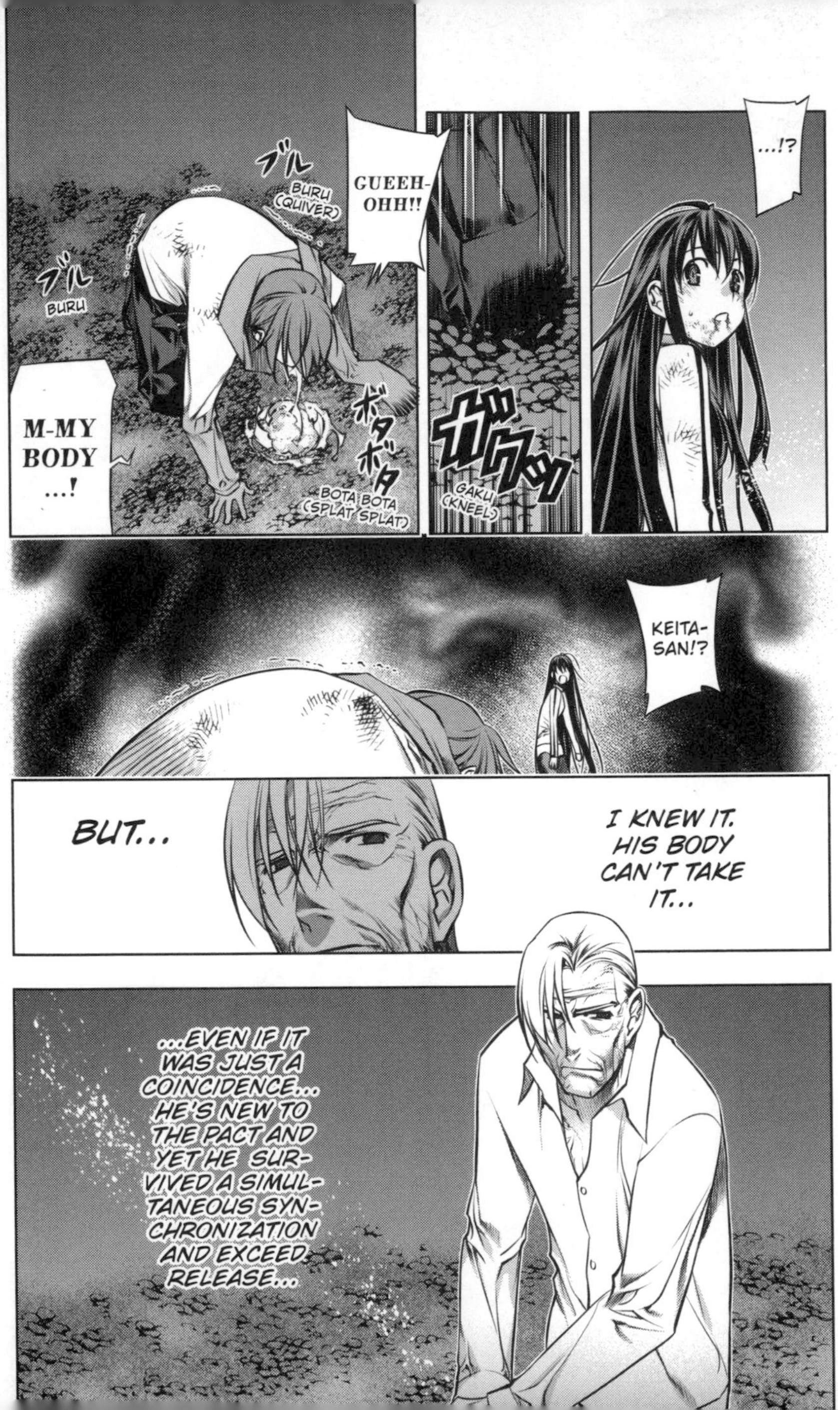
...!?
ガクッ
GAKU (KNEEL)
GUEEH-OHH!!
ブル
BURU (QUIVER)
ブル
BURU
ボタボタ
BOTA BOTA (SPLAT SPLAT)
M-MY BODY ...!
KEITA-SAN!?
I KNEW IT. HIS BODY CAN'T TAKE IT...
BUT...
...EVEN IF IT WAS JUST A COINCIDENCE... HE'S NEW TO THE PACT AND YET HE SURVIVED A SIMULTANEOUS SYNCHRONIZATION AND EXCEED RELEASE...

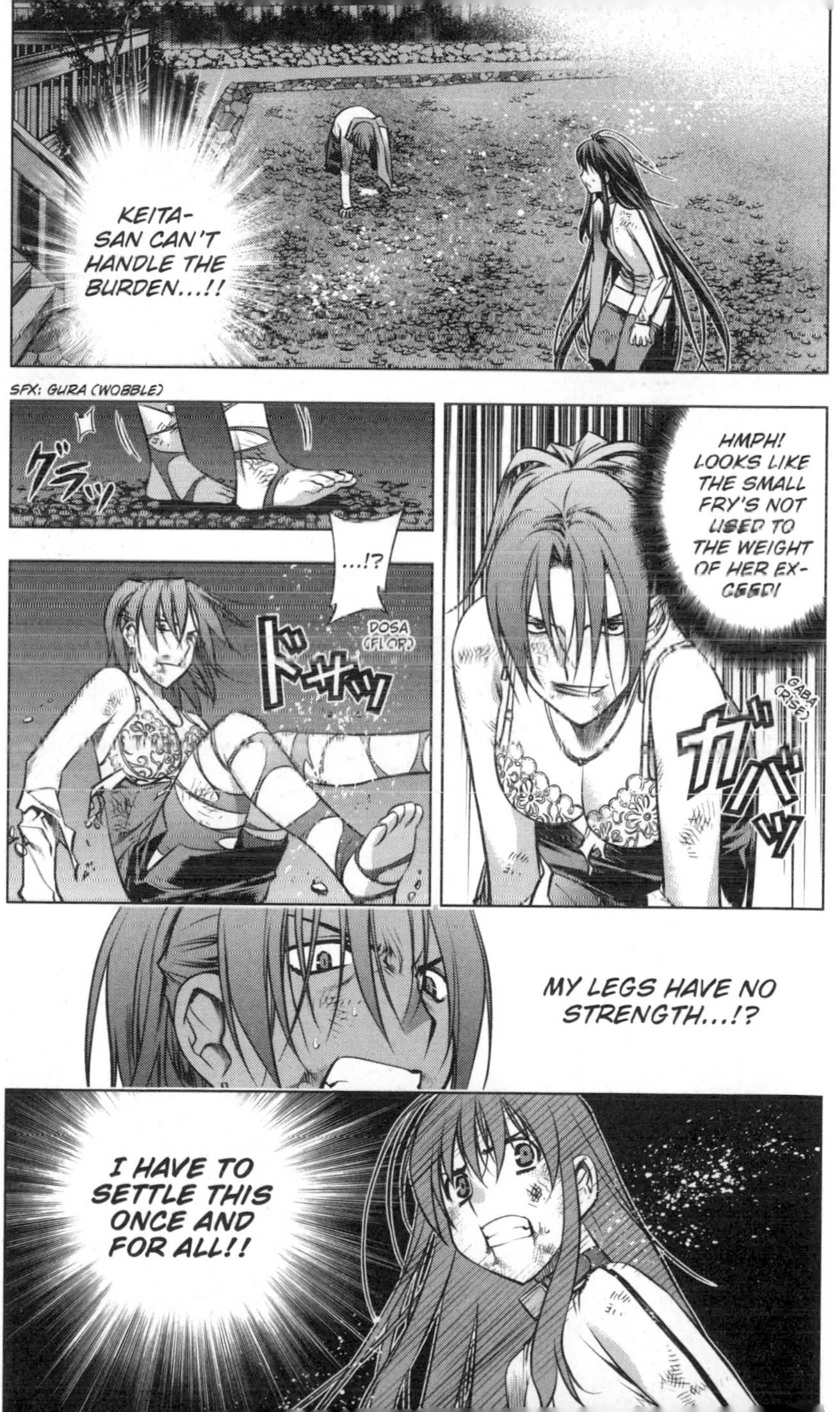
KEITA-SAN CAN'T HANDLE THE BURDEN...!!
SFX: GURA (WOBBLE)
HMPH! LOOKS LIKE THE SMALL FRY'S NOT USED TO THE WEIGHT OF HER EXCEED!
GABA (RISE)
ガバッ
グラッ
...!?
DOSA (FLOOR)
ドサッ
MY LEGS HAVE NO STRENGTH...!?
I HAVE TO SETTLE THIS ONCE AND FOR ALL!!

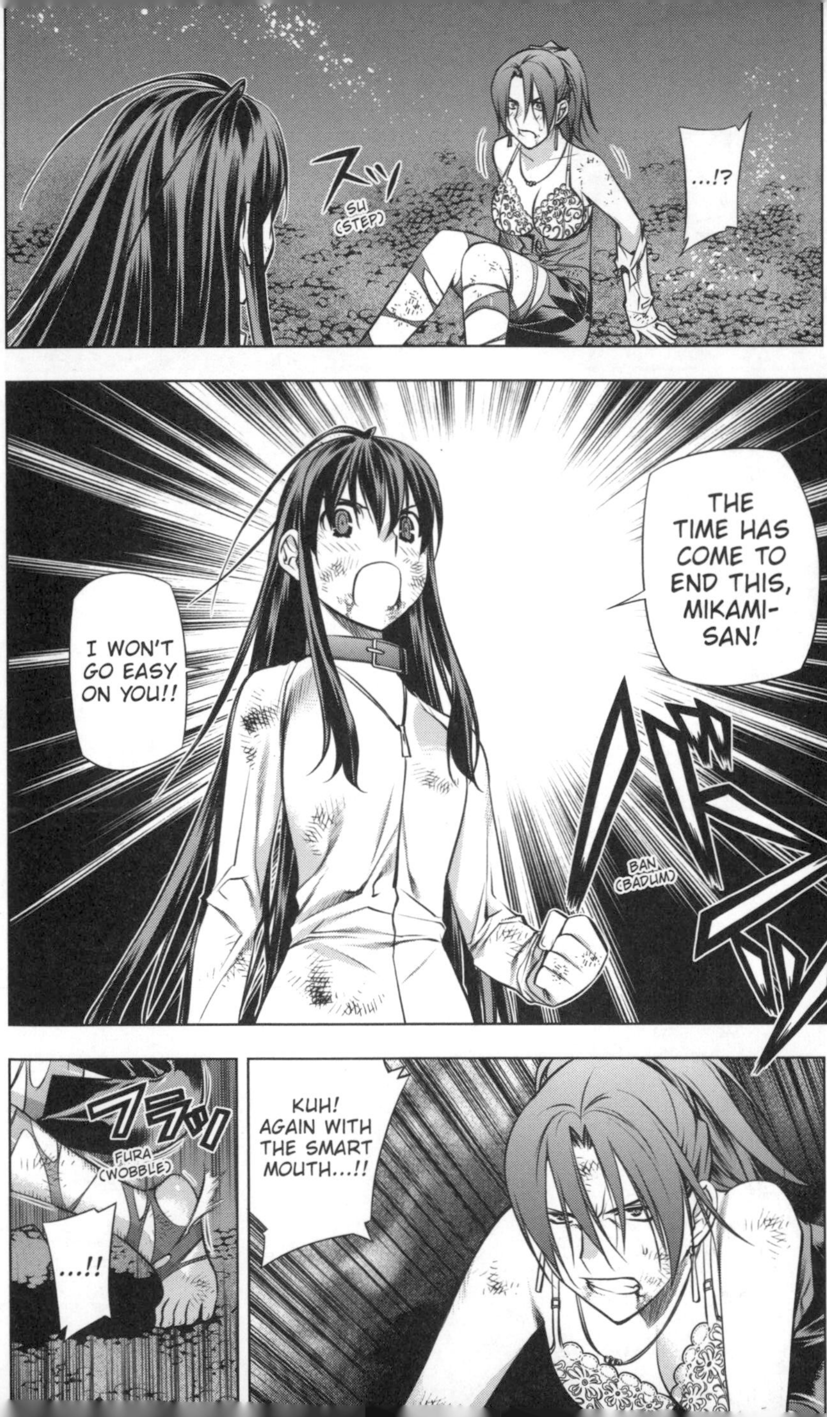
...!?
SU (STEP)
THE TIME HAS COME TO END THIS, MIKAMI-SAN!
BAN (BADUM)
I WON'T GO EASY ON YOU!!
KUH! AGAIN WITH THE SMART MOUTH...!!
FURA (WOBBLE)
...!!

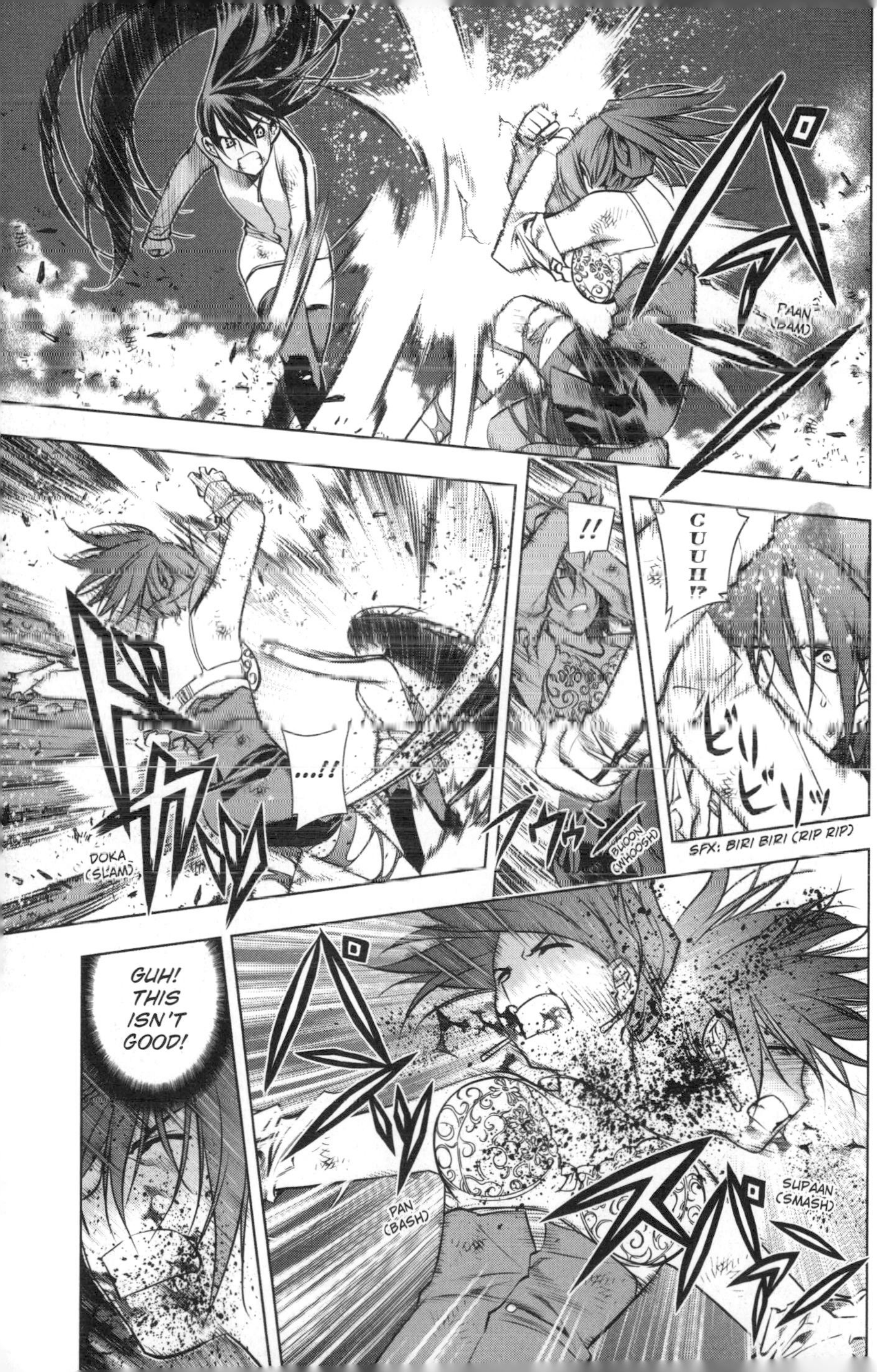
PAAN (BAM)
GUUH!?
SFX: BIRI BIRI (RIP RIP)
!!
BUOON (WHOOSH)
...!!
DOKA (SLAM)
SUPAAN (SMASH)
PAN (BASH)
GUH! THIS ISN'T GOOD!

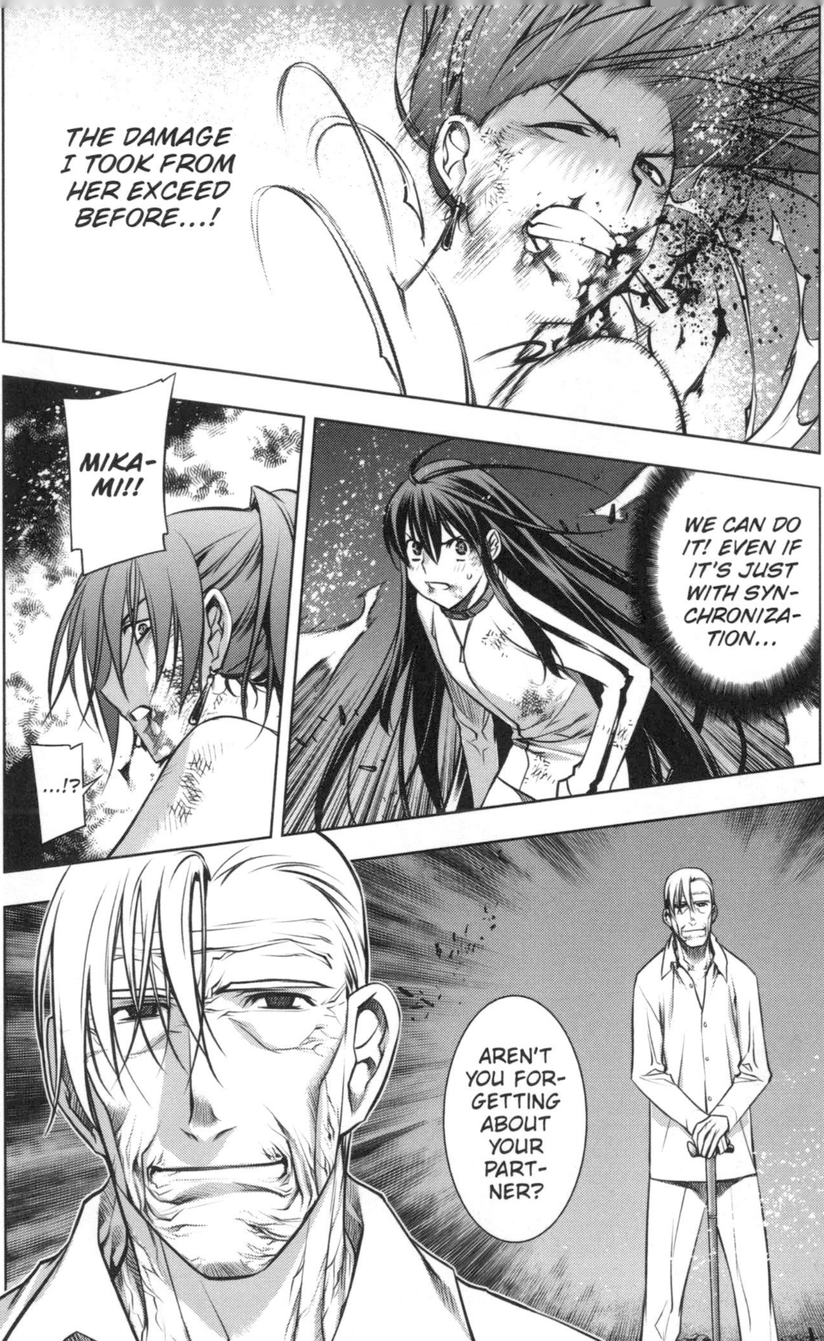
THE DAMAGE I TOOK FROM HER EXCEED BEFORE...!
WE CAN DO IT! EVEN IF IT'S JUST WITH SYN-CHRONIZA-TION...
MIKA-MI!!
...!?
AREN'T YOU FOR-GETTING ABOUT YOUR PART-NER?

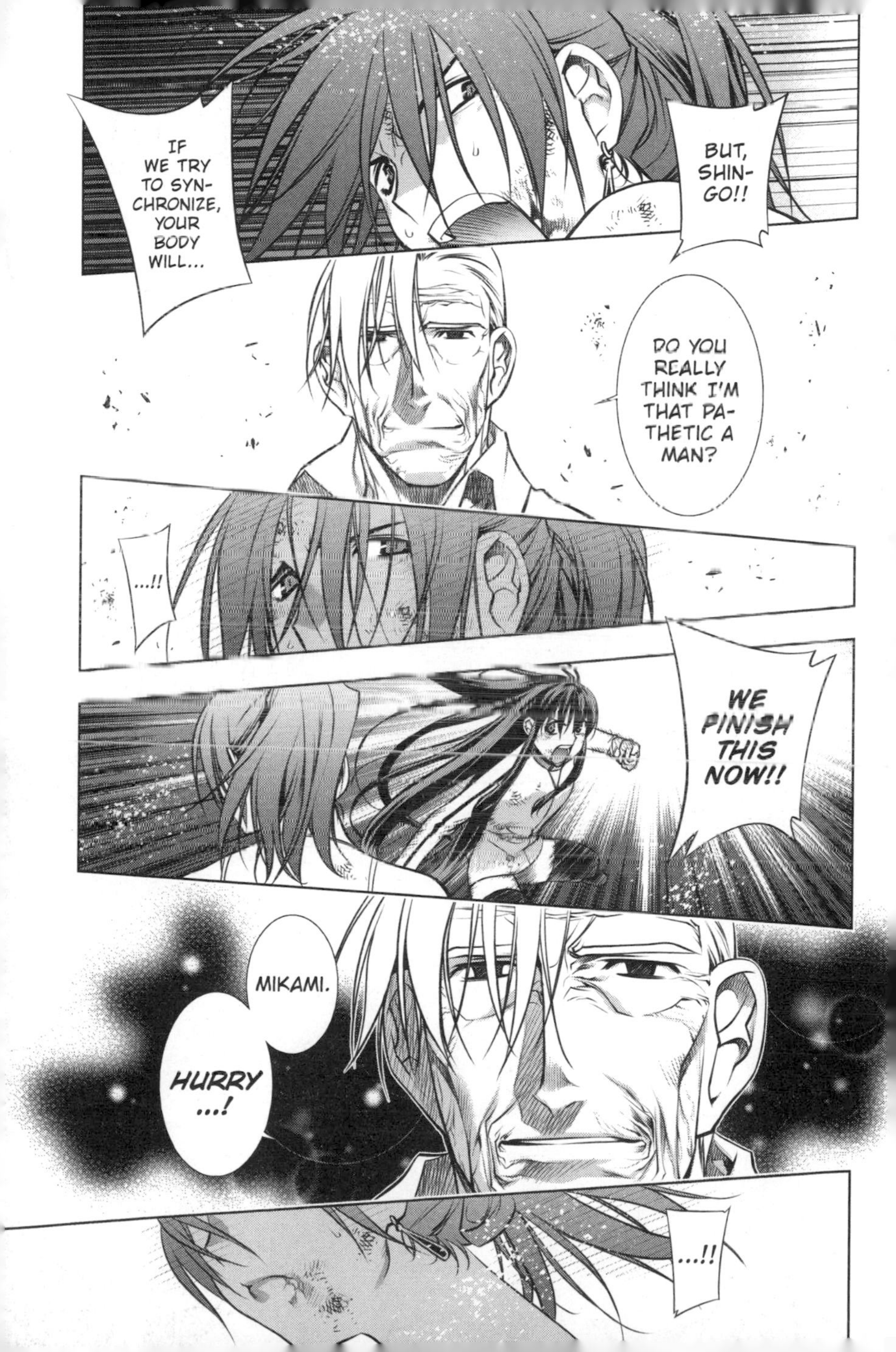
BUT, SHIN-GO!!
IF WE TRY TO SYN-CHRONIZE, YOUR BODY WILL...
DO YOU REALLY THINK I'M THAT PA-THETIC A MAN?
...!!
WE PINISH THIS NOW!!
MIKAMI.
HURRY ...!
...!!

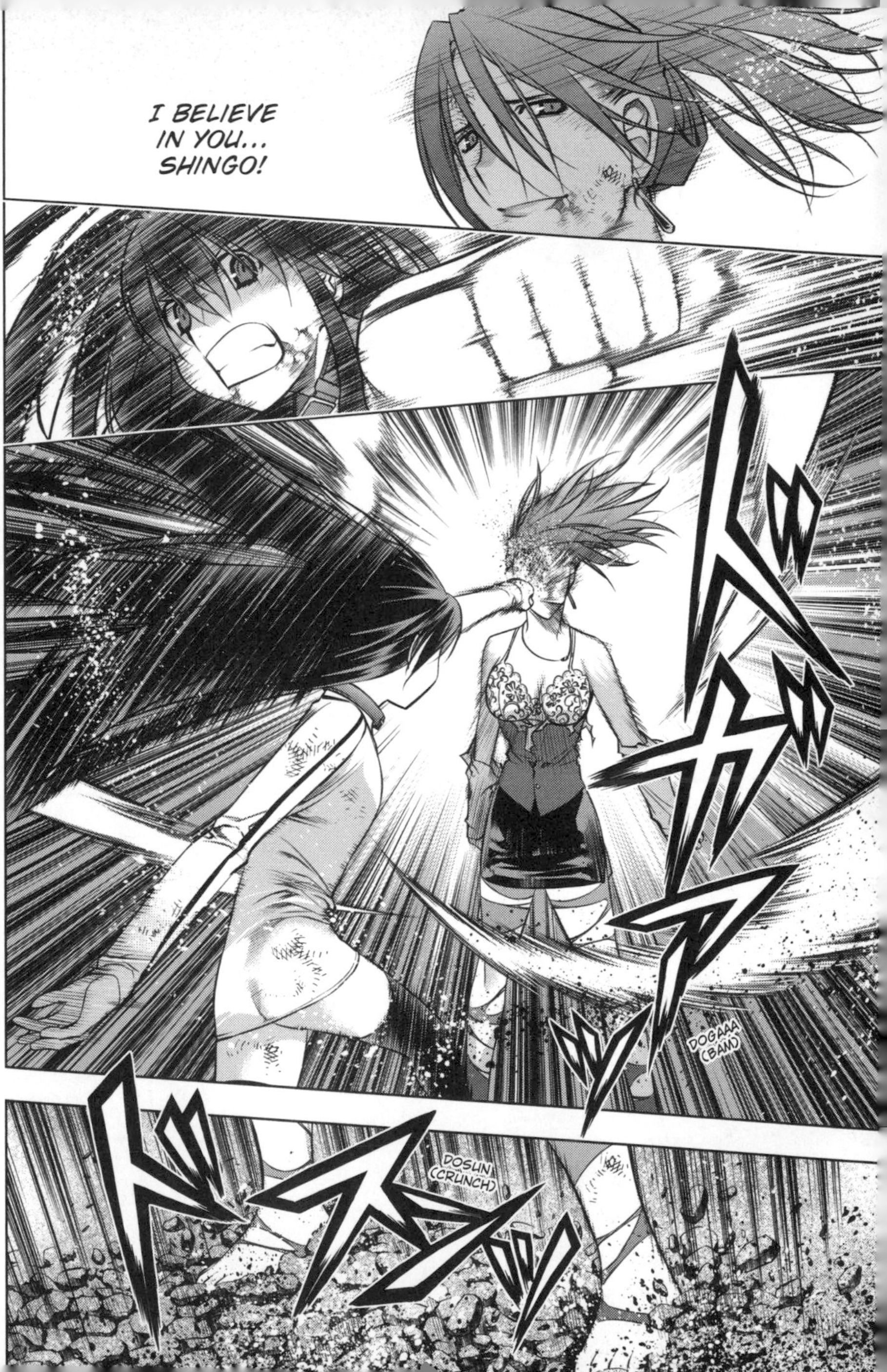
I BELIEVE IN YOU... SHINGO!
DOGAAA (BAN)
DOSUN (CRUNCH)

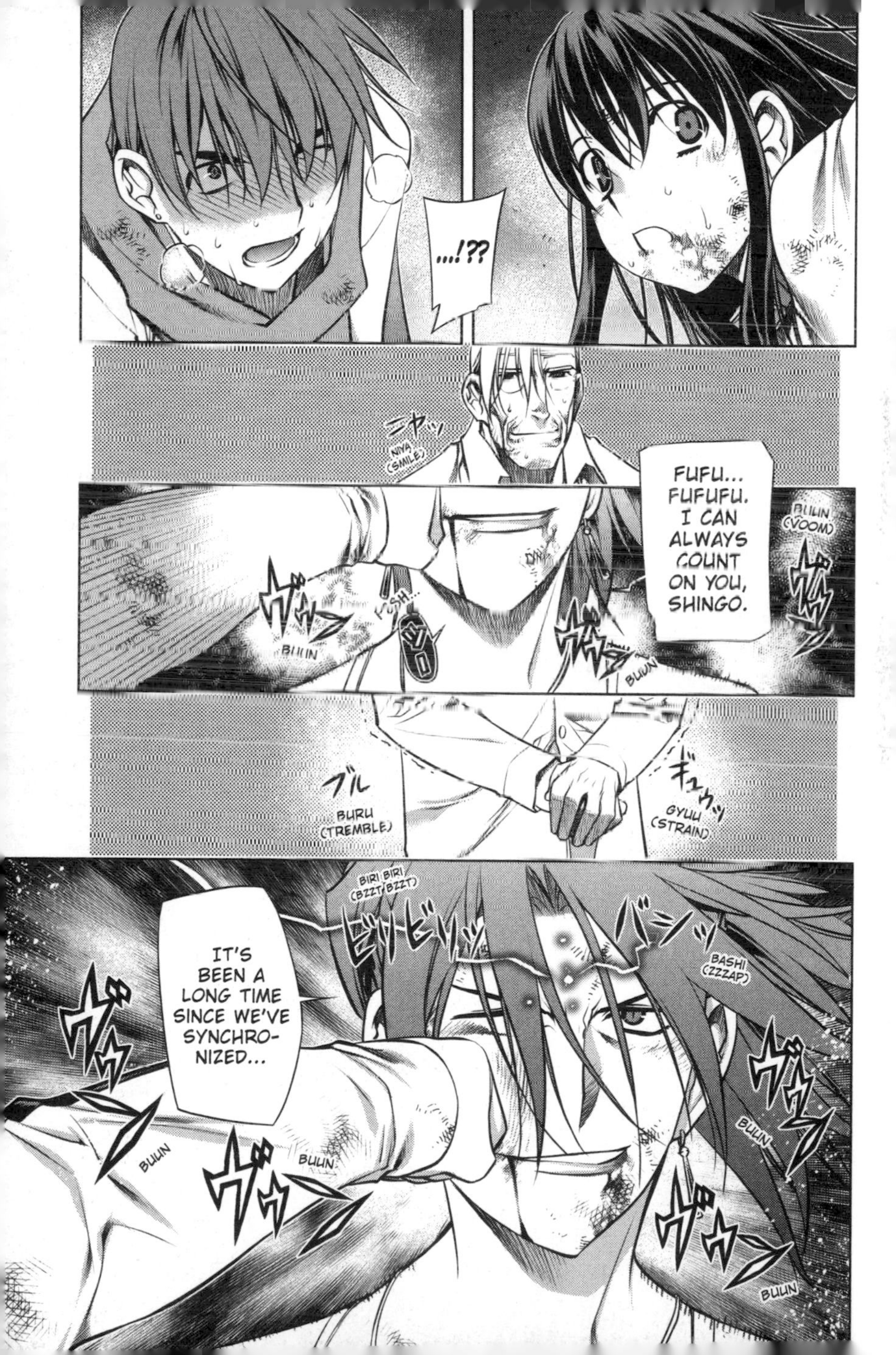
...!??
ニヤッ
NIYA (SMILE)
FUFU... FUFUFU. I CAN ALWAYS COUNT ON YOU, SHINGO.
BUUN (VOOM)
BUUN
PSH...
BUUN
GYUU (STRAIN)
ブル
BURU (TREMBLE)
BASHI (ZZZAP)
BIRI BIRI (BZZT BZZT)
IT'S BEEN A LONG TIME SINCE WE'VE SYNCHRO-NIZED...
BUUN
BUUN
BUUN
BUUN

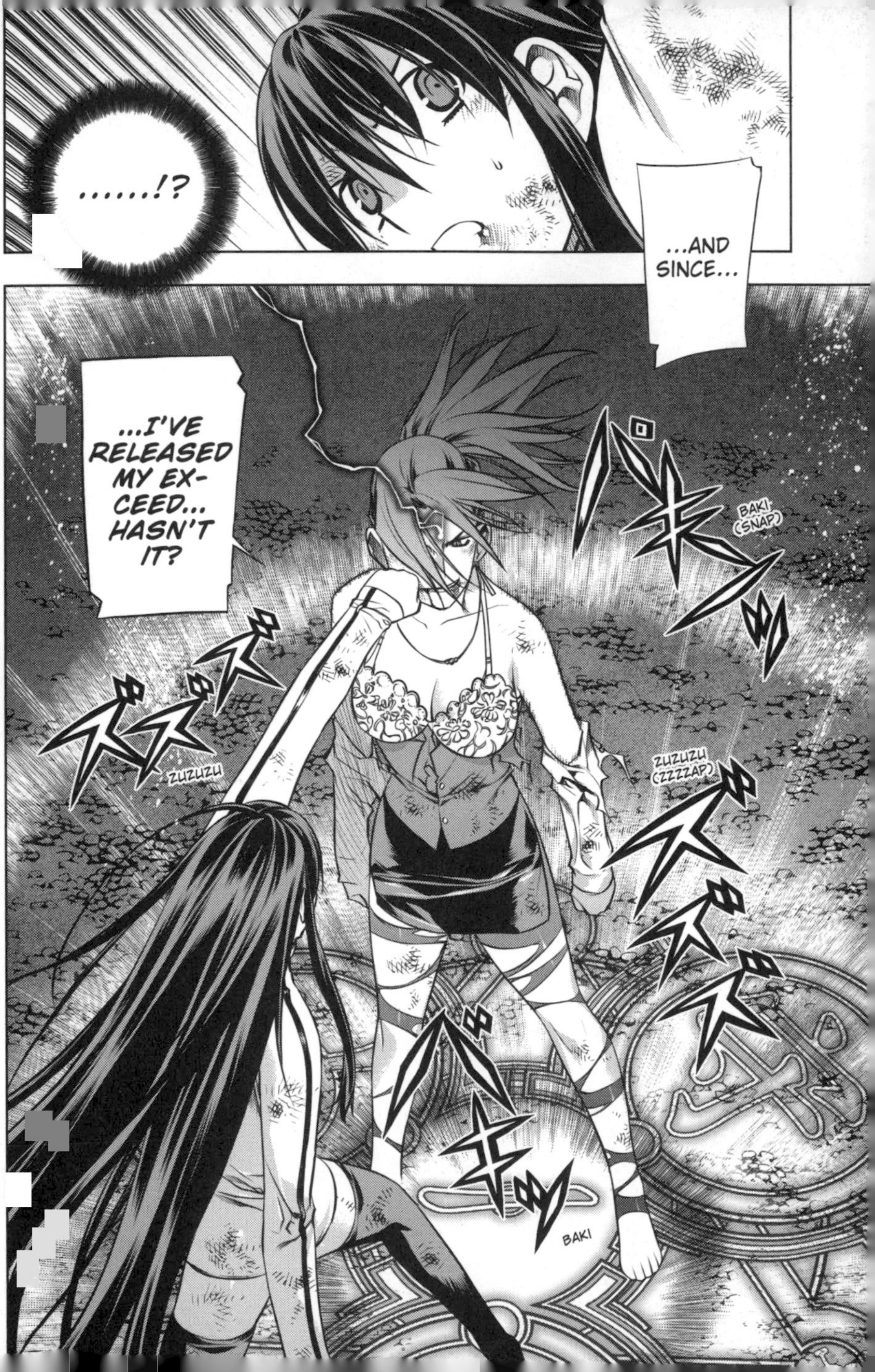
......!?
...AND SINCE...
...I'VE RELEASED MY EX-CEED... HASN'T IT?
BAKI (SNAP)
ZUZUZU (ZZZZAP)
ZUZUZU
BAKI

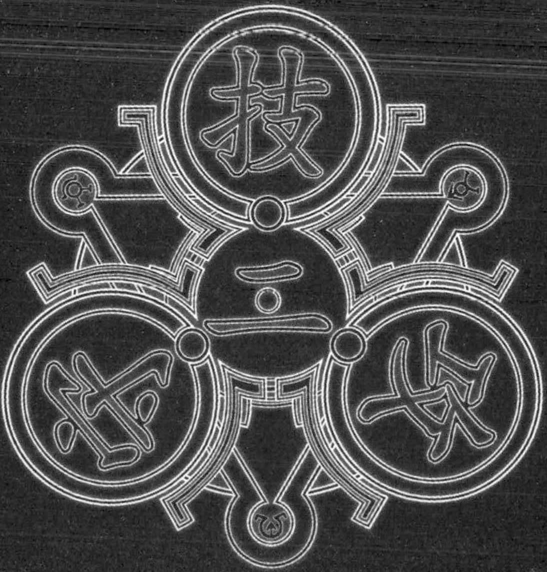
技

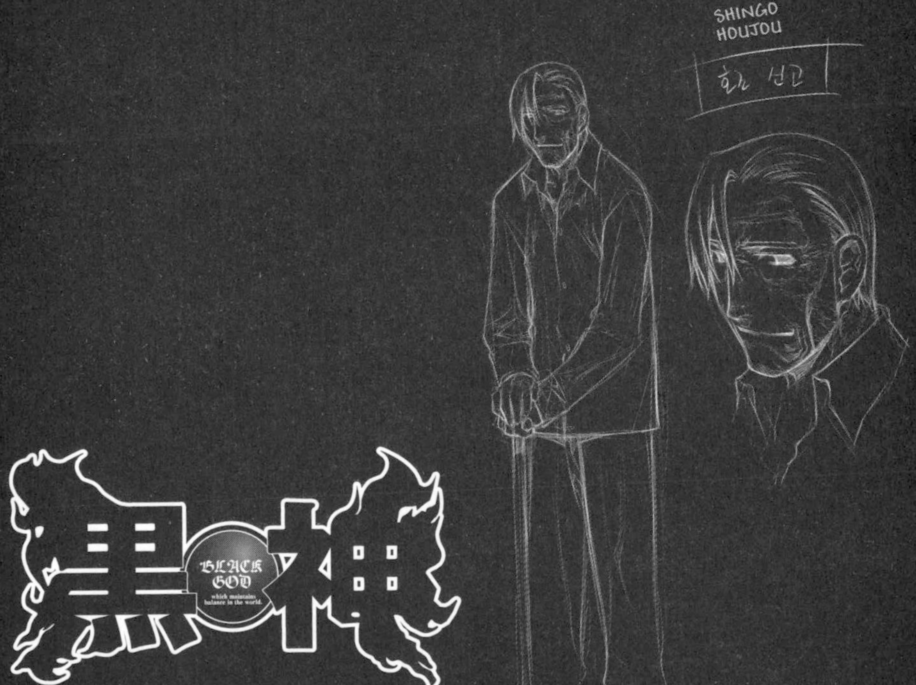
SHINGO
HOUJOU
BLACK
GOD
which maintains
balance in the world.

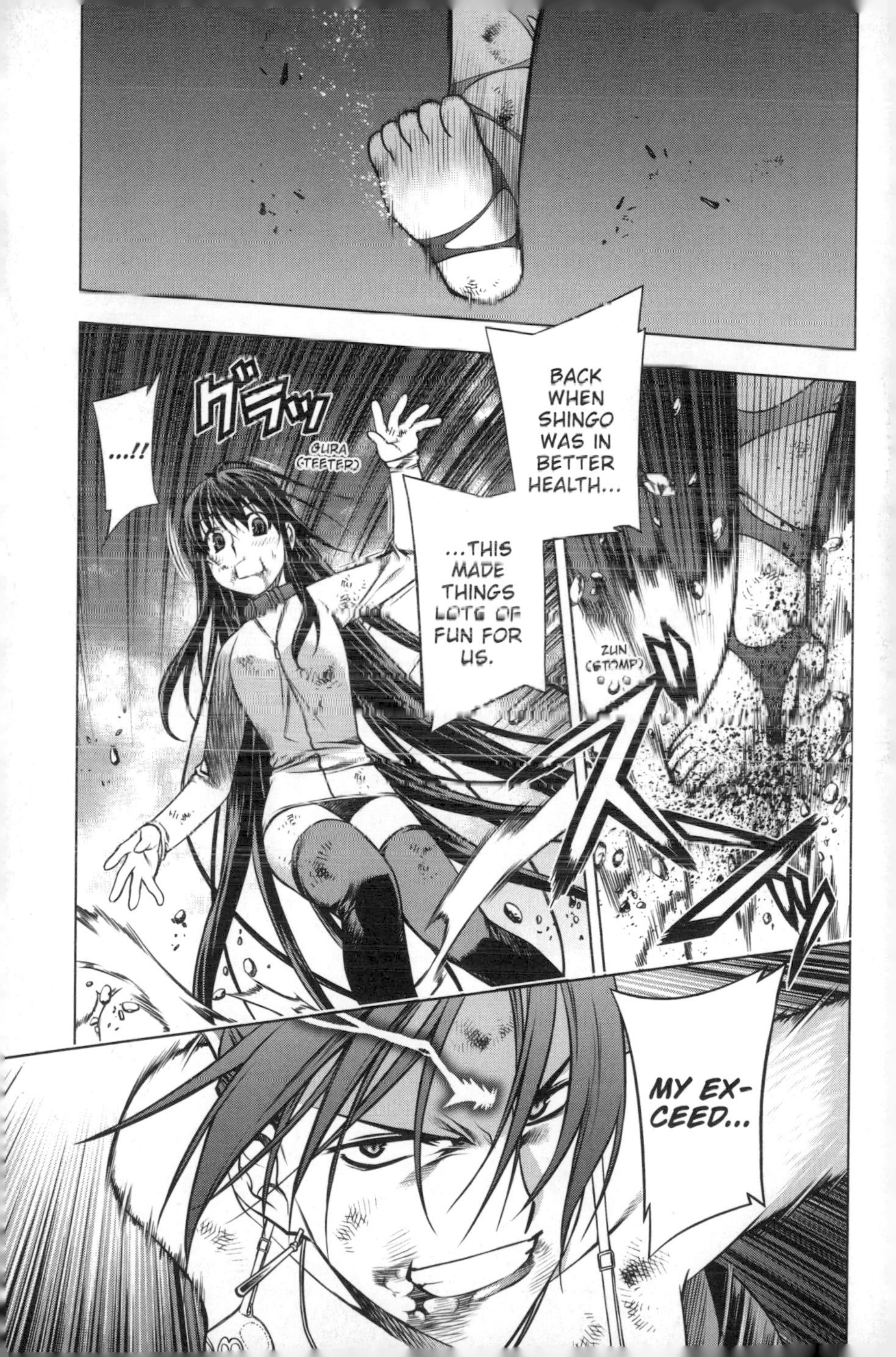
BACK WHEN SHINGO WAS IN BETTER HEALTH...
...THIS MADE THINGS LOTS OF FUN FOR US.
ZUN (STOMP)
グラッ
GURA (TEETER)
...!!
MY EX-CEED...

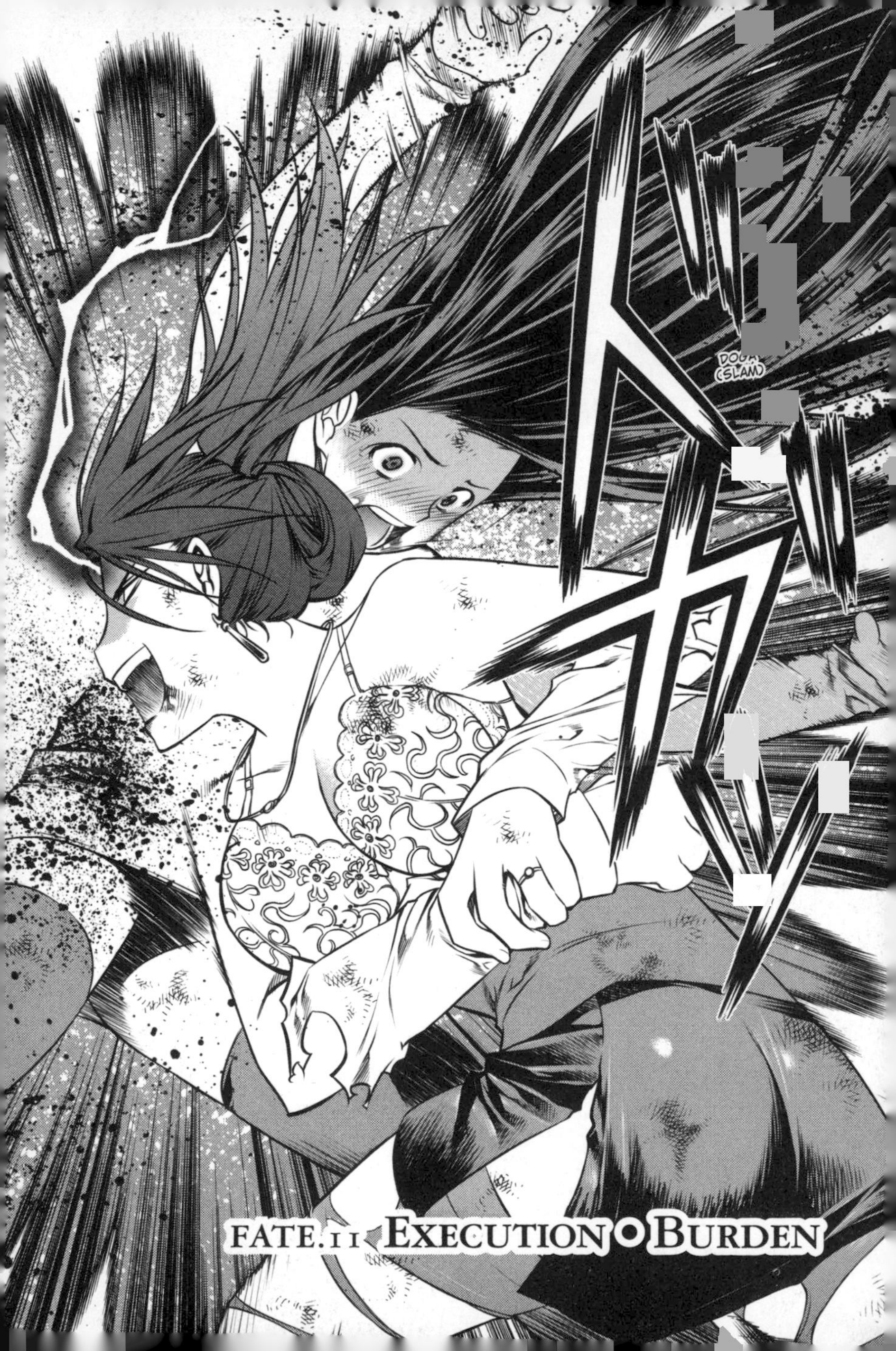
DOGA (SLAM)
FATE.11 EXECUTION • BURDEN

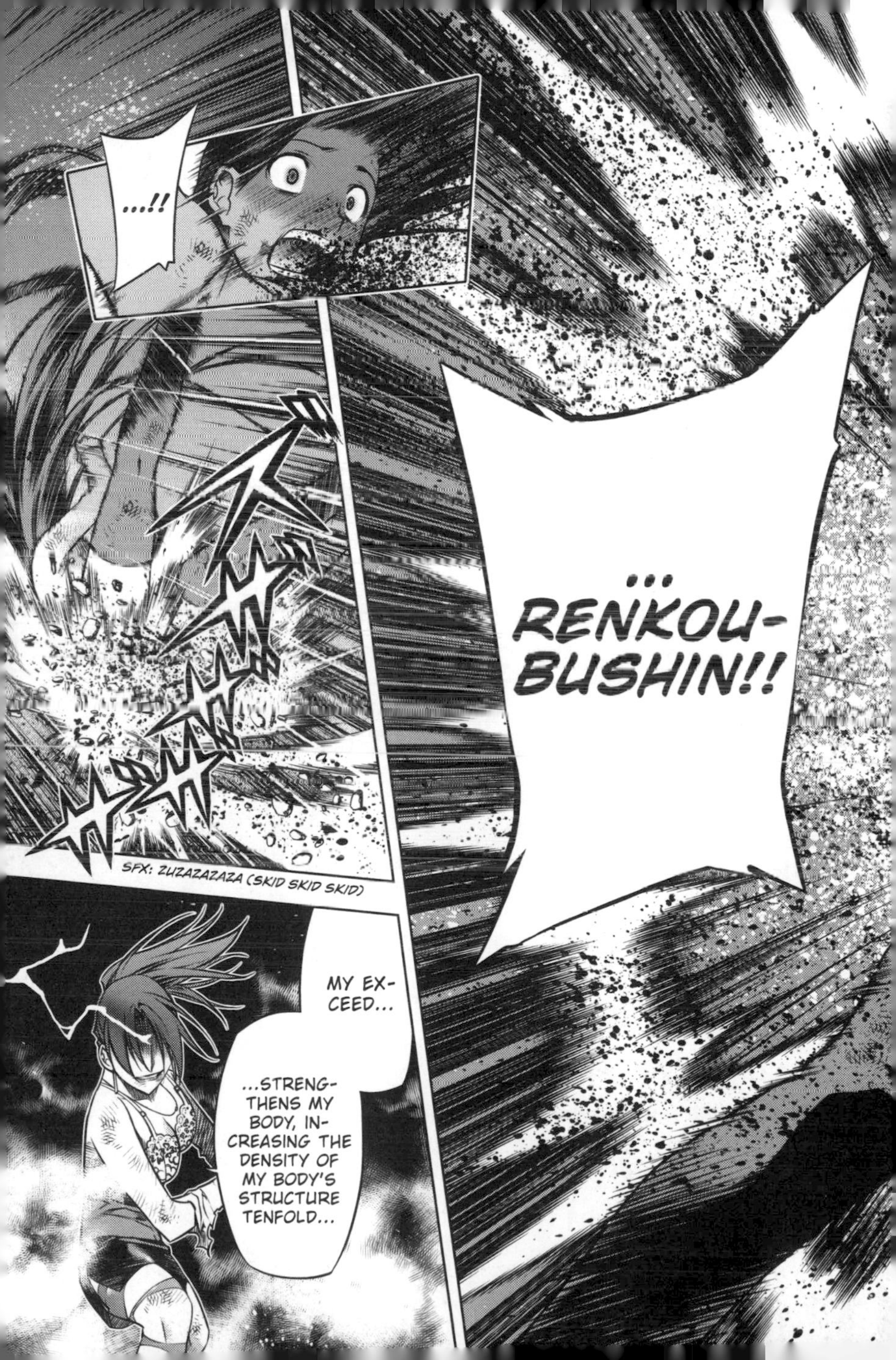
...RENKOU-BUSHIN!!
...!!
SFX: ZUZAZAZAZA (SKID SKID SKID)
MY EX-CEED...
...STRENG-THENS MY BODY, IN-CREASING THE DENSITY OF MY BODY'S STRUCTURE TENFOLD...

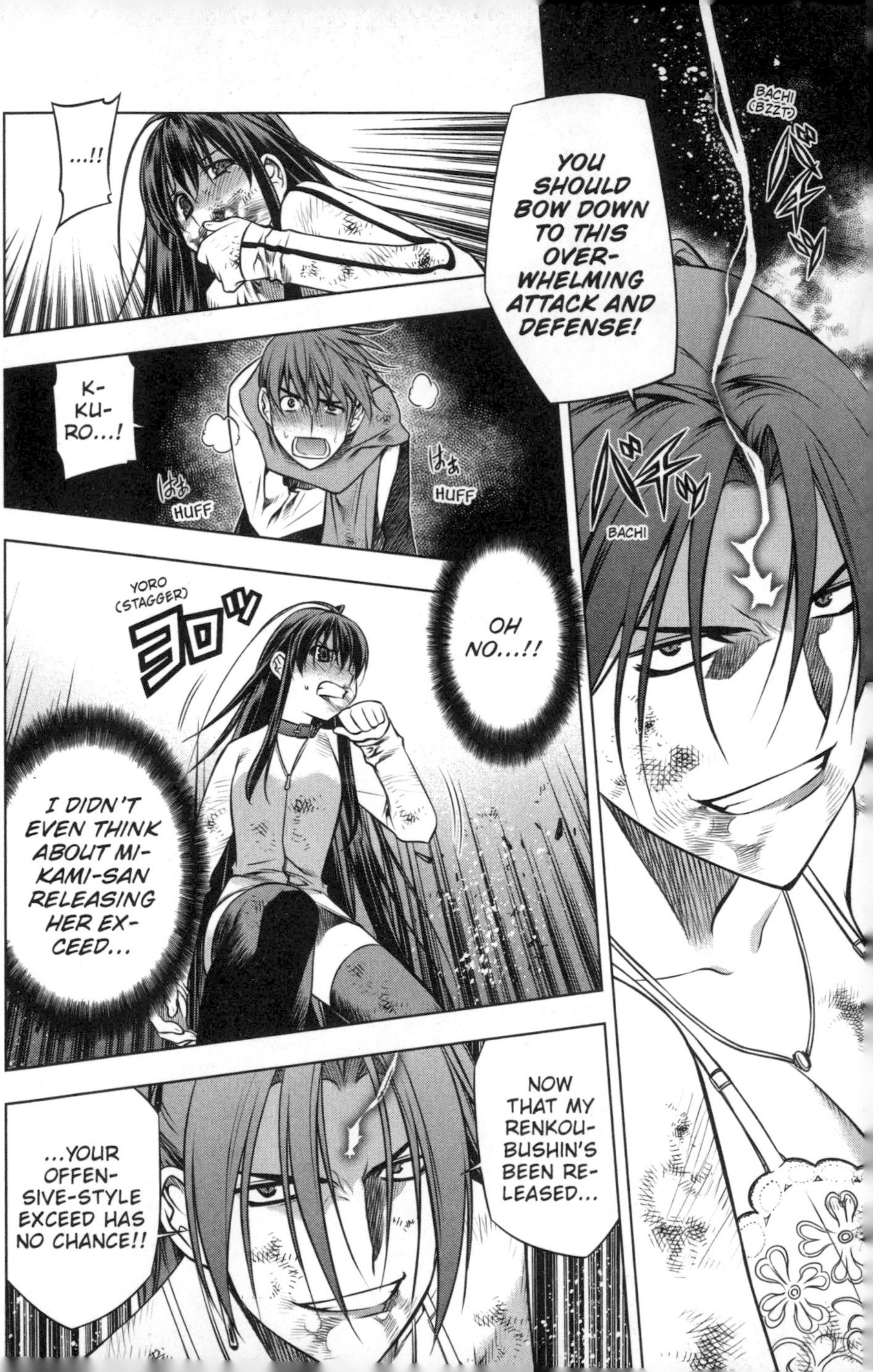
BACHI (BZZT)
YOU SHOULD BOW DOWN TO THIS OVER-WHELMING ATTACK AND DEFENSE!
BACHI
...!!
K-KU-RO...!
HUFF
HUFF
YORO (STAGGER)
OH NO...!!
I DIDN'T EVEN THINK ABOUT MI-KAMI-SAN RELEASING HER EX-CEED...
NOW THAT MY RENKOU-BUSHIN'S BEEN RE-LEASED...
...YOUR OFFEN-SIVE-STYLE EXCEED HAS NO CHANCE!!

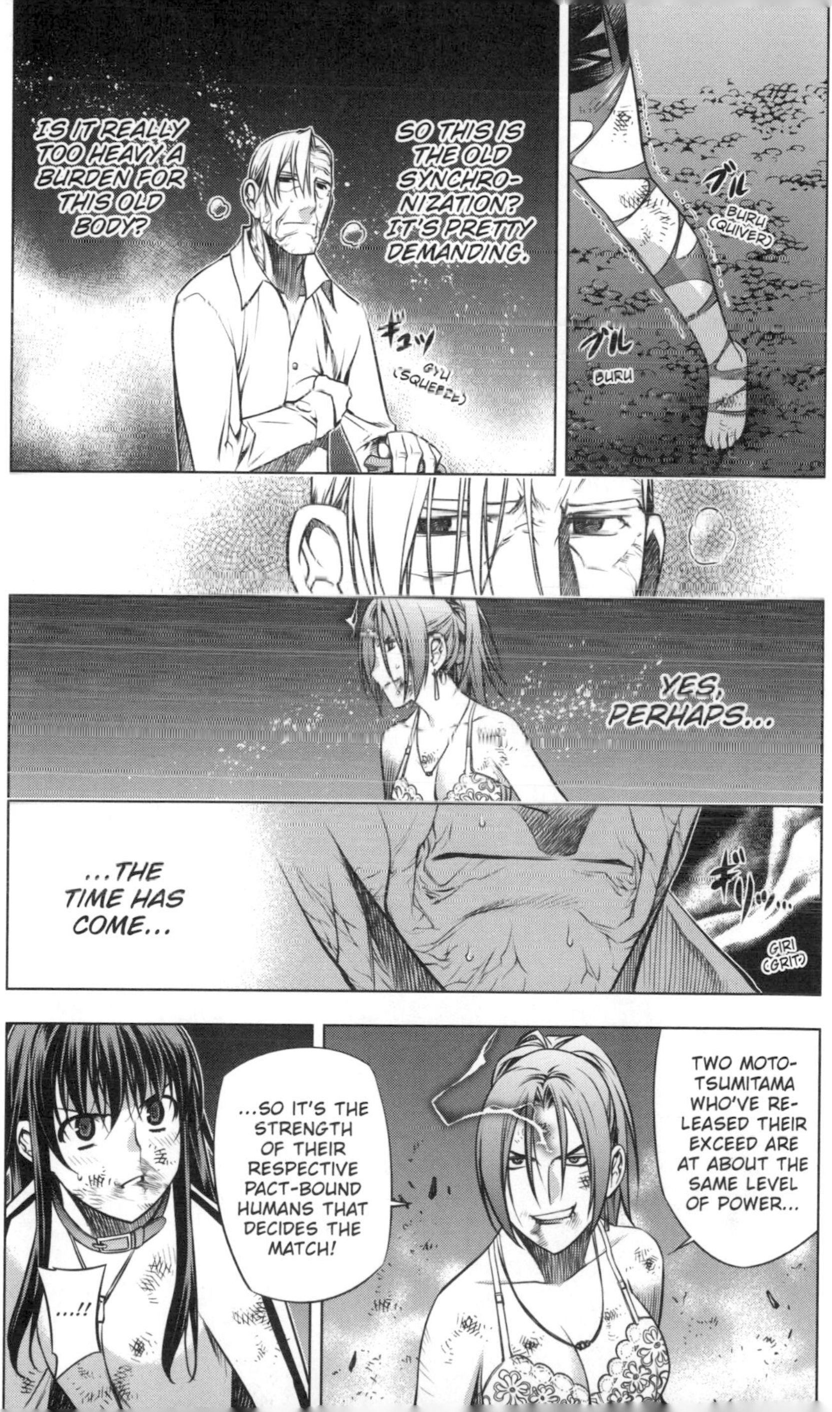
ブル
BURU (QUIVER)
ブル
BURU
SO THIS IS THE OLD SYNCHRONIZATION? IT'S PRETTY DEMANDING.
IS IT REALLY TOO HEAVY A BURDEN FOR THIS OLD BODY?
ギュッ
GYU (SQUEEZE)
YES, PERHAPS...
ギリッ…
GIRI (GRIT)
...THE TIME HAS COME...
TWO MOTO-TSUMITAMA WHO'VE RELEASED THEIR EXCEED ARE AT ABOUT THE SAME LEVEL OF POWER...
...SO IT'S THE STRENGTH OF THEIR RESPECTIVE PACT-BOUND HUMANS THAT DECIDES THE MATCH!
...!!

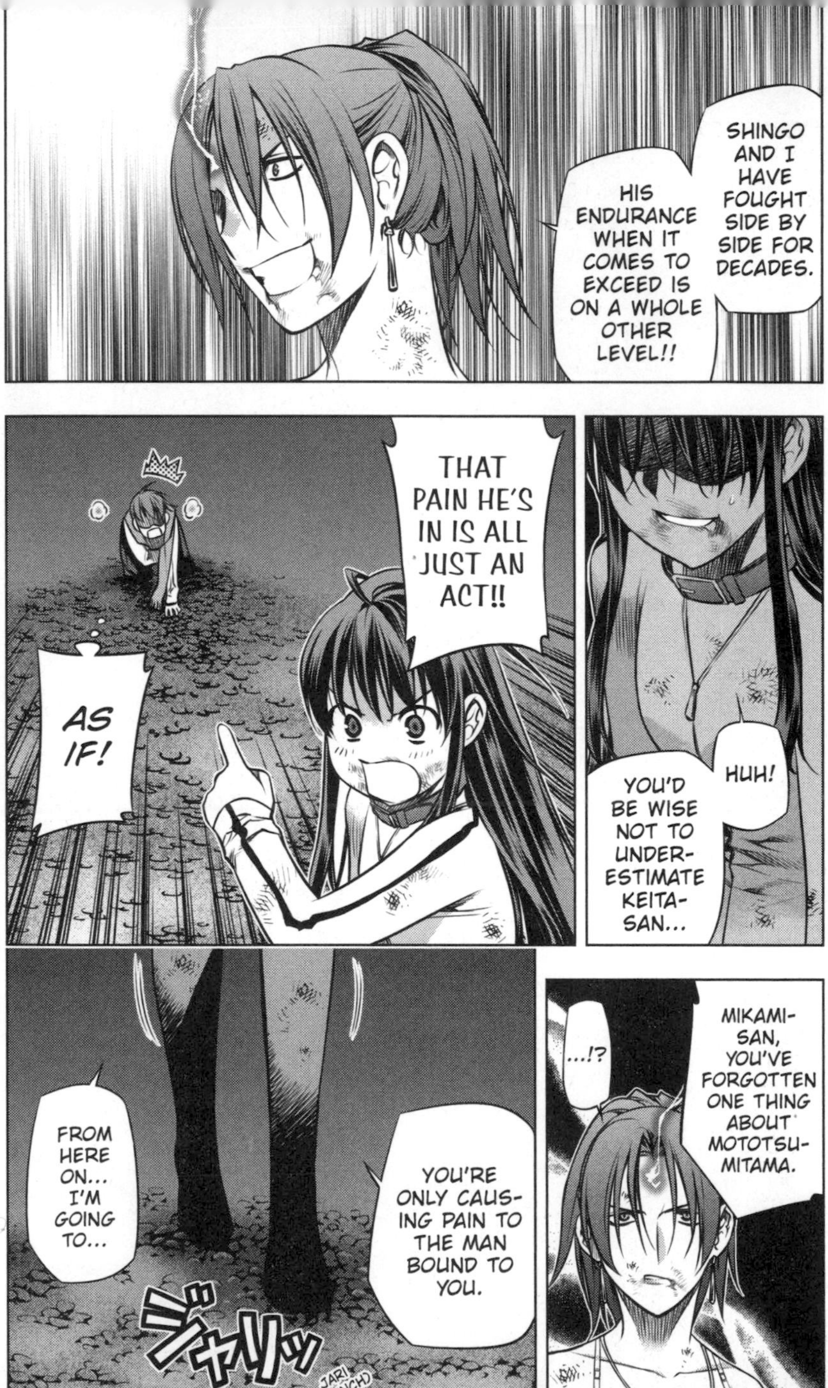
SHINGO AND I HAVE FOUGHT SIDE BY SIDE FOR DECADES.
HIS ENDURANCE WHEN IT COMES TO EXCEED IS ON A WHOLE OTHER LEVEL!!
HUH!
YOU'D BE WISE NOT TO UNDER-ESTIMATE KEITA-SAN...
THAT PAIN HE'S IN IS ALL JUST AN ACT!!
AS IF!
MIKAMI-SAN, YOU'VE FORGOTTEN ONE THING ABOUT MOTOTSU-MITAMA.
...!?
YOU'RE ONLY CAUSING PAIN TO THE MAN BOUND TO YOU.
FROM HERE ON... I'M GOING TO...
ジャリッ
JARI (CRUNCH)

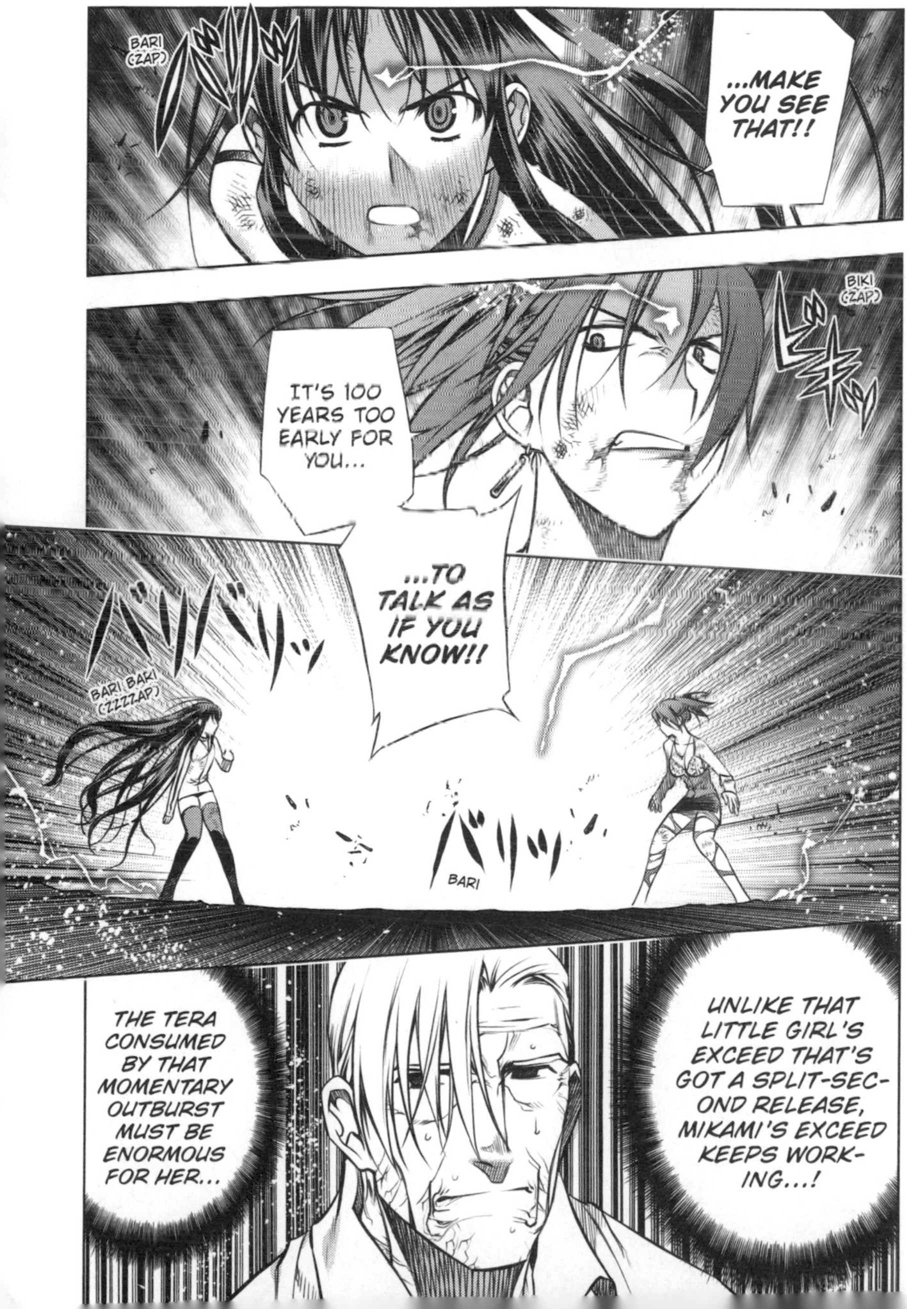
...MAKE YOU SEE THAT!!
BARI (ZAP)
BIKI (ZAP)
IT'S 100 YEARS TOO EARLY FOR YOU...
...TO TALK AS IF YOU KNOW!!
BARI
BARI BARI (ZZZZAP)
UNLIKE THAT LITTLE GIRL'S EXCEED THAT'S GOT A SPLIT-SEC-OND RELEASE, MIKAMI'S EXCEED KEEPS WORK-ING...!
THE TERA CONSUMED BY THAT MOMENTARY OUTBURST MUST BE ENORMOUS FOR HER...

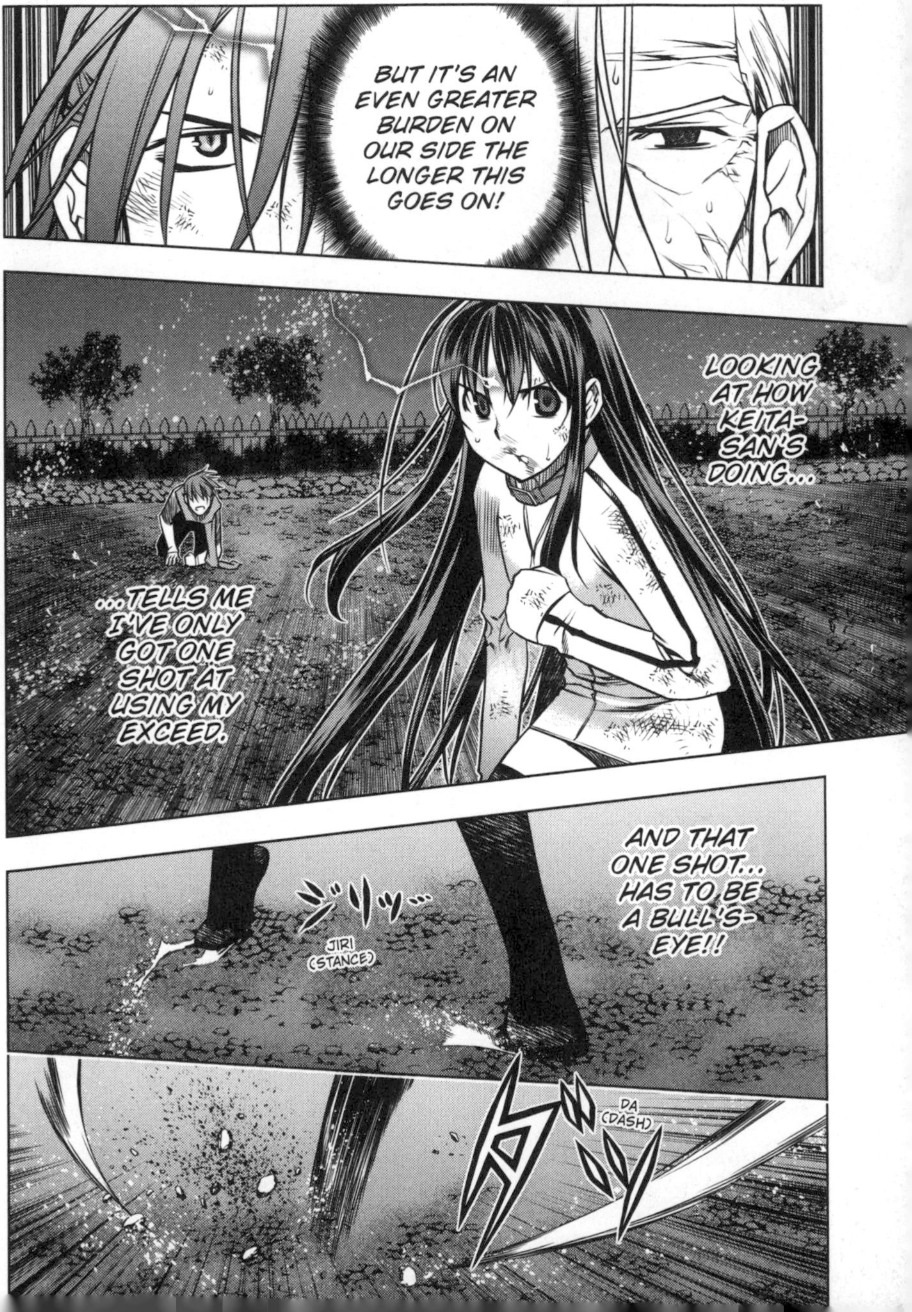
BUT IT'S AN EVEN GREATER BURDEN ON OUR SIDE THE LONGER THIS GOES ON!
LOOKING AT HOW KEITA-SAN'S DOING...
...TELLS ME I'VE ONLY GOT ONE SHOT AT USING MY EXCEED.
AND THAT ONE SHOT... HAS TO BE A BULL'S-EYE!!
ジリッ...
JIRI (STANCE)
ドッ
DA (DASH)

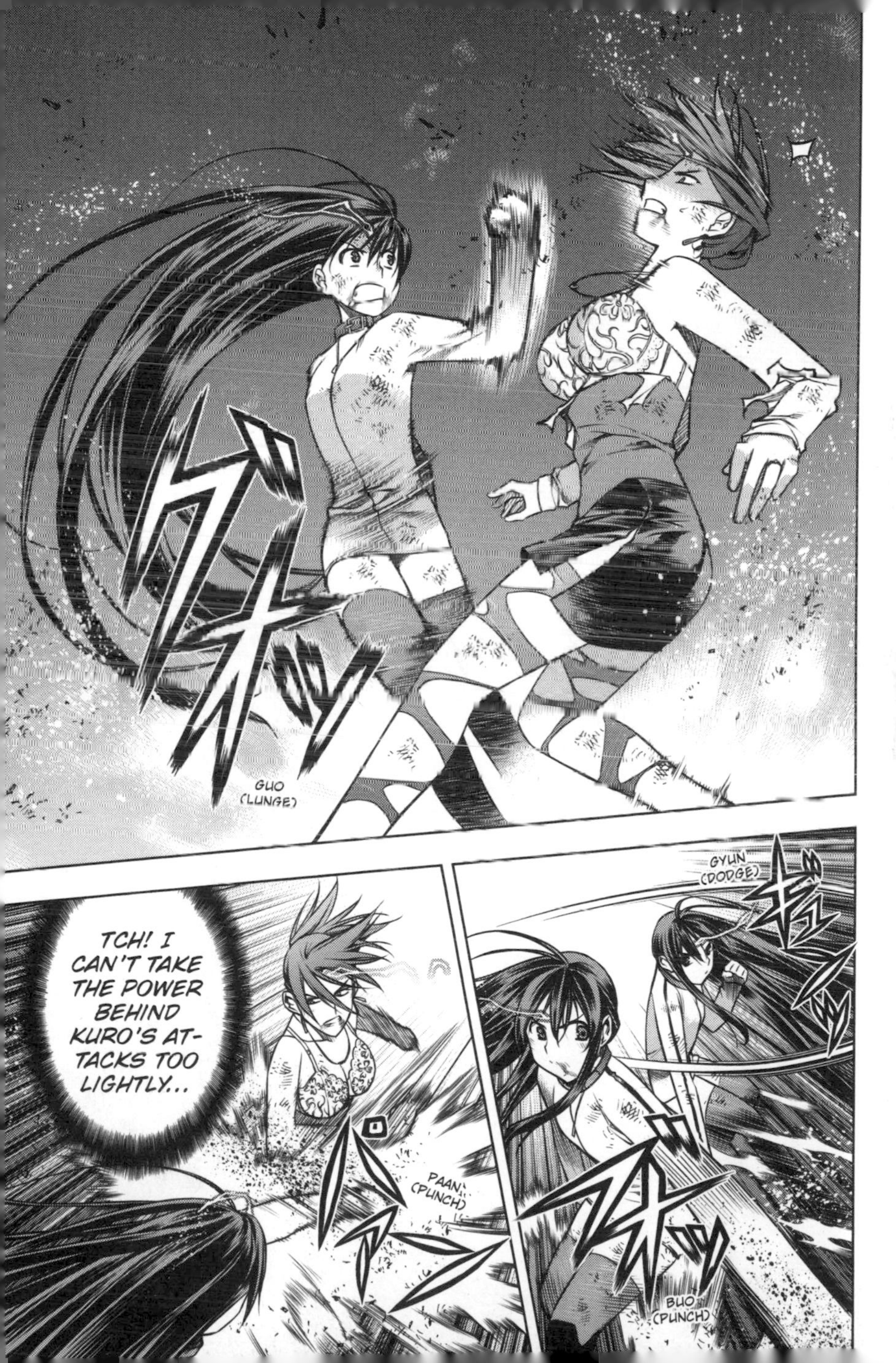
GUO
(LUNGE)
GYUN
(DODGE)
BUO
(PUNCH)
TCH! I CAN'T TAKE THE POWER BEHIND KURO'S AT-TACKS TOO LIGHTLY...
PAAN
(PUNCH)

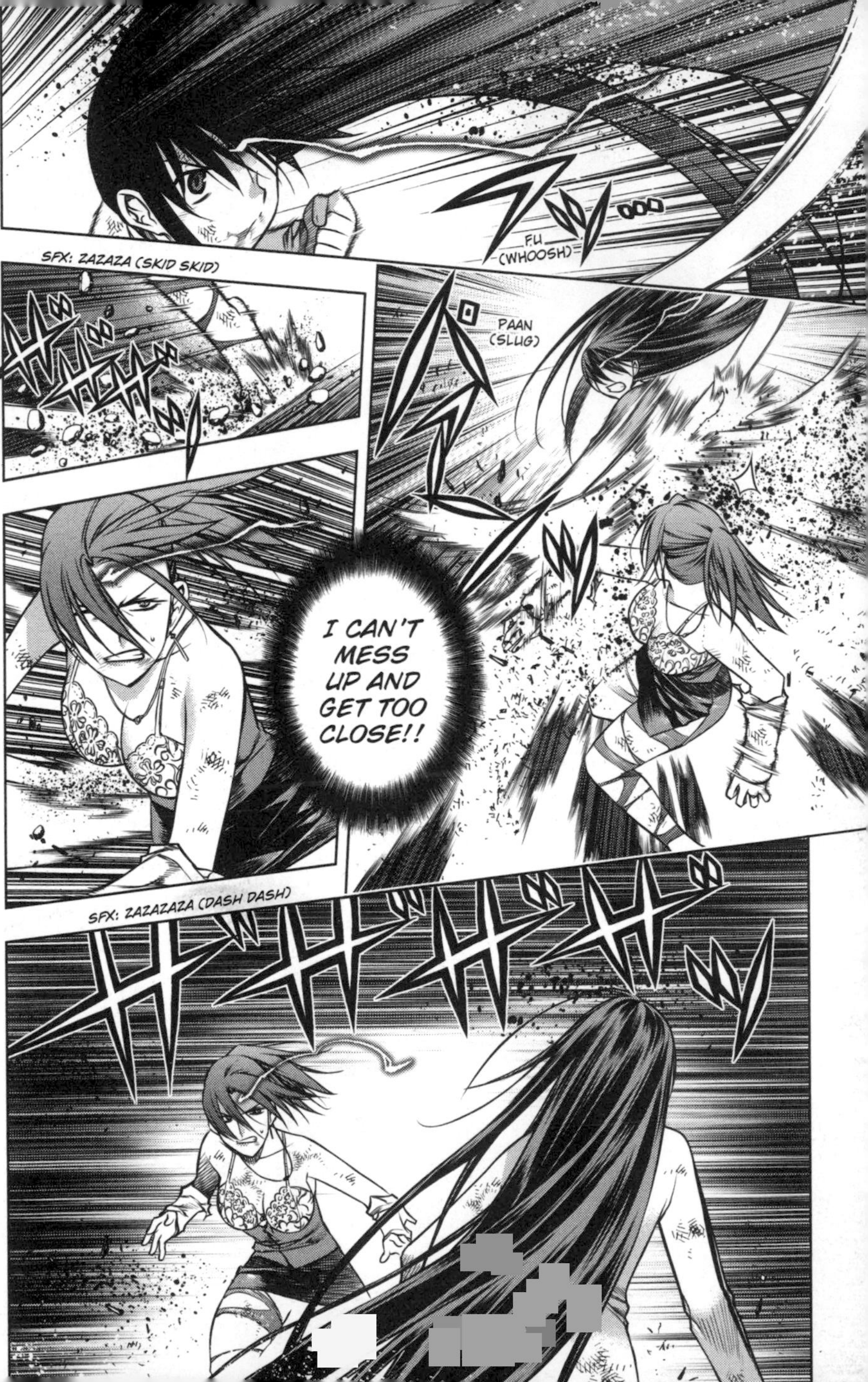
FU (WHOOSH)
PAAN (SLUG)
SFX: ZAZAZA (SKID SKID)
I CAN'T MESS UP AND GET TOO CLOSE!!
SFX: ZAZAZAZA (DASH DASH)

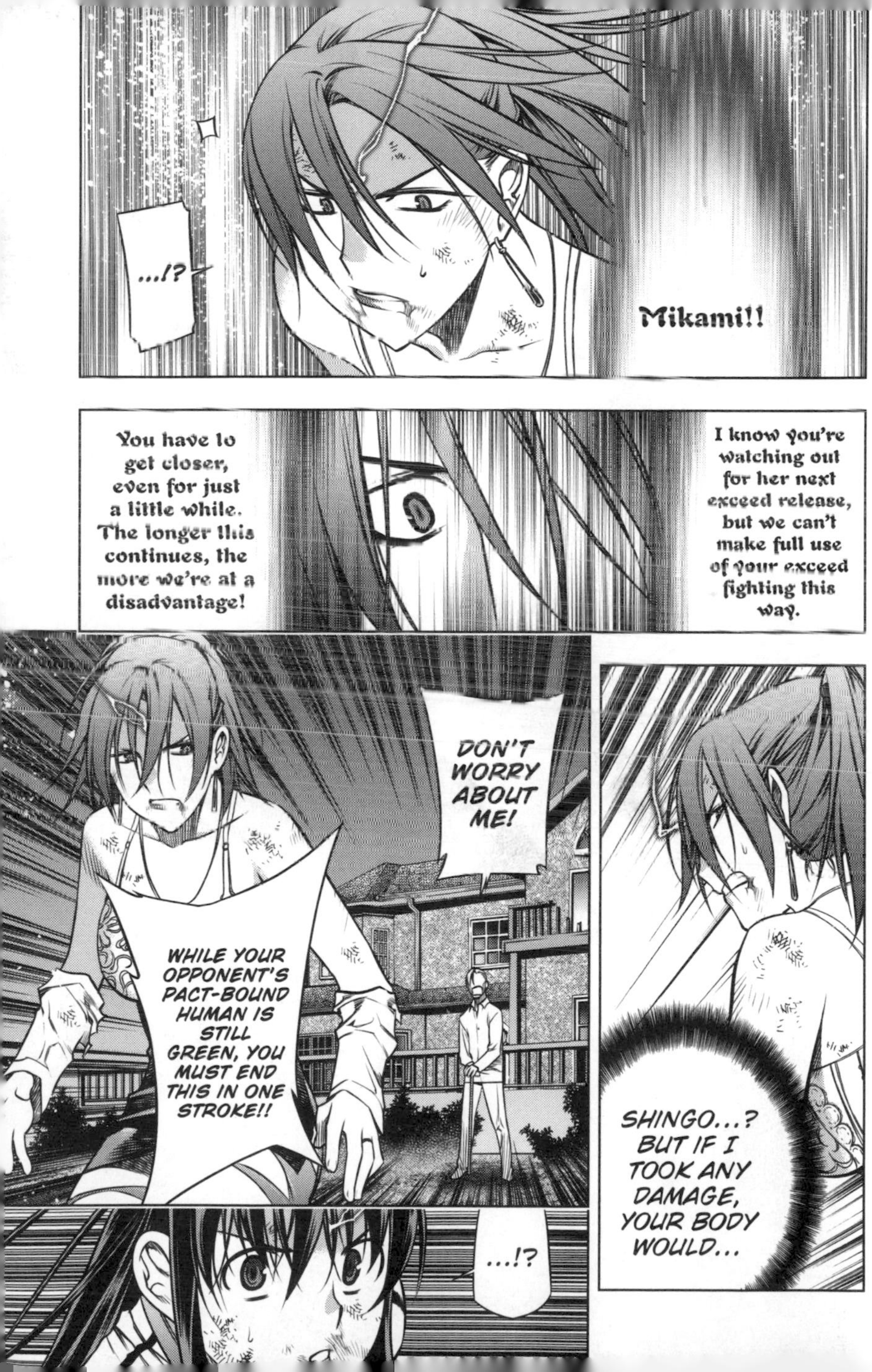
Mikami!!
...!?
I know you're watching out for her next exceed release, but we can't make full use of your exceed fighting this way.
You have to get closer, even for just a little while. The longer this continues, the more we're at a disadvantage!
SHINGO...? BUT IF I TOOK ANY DAMAGE, YOUR BODY WOULD...
DON'T WORRY ABOUT ME!
WHILE YOUR OPPONENT'S PACT-BOUND HUMAN IS STILL GREEN, YOU MUST END THIS IN ONE STROKE!!
...!?

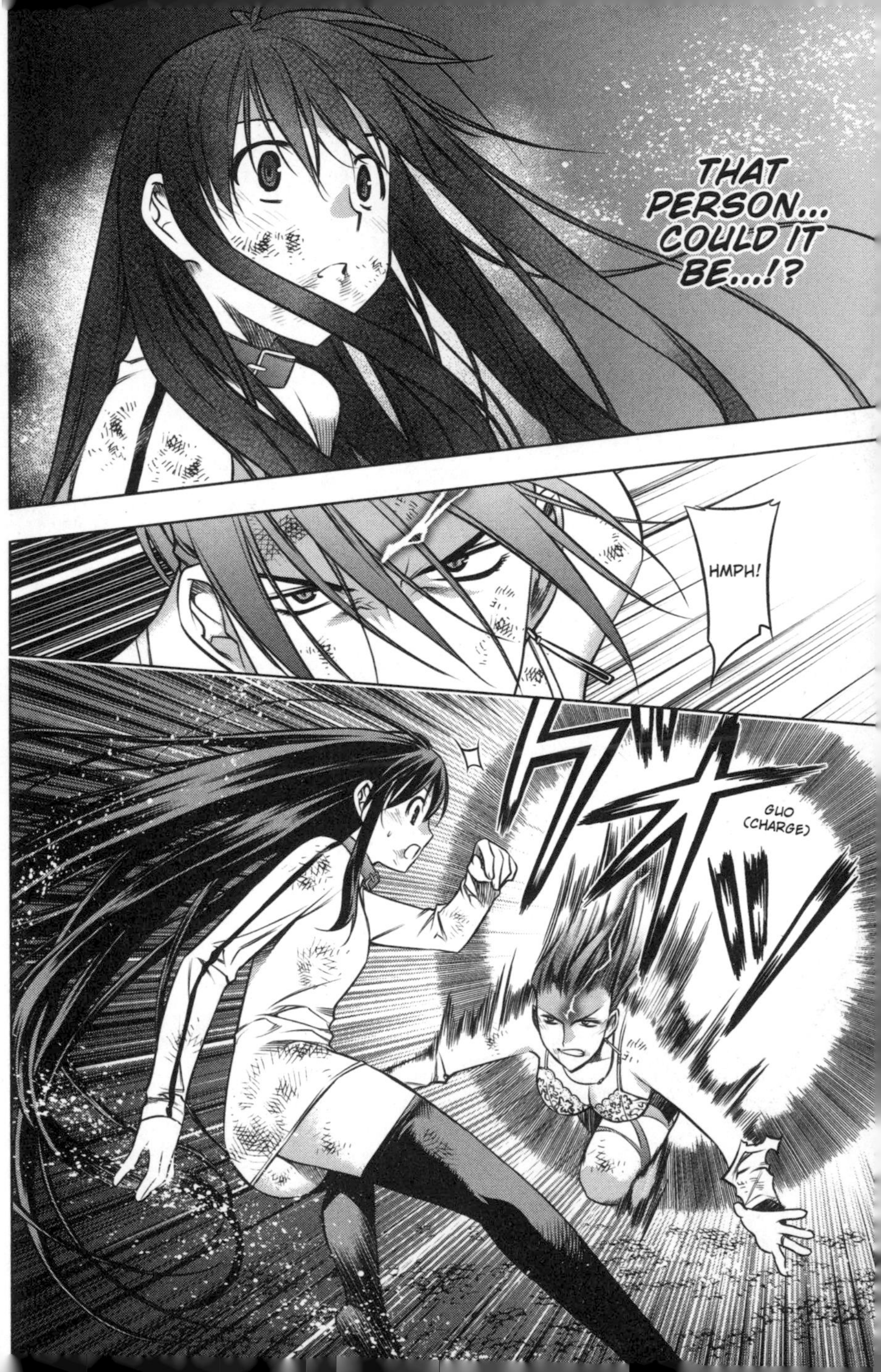
THAT PERSON... COULD IT BE...!?
HMPH!
GUO (CHARGE)

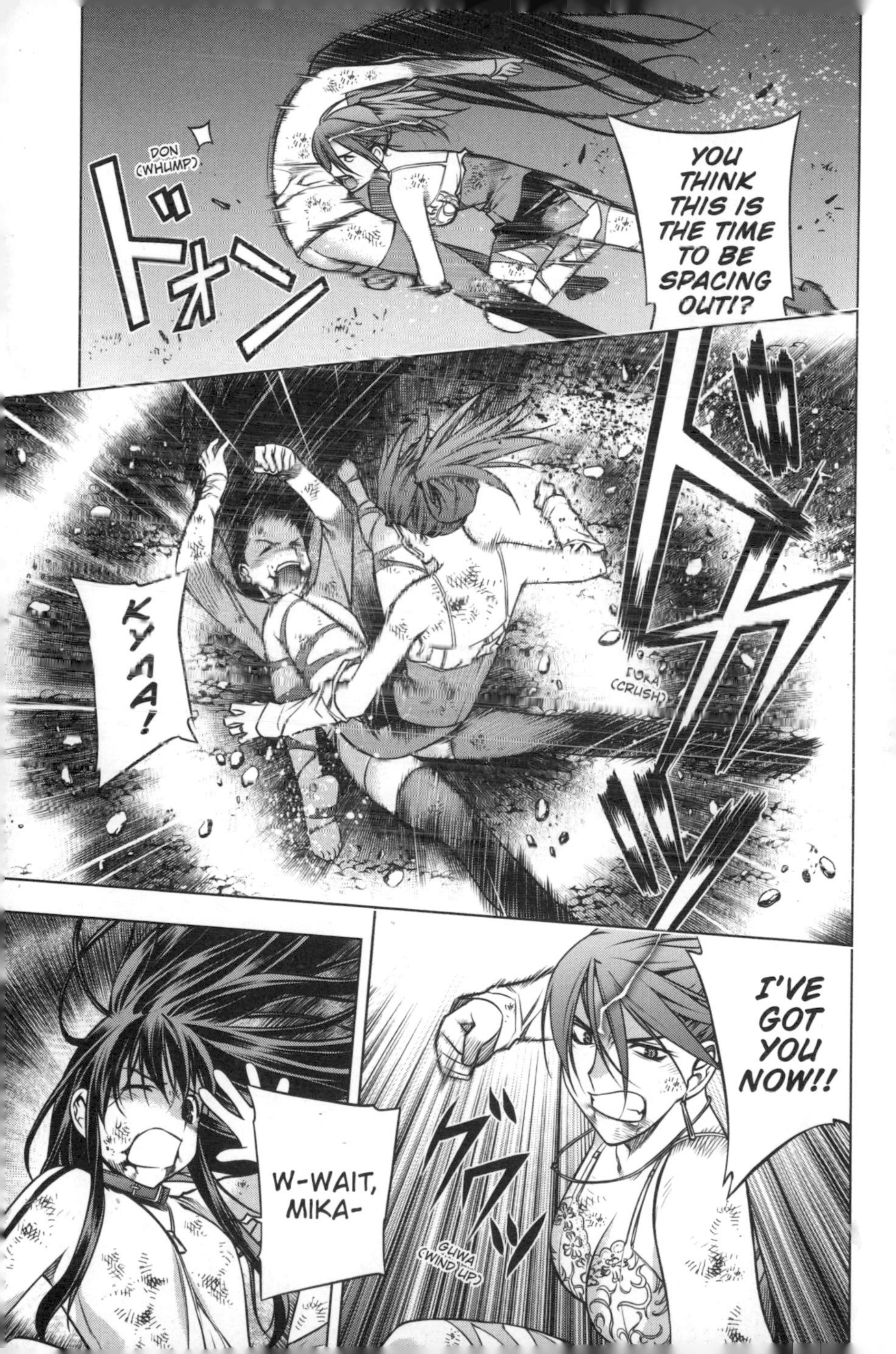
YOU THINK THIS IS THE TIME TO BE SPACING OUT!?
DON (WHUMP)
DOKA (CRUSH)
KYAA!
I'VE GOT YOU NOW!!
GUWA (WIND UP)
W-WAIT, MIKA-

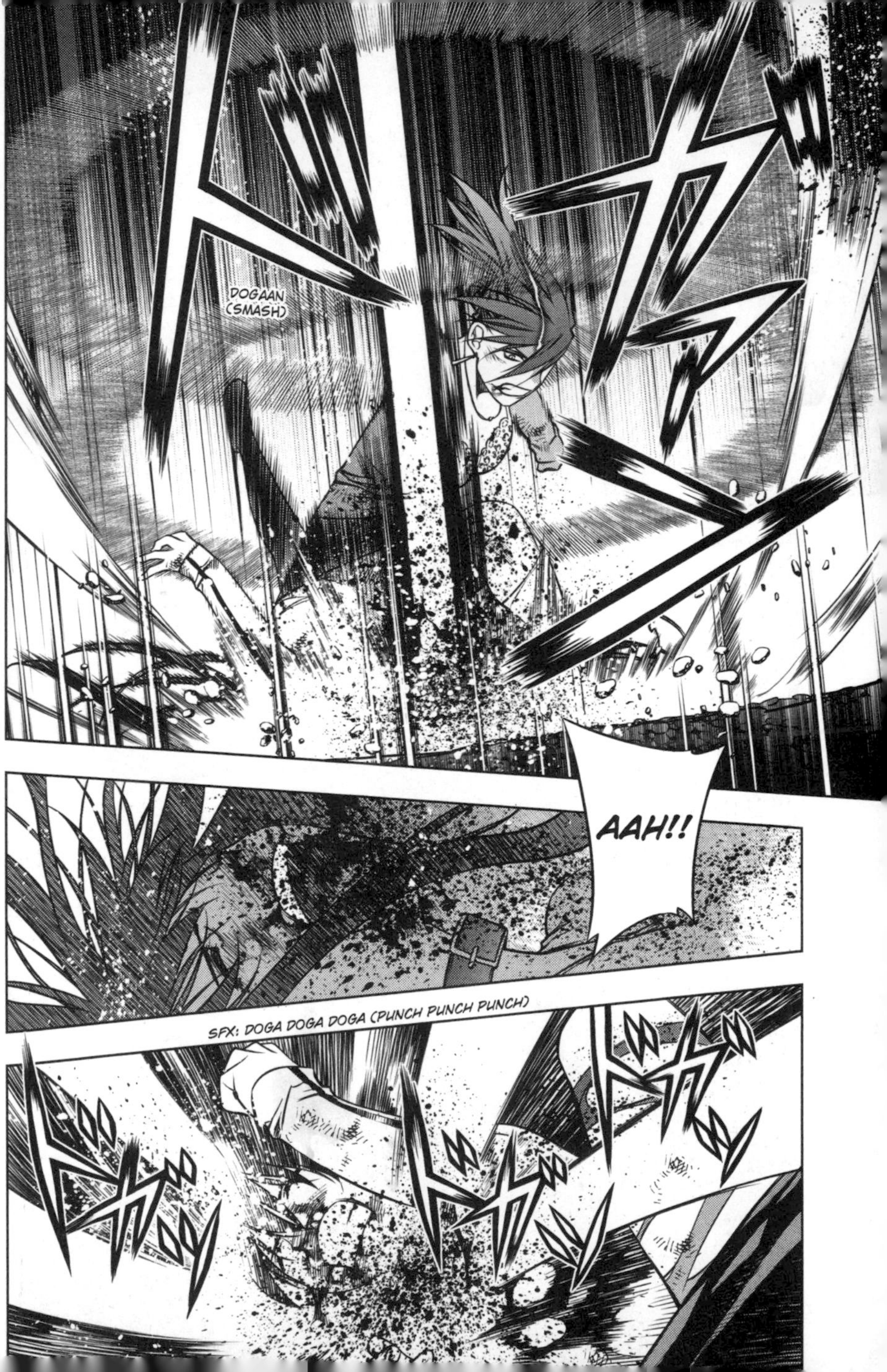
DOGAAN (SMASH)
AAH!!
SFX: DOGA DOGA DOGA (PUNCH PUNCH PUNCH)

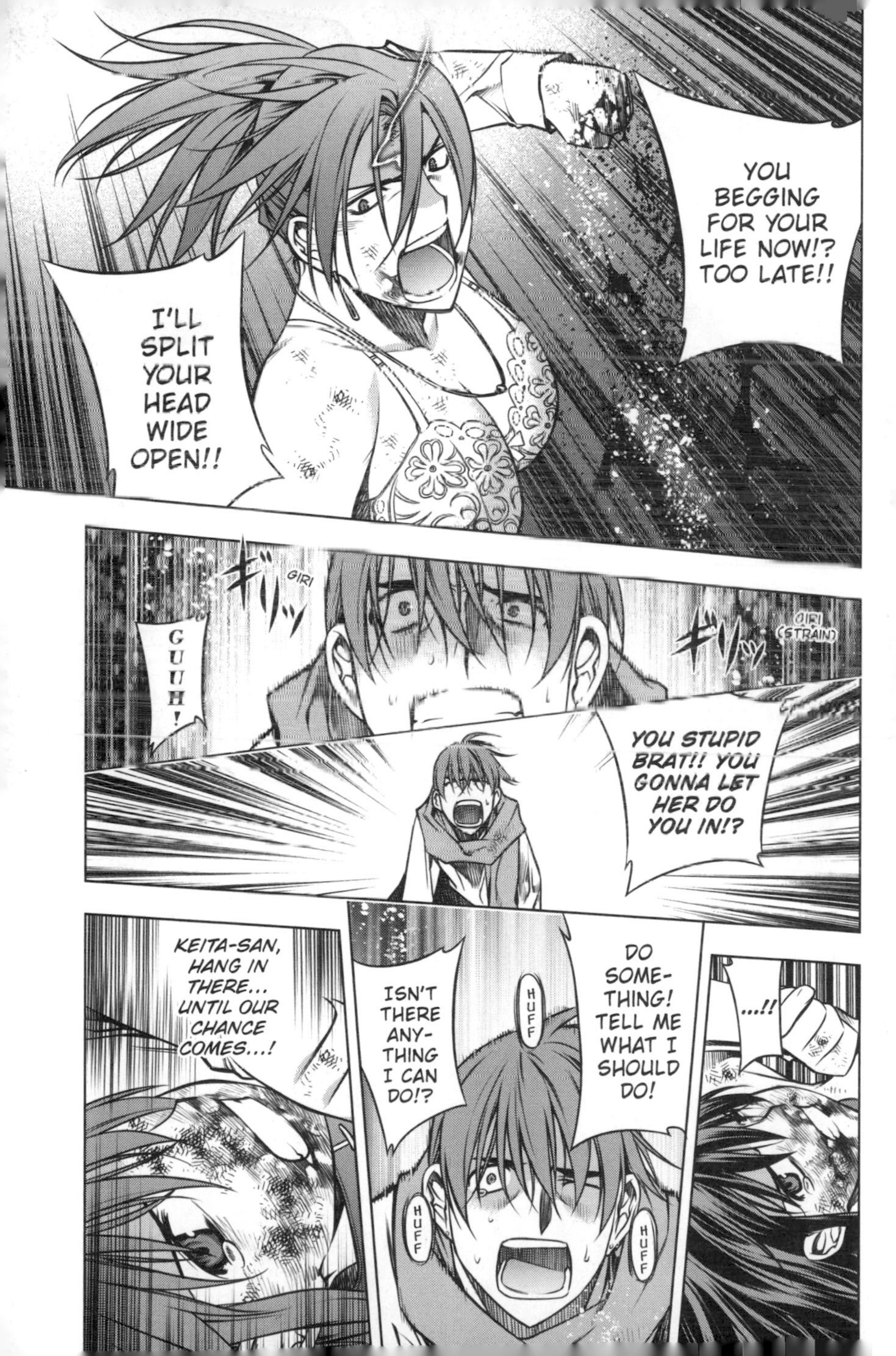
YOU BEGGING FOR YOUR LIFE NOW!? TOO LATE!!
I'LL SPLIT YOUR HEAD WIDE OPEN!!
GIRI (STRAIN)
GIRI
GUUH!
YOU STUPID BRAT!! YOU GONNA LET HER DO YOU IN!?
...!!
DO SOME-THING! TELL ME WHAT I SHOULD DO!
HUFF
ISN'T THERE ANY-THING I CAN DO!?
HUFF
HUFF
KEITA-SAN, HANG IN THERE... UNTIL OUR CHANCE COMES...!

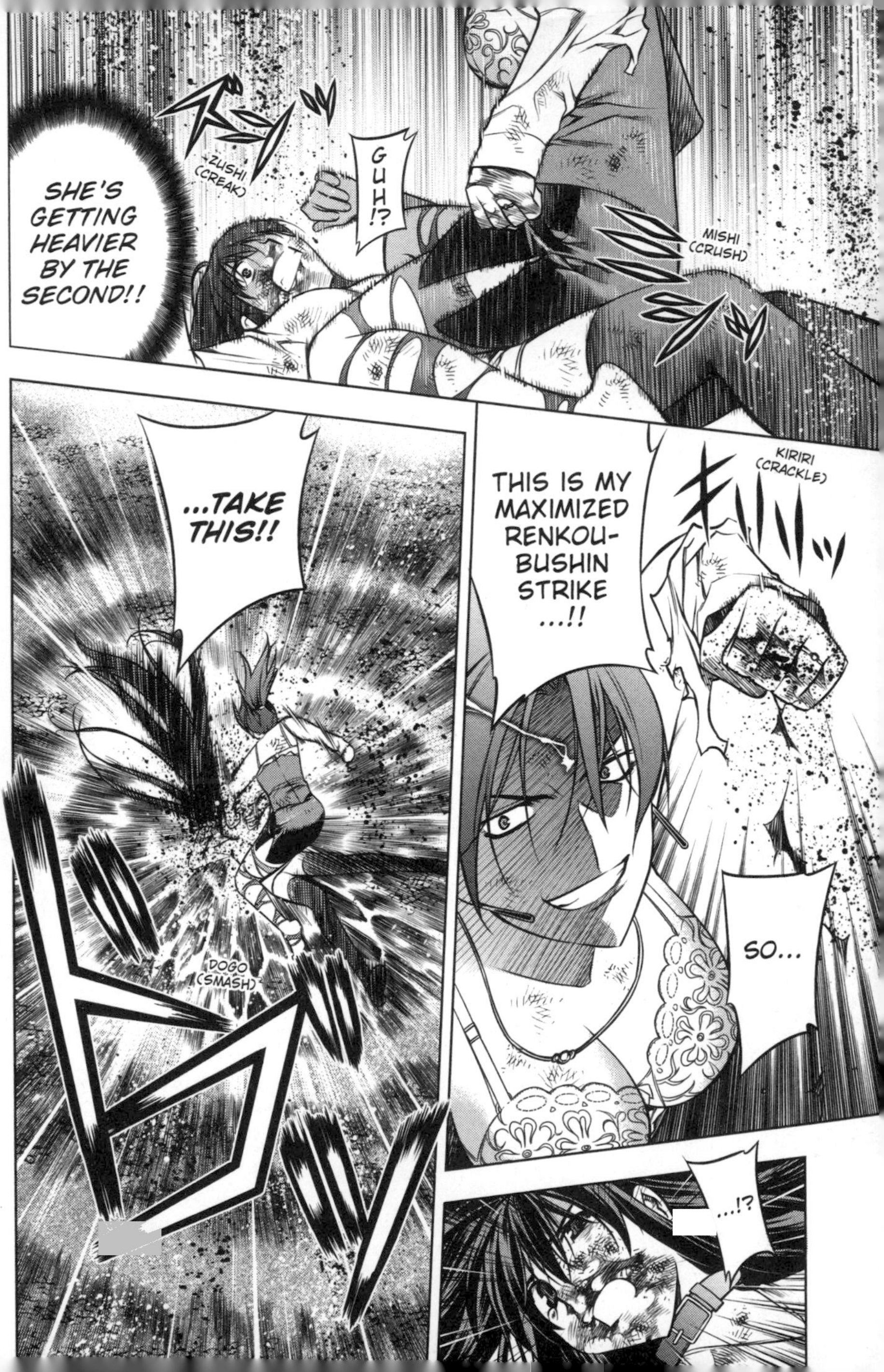
MISHI (CRUSH)
GUH!?
ZUSHI (CREAK)
SHE'S GETTING HEAVIER BY THE SECOND!!
KIRIRI (CRACKLE)
THIS IS MY MAXIMIZED RENKOU-BUSHIN STRIKE ...!!
SO...
...!?
...TAKE THIS!!
DOGO (SMASH)

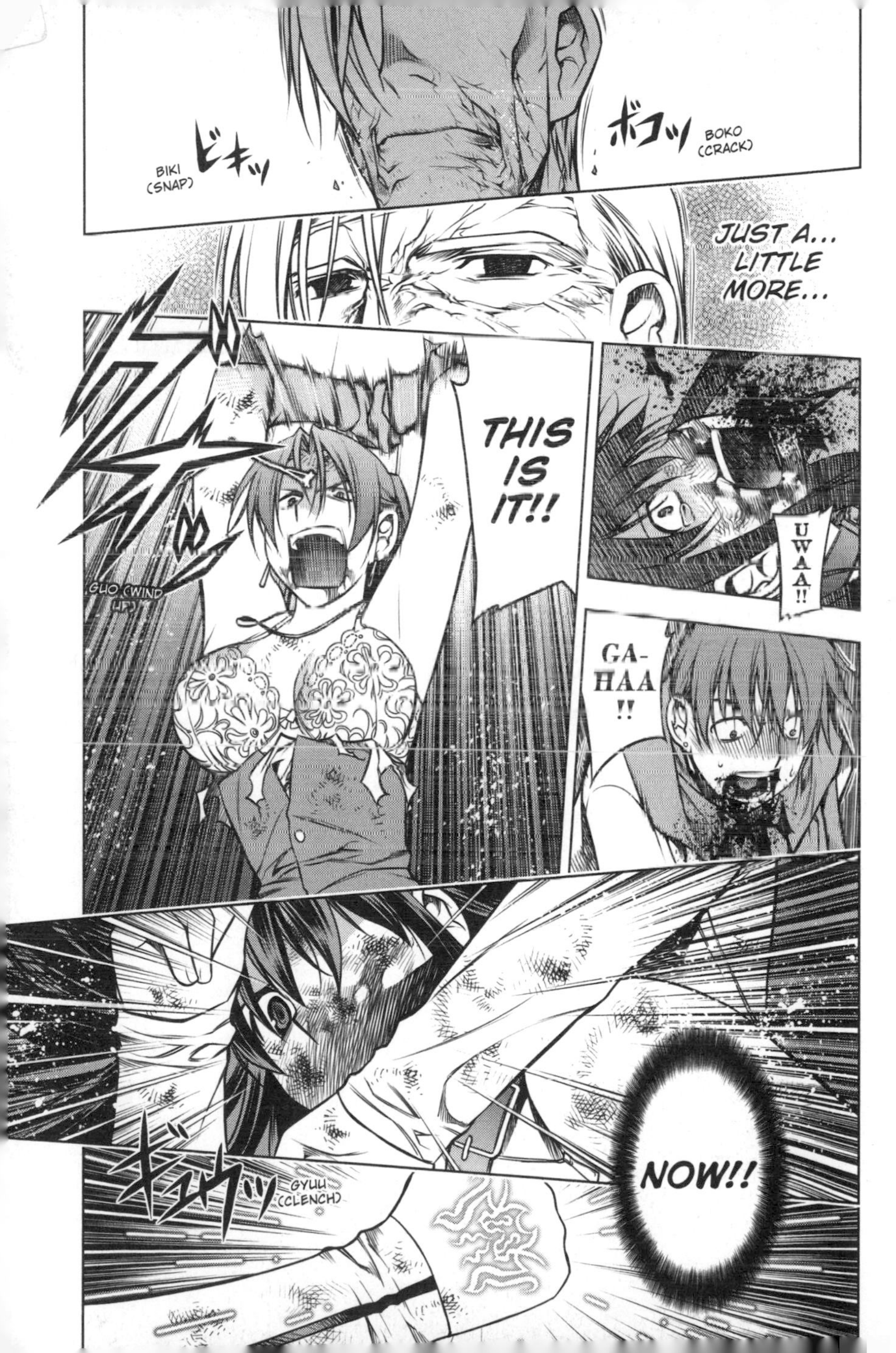

ボコッ
BOKO (CRACK)
ビキッ
BIKI (SNAP)
JUST A... LITTLE MORE...
UWAAA!!
GA-HAA!!
THIS IS IT!!
GUO (WIND UP)
NOW!!
ギュウッ
GYUU (CLENCH)

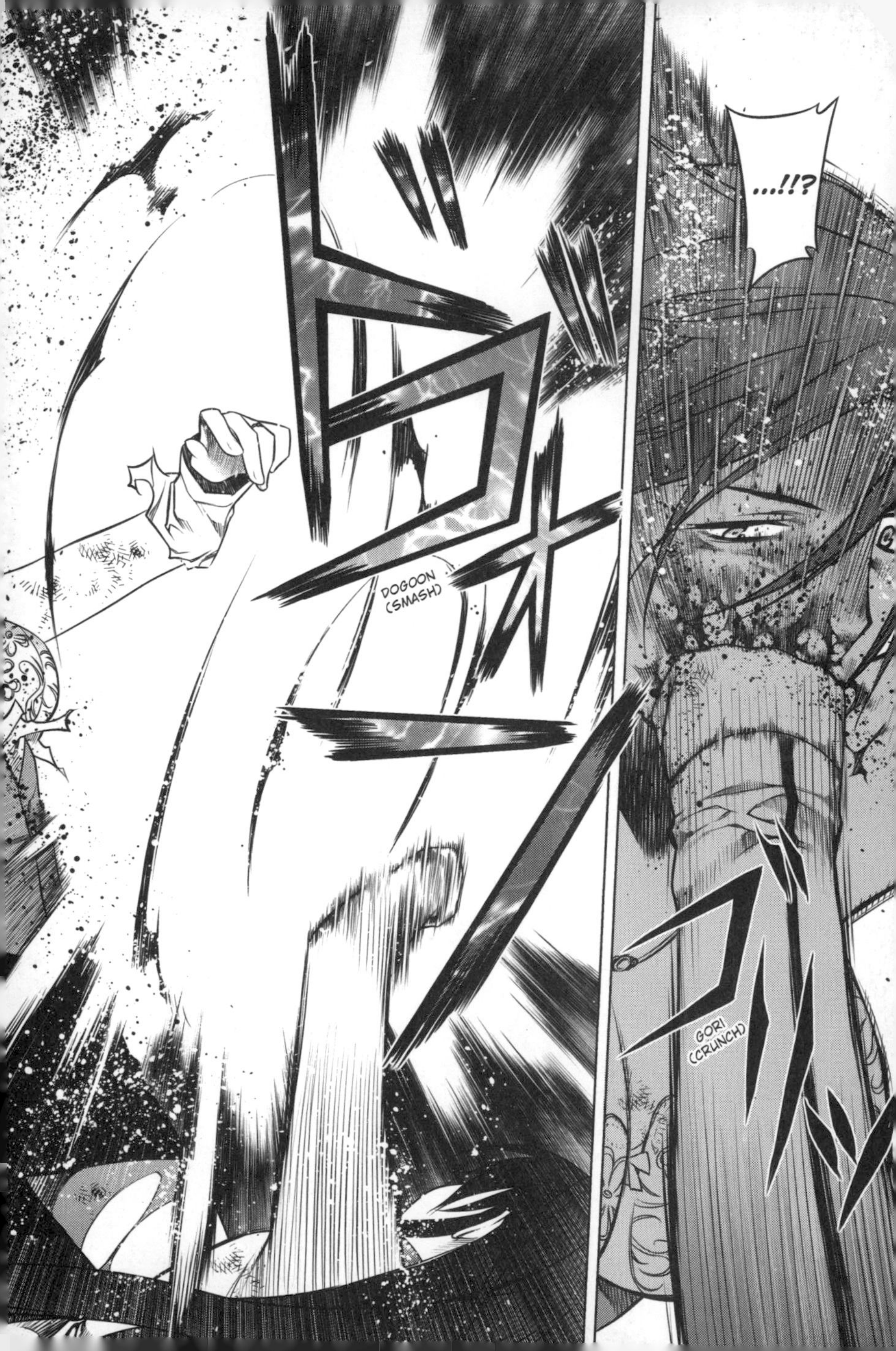
...!!?
GORI (CRUNCH)
DOGOON (SMASH)

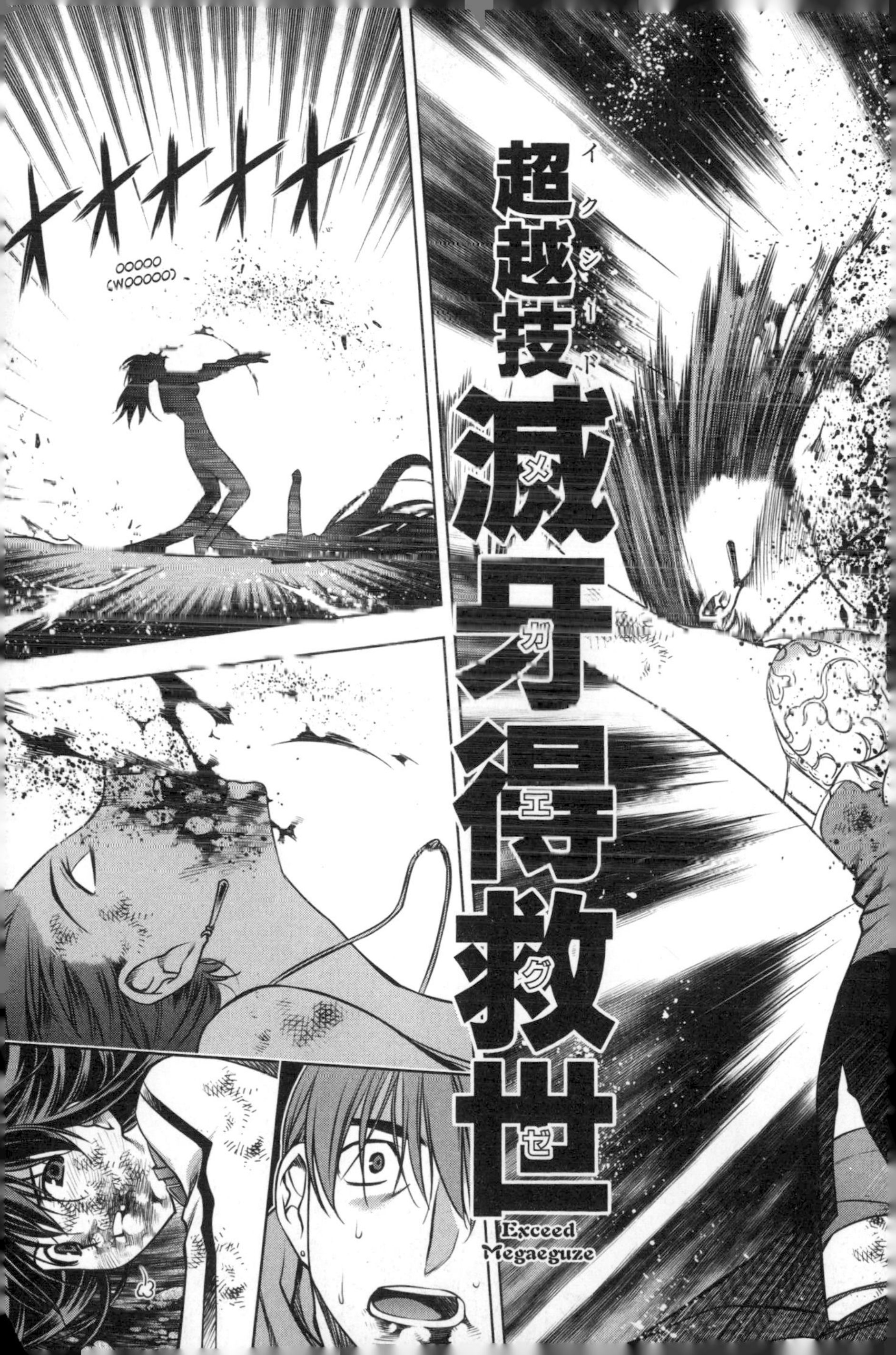

超越技(イクシード)滅牙得救世(メガエグゼ)
Exceed Megaeguze
オオオオオオ
OOOOO (WOOOOO)

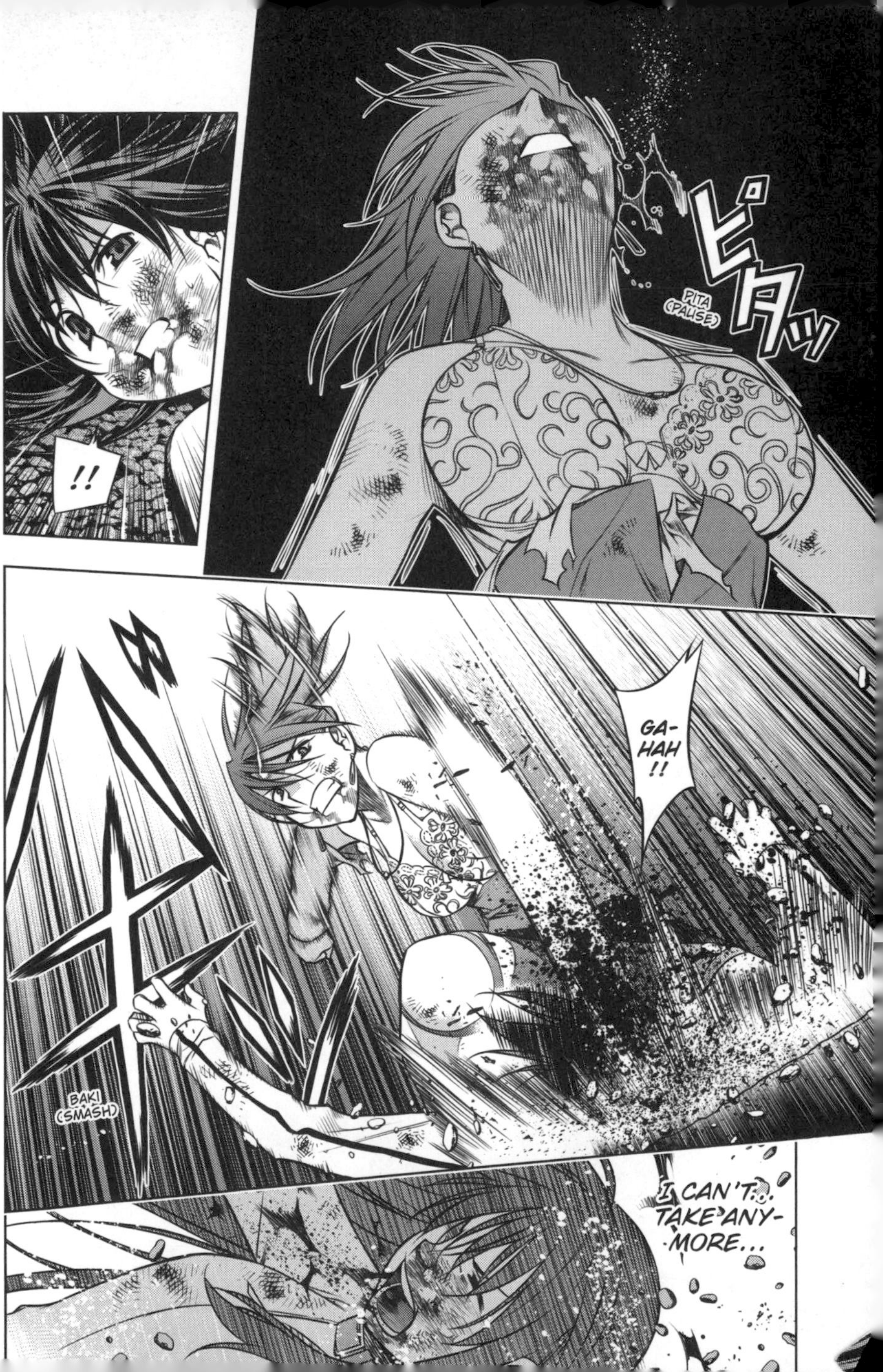
ピタッ
PITA (PAUSE)
!!
GA-HAH!!
BAKI (SMASH)
I CAN'T... TAKE ANY-MORE...

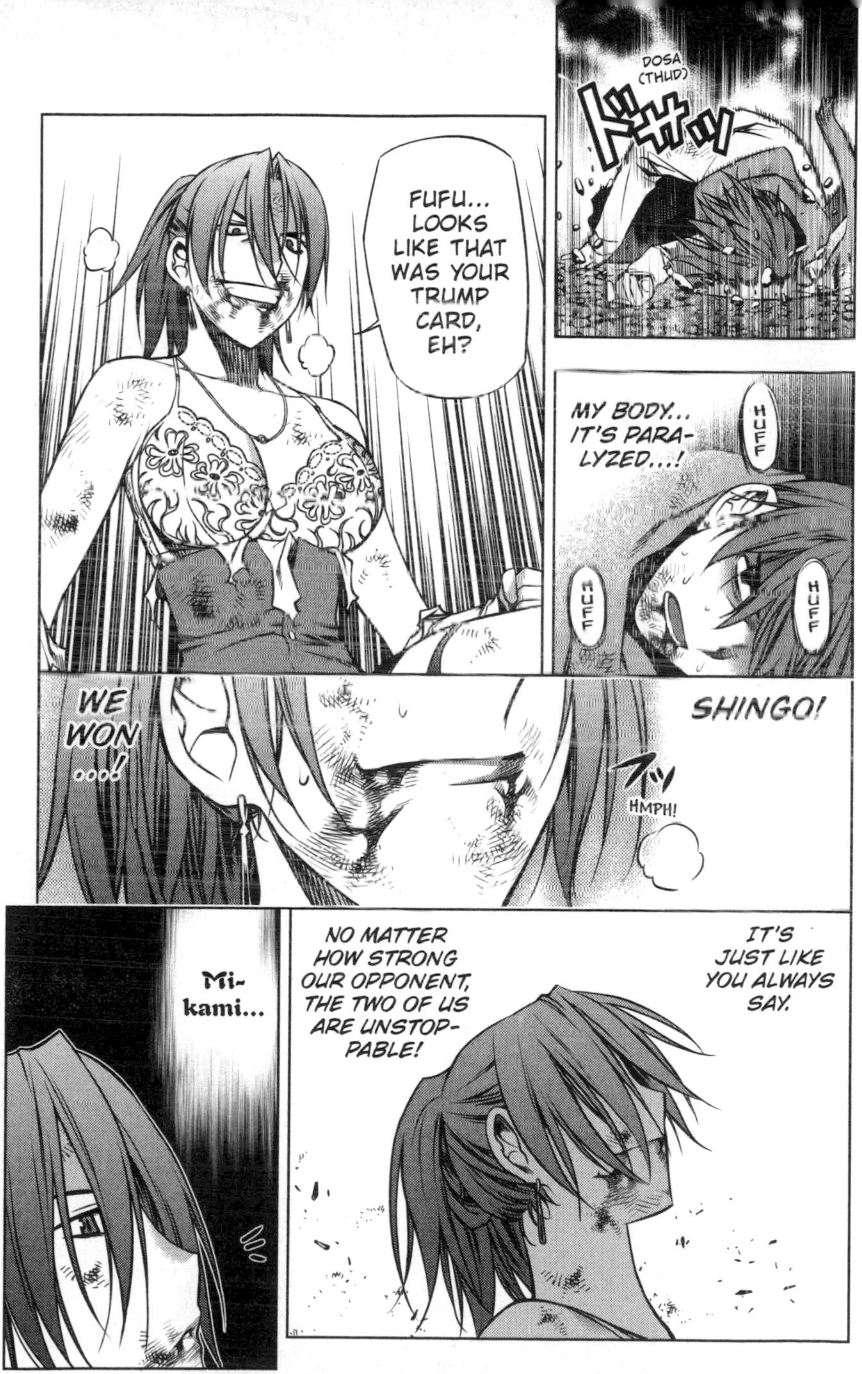
DOSA (THUD)
MY BODY... IT'S PARA-LYZED...!
HUFF
HUFF
HUFF
FUFU... LOOKS LIKE THAT WAS YOUR TRUMP CARD, EH?
SHINGO!
HMPH!
WE WON...!
IT'S JUST LIKE YOU ALWAYS SAY.
NO MATTER HOW STRONG OUR OPPONENT, THE TWO OF US ARE UNSTOP-PABLE!
Mi-kami...

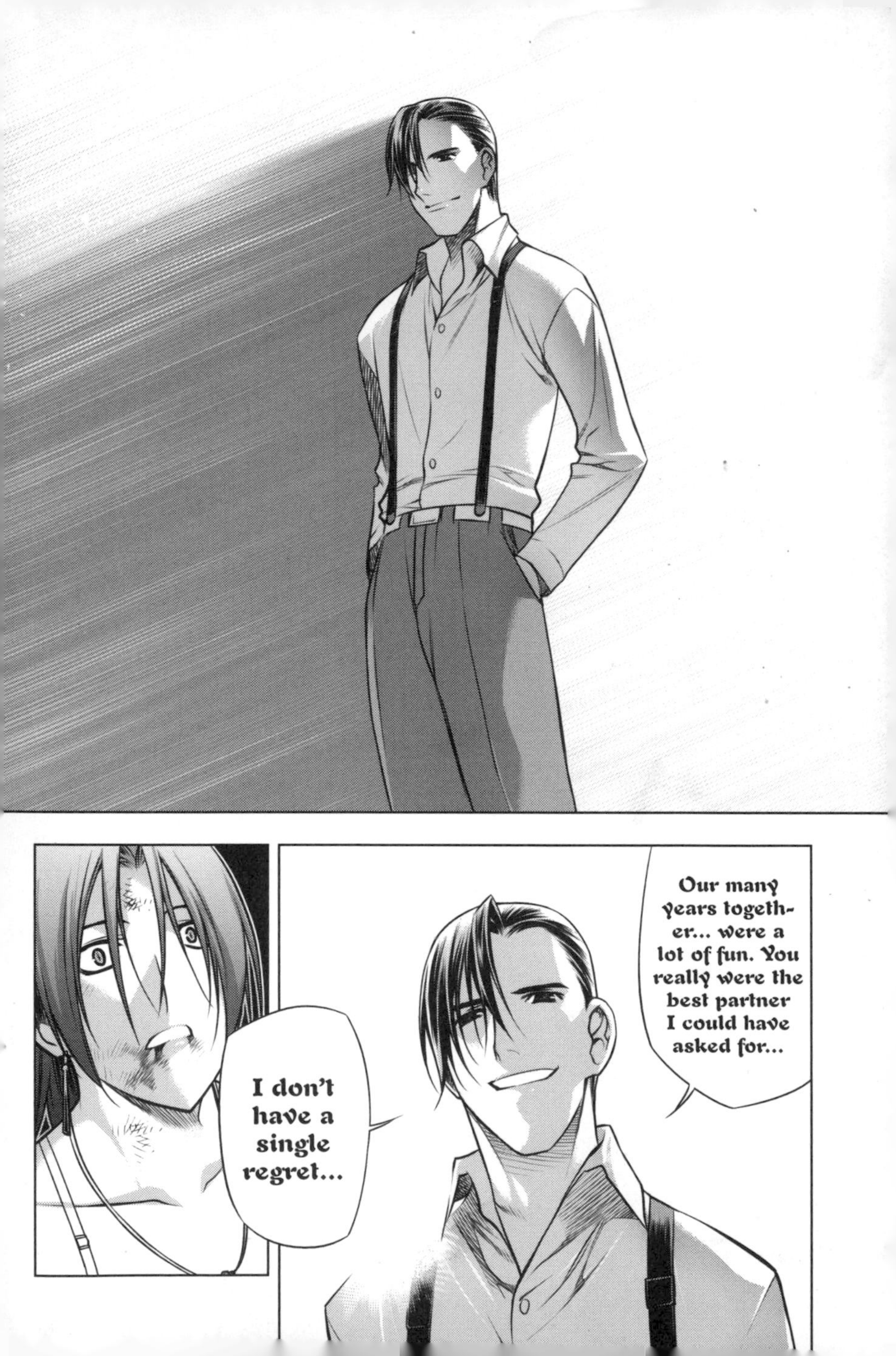
Our many years together... were a lot of fun. You really were the best partner I could have asked for...
I don't have a single regret...

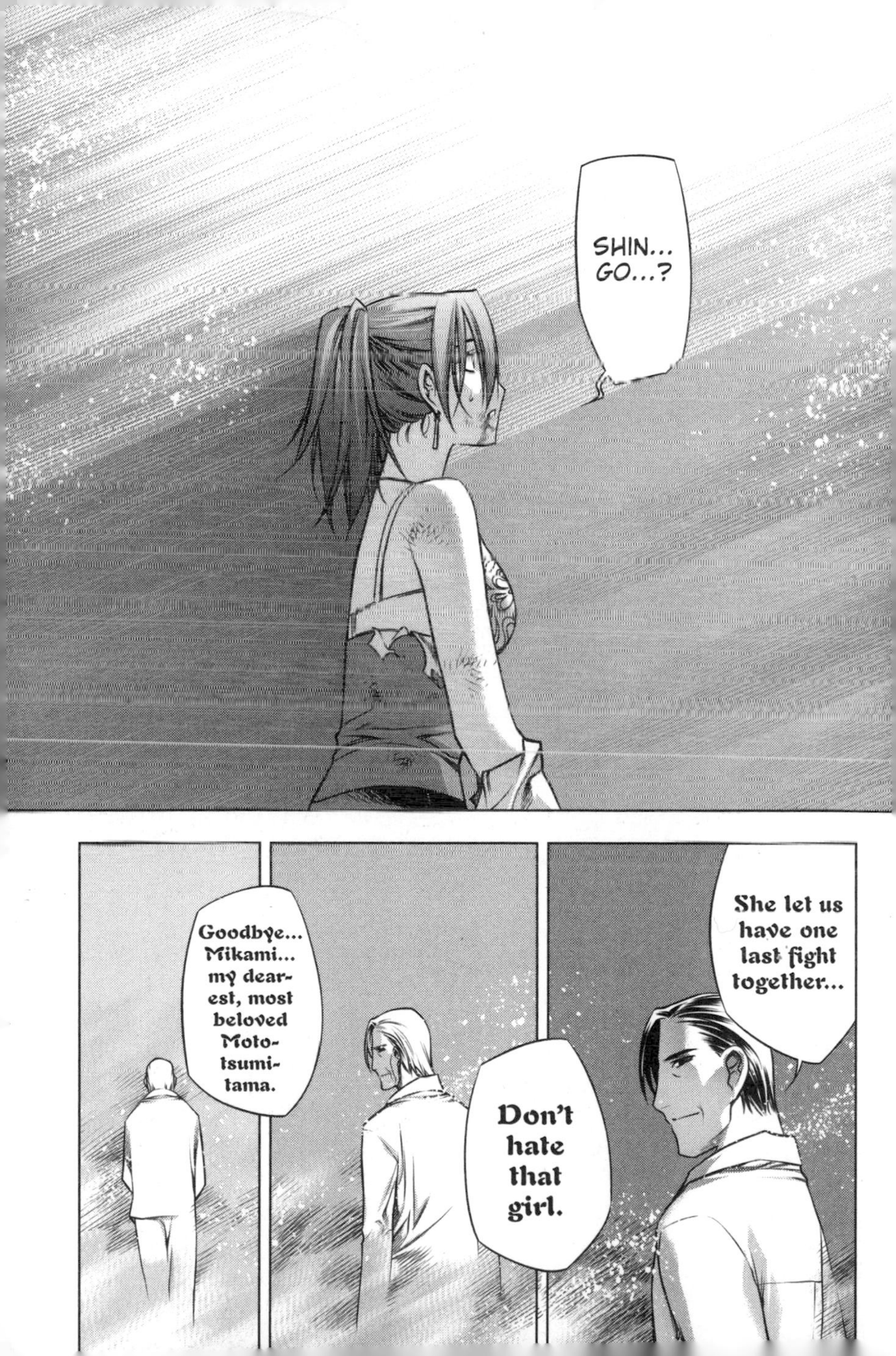
SHIN... GO...?
She let us have one last fight together...
Don't hate that girl.
Goodbye... Mikami... my dear-est, most beloved Moto-tsumi-tama.

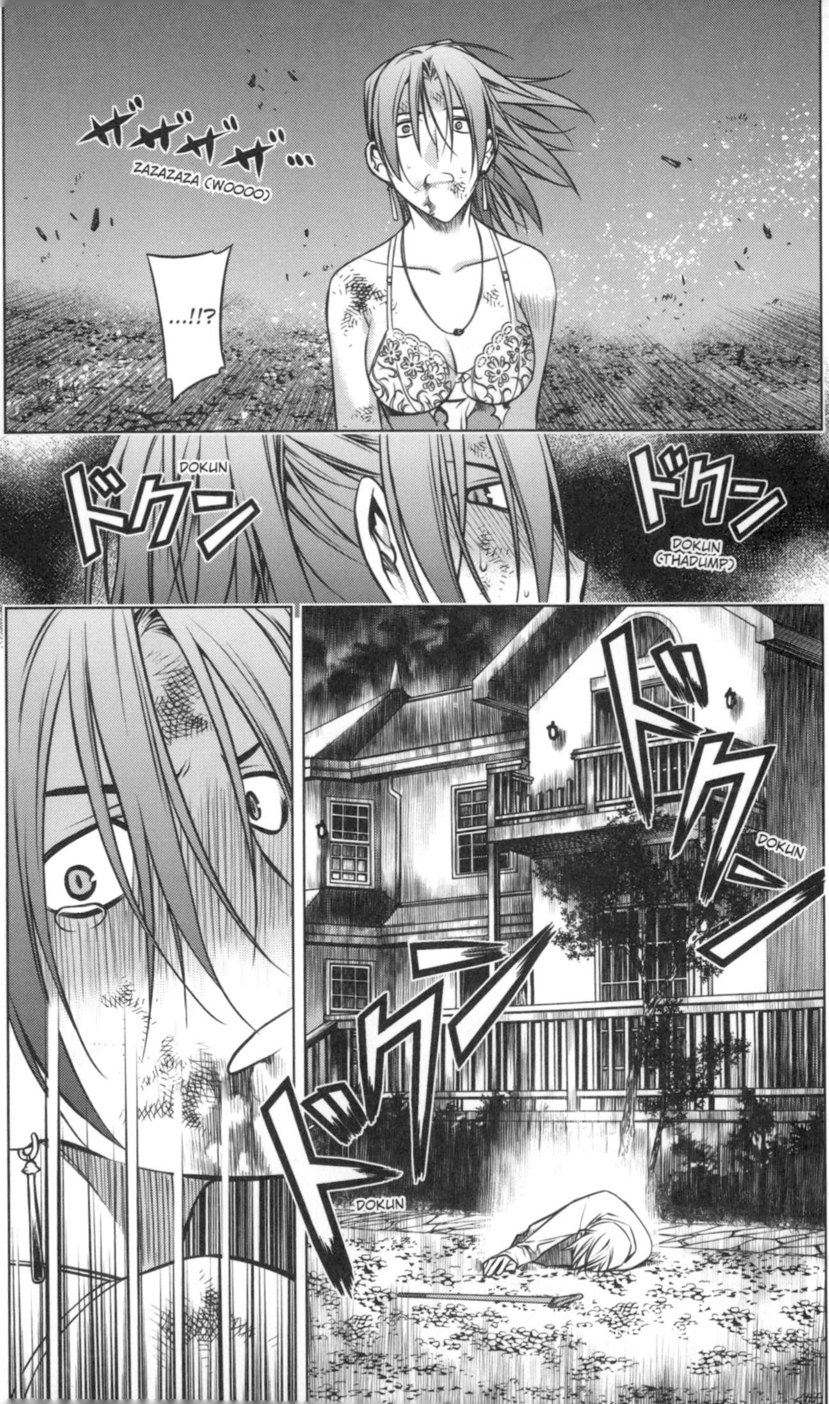
ザザザザ…
ZAZAZAZA (WOOOO)
...!!?
ドクン
DOKUN (THADUMP)
ドクン
DOKUN
ドクン
DOKUN
ドクン
DOKUN

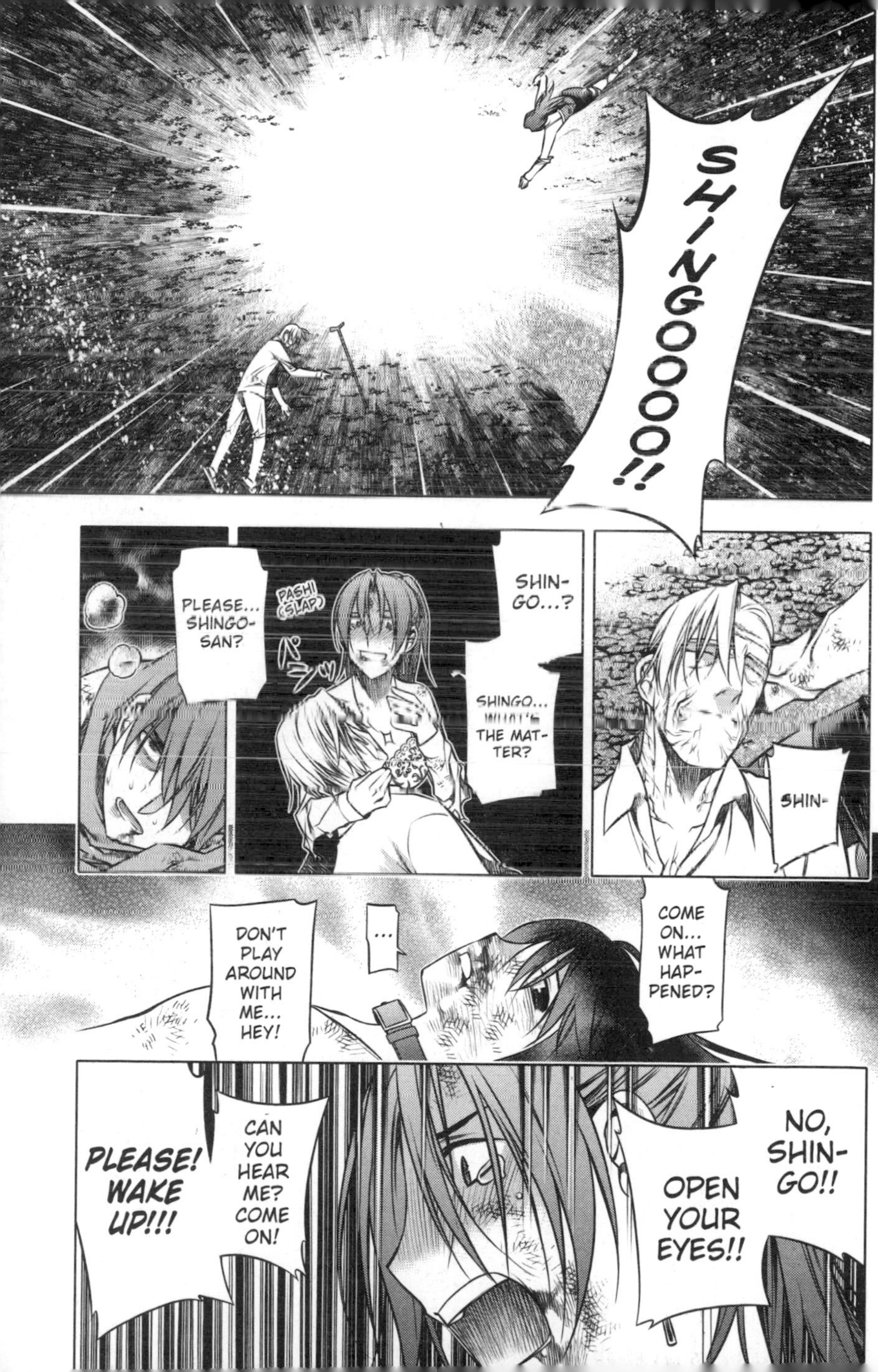
SHINGOOOOOO!!
SHIN-
SHIN-GO...?
SHINGO... WHAT'S THE MATTER?
PASHI (SLAP)
パシッ
PLEASE... SHINGO-SAN?
COME ON... WHAT HAP-PENED?
...
DON'T PLAY AROUND WITH ME... HEY!
NO, SHIN-GO!!
OPEN YOUR EYES!!
CAN YOU HEAR ME? COME ON!
PLEASE! WAKE UP!!!

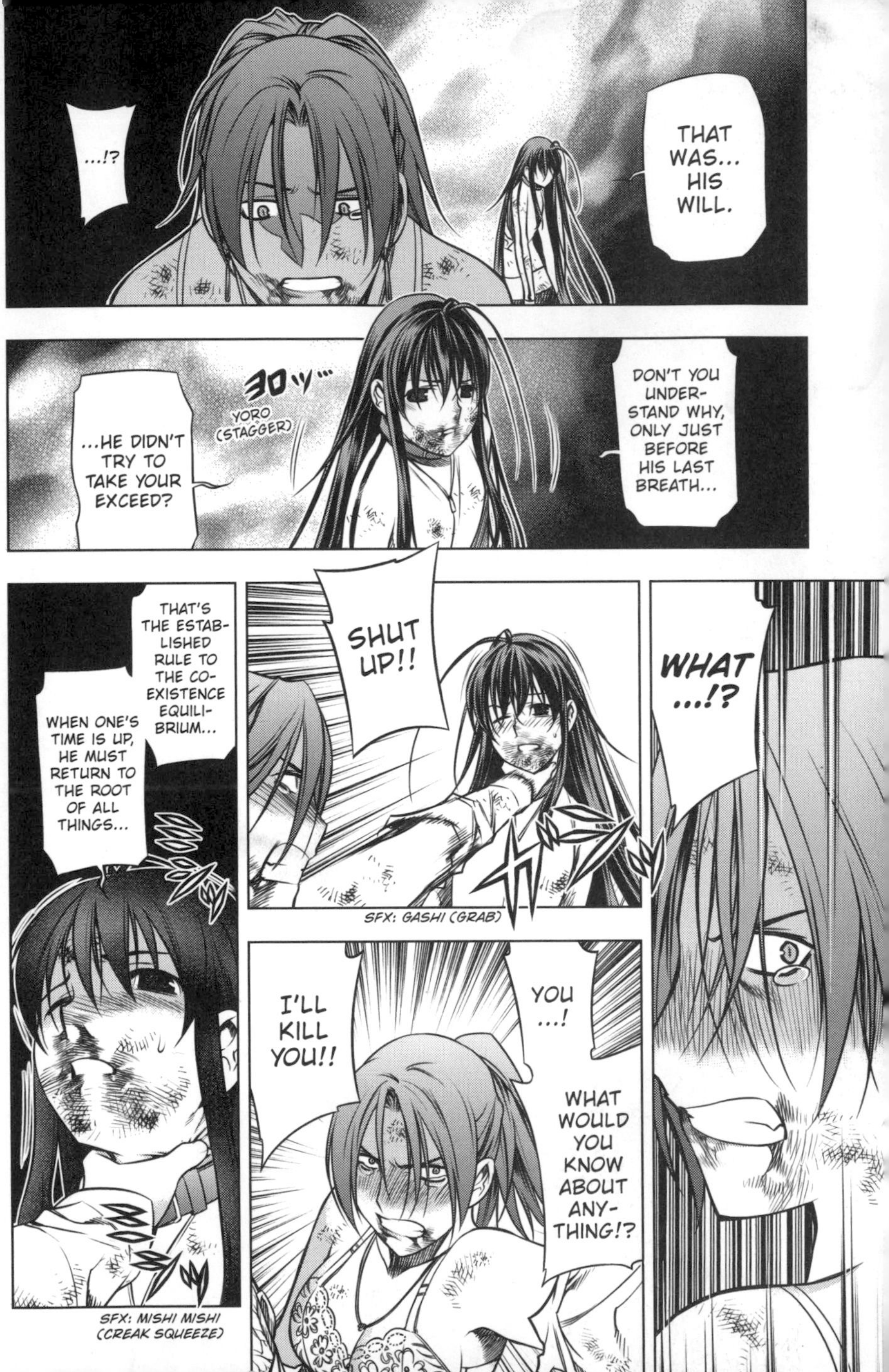
THAT WAS... HIS WILL.
...!?
DON'T YOU UNDER-STAND WHY, ONLY JUST BEFORE HIS LAST BREATH...
ヨロッ
YORO (STAGGER)
...HE DIDN'T TRY TO TAKE YOUR EXCEED?
WHAT ...!?
SHUT UP!!
SFX: GASHI (GRAB)
YOU ...!
WHAT WOULD YOU KNOW ABOUT ANY-THING!?
I'LL KILL YOU!!
THAT'S THE ESTAB-LISHED RULE TO THE CO-EXISTENCE EQUILI-BRIUM...
WHEN ONE'S TIME IS UP, HE MUST RETURN TO THE ROOT OF ALL THINGS...
SFX: MISHI MISHI (CREAK SQUEEZE)

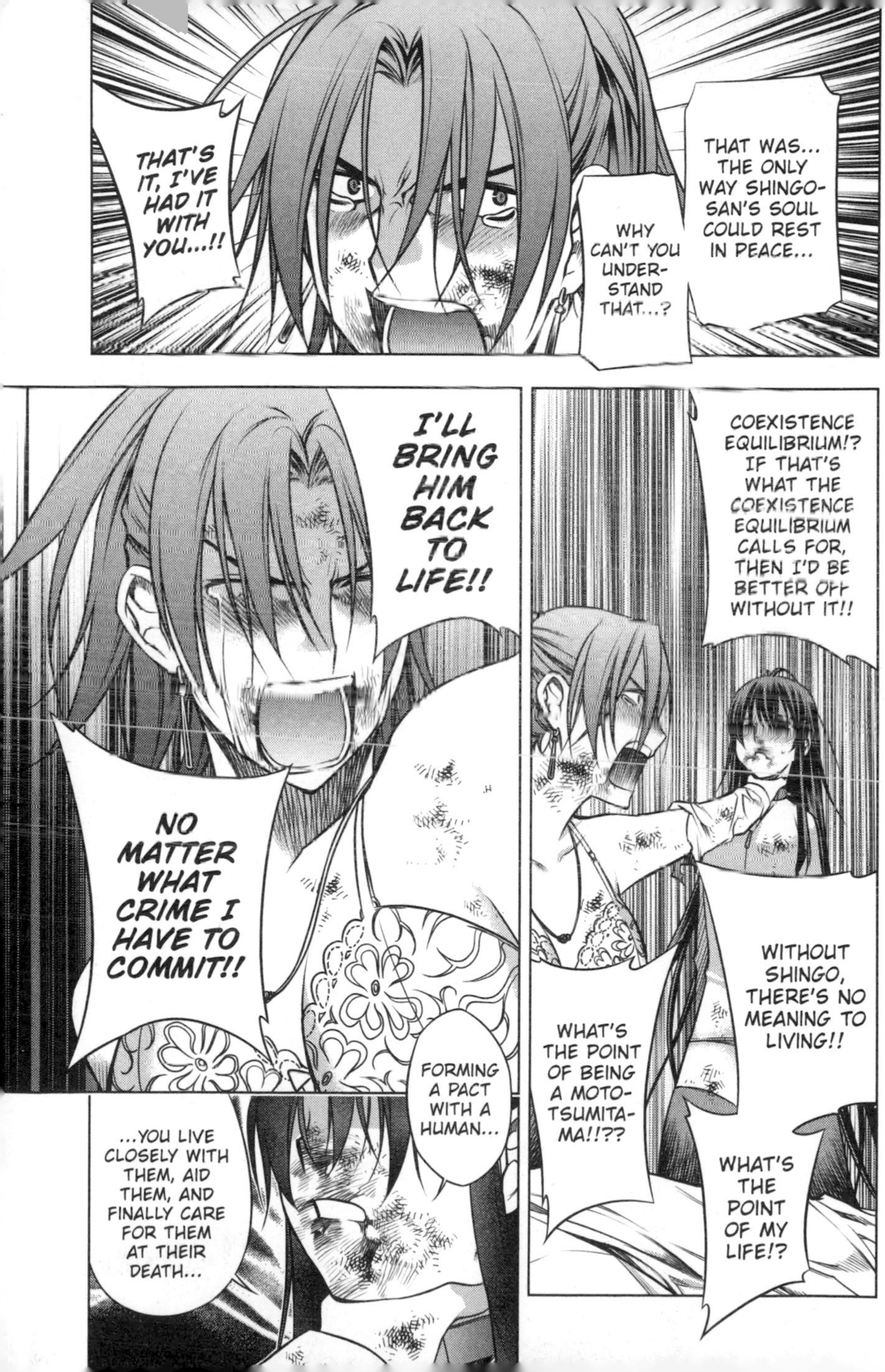
THAT WAS... THE ONLY WAY SHINGO-SAN'S SOUL COULD REST IN PEACE...
WHY CAN'T YOU UNDER-STAND THAT...?
THAT'S IT, I'VE HAD IT WITH YOU...!!
COEXISTENCE EQUILIBRIUM!? IF THAT'S WHAT THE COEXISTENCE EQUILIBRIUM CALLS FOR, THEN I'D BE BETTER OFF WITHOUT IT!!
WITHOUT SHINGO, THERE'S NO MEANING TO LIVING!!
WHAT'S THE POINT OF BEING A MOTO-TSUMITA-MA!!??
WHAT'S THE POINT OF MY LIFE!?
I'LL BRING HIM BACK TO LIFE!!
NO MATTER WHAT CRIME I HAVE TO COMMIT!!
FORMING A PACT WITH A HUMAN...
...YOU LIVE CLOSELY WITH THEM, AID THEM, AND FINALLY CARE FOR THEM AT THEIR DEATH...

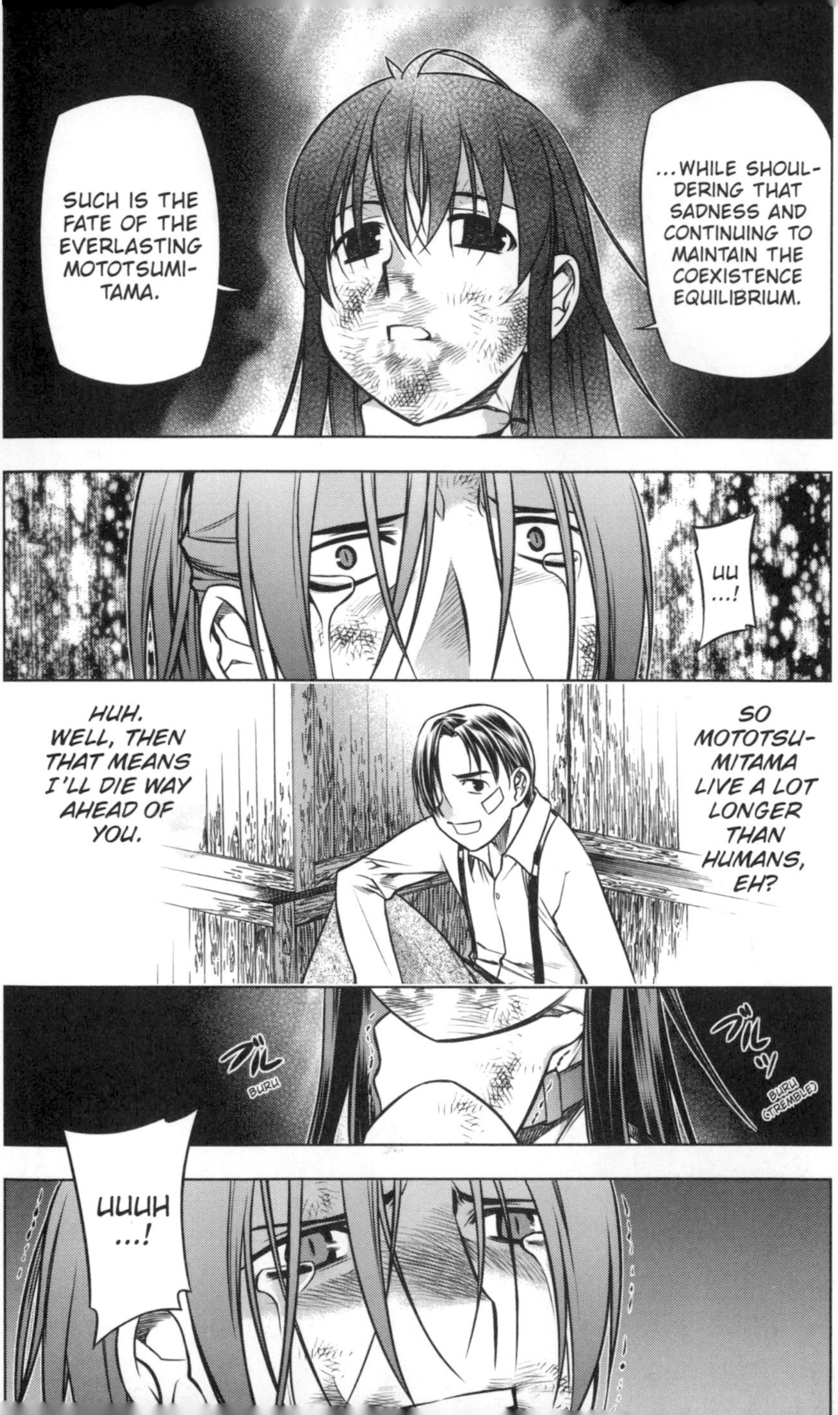
...WHILE SHOULDERING THAT SADNESS AND CONTINUING TO MAINTAIN THE COEXISTENCE EQUILIBRIUM.
SUCH IS THE FATE OF THE EVERLASTING MOTOTSUMITAMA.
UU ...!
SO MOTOTSUMITAMA LIVE A LOT LONGER THAN HUMANS, EH?
HUH. WELL, THEN THAT MEANS I'LL DIE WAY AHEAD OF YOU.
ブルッ
BURU (TREMBLE)
ブル
BURU
UUUH ...!

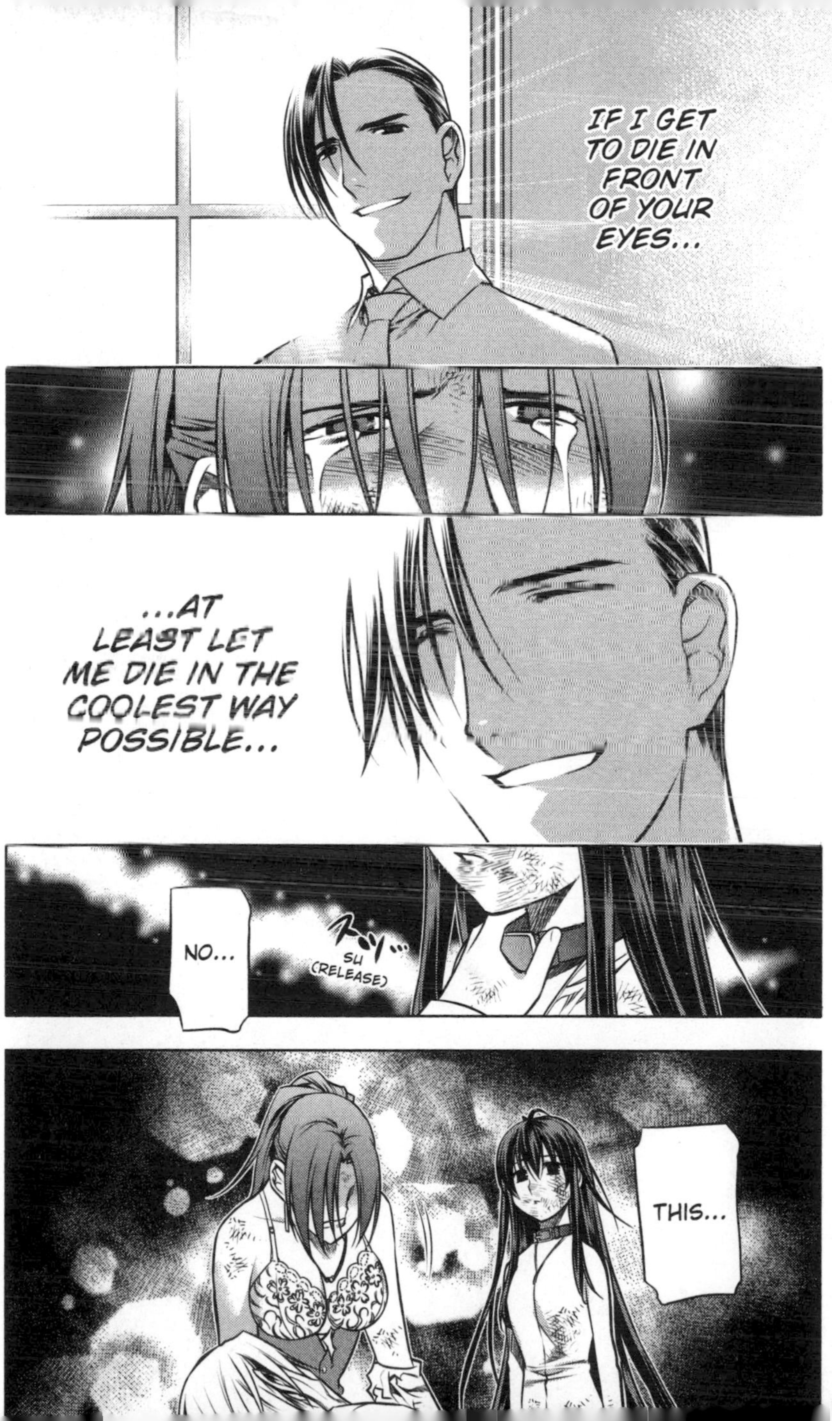
IF I GET TO DIE IN FRONT OF YOUR EYES...
...AT LEAST LET ME DIE IN THE COOLEST WAY POSSIBLE...
SU (RELEASE)
NO...
THIS...

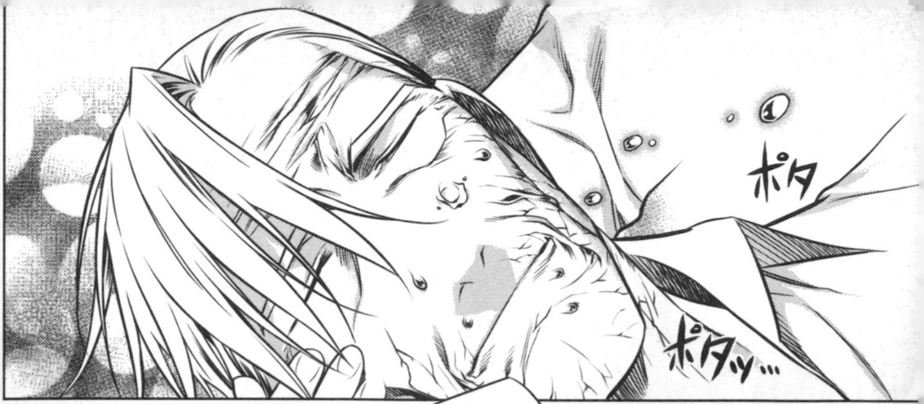
ポタ
ポタッ…

SFX: POTA POTA (PLIP PLIP)

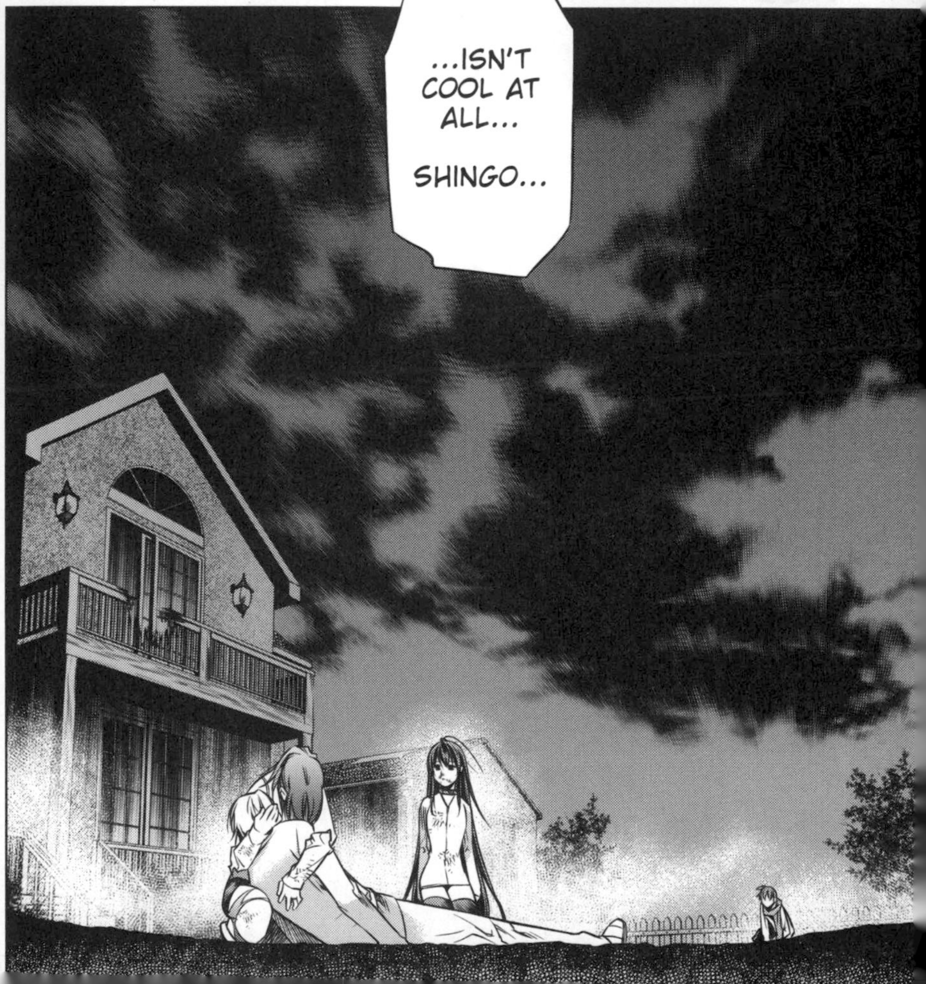
...ISN'T COOL AT ALL...
SHINGO...

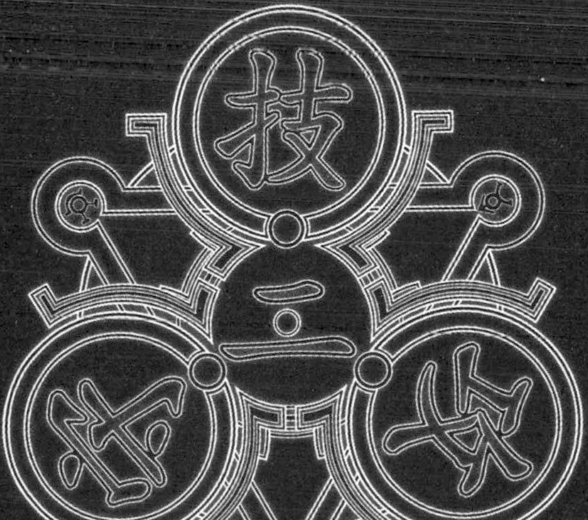
技

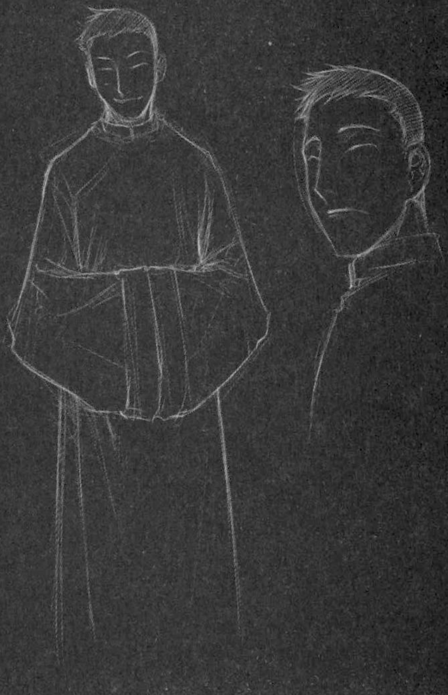

BLACK GOD
which maintains balance in the world.

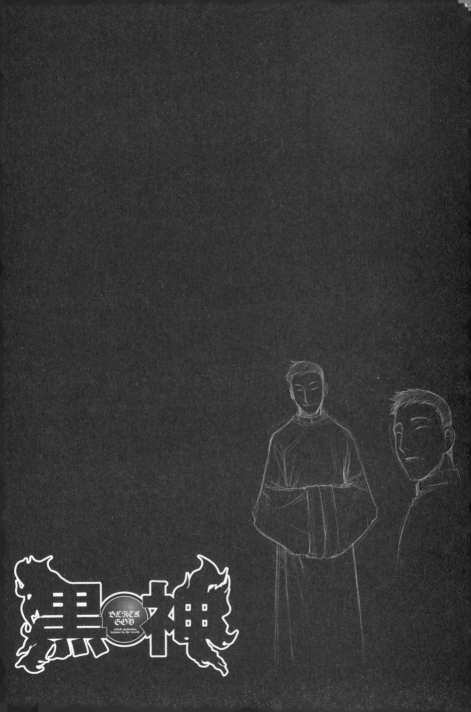

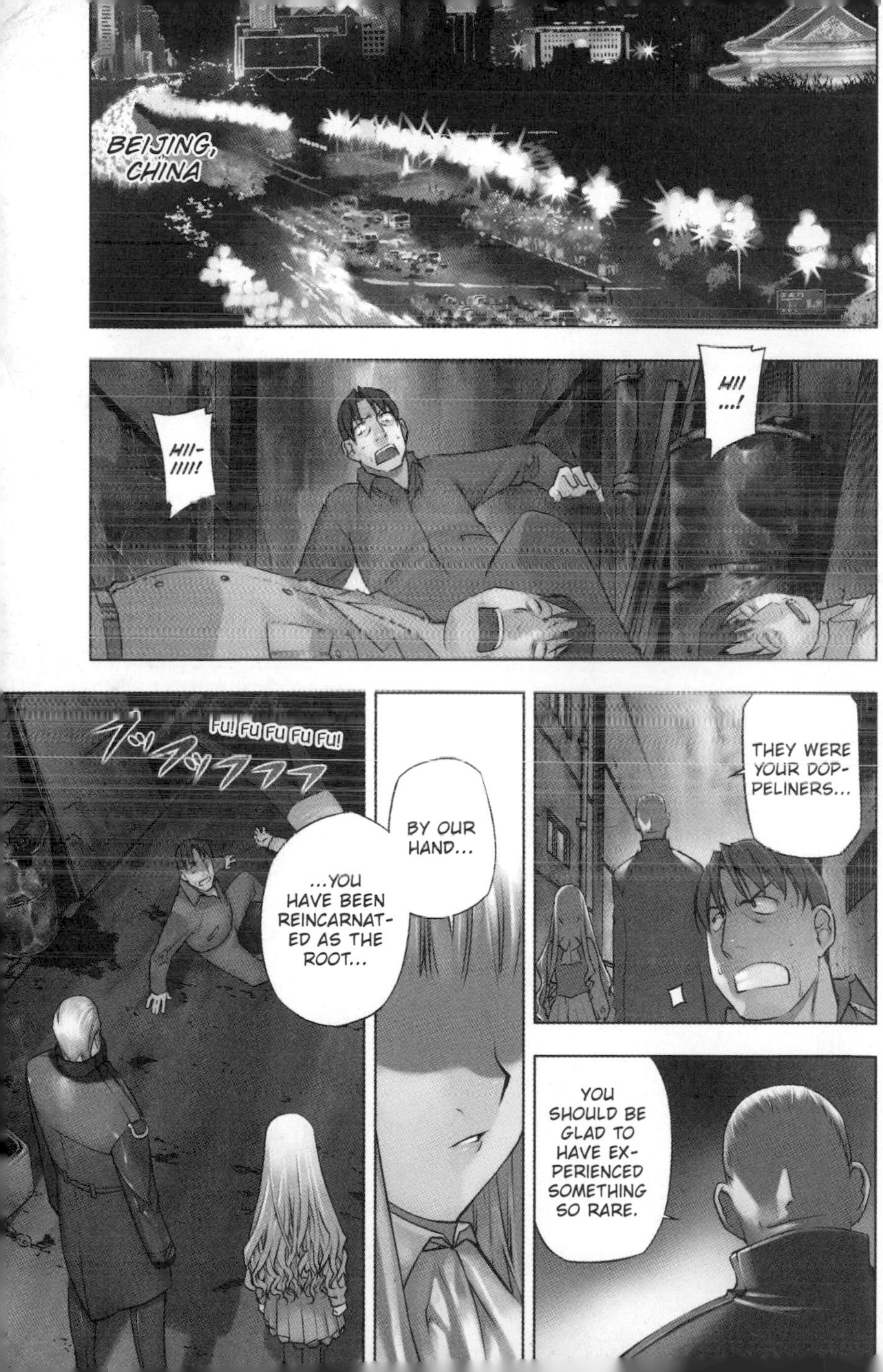
BEIJING, CHINA
HII ...!
HII-IIII!
THEY WERE YOUR DOP-PELINERS...
YOU SHOULD BE GLAD TO HAVE EX-PERIENCED SOMETHING SO RARE.
BY OUR HAND...
...YOU HAVE BEEN REINCARNAT-ED AS THE ROOT...
FU! FU FU FU FU!

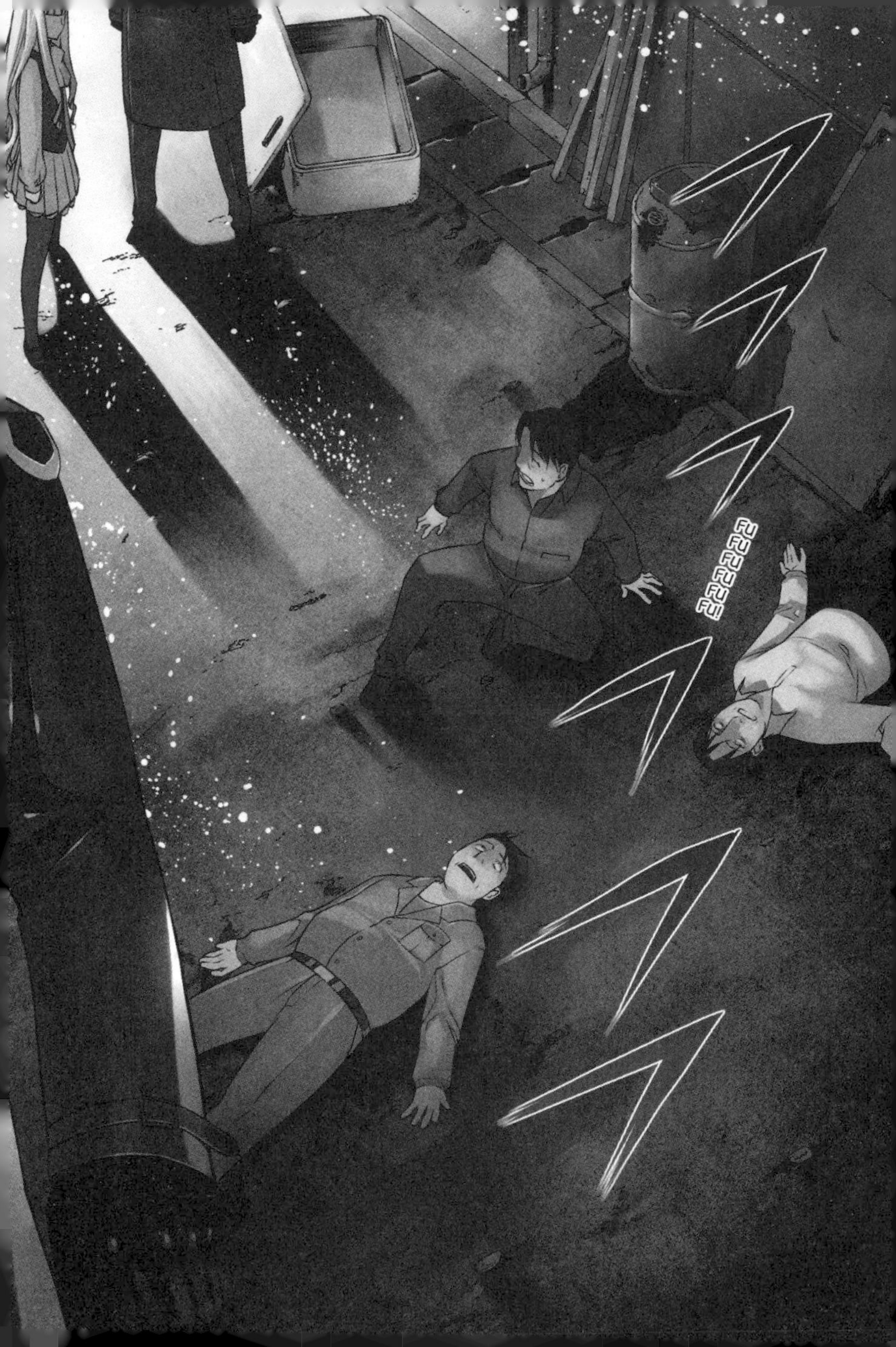
FU FU FU FU FU FU!

FATE.12 REST • TRAINING

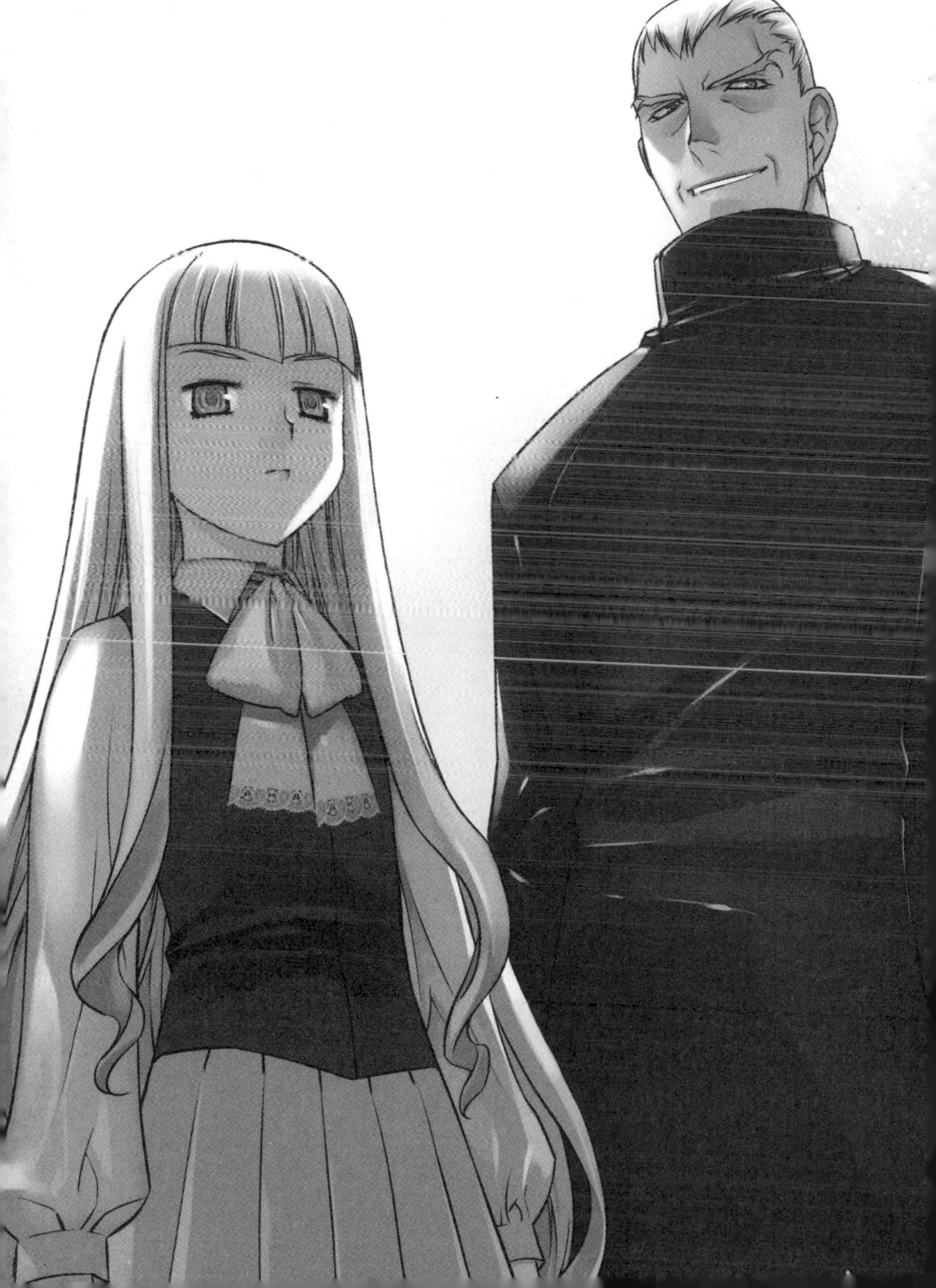

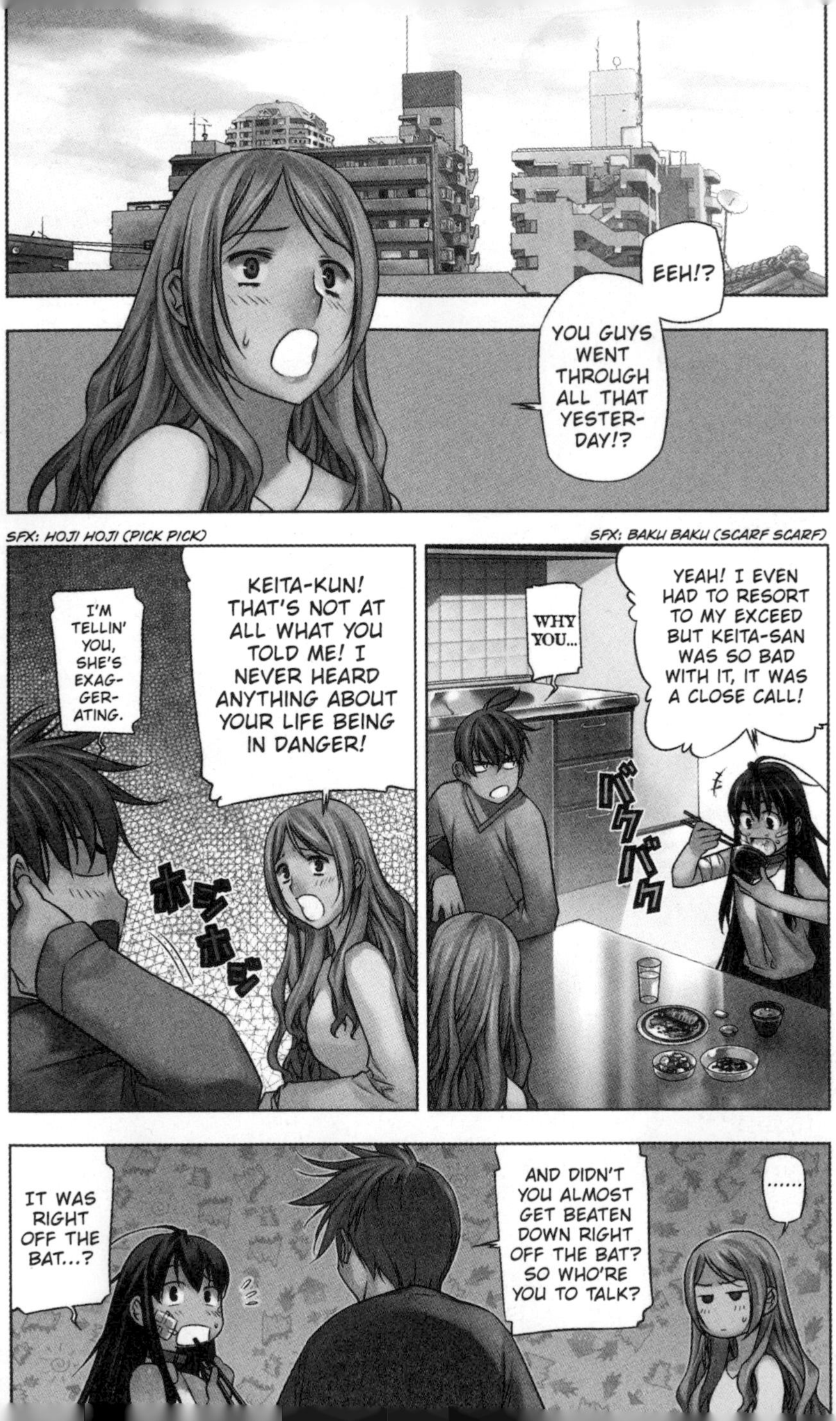
EEH!?
YOU GUYS WENT THROUGH ALL THAT YESTER-DAY!?
SFX: BAKU BAKU (SCARF SCARF)
YEAH! I EVEN HAD TO RESORT TO MY EXCEED BUT KEITA-SAN WAS SO BAD WITH IT, IT WAS A CLOSE CALL!
WHY YOU...
SFX: HOJI HOJI (PICK PICK)
KEITA-KUN! THAT'S NOT AT ALL WHAT YOU TOLD ME! I NEVER HEARD ANYTHING ABOUT YOUR LIFE BEING IN DANGER!
I'M TELLIN' YOU, SHE'S EXAG-GER-ATING.
......
AND DIDN'T YOU ALMOST GET BEATEN DOWN RIGHT OFF THE BAT? SO WHO'RE YOU TO TALK?
IT WAS RIGHT OFF THE BAT...?

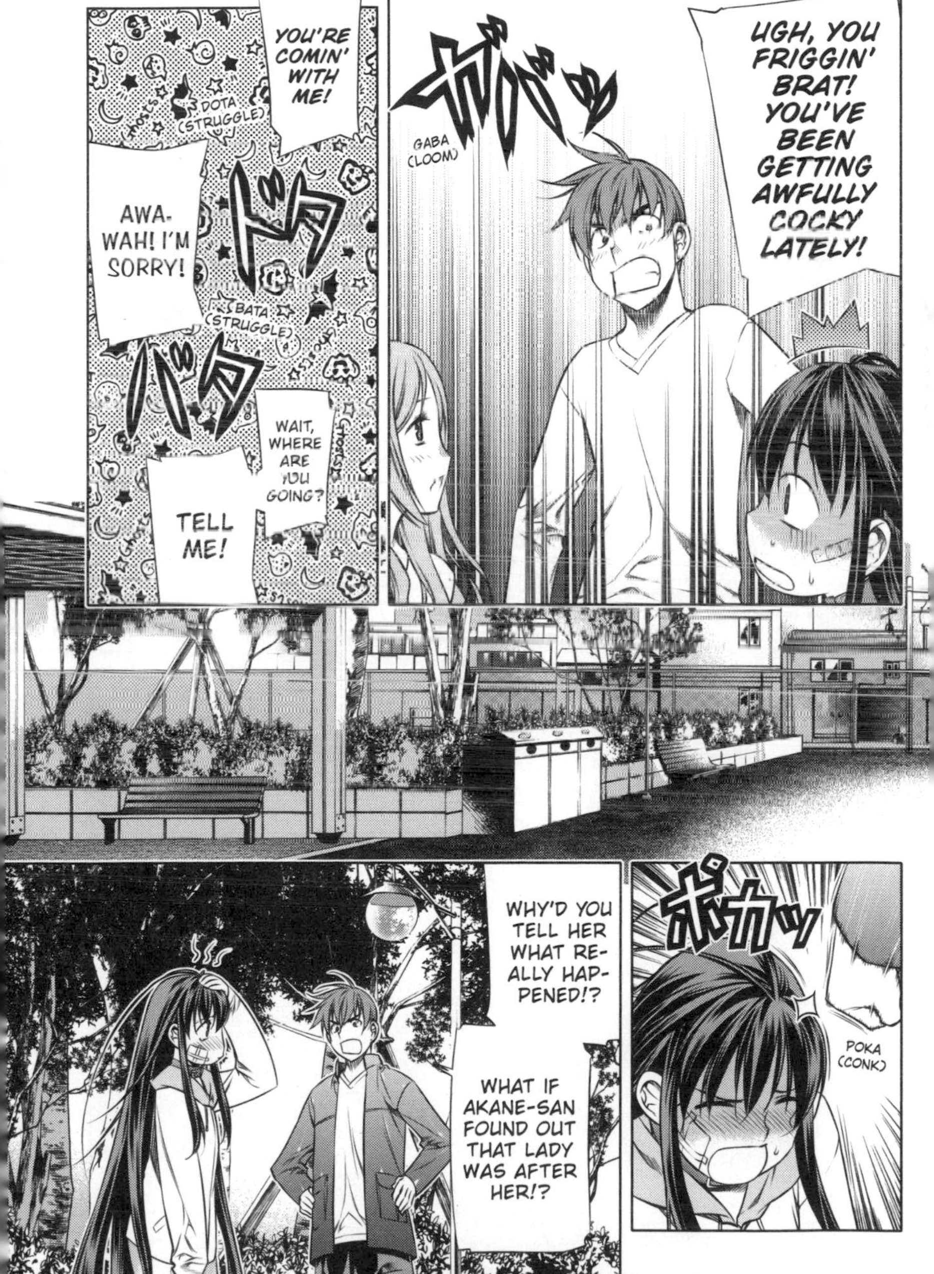
UGH, YOU FRIGGIN' BRAT! YOU'VE BEEN GETTING AWFULLY COCKY LATELY!
GABA (LOOM)
YOU'RE COMIN' WITH ME!
DOTA (STRUGGLE)
AWA-WAH! I'M SORRY!
BATA (STRUGGLE)
WAIT, WHERE ARE YOU GOING?
TELL ME!
POKA (CONK)
WHY'D YOU TELL HER WHAT RE-ALLY HAP-PENED!?
WHAT IF AKANE-SAN FOUND OUT THAT LADY WAS AFTER HER!?

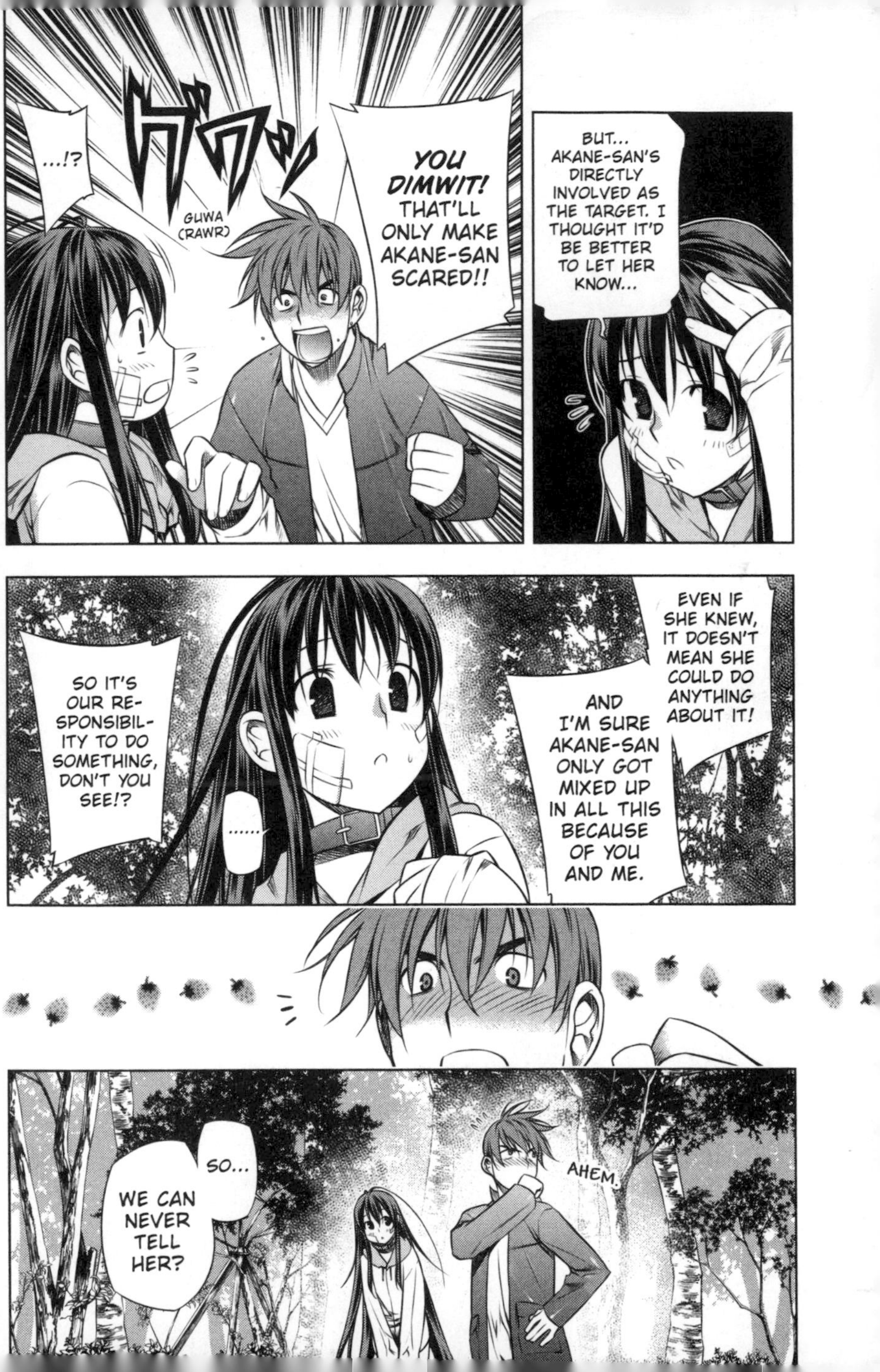
BUT... AKANE-SAN'S DIRECTLY INVOLVED AS THE TARGET. I THOUGHT IT'D BE BETTER TO LET HER KNOW...
YOU DIMWIT! THAT'LL ONLY MAKE AKANE-SAN SCARED!!
GUWA (RAWR)
...!?
EVEN IF SHE KNEW, IT DOESN'T MEAN SHE COULD DO ANYTHING ABOUT IT!
AND I'M SURE AKANE-SAN ONLY GOT MIXED UP IN ALL THIS BECAUSE OF YOU AND ME.
......
SO IT'S OUR RE-SPONSIBIL-ITY TO DO SOMETHING, DON'T YOU SEE!?
AHEM.
SO...
WE CAN NEVER TELL HER?

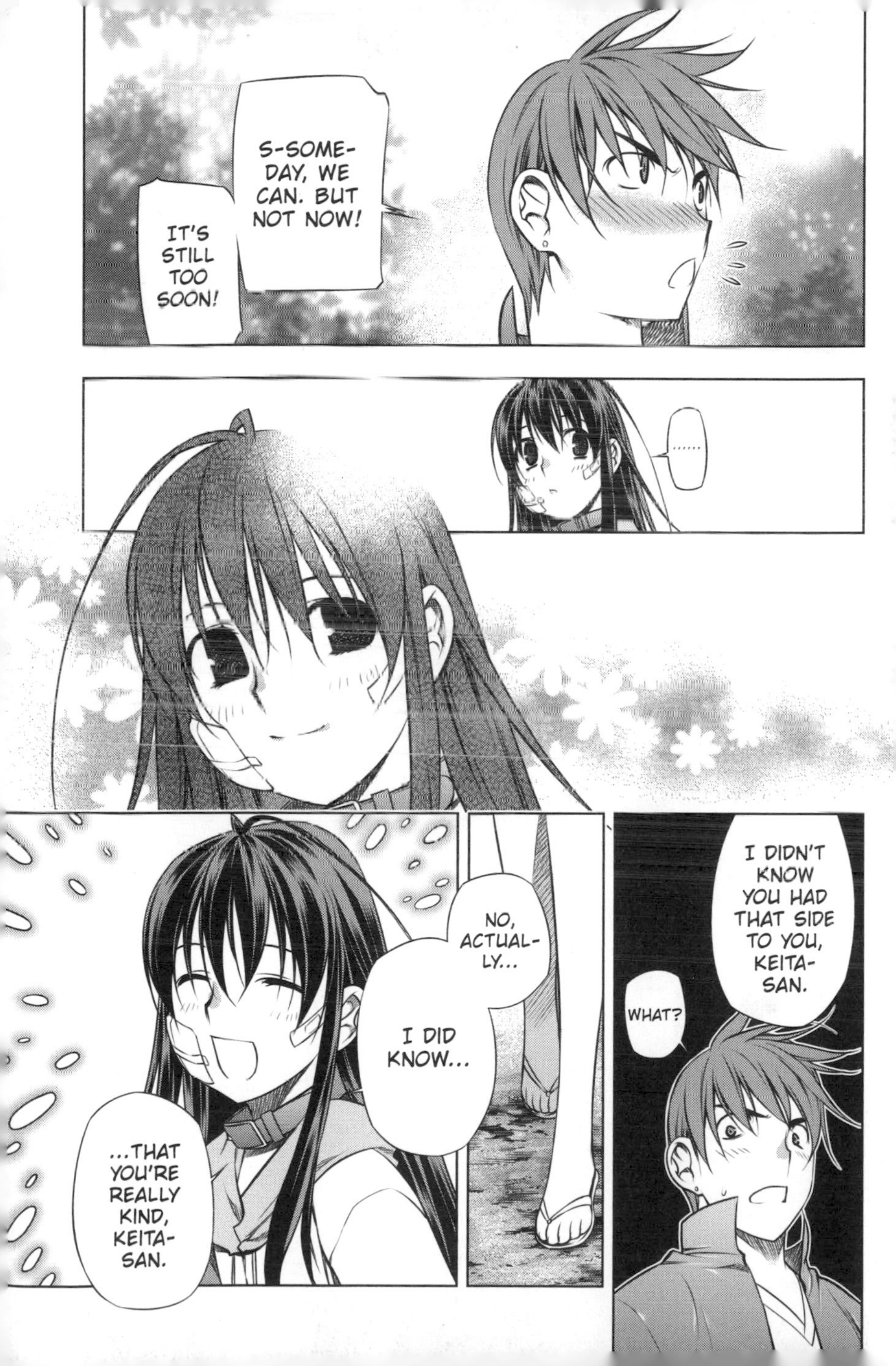
S-SOME-DAY, WE CAN. BUT NOT NOW!
IT'S STILL TOO SOON!
......
I DIDN'T KNOW YOU HAD THAT SIDE TO YOU, KEITA-SAN.
WHAT?
NO, ACTUAL-LY...
I DID KNOW...
...THAT YOU'RE REALLY KIND, KEITA-SAN.

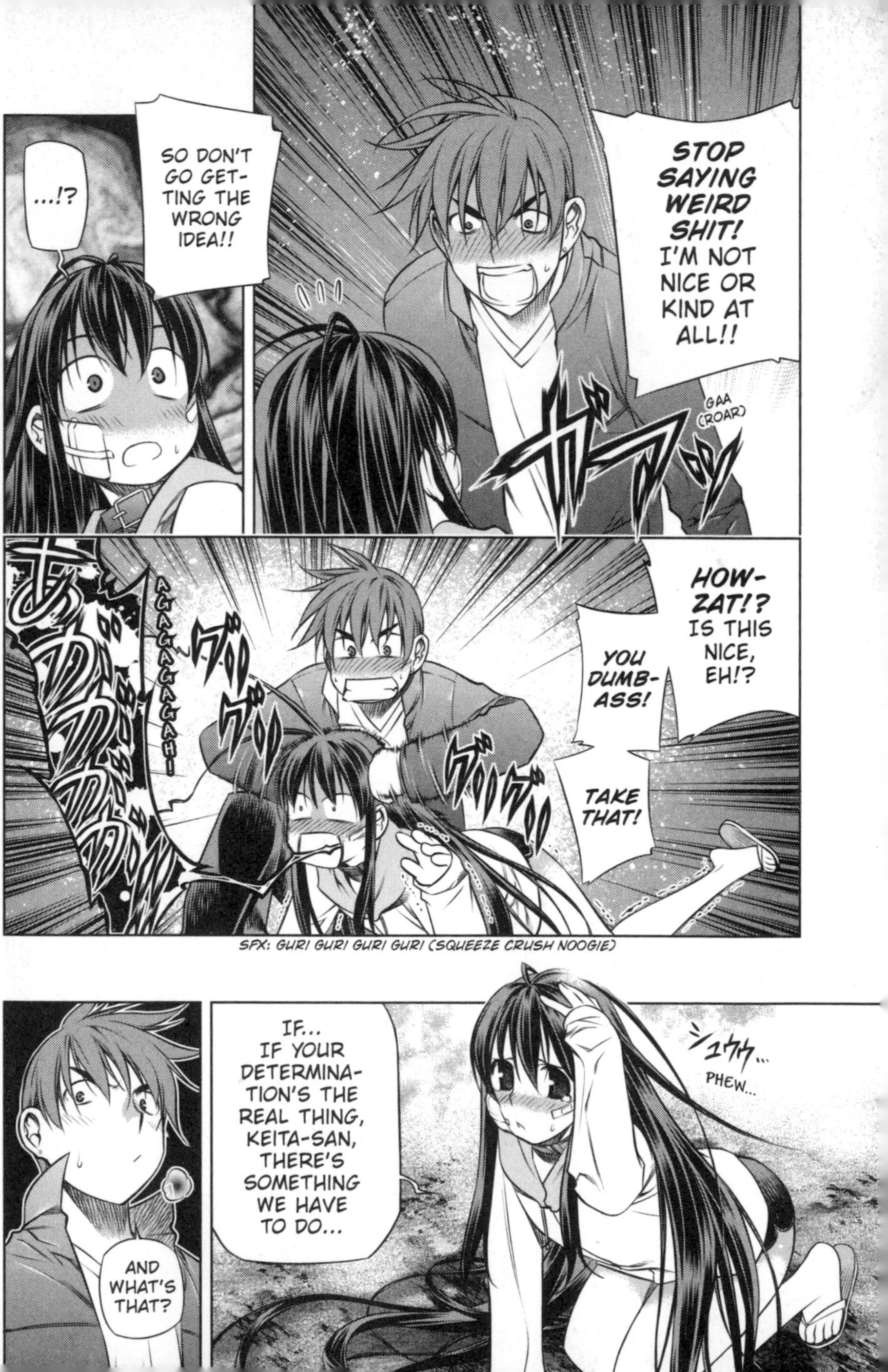
STOP SAYING WEIRD SHIT! I'M NOT NICE OR KIND AT ALL!!
GAA (ROAR)
SO DON'T GO GETTING THE WRONG IDEA!!
...!?
HOW-ZAT!? IS THIS NICE, EH!?
YOU DUMB-ASS!
TAKE THAT!
AGAGAGAGAGAH!
SFX: GURI GURI GURI GURI (SQUEEZE CRUSH NOOGIE)
PHEW...
IF... IF YOUR DETERMINATION'S THE REAL THING, KEITA-SAN, THERE'S SOMETHING WE HAVE TO DO...
AND WHAT'S THAT?

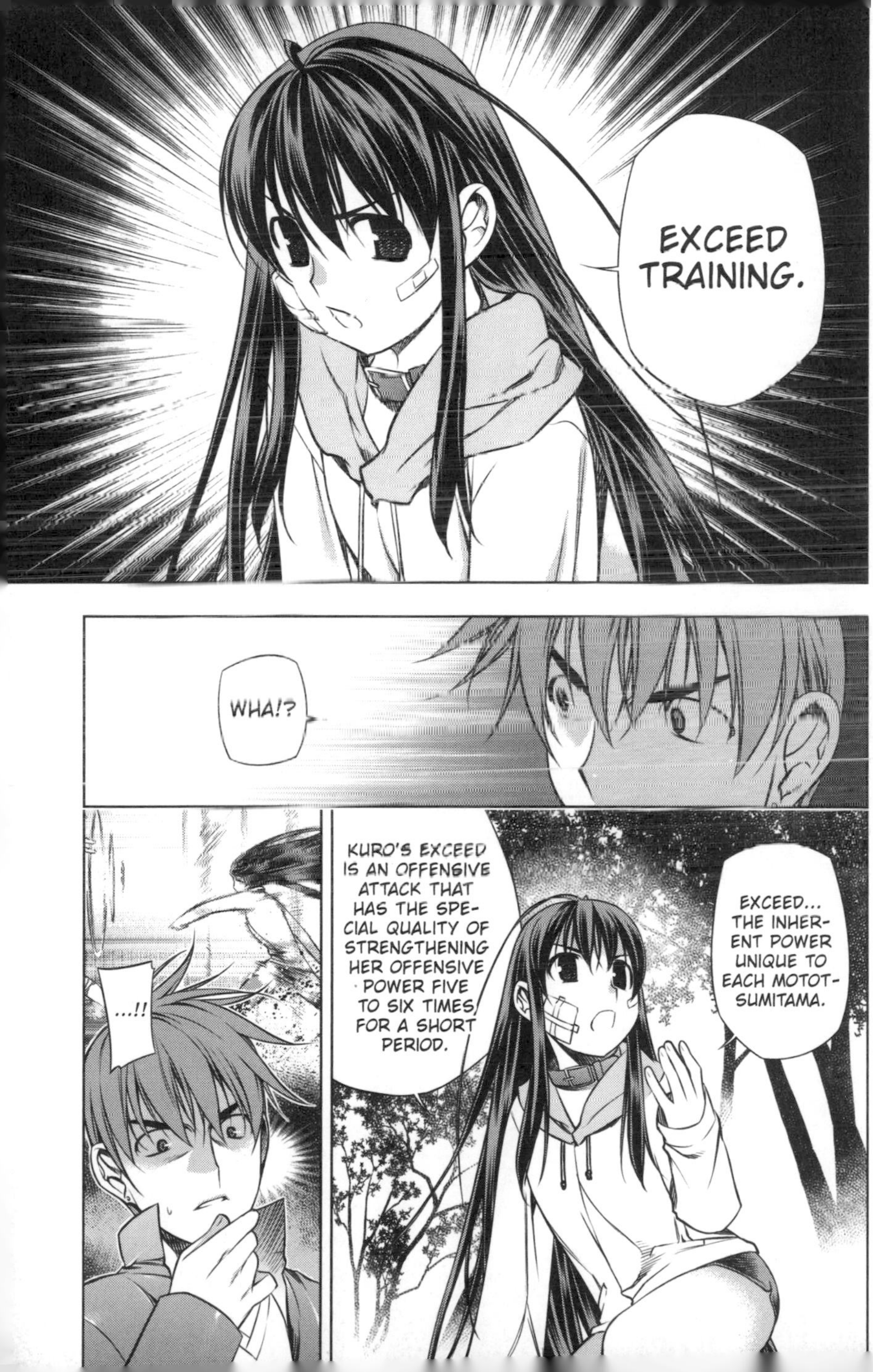
EXCEED TRAINING.
WHA!?
EXCEED... THE INHERENT POWER UNIQUE TO EACH MOTOT-SUMITAMA.
KURO'S EXCEED IS AN OFFENSIVE ATTACK THAT HAS THE SPE-CIAL QUALITY OF STRENGTHENING HER OFFENSIVE POWER FIVE TO SIX TIMES FOR A SHORT PERIOD.
...!!

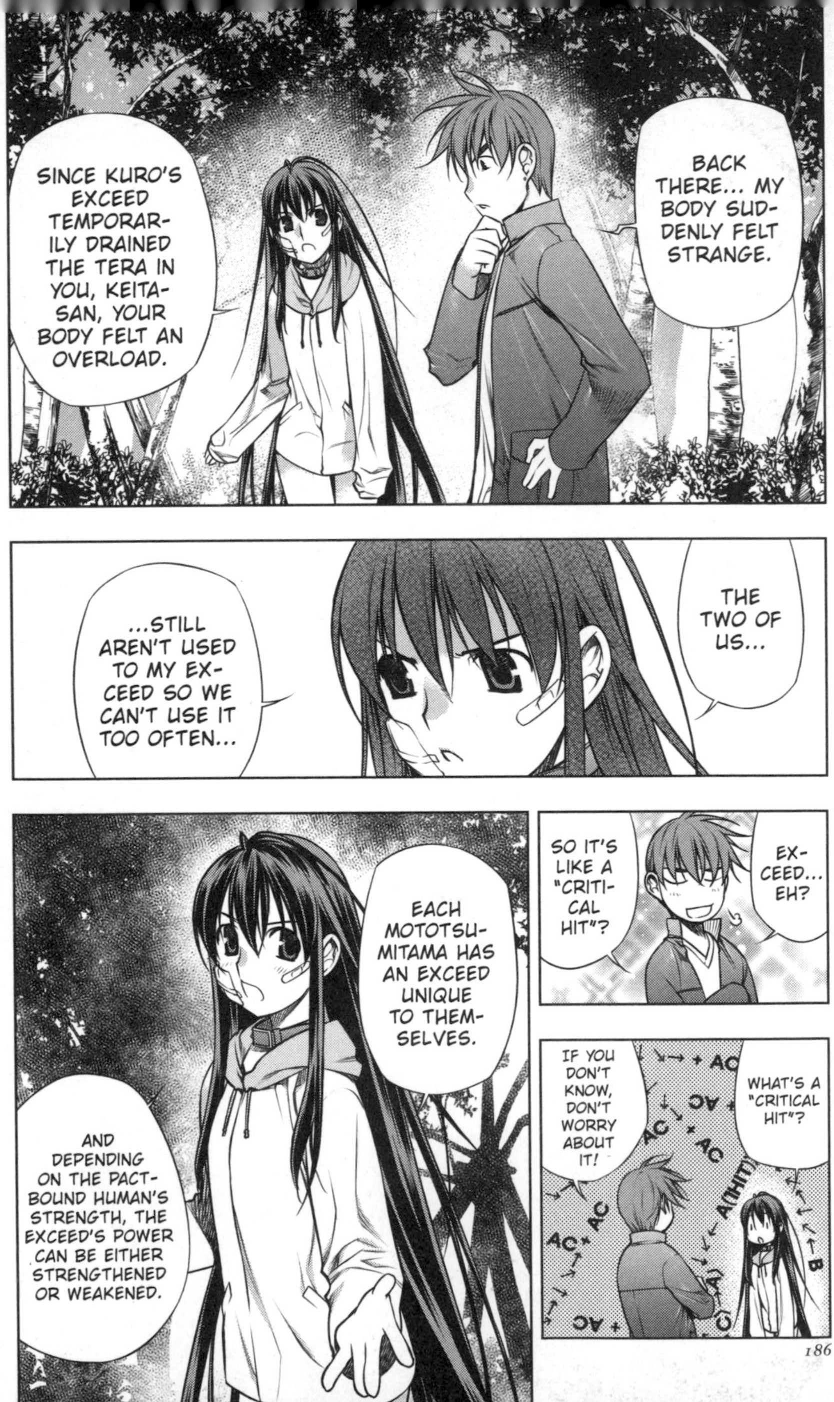
BACK THERE... MY BODY SUDDENLY FELT STRANGE.
SINCE KURO'S EXCEED TEMPORARILY DRAINED THE TERA IN YOU, KEITA-SAN, YOUR BODY FELT AN OVERLOAD.
THE TWO OF US...
...STILL AREN'T USED TO MY EXCEED SO WE CAN'T USE IT TOO OFTEN...
EXCEED... EH?
SO IT'S LIKE A "CRITICAL HIT"?
WHAT'S A "CRITICAL HIT"?
IF YOU DON'T KNOW, DON'T WORRY ABOUT IT!
EACH MOTOTSUMITAMA HAS AN EXCEED UNIQUE TO THEMSELVES.
AND DEPENDING ON THE PACT-BOUND HUMAN'S STRENGTH, THE EXCEED'S POWER CAN BE EITHER STRENGTHENED OR WEAKENED.

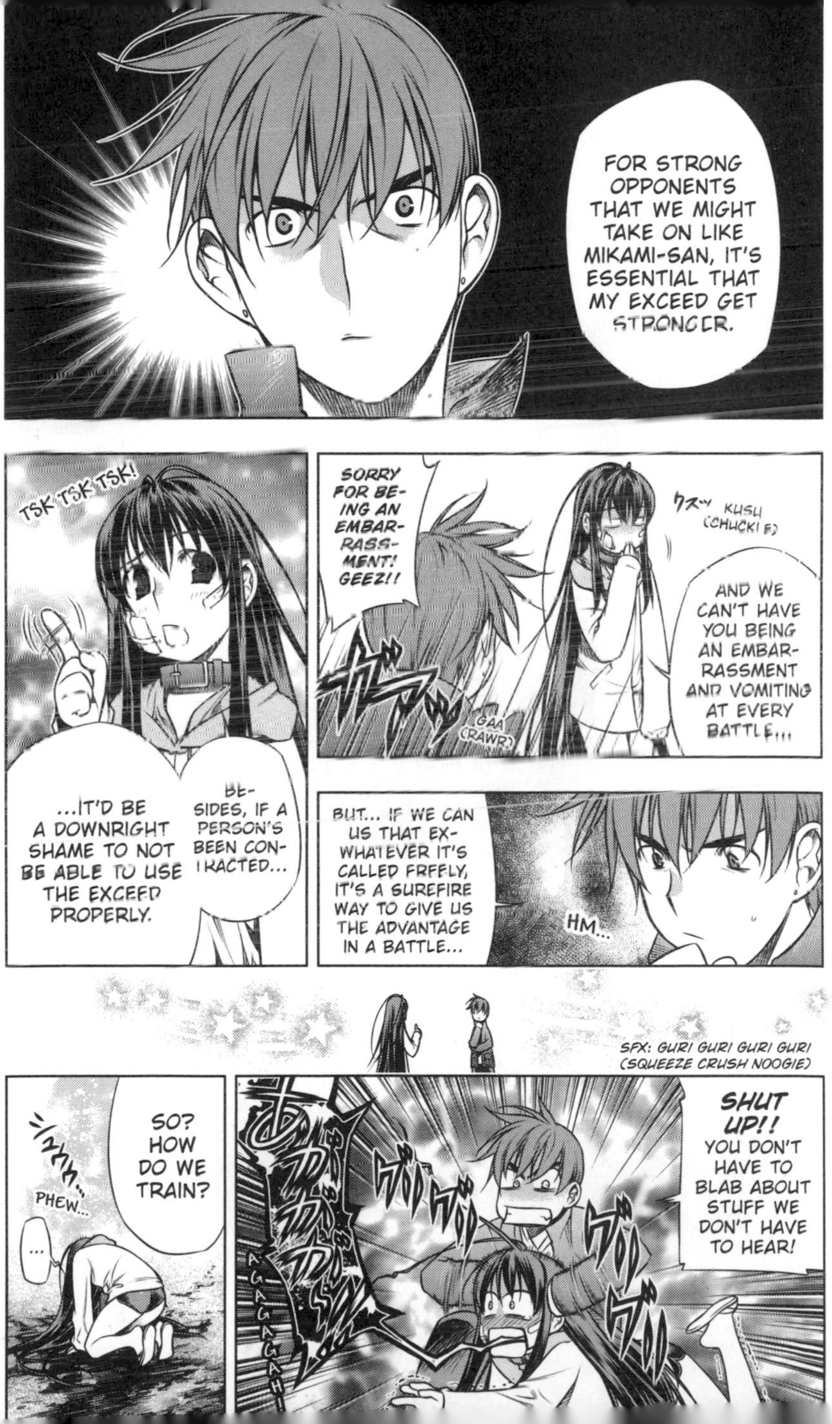
FOR STRONG OPPONENTS THAT WE MIGHT TAKE ON LIKE MIKAMI-SAN, IT'S ESSENTIAL THAT MY EXCEED GET STRONGER.
クスッ KUSU (CHUCKLE)
AND WE CAN'T HAVE YOU BEING AN EMBARRASSMENT AND VOMITING AT EVERY BATTLE...
SORRY FOR BEING AN EMBARRASSMENT! GEEZ!!
GAA (RAWR)
TSK TSK TSK!
BESIDES, IF A PERSON'S BEEN CONTRACTED...
...IT'D BE A DOWNRIGHT SHAME TO NOT BE ABLE TO USE THE EXCEED PROPERLY.
BUT... IF WE CAN US THAT EX-WHATEVER IT'S CALLED FREELY, IT'S A SUREFIRE WAY TO GIVE US THE ADVANTAGE IN A BATTLE...
HM...
SFX: GURI GURI GURI GURI (SQUEEZE CRUSH NOOGIE)
SHUT UP!! YOU DON'T HAVE TO BLAB ABOUT STUFF WE DON'T HAVE TO HEAR!
AGAGAGAGAH
SO? HOW DO WE TRAIN?
PHEW...
...

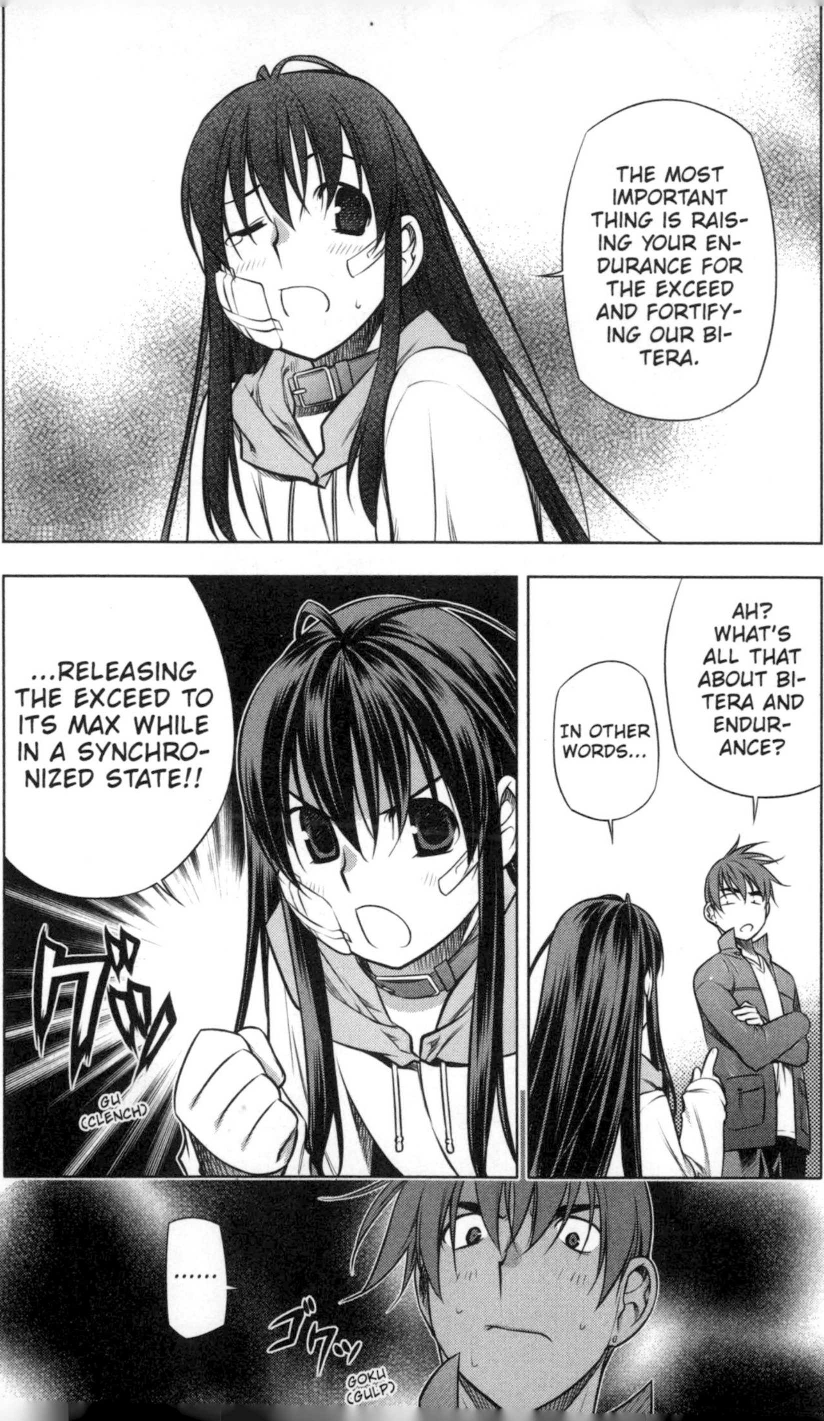

THE MOST IMPORTANT THING IS RAISING YOUR ENDURANCE FOR THE EXCEED AND FORTIFYING OUR BITERA.
AH? WHAT'S ALL THAT ABOUT BITERA AND ENDURANCE?
IN OTHER WORDS...
...RELEASING THE EXCEED TO ITS MAX WHILE IN A SYNCHRONIZED STATE!!
GU (CLENCH)
......
GOKU (GULP)

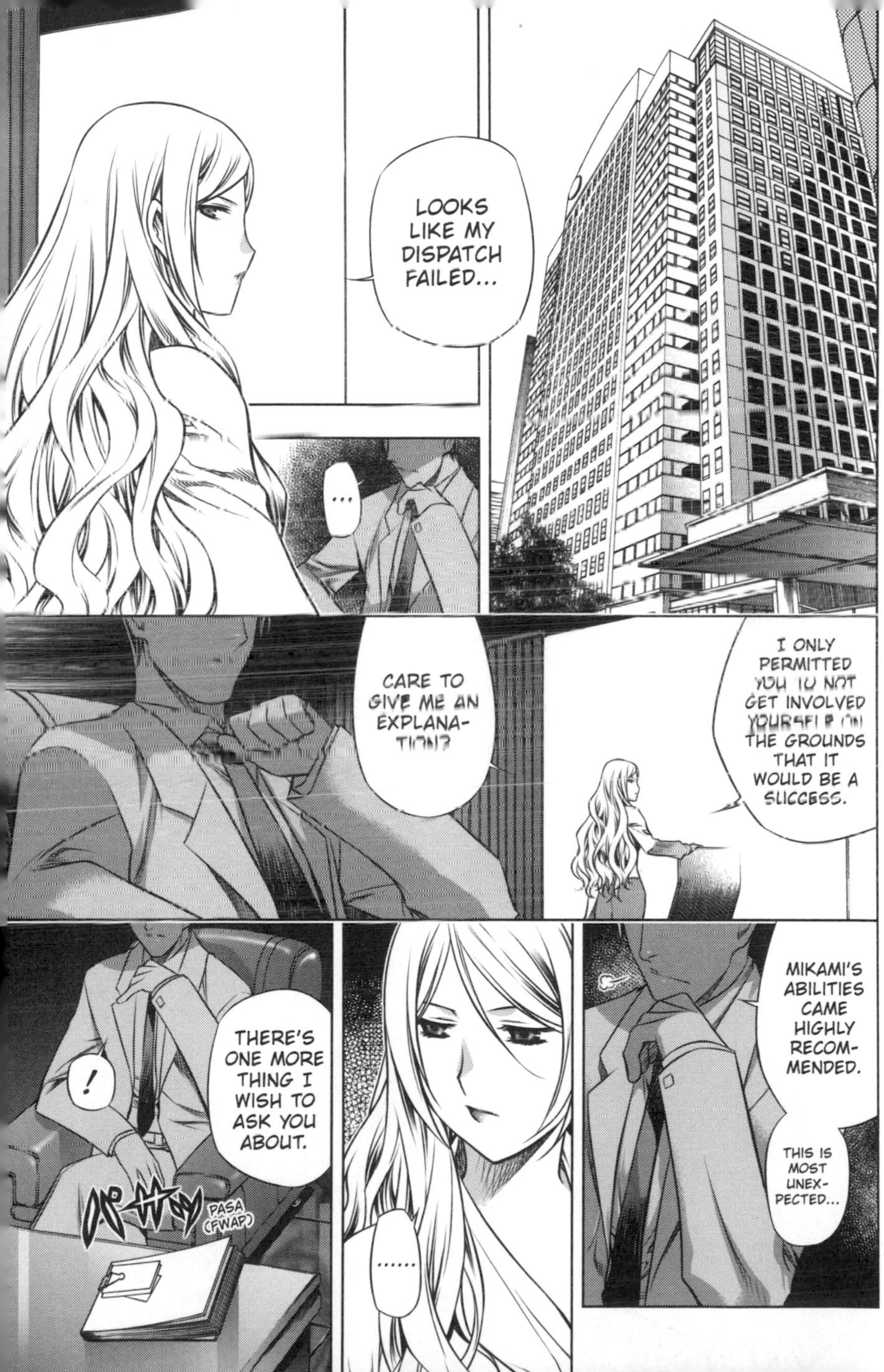
LOOKS LIKE MY DISPATCH FAILED...
...
I ONLY PERMITTED YOU TO NOT GET INVOLVED YOURSELF ON THE GROUNDS THAT IT WOULD BE A SUCCESS.
CARE TO GIVE ME AN EXPLANATION?
MIKAMI'S ABILITIES CAME HIGHLY RECOMMENDED.
THIS IS MOST UNEXPECTED...
......
THERE'S ONE MORE THING I WISH TO ASK YOU ABOUT.
!
PASA (FWAP)

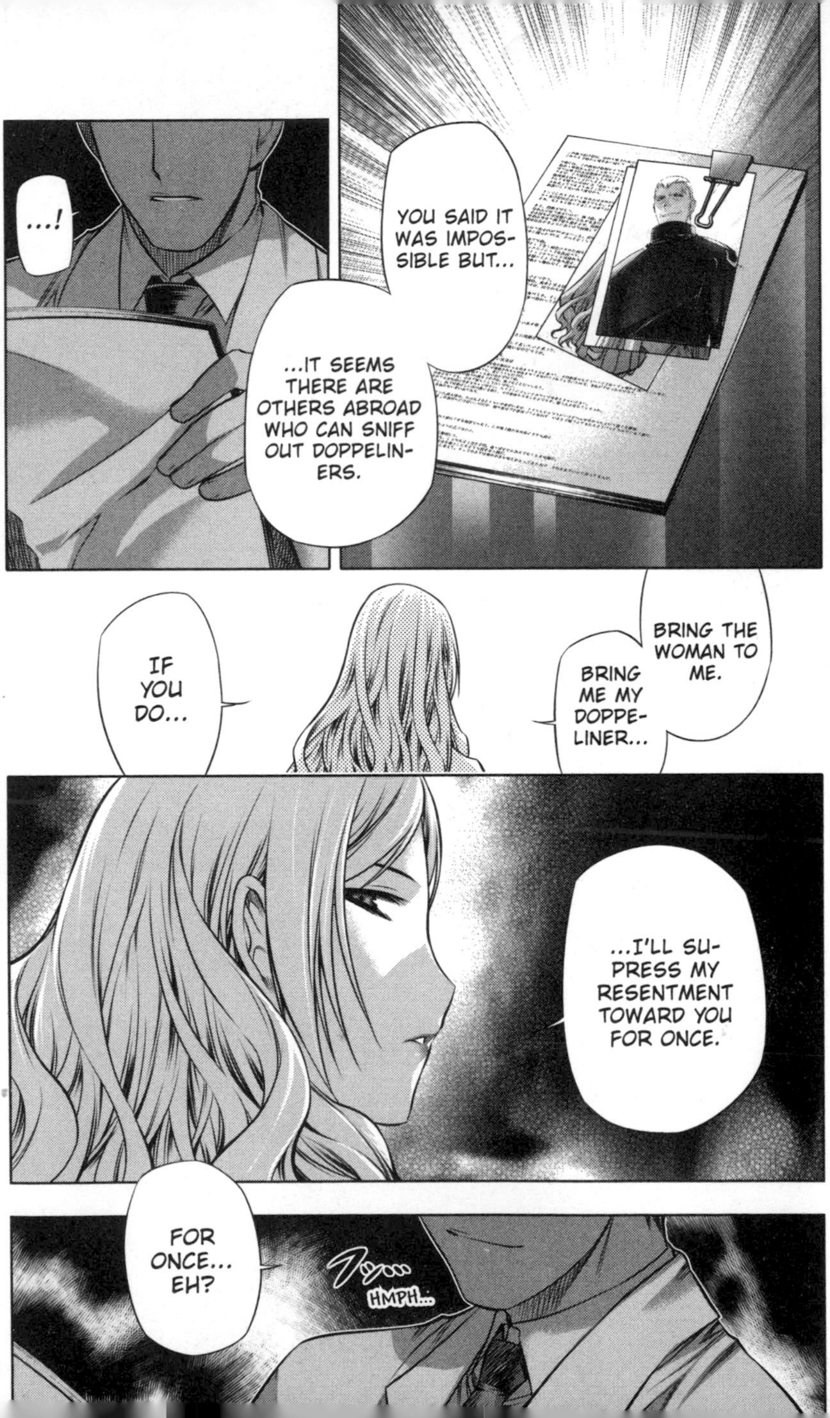
YOU SAID IT WAS IMPOSSIBLE BUT...
...IT SEEMS THERE ARE OTHERS ABROAD WHO CAN SNIFF OUT DOPPELINERS.
...!
BRING THE WOMAN TO ME.
BRING ME MY DOPPELINER...
IF YOU DO...
...I'LL SUPRESS MY RESENTMENT TOWARD YOU FOR ONCE.
FOR ONCE... EH?
HMPH...

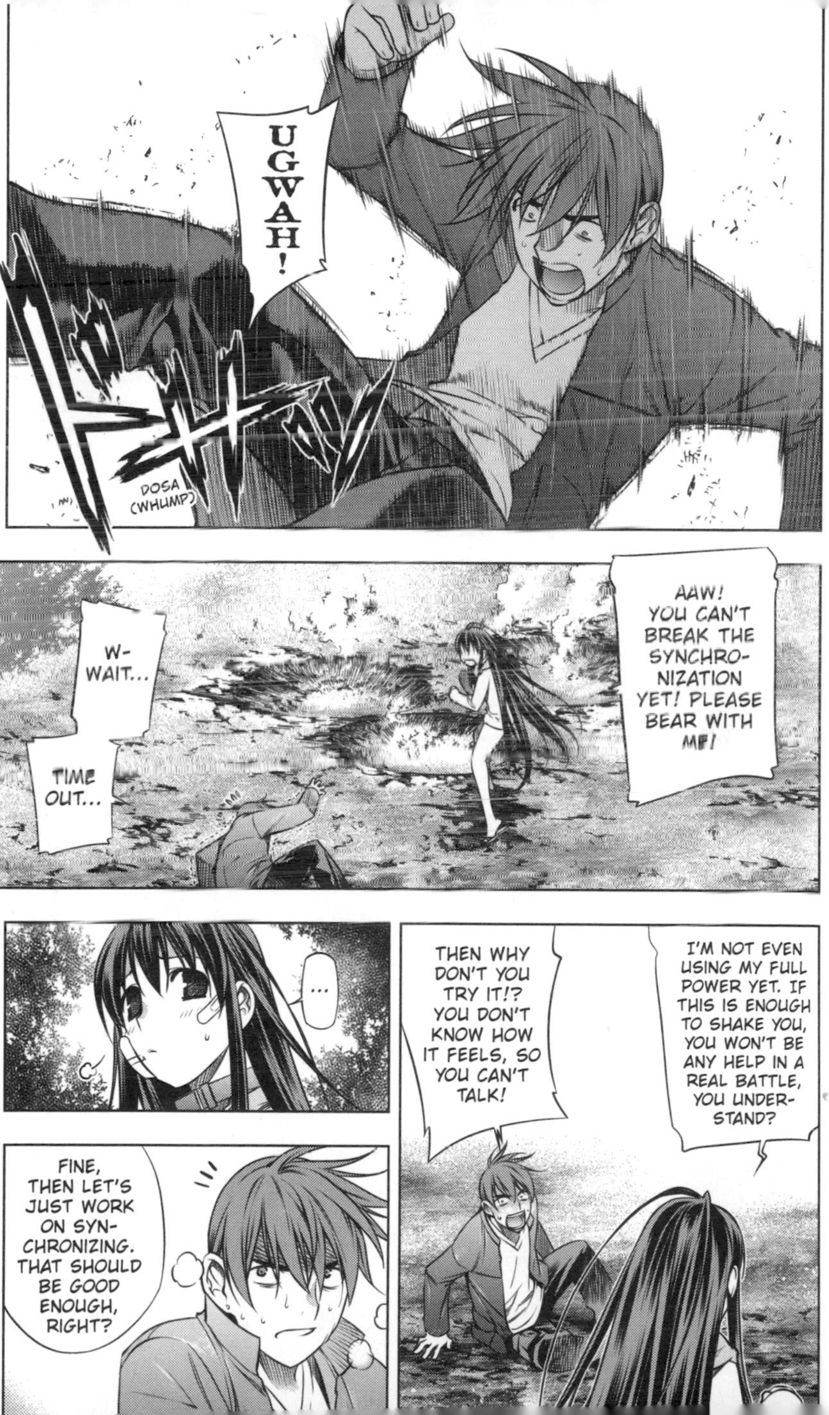
UGWAH!
DOSA (WHUMP)
AAW! YOU CAN'T BREAK THE SYNCHRO-NIZATION YET! PLEASE BEAR WITH ME!
W-WAIT...
TIME OUT...
I'M NOT EVEN USING MY FULL POWER YET. IF THIS IS ENOUGH TO SHAKE YOU, YOU WON'T BE ANY HELP IN A REAL BATTLE, YOU UNDER-STAND?
THEN WHY DON'T YOU TRY IT!? YOU DON'T KNOW HOW IT FEELS, SO YOU CAN'T TALK!
...
FINE, THEN LET'S JUST WORK ON SYN-CHRONIZING. THAT SHOULD BE GOOD ENOUGH, RIGHT?

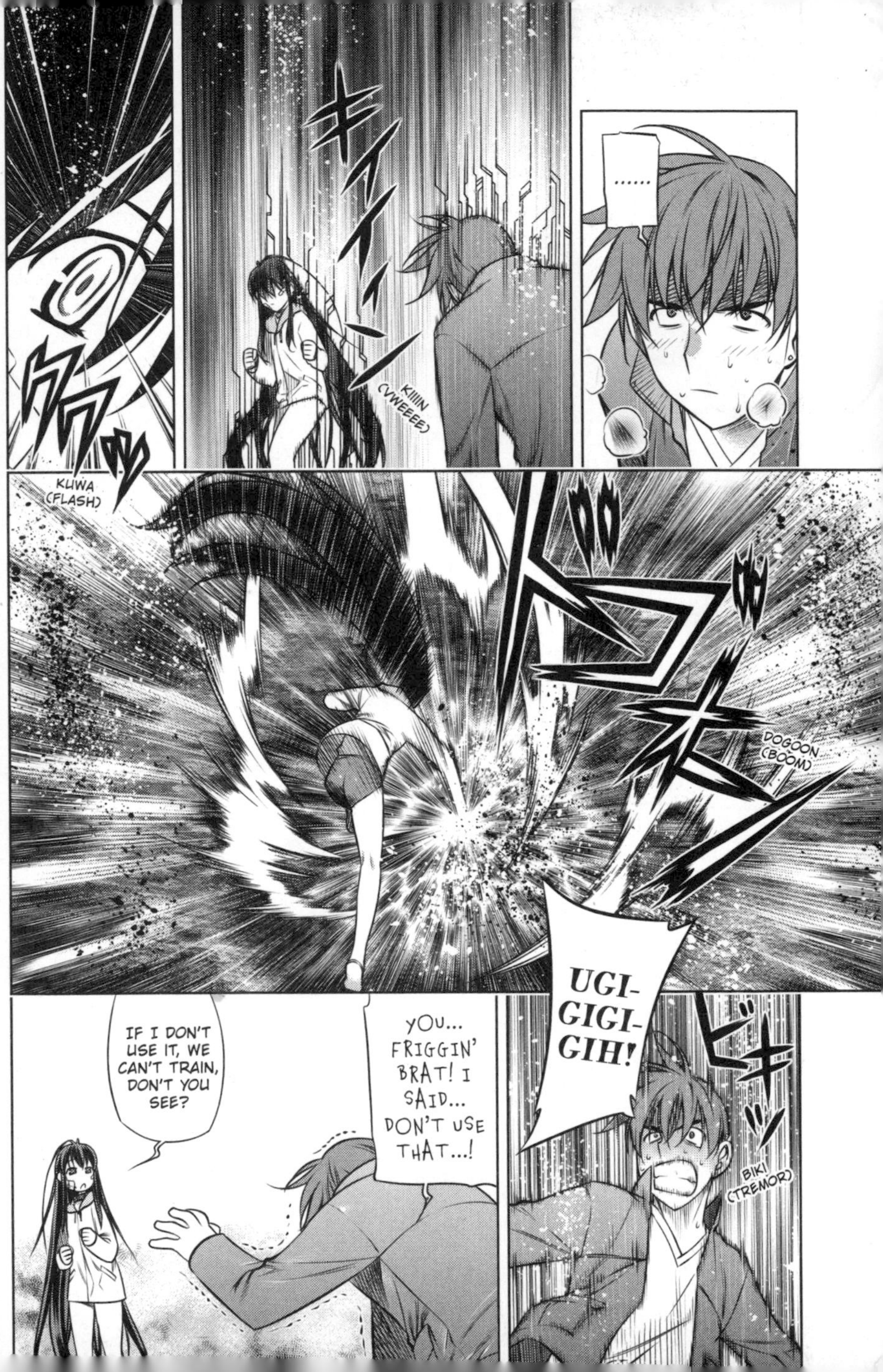
......
KIIIN (VWEEEE)
KUWA (FLASH)
DOGOON (BOOM)
UGI-GIGI-GIGIH!
BIKI (TREMOR)
YOU... FRIGGIN' BRAT! I SAID... DON'T USE THAT...!
IF I DON'T USE IT, WE CAN'T TRAIN, DON'T YOU SEE?

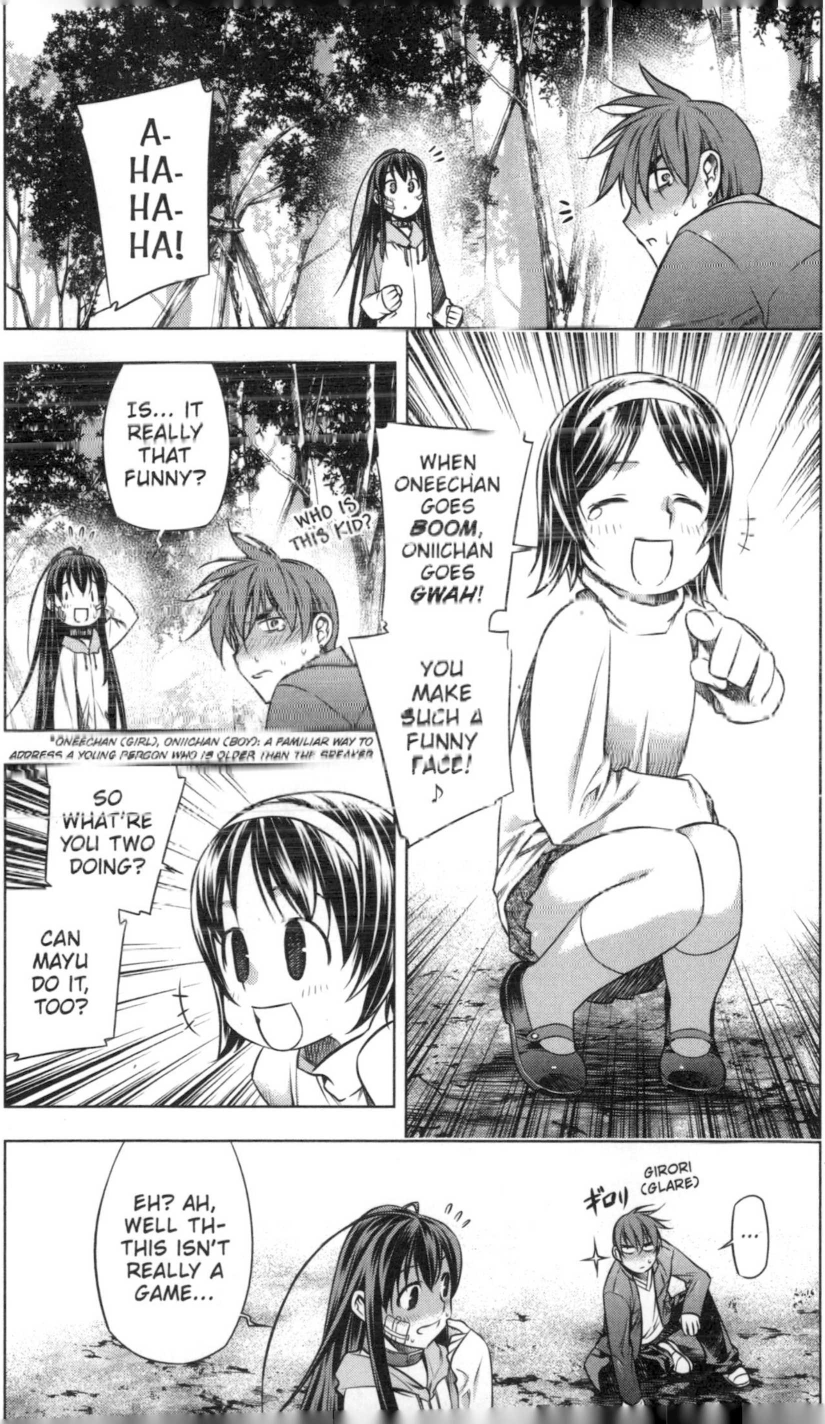
A-HA-HA-HA!
WHEN ONEECHAN GOES BOOM, ONIICHAN GOES GWAH!
YOU MAKE SUCH A FUNNY FACE! ♪
IS... IT REALLY THAT FUNNY?
WHO IS THIS KID?
*ONEECHAN (GIRL), ONIICHAN (BOY): A FAMILIAR WAY TO ADDRESS A YOUNG PERSON WHO IS OLDER THAN THE SPEAKER
SO WHAT'RE YOU TWO DOING?
CAN MAYU DO IT, TOO?
GIRORI (GLARE)
ギロリ
...
EH? AH, WELL TH-THIS ISN'T REALLY A GAME...

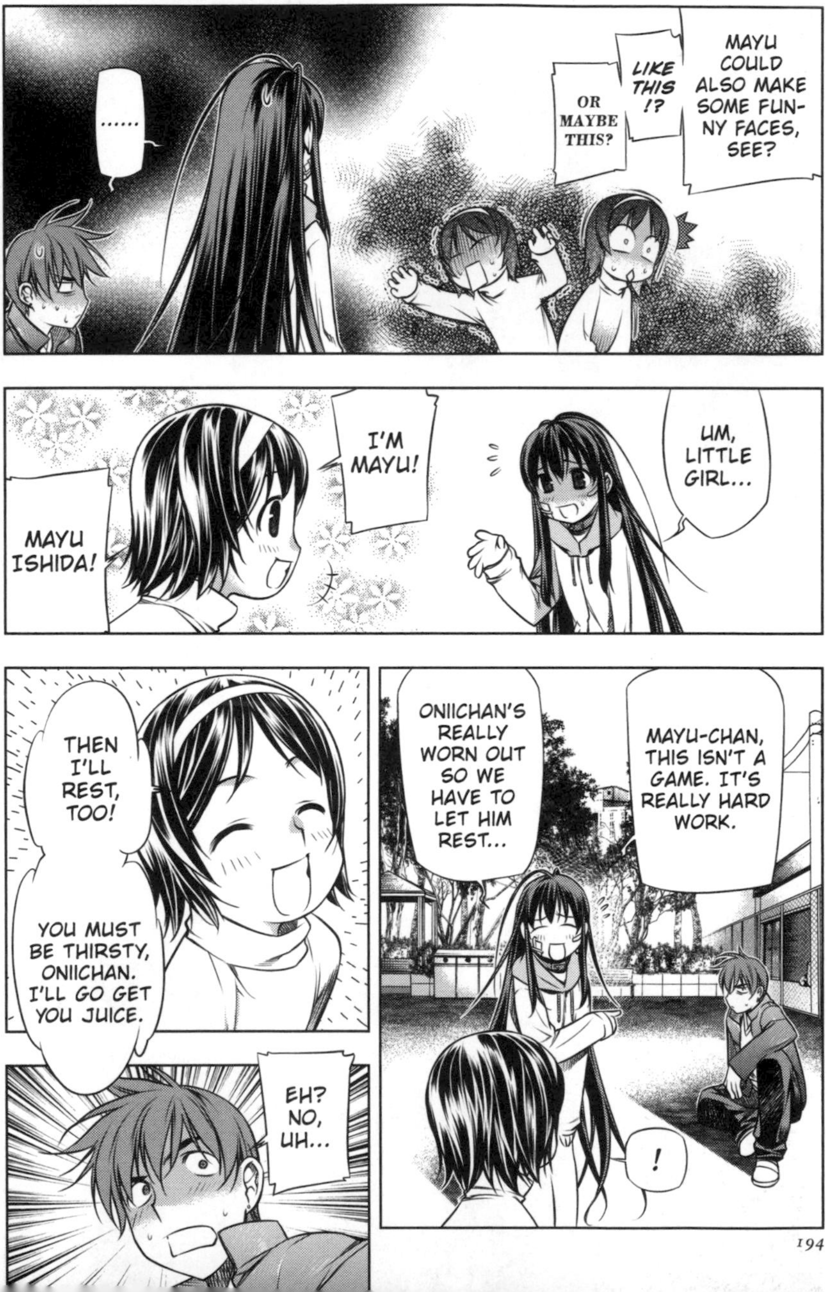
MAYU COULD ALSO MAKE SOME FUN-NY FACES, SEE?
LIKE THIS!?
OR MAYBE THIS?
......
UM, LITTLE GIRL...
I'M MAYU!
MAYU ISHIDA!
MAYU-CHAN, THIS ISN'T A GAME. IT'S REALLY HARD WORK.
ONIICHAN'S REALLY WORN OUT SO WE HAVE TO LET HIM REST...
!
THEN I'LL REST, TOO!
YOU MUST BE THIRSTY, ONIICHAN. I'LL GO GET YOU JUICE.
EH? NO, UH...

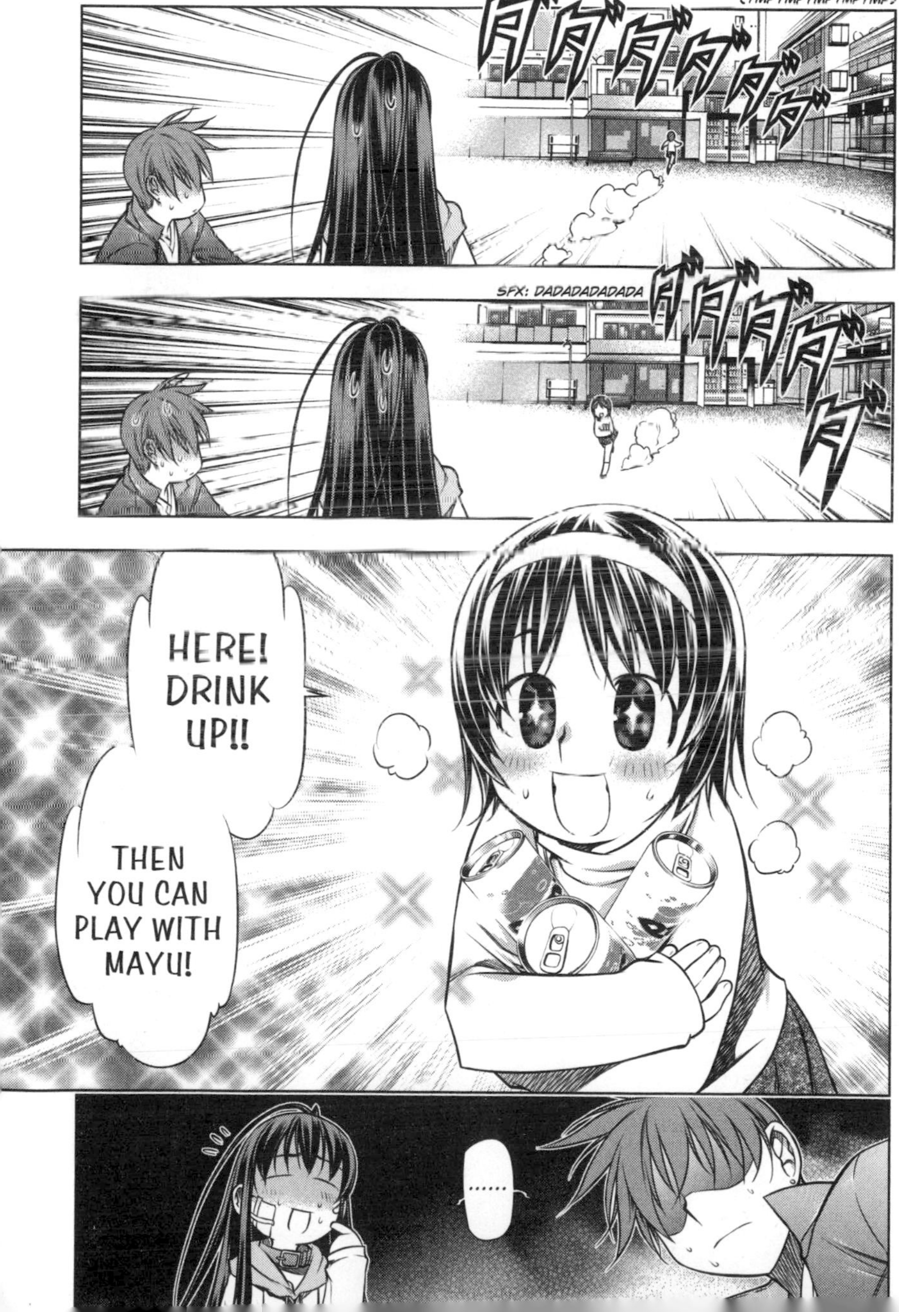
SFX: DADADADADADA (TMPTMPTMPTMPTMP)
SFX: DADADADADADA
HERE! DRINK UP!!
THEN YOU CAN PLAY WITH MAYU!
......

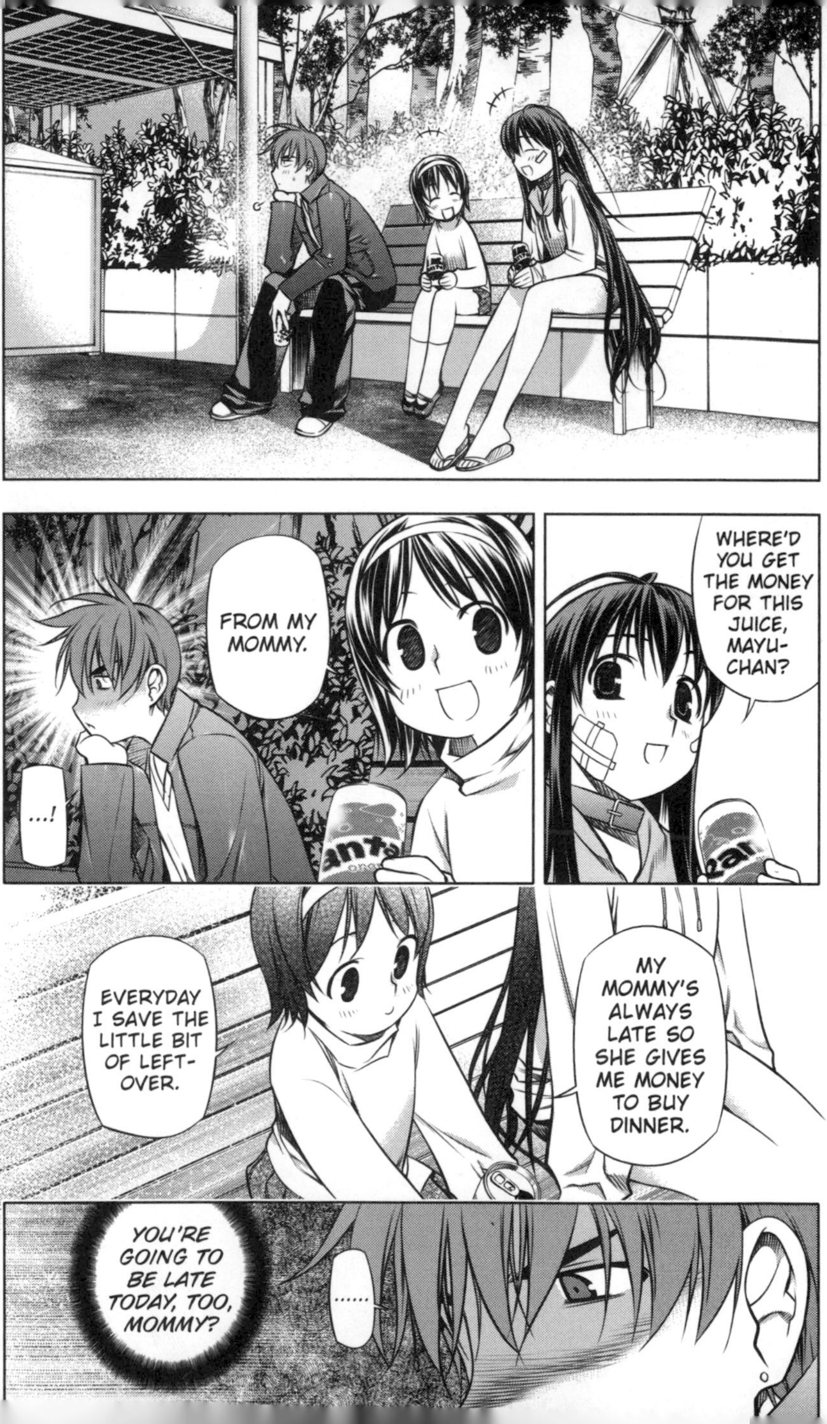
WHERE'D YOU GET THE MONEY FOR THIS JUICE, MAYU-CHAN?
FROM MY MOMMY.
...!
MY MOMMY'S ALWAYS LATE SO SHE GIVES ME MONEY TO BUY DINNER.
EVERYDAY I SAVE THE LITTLE BIT OF LEFT-OVER.
......
YOU'RE GOING TO BE LATE TODAY, TOO, MOMMY?

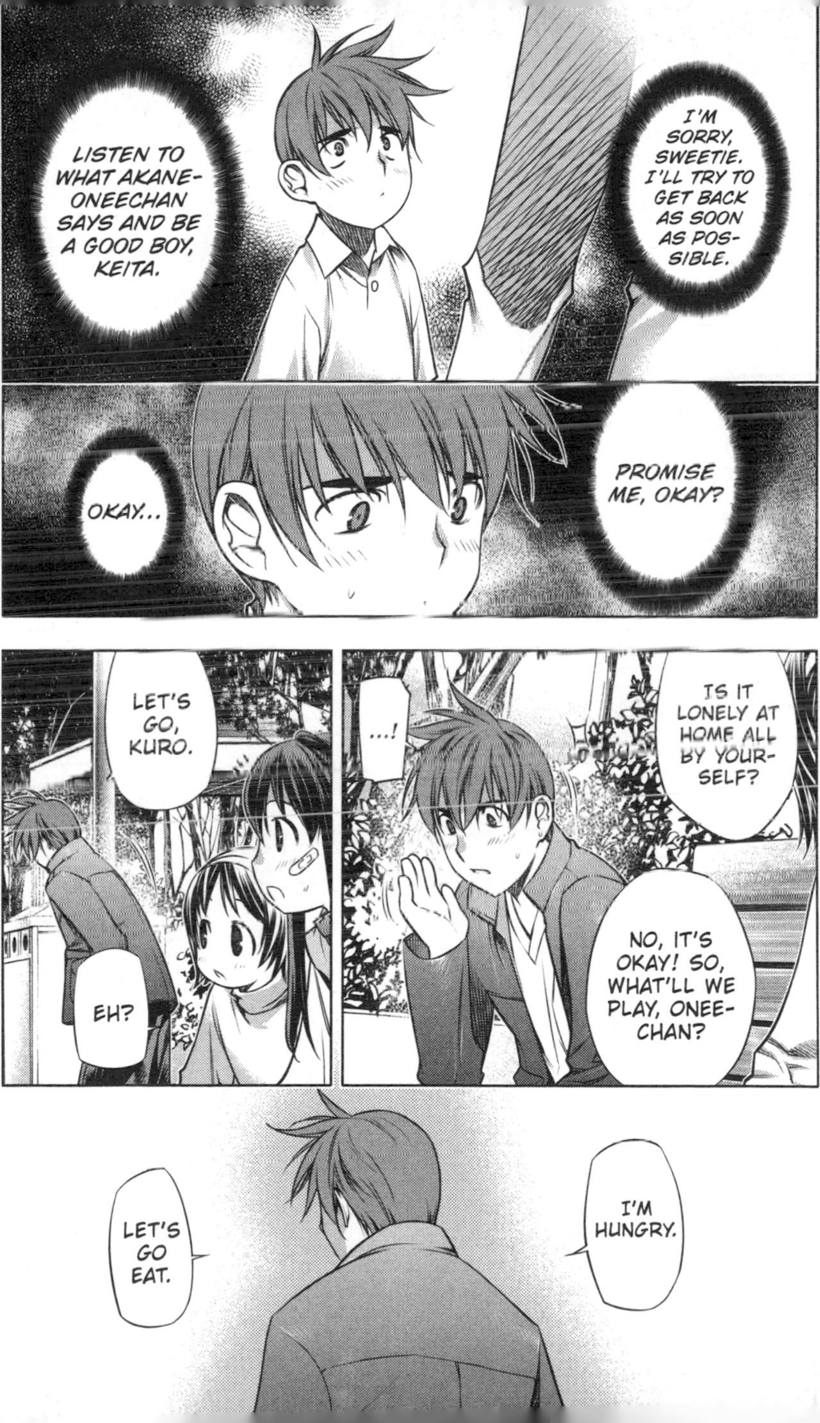
I'M SORRY, SWEETIE. I'LL TRY TO GET BACK AS SOON AS POSSIBLE.
LISTEN TO WHAT AKANE-ONEECHAN SAYS AND BE A GOOD BOY, KEITA.
PROMISE ME, OKAY?
OKAY...
IS IT LONELY AT HOME ALL BY YOURSELF?
...!
NO, IT'S OKAY! SO, WHAT'LL WE PLAY, ONEE-CHAN?
LET'S GO, KURO.
EH?
I'M HUNGRY.
LET'S GO EAT.

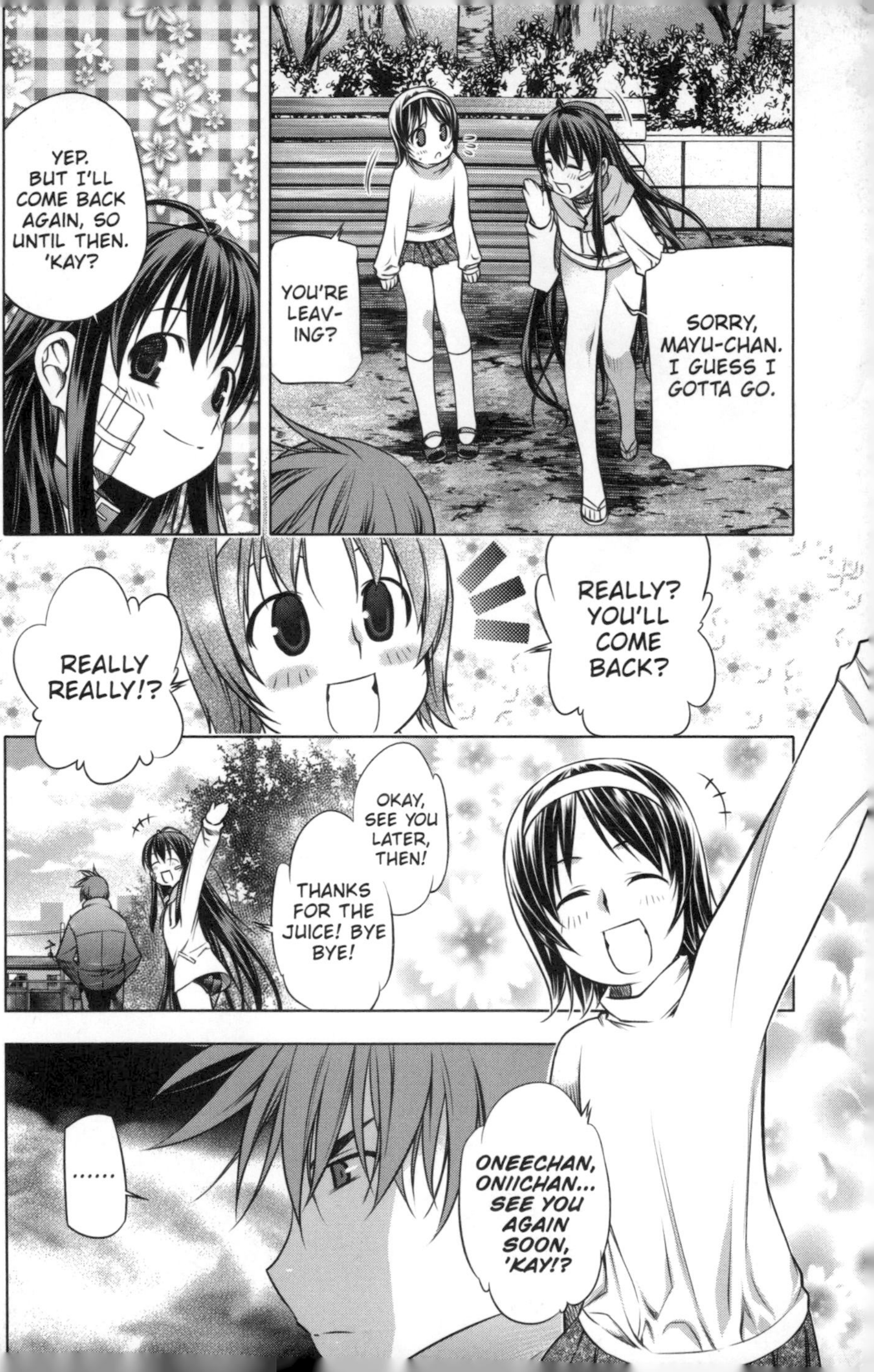
SORRY, MAYU-CHAN. I GUESS I GOTTA GO.
YOU'RE LEAV-ING?
YEP. BUT I'LL COME BACK AGAIN, SO UNTIL THEN. 'KAY?
REALLY? YOU'LL COME BACK?
REALLY REALLY!?
OKAY, SEE YOU LATER, THEN!
THANKS FOR THE JUICE! BYE BYE!
ONEECHAN, ONIICHAN... SEE YOU AGAIN SOON, 'KAY!?
....

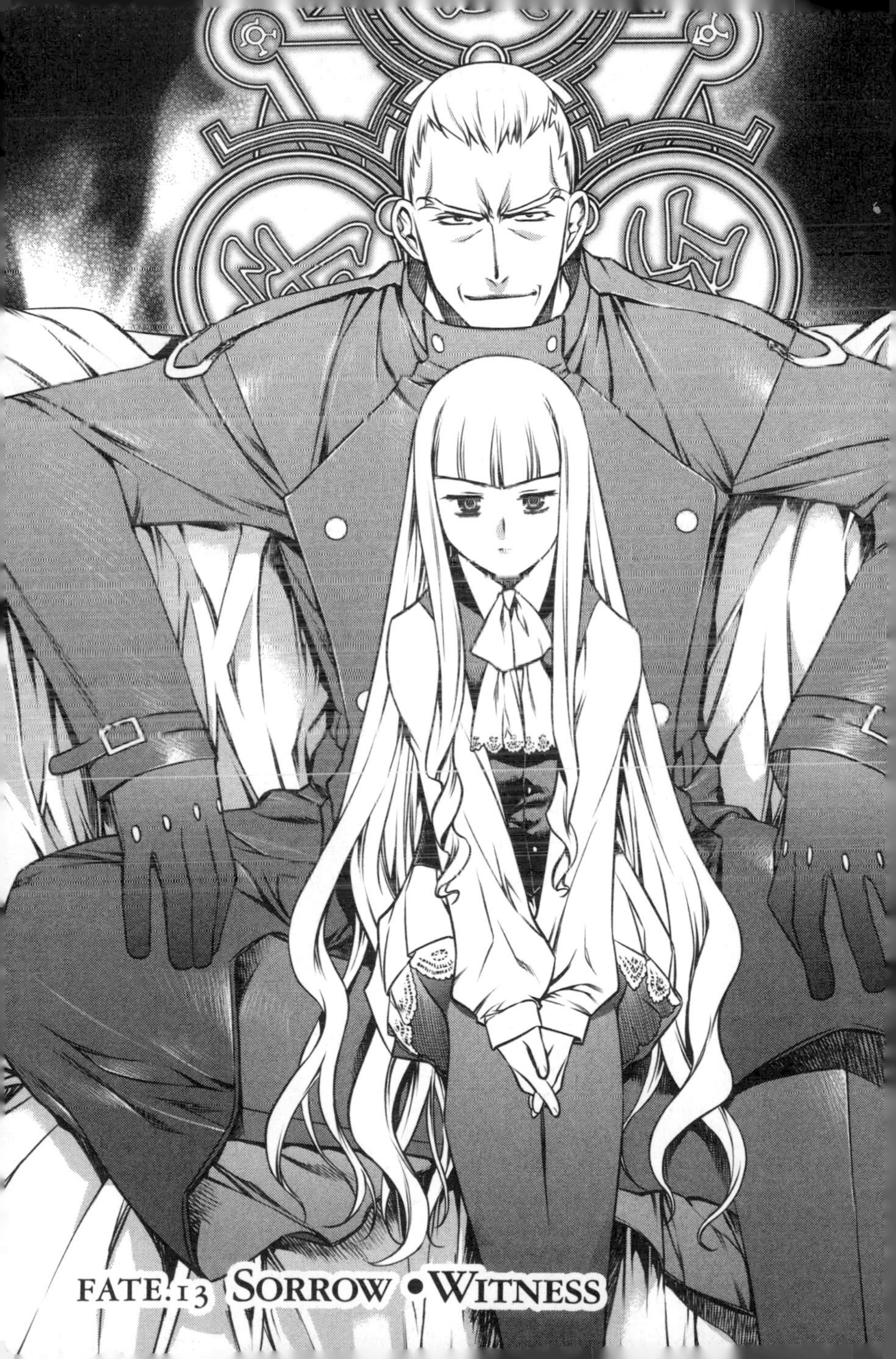

FATE.13 SORROW • WITNESS

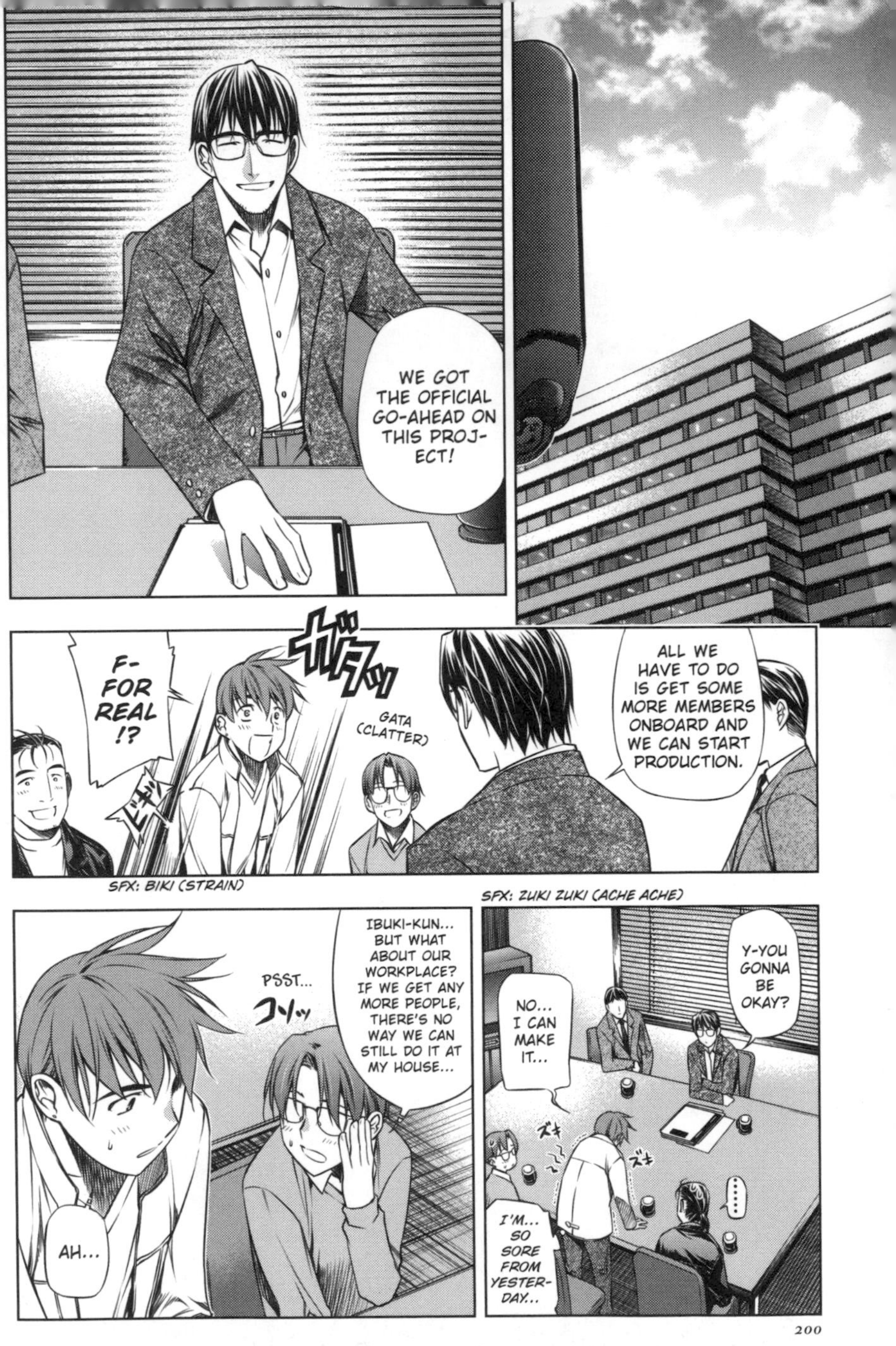
WE GOT THE OFFICIAL GO-AHEAD ON THIS PROJ-ECT!
ALL WE HAVE TO DO IS GET SOME MORE MEMBERS ONBOARD AND WE CAN START PRODUCTION.
GATA (CLATTER)
F-FOR REAL!?
SFX: BIKI (STRAIN)
SFX: ZUKI ZUKI (ACHE ACHE)
Y-YOU GONNA BE OKAY?
NO... I CAN MAKE IT...
......
I'M... SO SORE FROM YESTER-DAY...
IBUKI-KUN... BUT WHAT ABOUT OUR WORKPLACE? IF WE GET ANY MORE PEOPLE, THERE'S NO WAY WE CAN STILL DO IT AT MY HOUSE...
PSST...
AH...

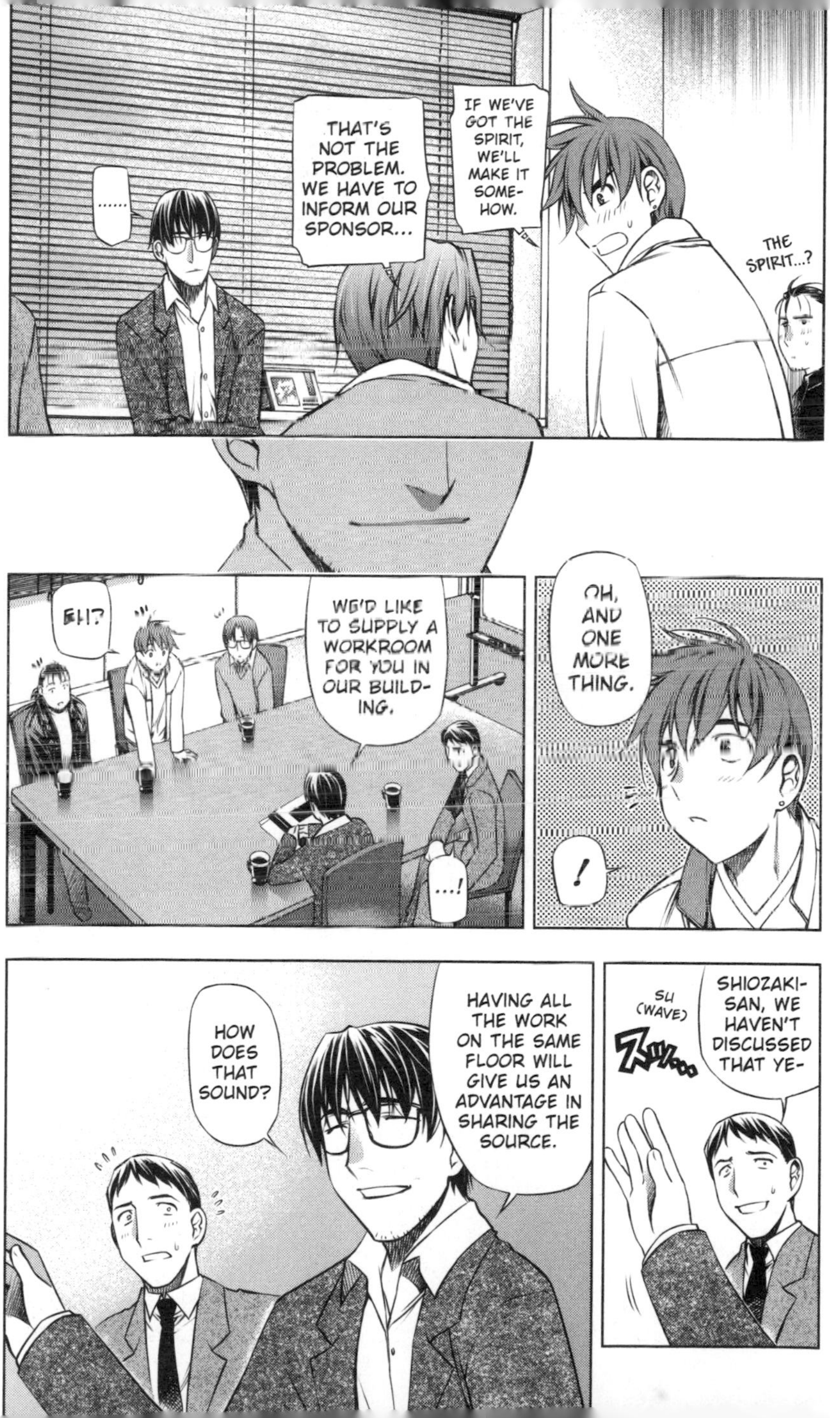
IF WE'VE GOT THE SPIRIT, WE'LL MAKE IT SOME-HOW.
THE SPIRIT...?
THAT'S NOT THE PROBLEM. WE HAVE TO INFORM OUR SPONSOR...
......
OH, AND ONE MORE THING.
!
WE'D LIKE TO SUPPLY A WORKROOM FOR YOU IN OUR BUILD-ING.
EH!?
...!
SHIOZAKI-SAN, WE HAVEN'T DISCUSSED THAT YE-
SU (WAVE)
HAVING ALL THE WORK ON THE SAME FLOOR WILL GIVE US AN ADVANTAGE IN SHARING THE SOURCE.
HOW DOES THAT SOUND?

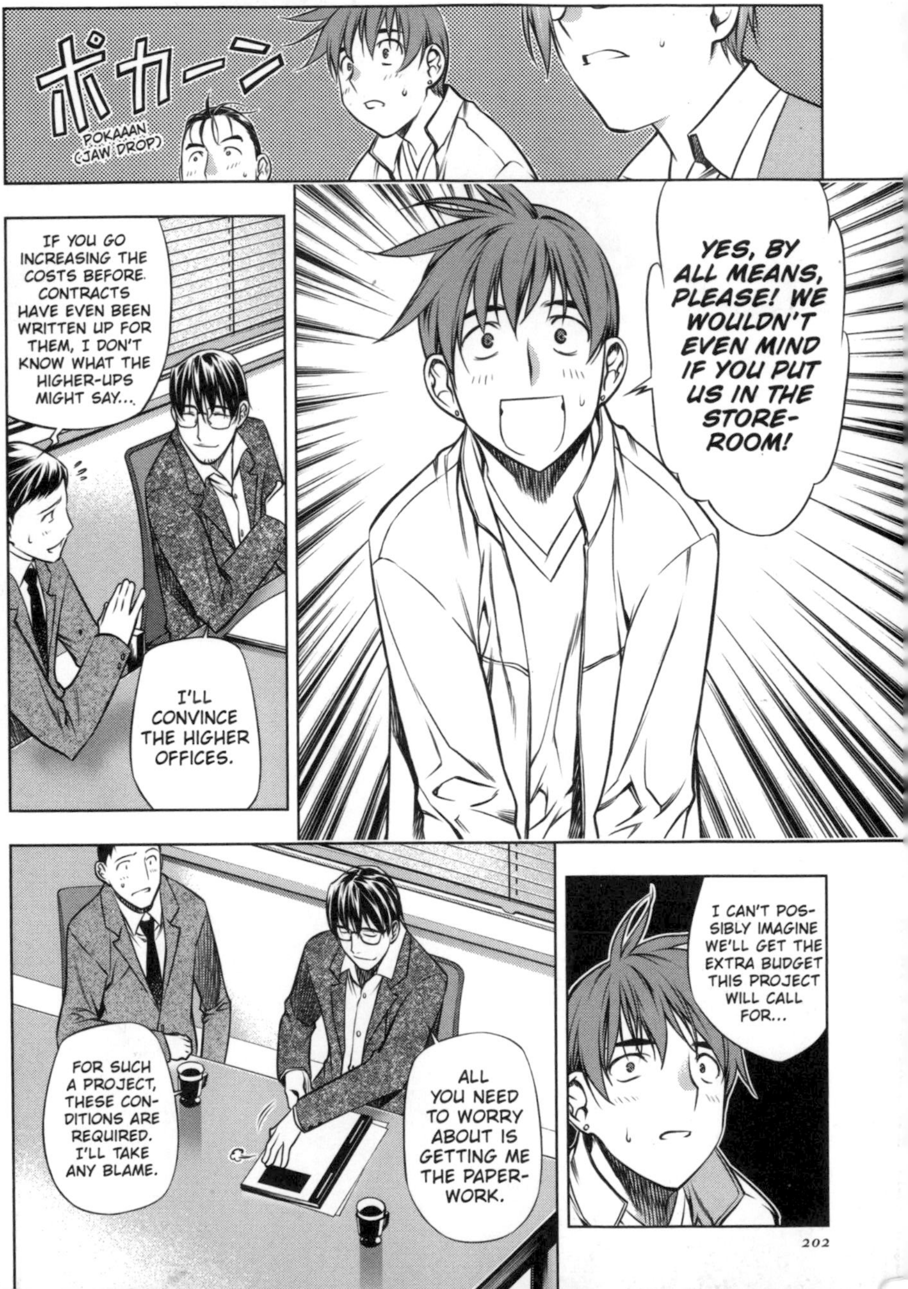
ポカーン
POKAAAN (JAW DROP)
YES, BY ALL MEANS, PLEASE! WE WOULDN'T EVEN MIND IF YOU PUT US IN THE STORE-ROOM!
IF YOU GO INCREASING THE COSTS BEFORE. CONTRACTS HAVE EVEN BEEN WRITTEN UP FOR THEM, I DON'T KNOW WHAT THE HIGHER-UPS MIGHT SAY...
I'LL CONVINCE THE HIGHER OFFICES.
I CAN'T POS-SIBLY IMAGINE WE'LL GET THE EXTRA BUDGET THIS PROJECT WILL CALL FOR...
ALL YOU NEED TO WORRY ABOUT IS GETTING ME THE PAPER-WORK.
FOR SUCH A PROJECT, THESE CON-DITIONS ARE REQUIRED. I'LL TAKE ANY BLAME.

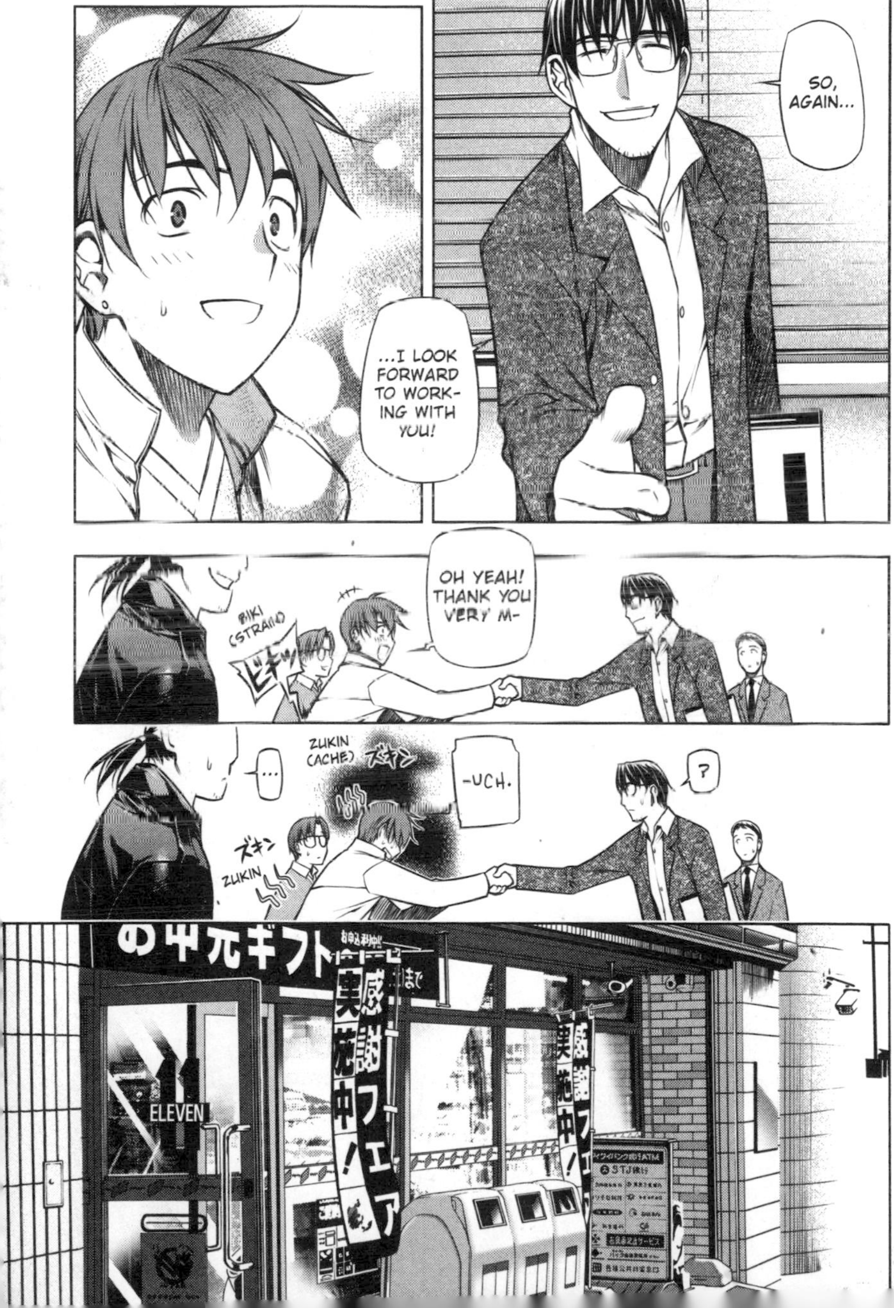
SO, AGAIN...
...I LOOK FORWARD TO WORK-ING WITH YOU!
OH YEAH! THANK YOU VERY M-
ビキッ
BIKI (STRAIN)
?
-UCH.
ズキン
ZUKIN (ACHE)
...
ズキン
ZUKIN
感謝フェア実施中!
ELEVEN
感謝フェア実施中!

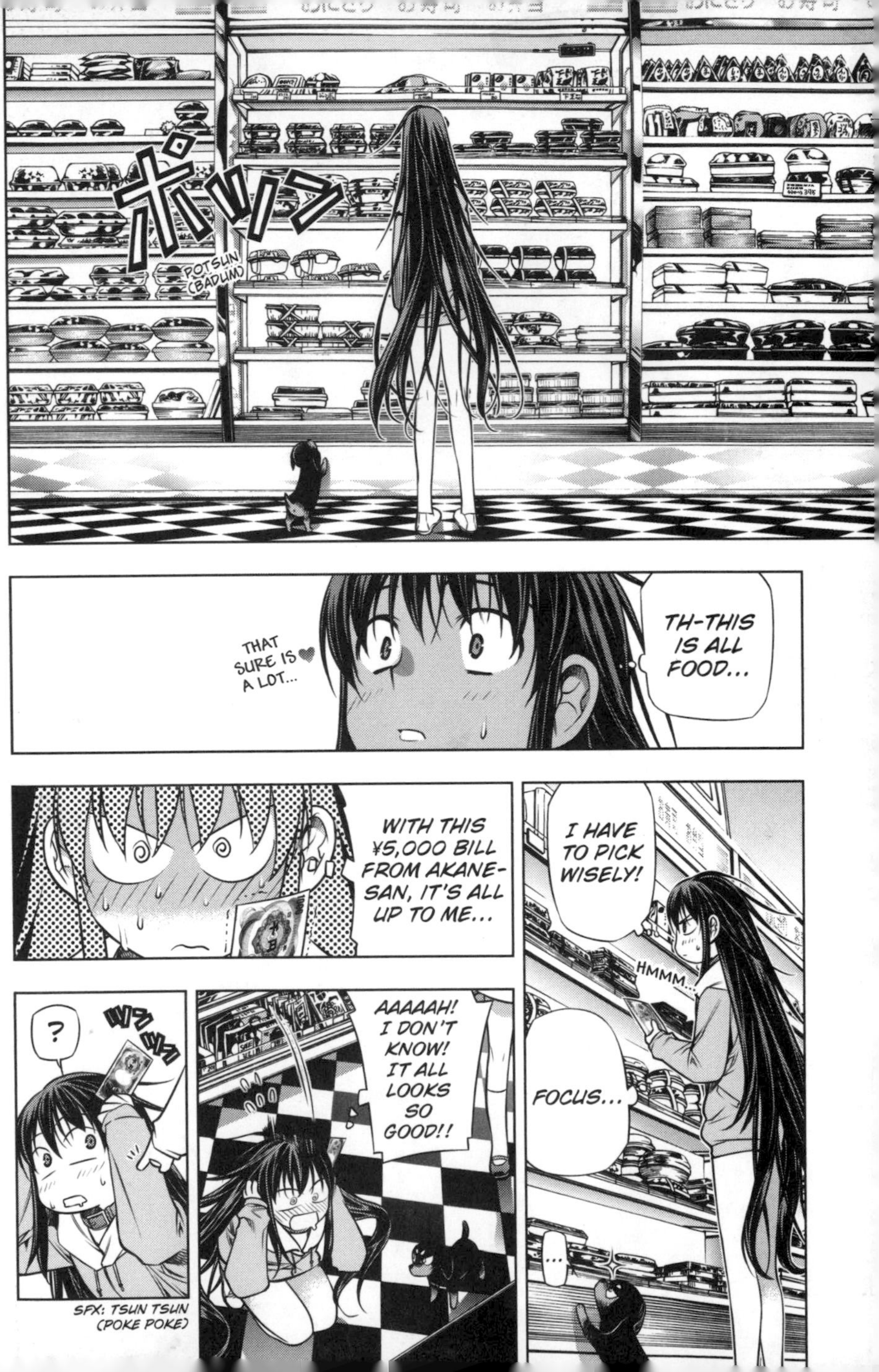

ポツン
POTSUN (BADUM)
TH-THIS IS ALL FOOD...
THAT SURE IS A LOT...♥
I HAVE TO PICK WISELY!
HMMM...
FOCUS...
...
WITH THIS ¥5,000 BILL FROM AKANE-SAN, IT'S ALL UP TO ME...
AAAAAH! I DON'T KNOW! IT ALL LOOKS SO GOOD!!
?
ツンツン
SFX: TSUN TSUN (POKE POKE)

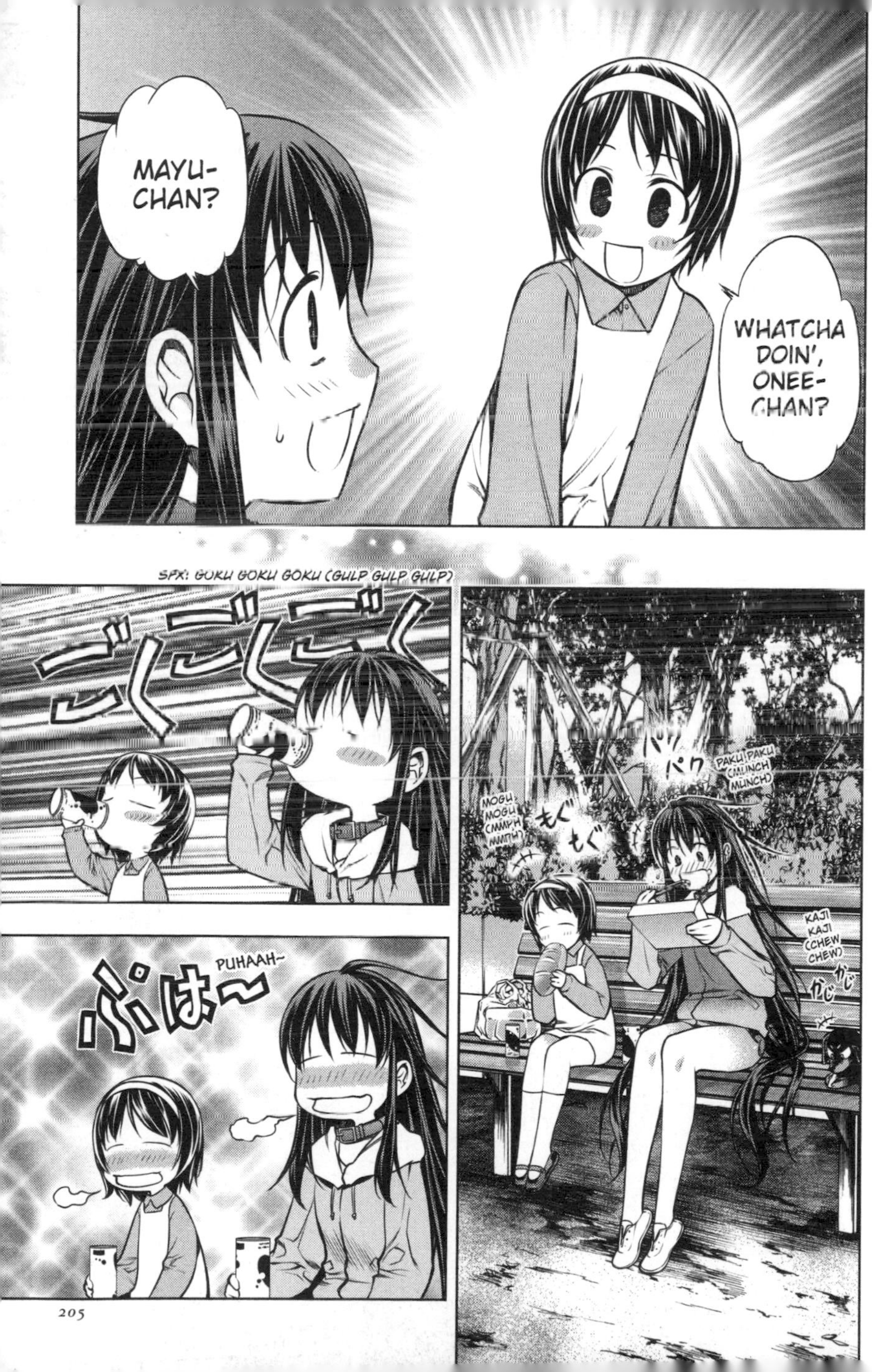
WHATCHA DOIN', ONEE-CHAN?
MAYU-CHAN?
パクパク
PAKU PAKU (MUNCH MUNCH)
もぐもぐ
MOGU MOGU (MMPH MMPH)
かじかじ
KAJI KAJI (CHEW CHEW)
SFX: GOKU GOKU GOKU (GULP GULP GULP)
ごくごくごく
ぷは～
PUHAAH~

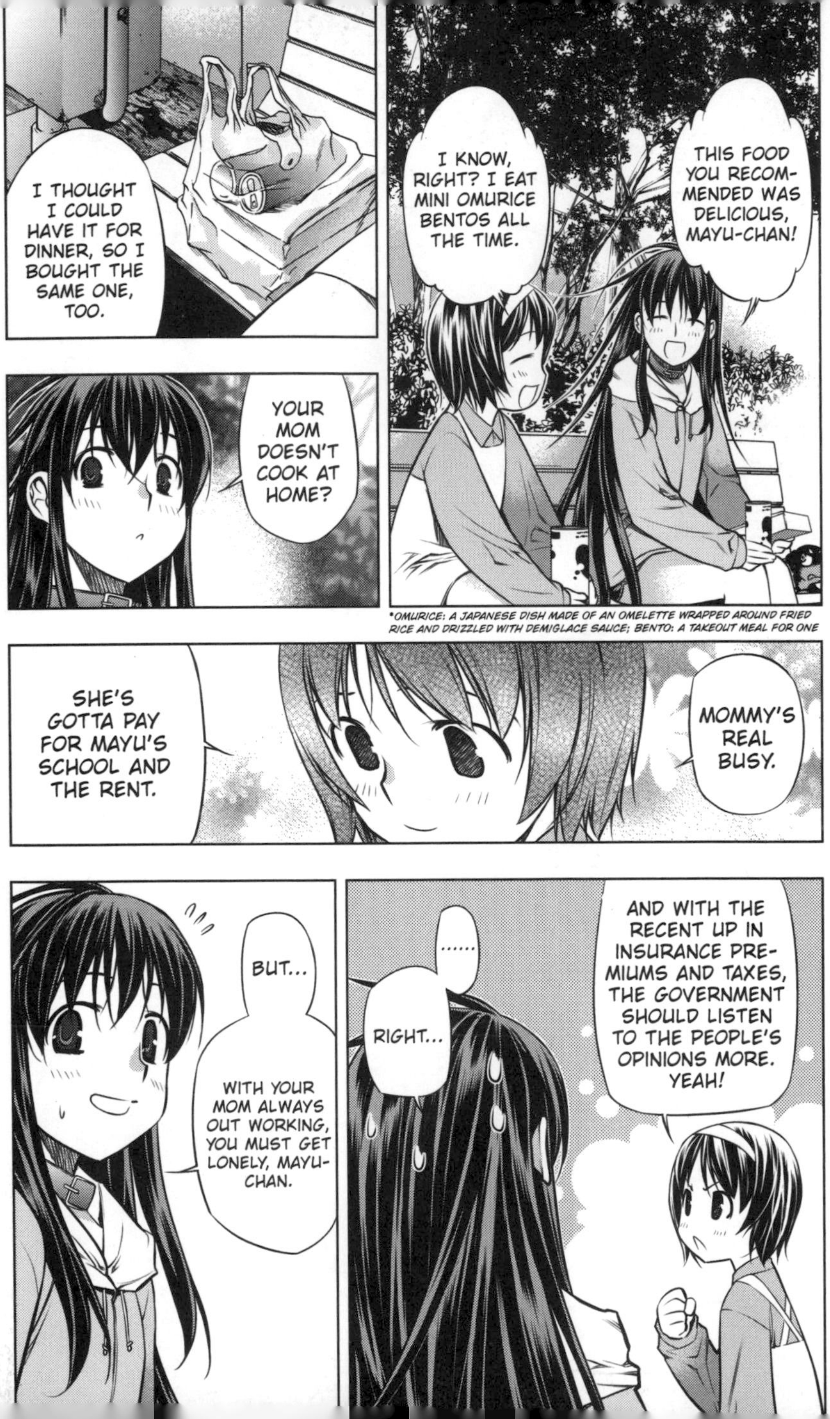
THIS FOOD YOU RECOMMENDED WAS DELICIOUS, MAYU-CHAN!
I KNOW, RIGHT? I EAT MINI OMURICE BENTOS ALL THE TIME.
I THOUGHT I COULD HAVE IT FOR DINNER, SO I BOUGHT THE SAME ONE, TOO.
YOUR MOM DOESN'T COOK AT HOME?
MOMMY'S REAL BUSY.
SHE'S GOTTA PAY FOR MAYU'S SCHOOL AND THE RENT.
AND WITH THE RECENT UP IN INSURANCE PREMIUMS AND TAXES, THE GOVERNMENT SHOULD LISTEN TO THE PEOPLE'S OPINIONS MORE. YEAH!
......
RIGHT...
BUT...
WITH YOUR MOM ALWAYS OUT WORKING, YOU MUST GET LONELY, MAYU-CHAN.

*OMURICE: A JAPANESE DISH MADE OF AN OMELETTE WRAPPED AROUND FRIED RICE AND DRIZZLED WITH DEMIGLACE SAUCE; BENTO: A TAKEOUT MEAL FOR ONE

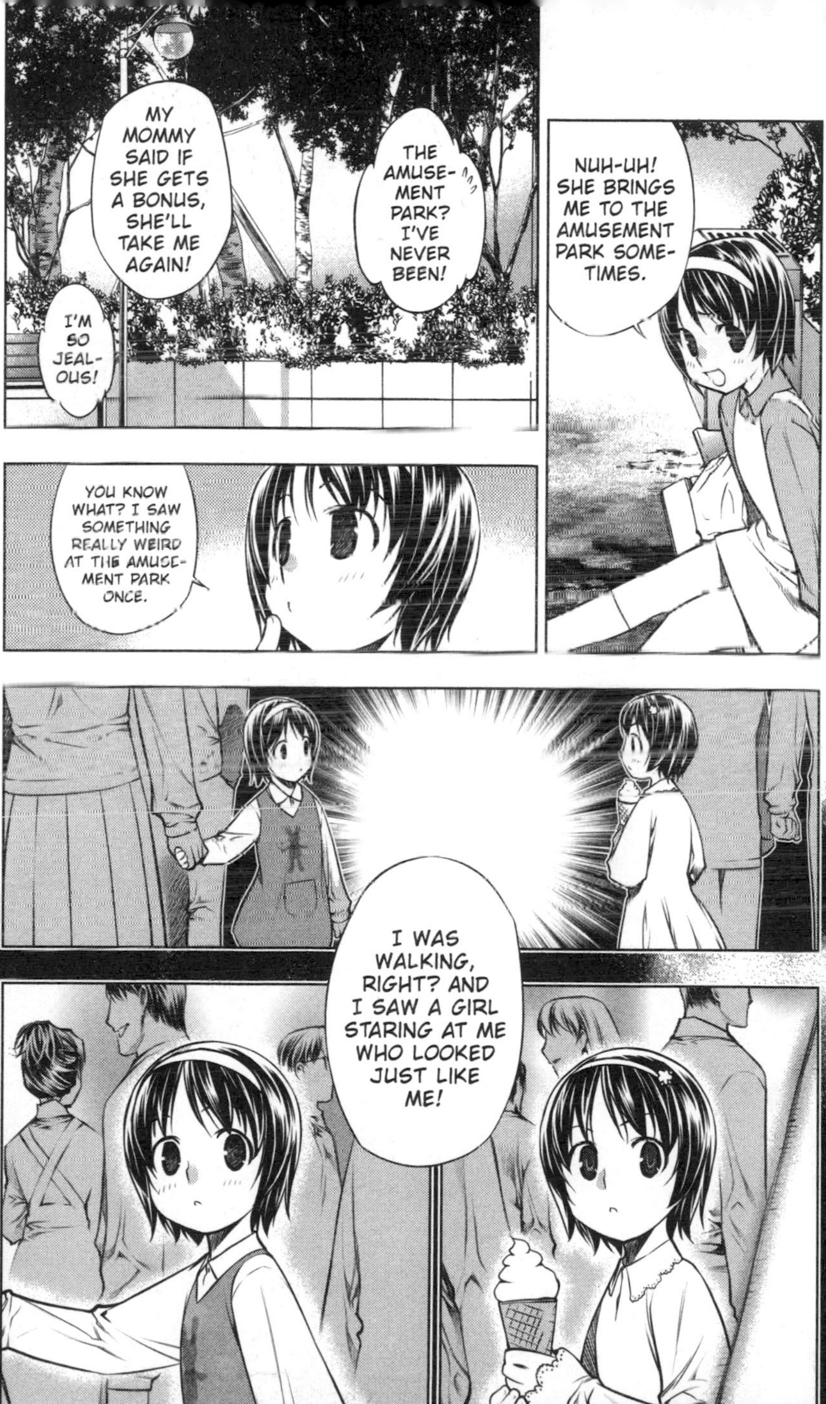
NUH-UH! SHE BRINGS ME TO THE AMUSEMENT PARK SOME-TIMES.
THE AMUSE-MENT PARK? I'VE NEVER BEEN!
MY MOMMY SAID IF SHE GETS A BONUS, SHE'LL TAKE ME AGAIN!
I'M SO JEAL-OUS!
YOU KNOW WHAT? I SAW SOMETHING REALLY WEIRD AT THE AMUSE-MENT PARK ONCE.
I WAS WALKING, RIGHT? AND I SAW A GIRL STARING AT ME WHO LOOKED JUST LIKE ME!

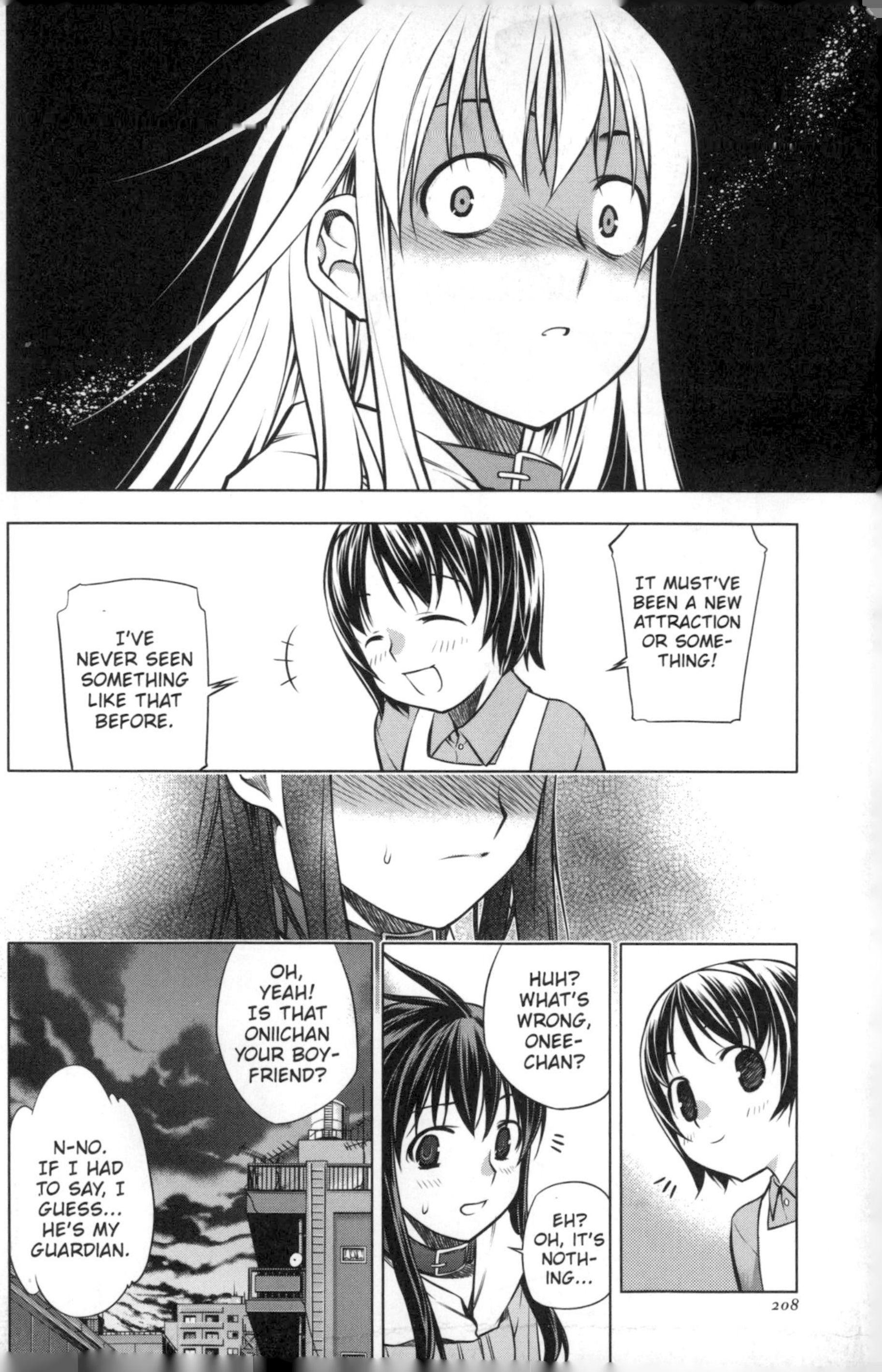
IT MUST'VE BEEN A NEW ATTRACTION OR SOME-THING!
I'VE NEVER SEEN SOMETHING LIKE THAT BEFORE.
HUH? WHAT'S WRONG, ONEE-CHAN?
EH? OH, IT'S NOTH-ING...
OH, YEAH! IS THAT ONIICHAN YOUR BOY-FRIEND?
N-NO. IF I HAD TO SAY, I GUESS... HE'S MY GUARDIAN.

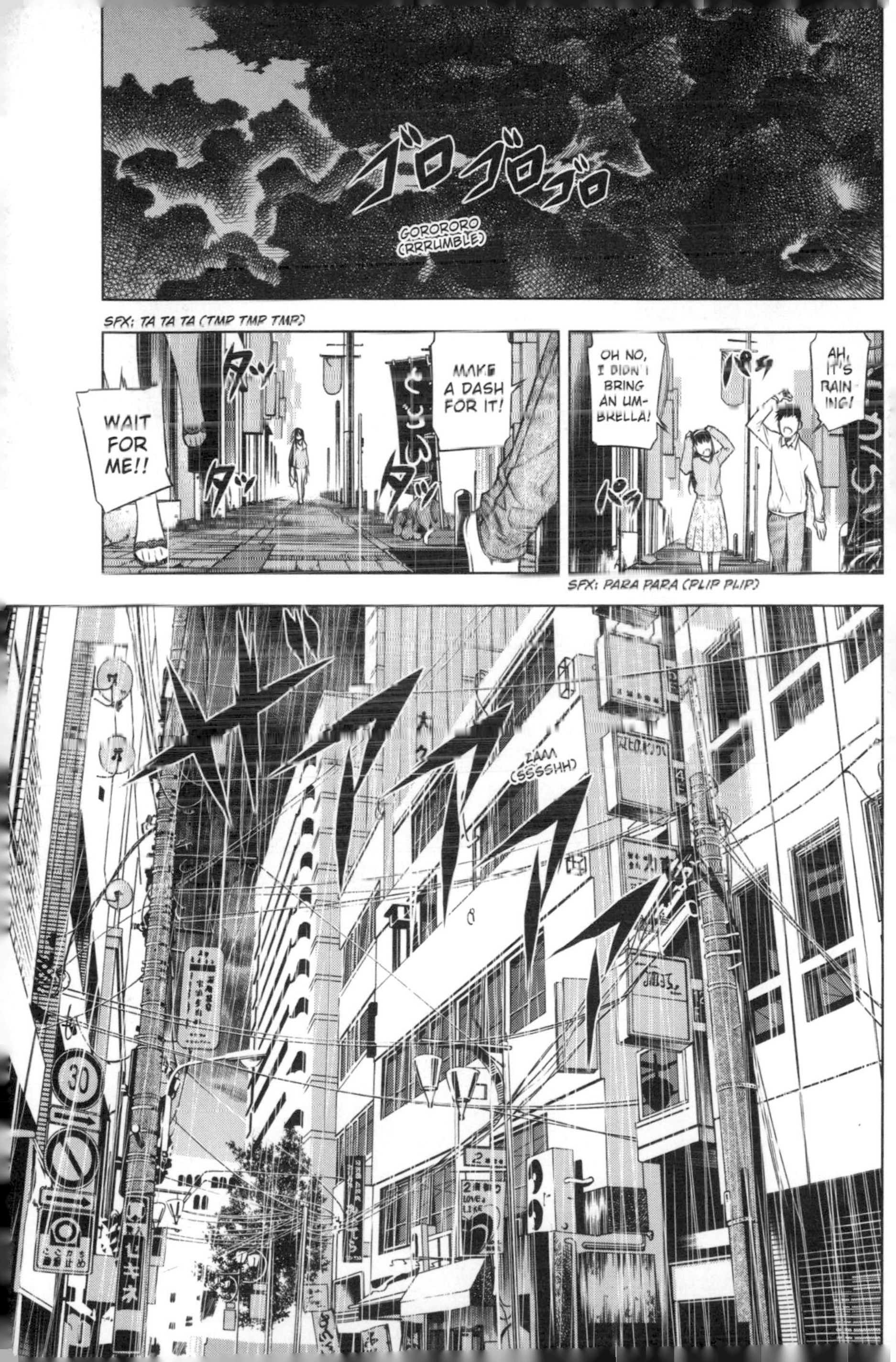
GORORORO (RRRUMBLE)
AH, IT'S RAINING!
OH NO, I DIDN'T BRING AN UMBRELLA!
SFX: PARA PARA (PLIP PLIP)
MAKE A DASH FOR IT!
WAIT FOR ME!!
SFX: TA TA TA (TMP TMP TMP)
ZAM (SSSSHH)

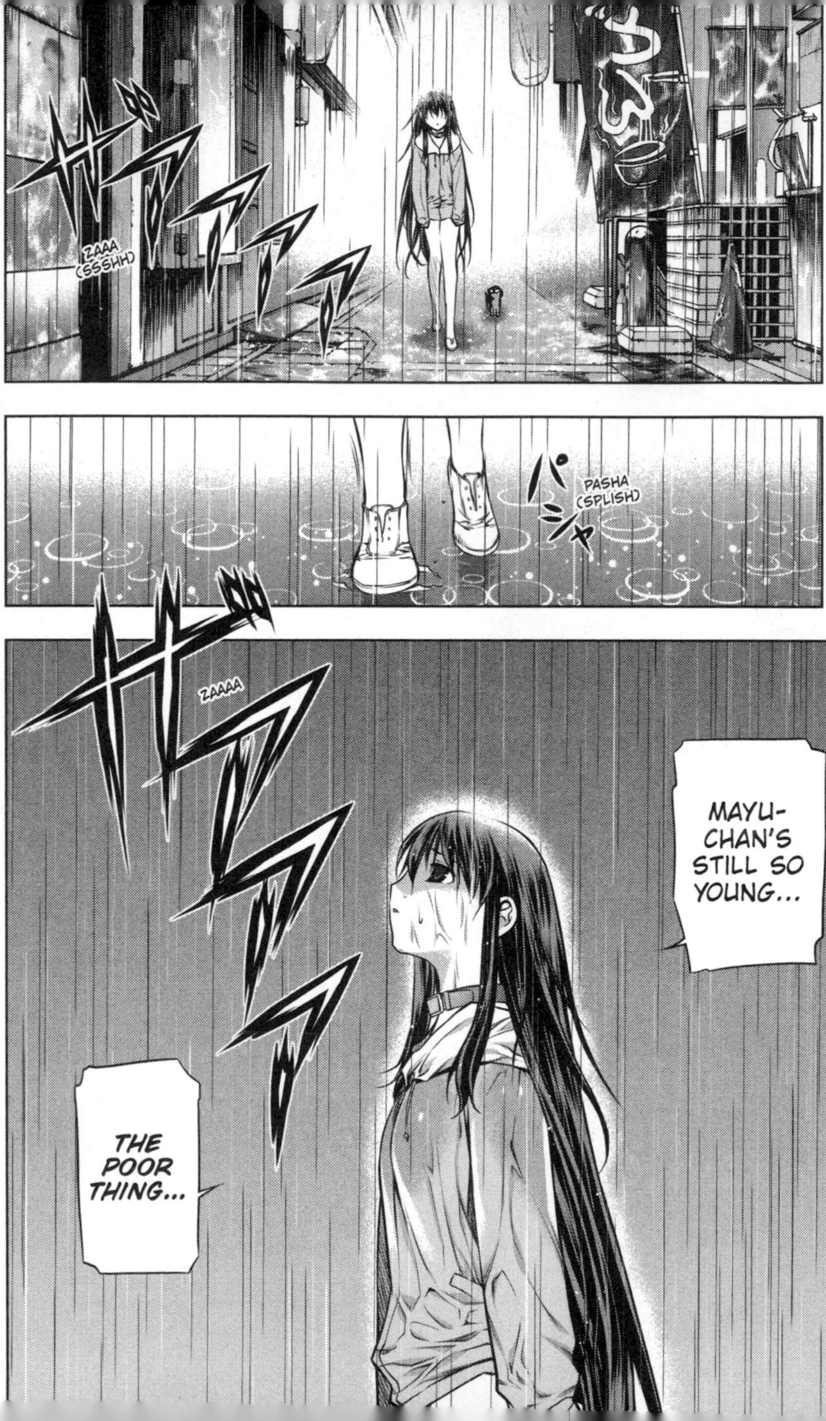
ZAAA
(SSSHH)
PASHA
(SPLISH)
ZAAAA
MAYU-CHAN'S STILL SO YOUNG...
THE POOR THING...

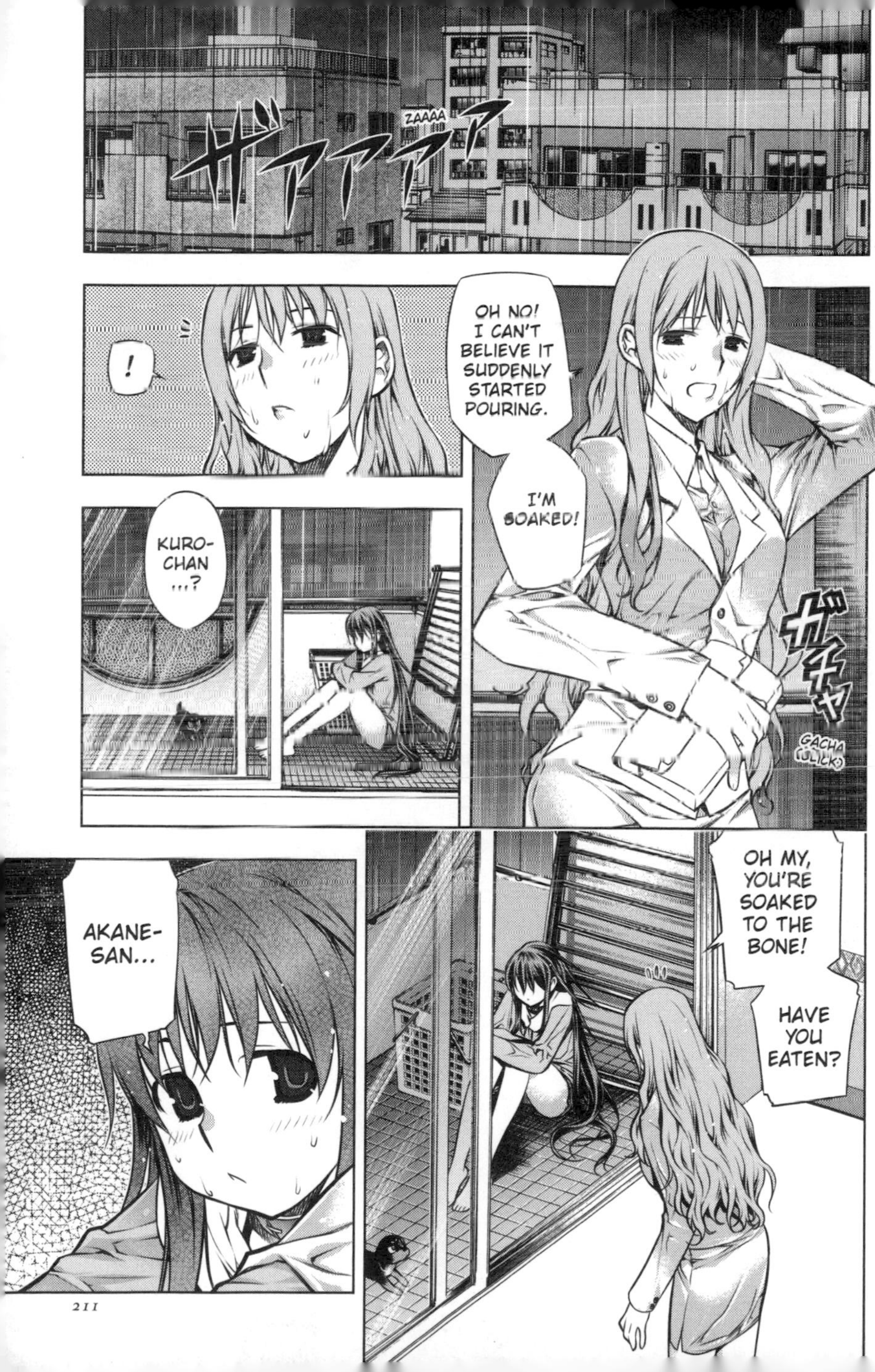
ザアアア
ZAAAA
OH NO! I CAN'T BELIEVE IT SUDDENLY STARTED POURING.
I'M SOAKED!
ガチャ
GACHA (CLICK)
!
KURO-CHAN ...?
OH MY, YOU'RE SOAKED TO THE BONE!
HAVE YOU EATEN?
AKANE-SAN...

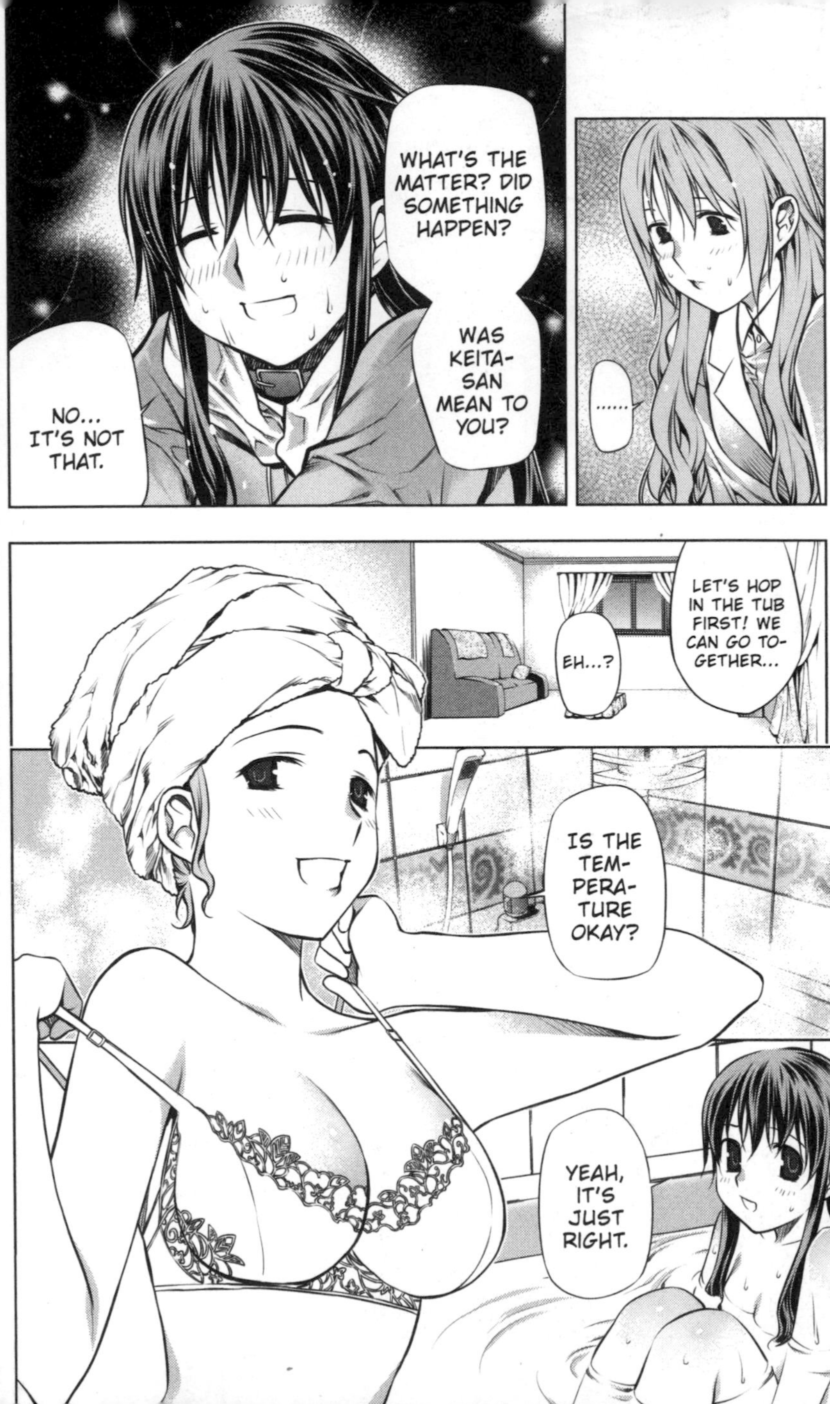
......
WHAT'S THE MATTER? DID SOMETHING HAPPEN?
WAS KEITA-SAN MEAN TO YOU?
NO... IT'S NOT THAT.
LET'S HOP IN THE TUB FIRST! WE CAN GO TO-GETHER...
EH...?
IS THE TEM-PERA-TURE OKAY?
YEAH, IT'S JUST RIGHT.

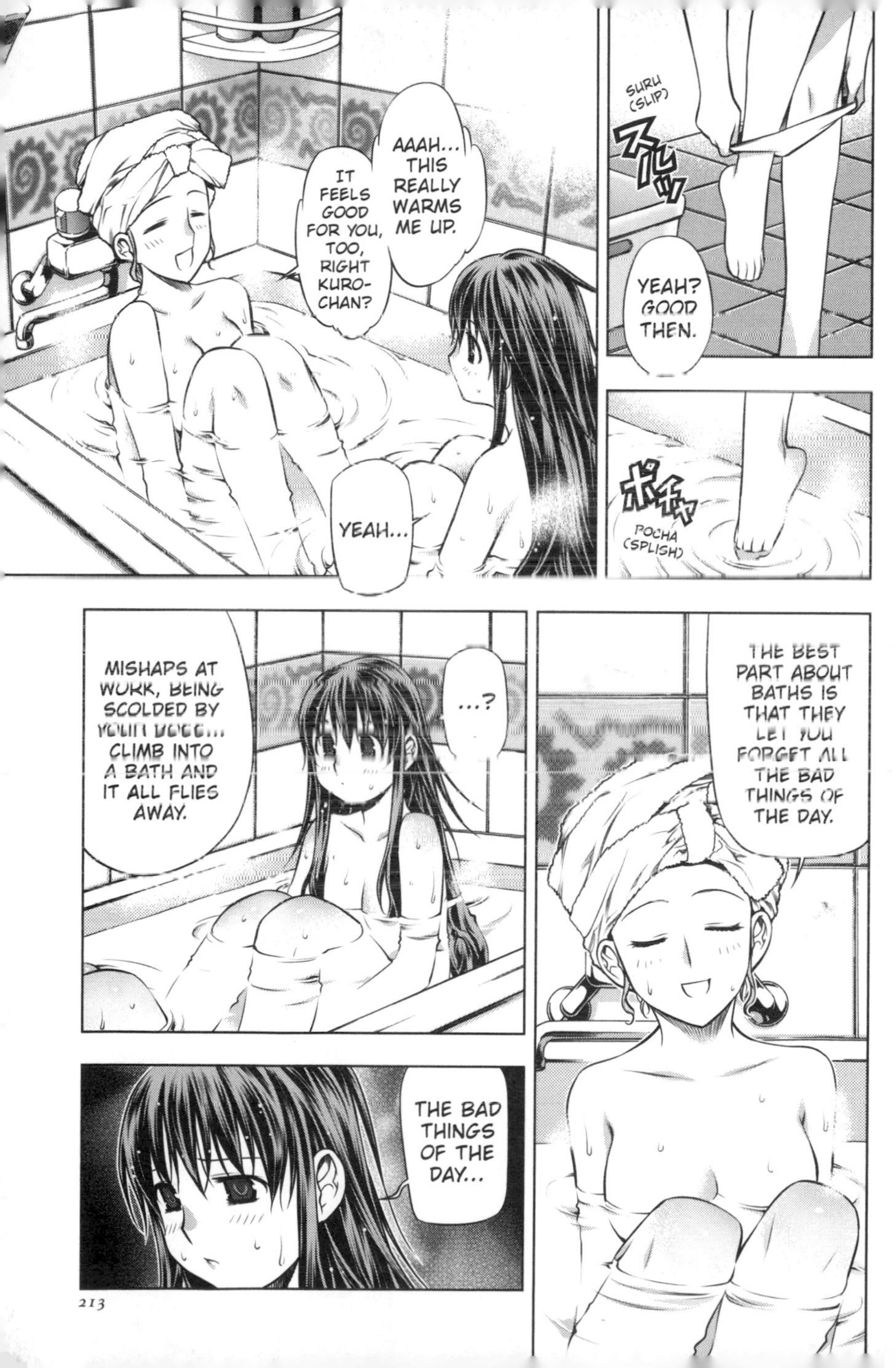
SURU (SLIP)
スルッ
YEAH? GOOD THEN.
ポチャ
POCHA (SPLISH)
AAAH... THIS REALLY WARMS ME UP.
IT FEELS GOOD FOR YOU, TOO, RIGHT KURO-CHAN?
YEAH...
THE BEST PART ABOUT BATHS IS THAT THEY LET YOU FORGET ALL THE BAD THINGS OF THE DAY.
...?
MISHAPS AT WORK, BEING SCOLDED BY YOUR BOSS... CLIMB INTO A BATH AND IT ALL FLIES AWAY.
THE BAD THINGS OF THE DAY...

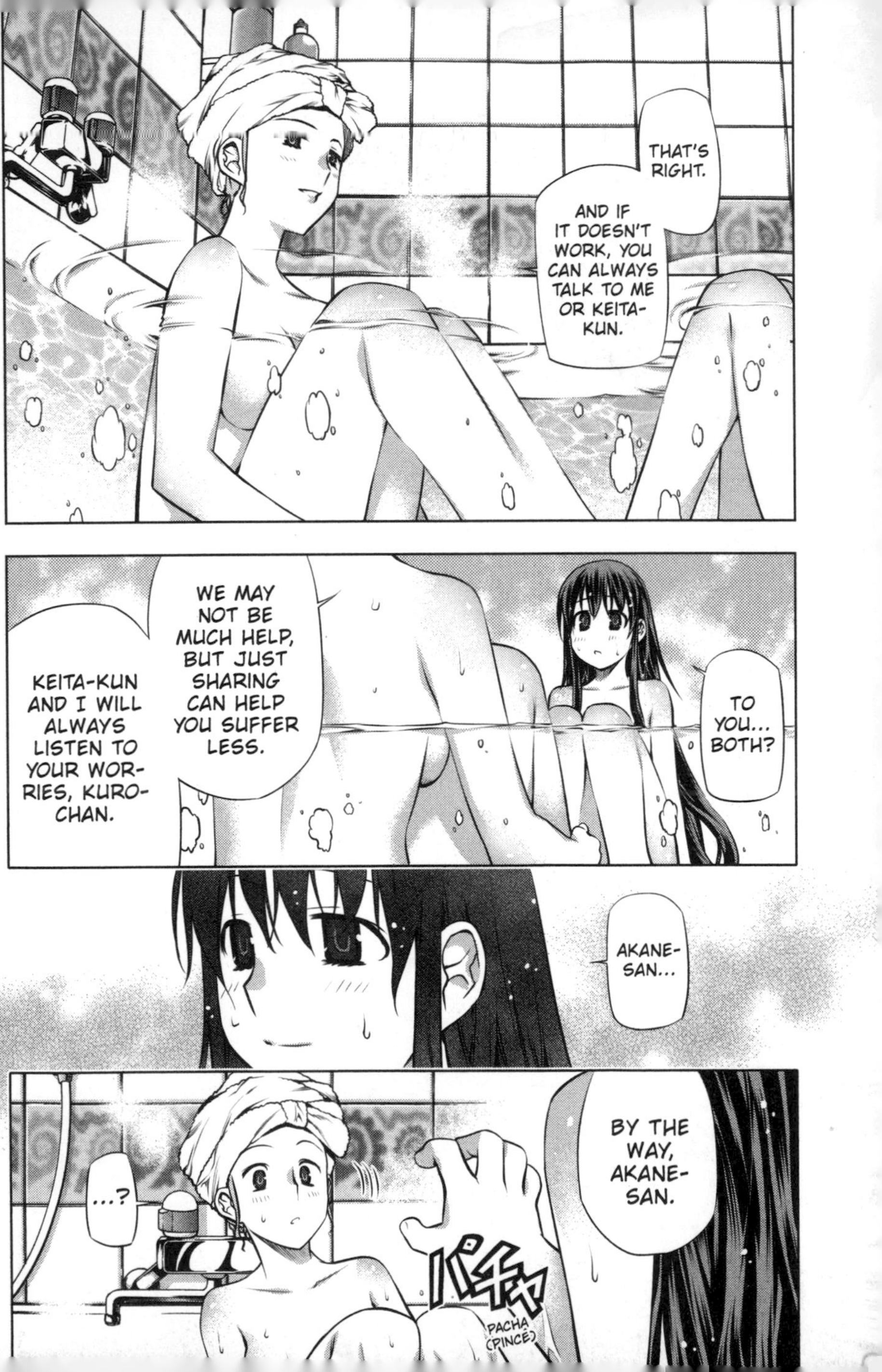
THAT'S RIGHT.
AND IF IT DOESN'T WORK, YOU CAN ALWAYS TALK TO ME OR KEITA-KUN.
WE MAY NOT BE MUCH HELP, BUT JUST SHARING CAN HELP YOU SUFFER LESS.
KEITA-KUN AND I WILL ALWAYS LISTEN TO YOUR WOR-RIES, KURO-CHAN.
TO YOU... BOTH?
AKANE-SAN...
BY THE WAY, AKANE-SAN.
...?
パチャ
PACHA (PINCE)

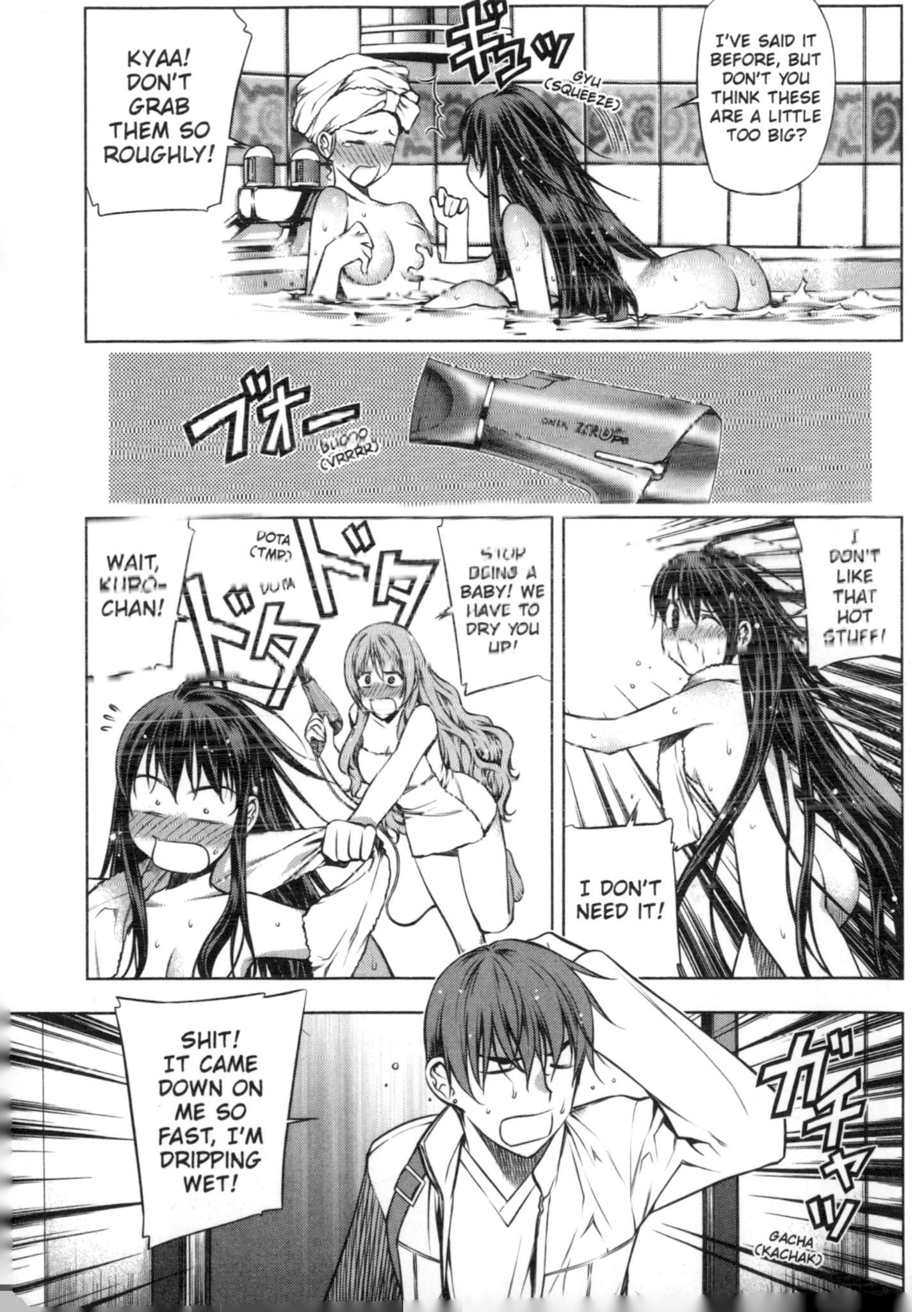
I'VE SAID IT BEFORE, BUT DON'T YOU THINK THESE ARE A LITTLE TOO BIG?
GYU (SQUEEZE)
KYAA! DON'T GRAB THEM SO ROUGHLY!
BUOOO (VRRRR)
I DON'T LIKE THAT HOT STUFF!
I DON'T NEED IT!
STOP BEING A BABY! WE HAVE TO DRY YOU UP!
DOTA (TMP)
DOTA
WAIT, KURO-CHAN!
GACHA (KACHAK)
SHIT! IT CAME DOWN ON ME SO FAST, I'M DRIPPING WET!

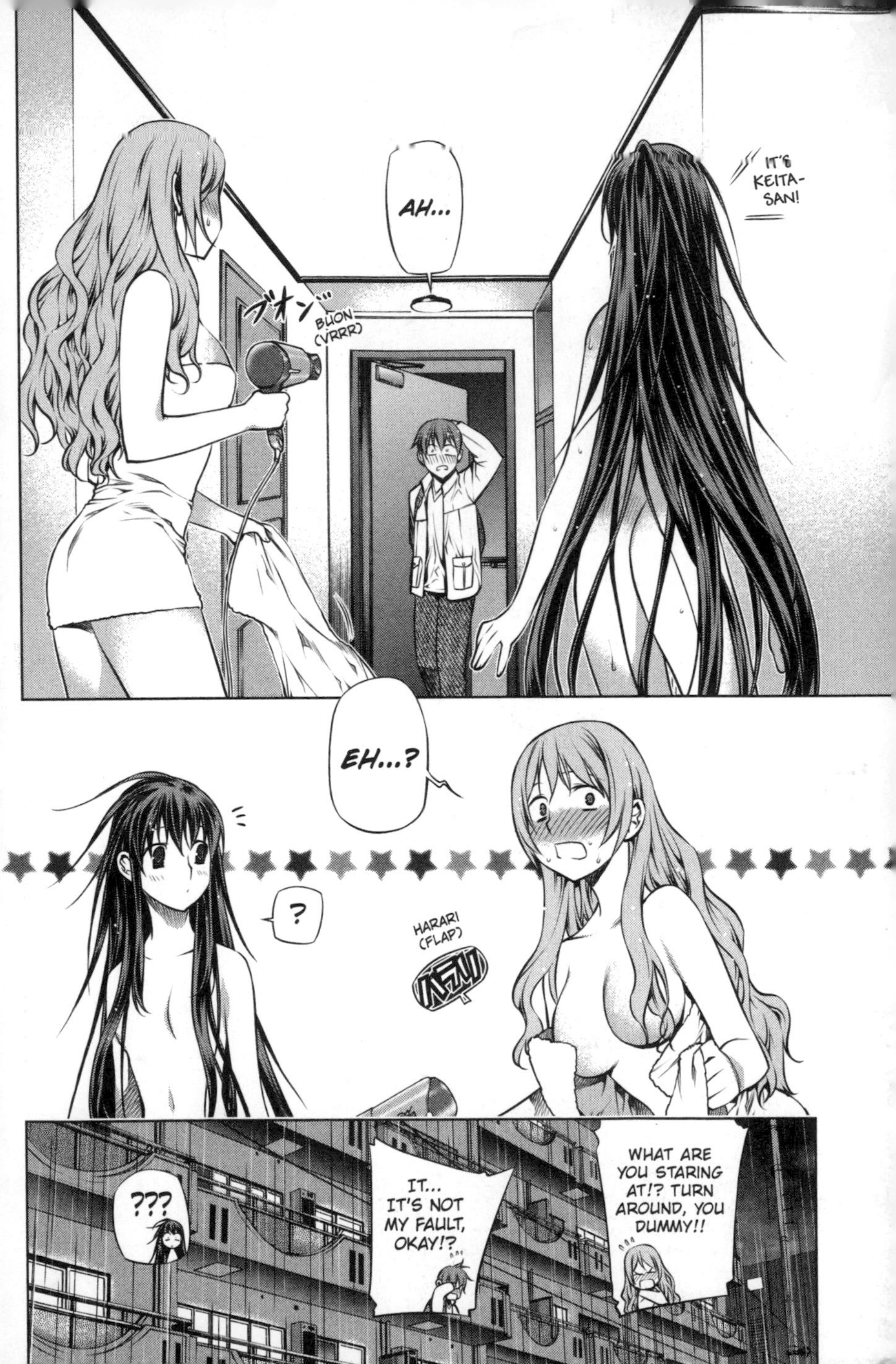
IT'S KEITA-SAN!
AH...
ブォン
BUON (VRRR)
EH...?
?
HARARI (FLAP)
WHAT ARE YOU STARING AT!? TURN AROUND, YOU DUMMY!!
IT... IT'S NOT MY FAULT, OKAY!?
???

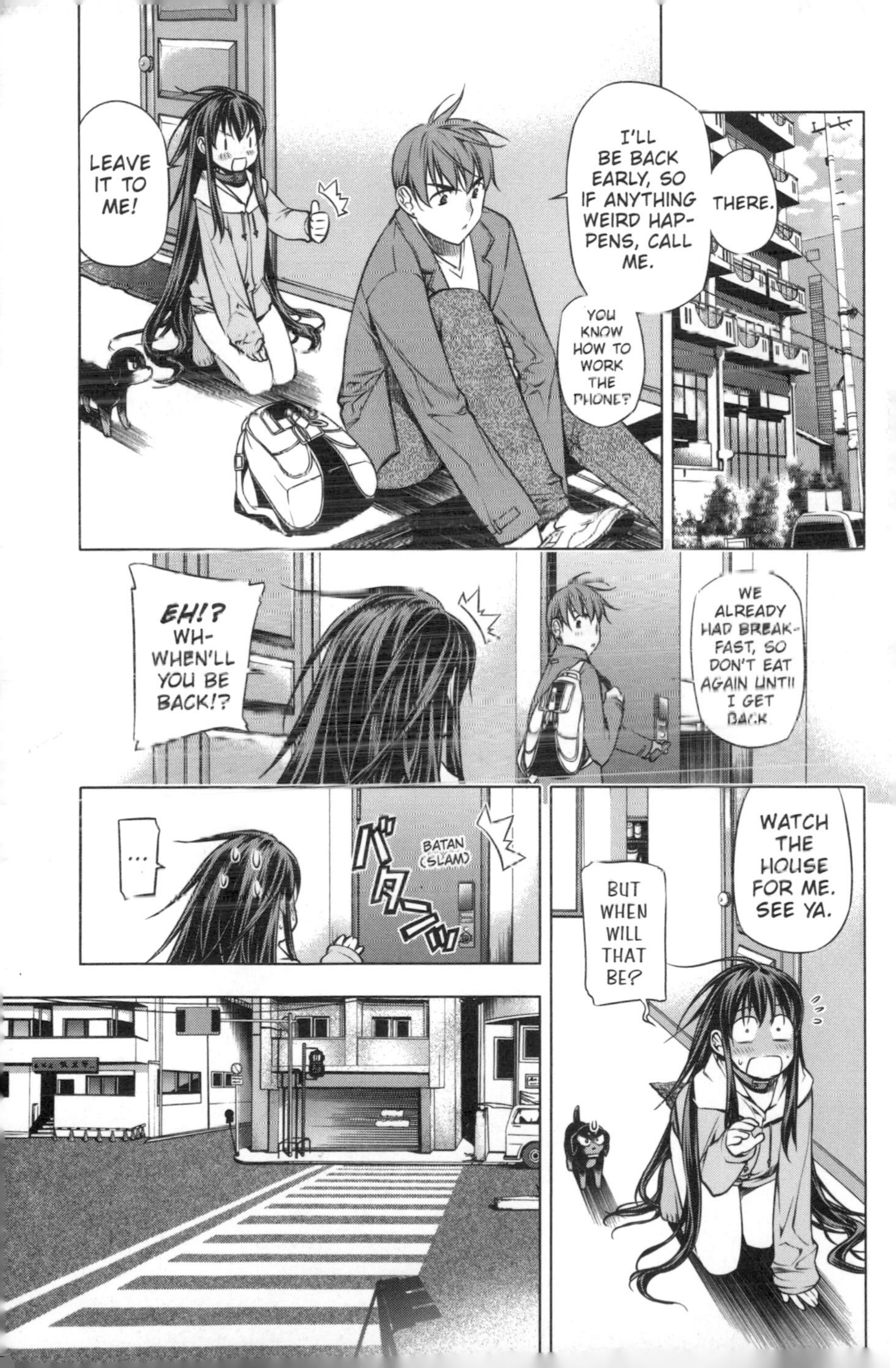
THERE.
I'LL BE BACK EARLY, SO IF ANYTHING WEIRD HAP-PENS, CALL ME.
YOU KNOW HOW TO WORK THE PHONE?
LEAVE IT TO ME!
WE ALREADY HAD BREAK-FAST, SO DON'T EAT AGAIN UNTIL I GET BACK.
EH!? WH-WHEN'LL YOU BE BACK!?
WATCH THE HOUSE FOR ME. SEE YA.
BUT WHEN WILL THAT BE?
BATAN (SLAM)
...

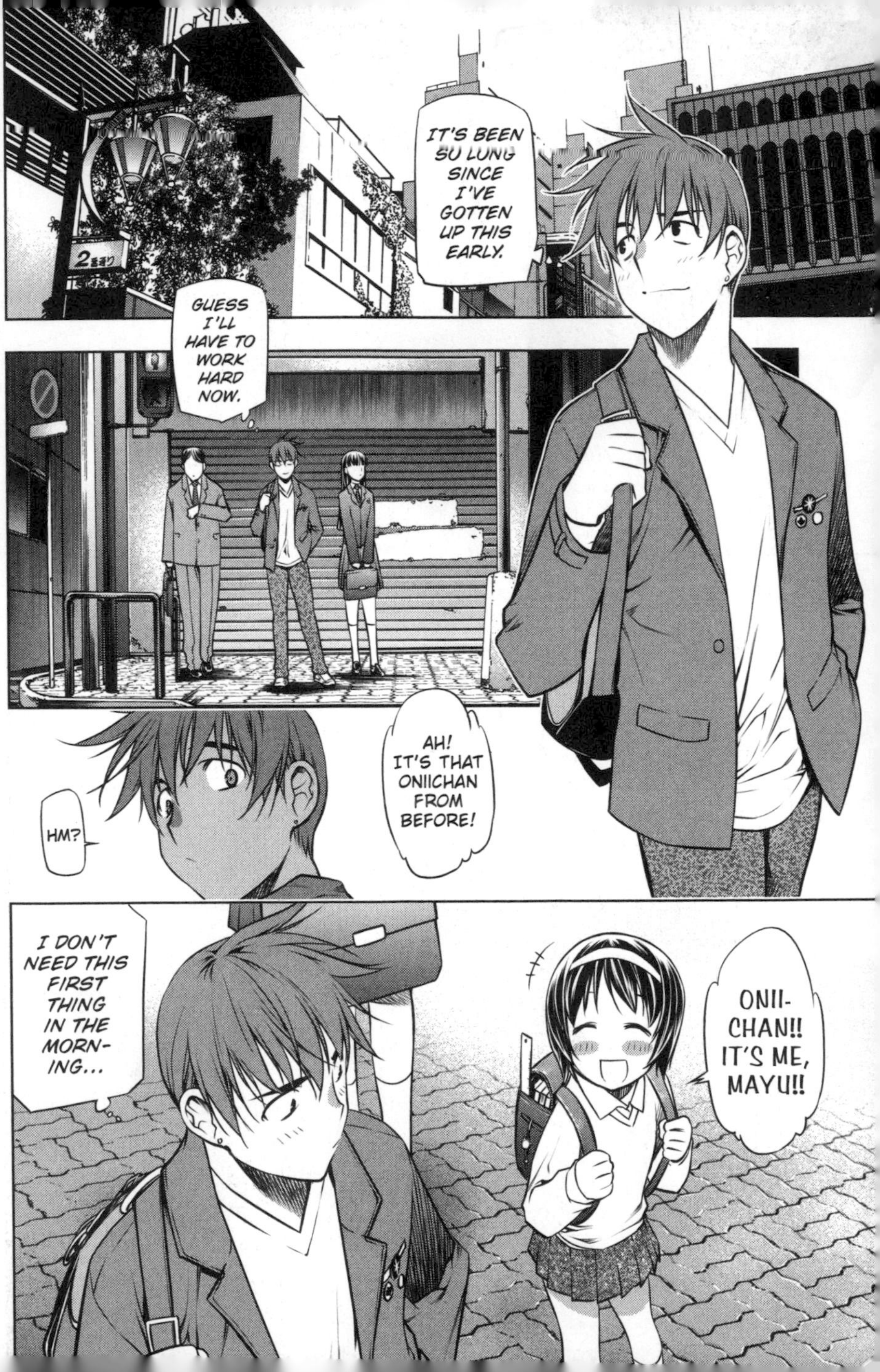
IT'S BEEN SO LONG SINCE I'VE GOTTEN UP THIS EARLY.
GUESS I'LL HAVE TO WORK HARD NOW.
AH! IT'S THAT ONIICHAN FROM BEFORE!
HM?
ONII-CHAN!! IT'S ME, MAYU!!
I DON'T NEED THIS FIRST THING IN THE MORN-ING...

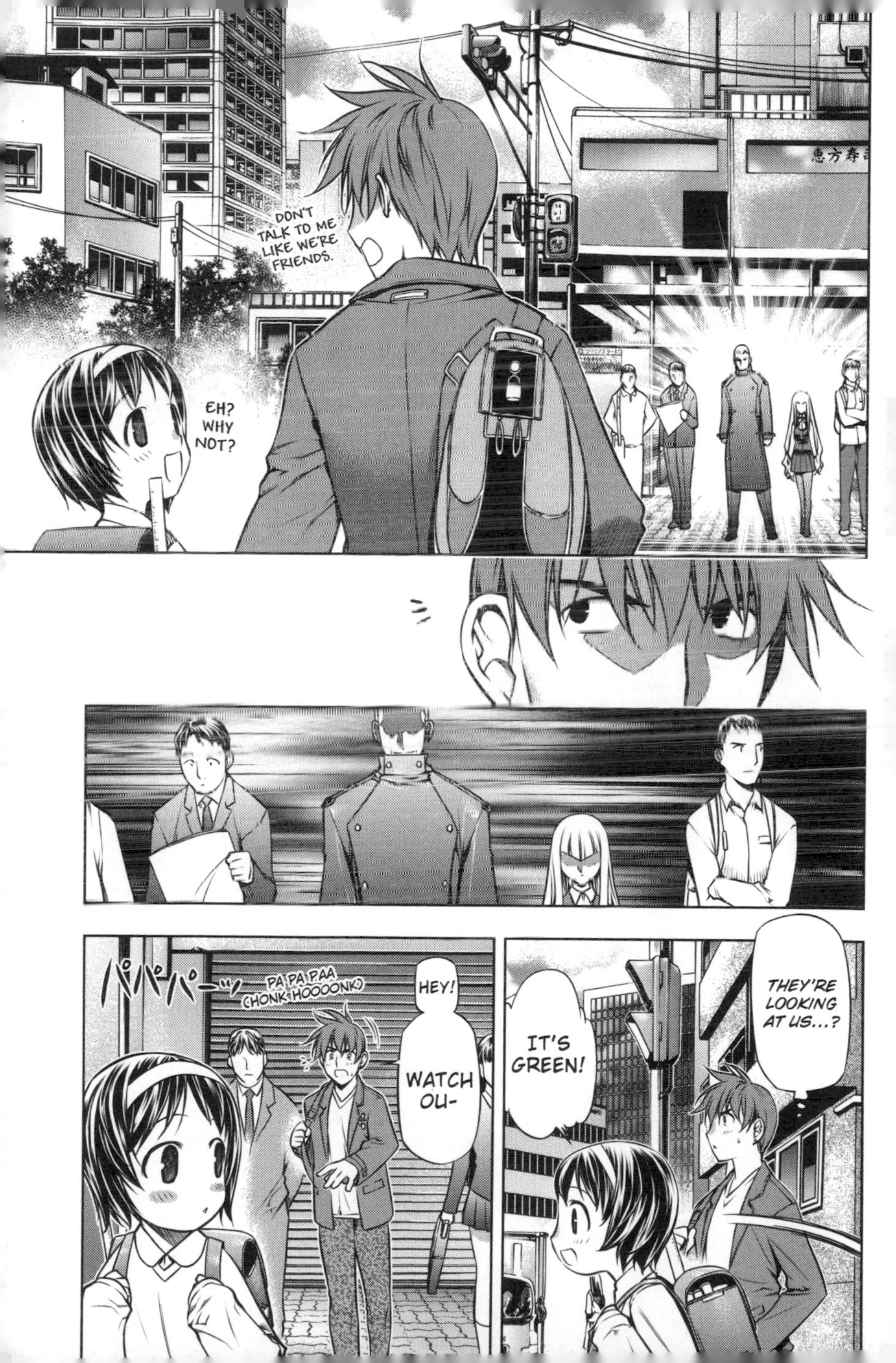
DON'T TALK TO ME LIKE WE'RE FRIENDS.
EH? WHY NOT?
THEY'RE LOOKING AT US...?
IT'S GREEN!
HEY!
WATCH OU-
パパパーッ
PA PA PAA (HONK HOOOONK)

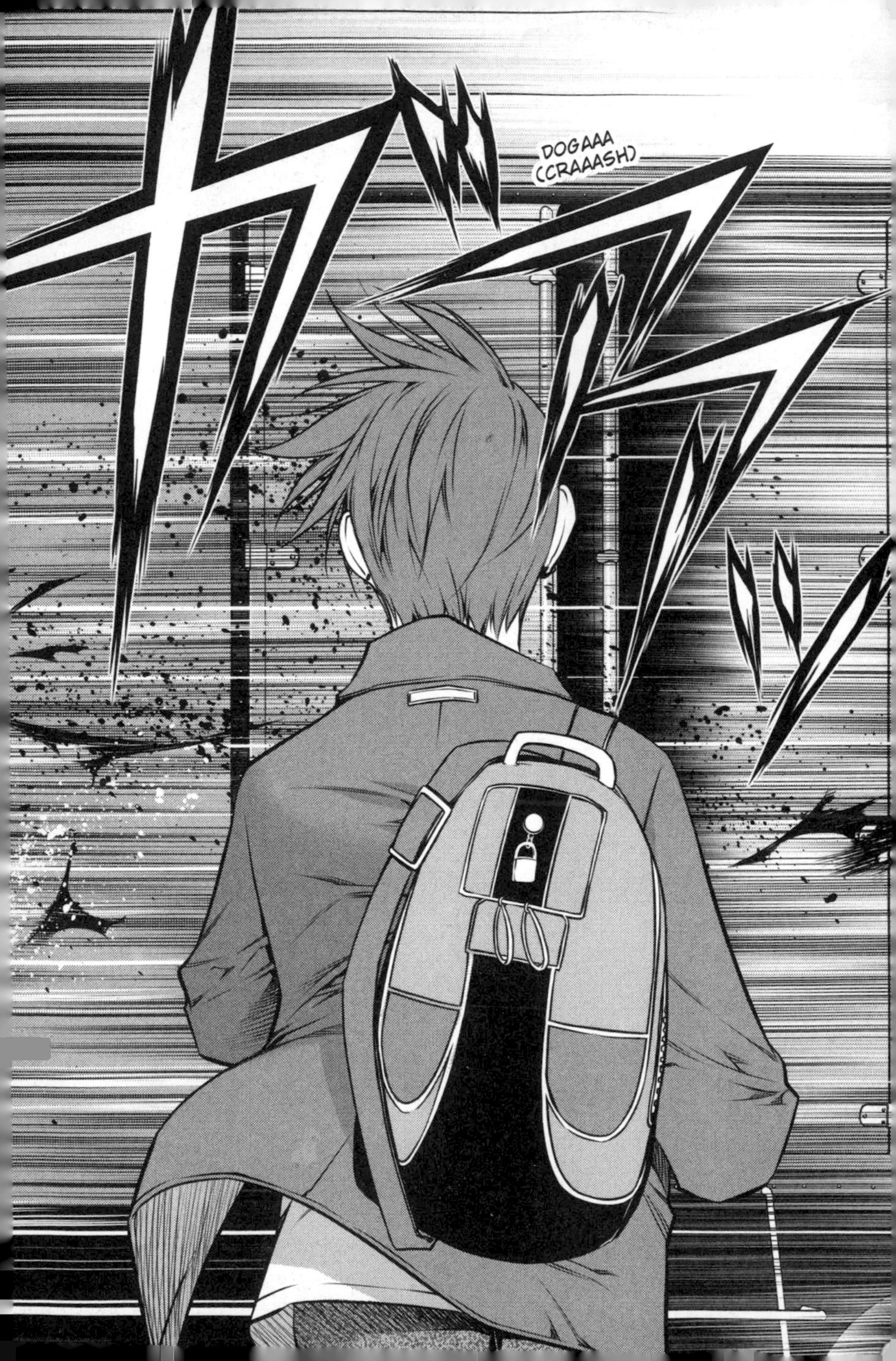
DOGAAA (CRAAASH)

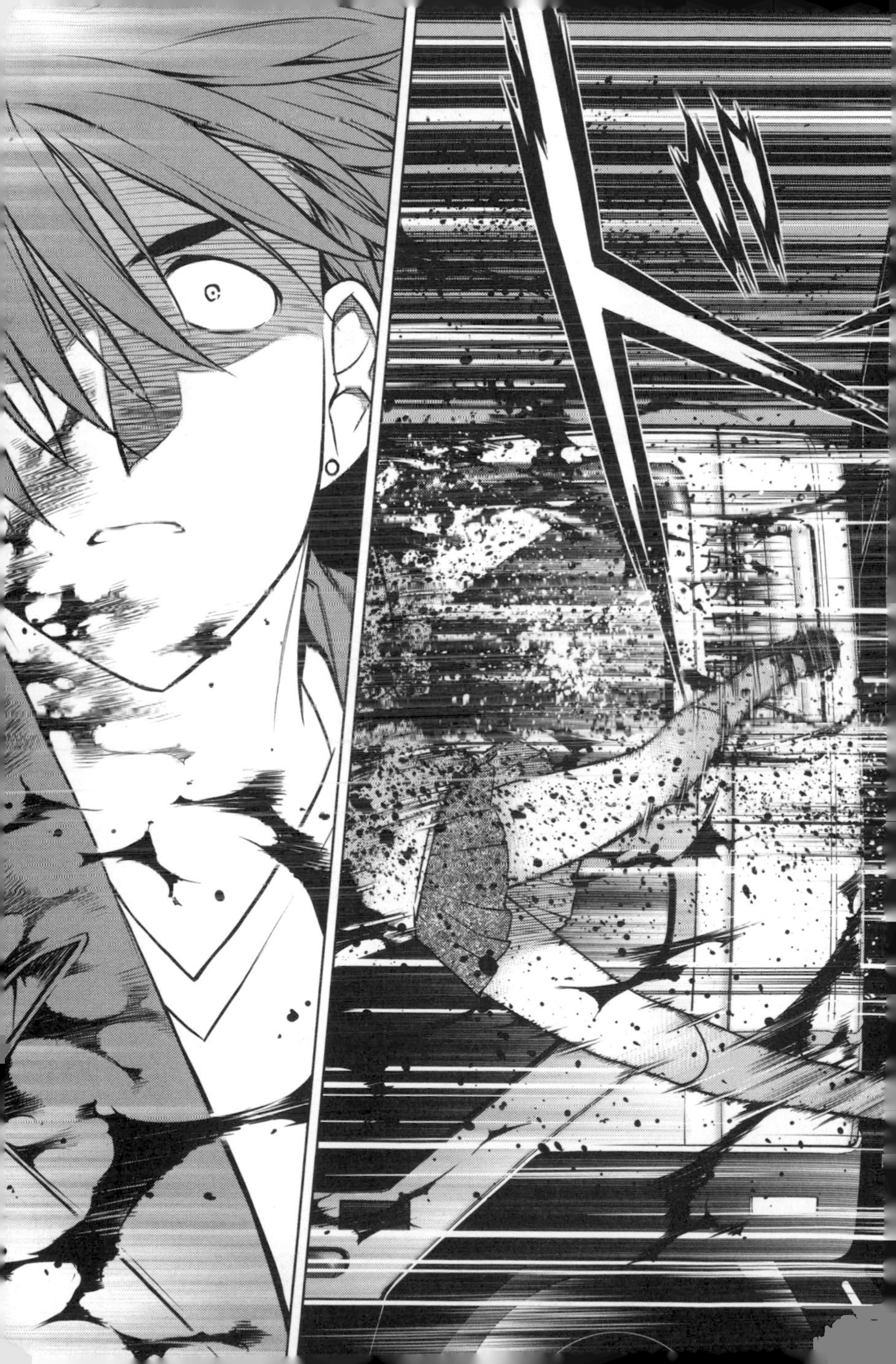

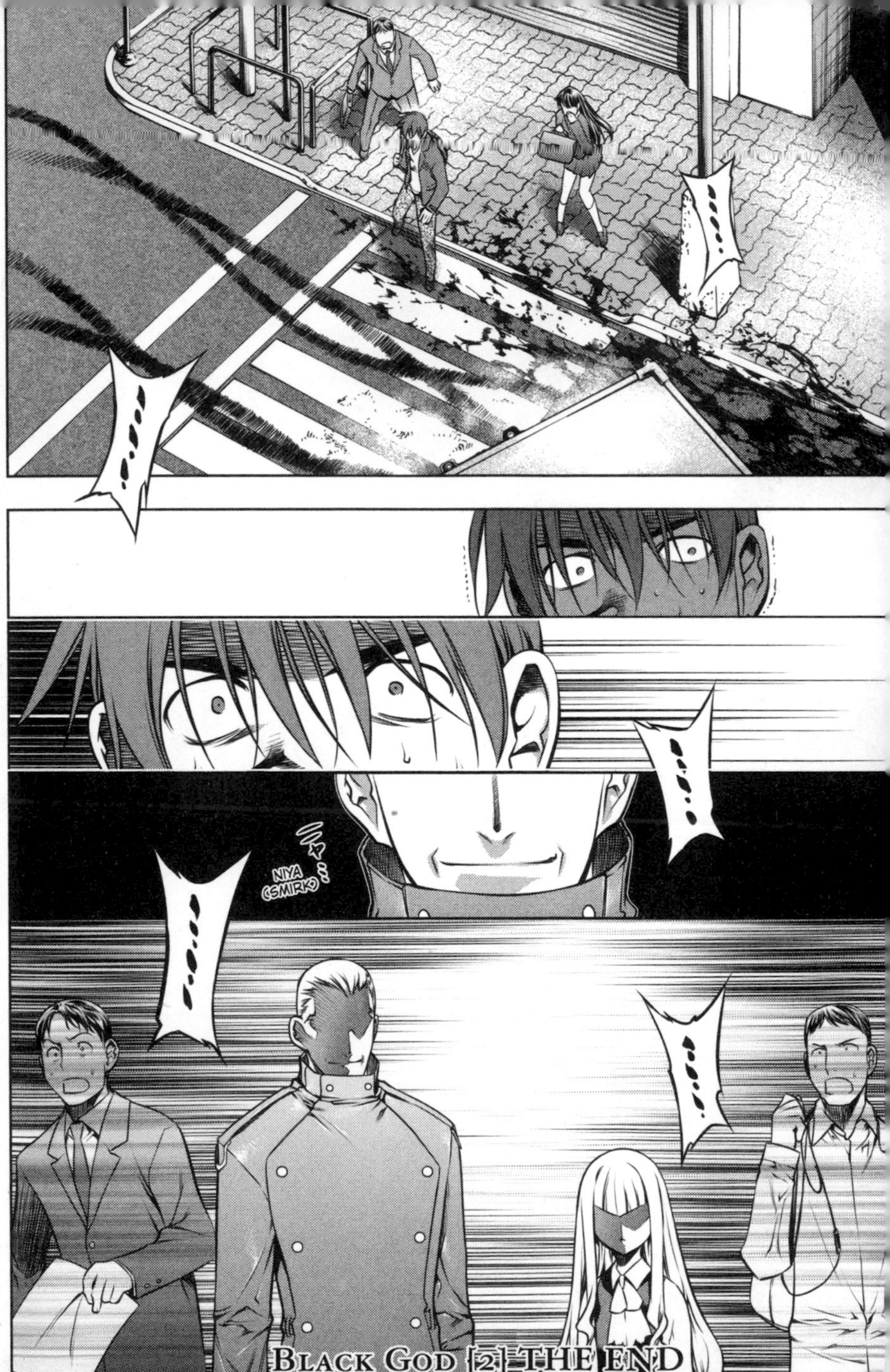
NIYA (SMIRK)

BLACK GOD [2] THE END

●Drawing Staff（作画スタッフ）
Do Young Shin
Shin Yun Hee
Jung Jin Ju
Kim Do Kyoung
Kwon Hyuck Jin
——Studio Zero——

●Manager（マネージャー）
Park Jin Woo

●Project Cooperator（企画協力）
Lee Hyun Seok（warmania）

●Translator（翻訳）
Jang Jong Choul（張綜哲）

BLACK GOD

2

Dall-Young Lim and Sung-Woo Park

Translation: Christine Schilling
Lettering: Keiran O'Leary

) Vol. 2 © 2005 Lim Dall Young, Park Sung Woo / SQUARE
jhts reserved. First published in Japan in 2005 by SQUARE
'D. English translation rights arranged with SQUARE ENIX
d Hachette Book Group USA through Tuttle-Mori Agency,
Translation © 2007 by SQUARE ENIX CO., LTD.

Yen Press
Hachette Book Group USA
237 Park Avenue, New York, NY 10017

ur Web sites at www.HachetteBookGroupUSA.com and
www.YenPress.com.

Press is a division of Hachette Book Group USA, Inc.
The Yen Press name and logo is a trademark of
Hachette Book Group USA, Inc.

First Edition: February 2008

9000001003 8192